Brook Farm

STERLING F. DELANO

Brook Farm

THE DARK SIDE
OF UTOPIA

THE BELKNAP PRESS OF
HARVARD UNIVERSITY PRESS
Cambridge, Massachusetts, and London, England
2004

PRINTED IN THE UNITED STATES OF AMERICA

Library of Congress Cataloging-in-Publication Data
Delano, Sterling F., 1942–
Brook Farm : the dark side of utopia / Sterling F. Delano.
p. cm.
Includes bibliographical references and index.
ISBN 0-674-01160-0 (alk. paper)
1. Brook Farm Phalanx (West Roxbury, Boston, Mass.)
2. Collective settlements—Massachusetts—Boston—History.
3. Transcendentalism (New England)—History.
I. Title.
HX656.B8D45 2004
307.77′09744′61—dc22
2003057008

In loving memory of
Margaret and Sterling Delano,
Leonard and Karen Kleinman, and
Solomon and Naomi Kleinman

Contents

Illustrations

Preface

Among the dozens of surviving reminiscences of the celebrated antebellum utopian experiment that was known as Brook Farm (1841–1847), one feature stands out above all others: invariably the community is nostalgically recalled as a bucolic retreat in which the days began with choruses of Mozart and Haydn by the Brook Farm choir, afternoons were interrupted in order to read Dante's great work in the original, and evenings featured dramatic tableaux, lectures, and dancing. Life at Brook Farm often did resemble an Arcadian adventure, but what is never acknowledged in the numerous surviving accounts of the West Roxbury, Massachusetts, community is the desperation that came from unrelieved financial pressures, the loss of faith in Brook Farm's leaders, and the class antagonisms that often smoldered beneath the surface of community civility—what my title refers to as "the dark side of Utopia." This study includes many of the anecdotes that have contributed to the nostalgic view of the community. Where it departs from all previous treatments of Brook Farm is in the effort to tell the story whole, to document the persistent struggle, even from the earliest days of the community's existence, to prevent it from going under. *Brook Farm: The Dark Side of Utopia* is therefore not only a corrective study; it is a revisionary one as well.

I first became aware of Brook Farm's internal turmoil when I orga-

nized an exhibition at Villanova University in 1991 to commemorate the 150th anniversary of the founding of the community. That
prompted me to read through virtually all of the more than 300 articles and the dozen or more books that deal with one aspect or another
of America's most renowned utopian experiment. It was quite an experience. Not one of the numerous resources, I quickly realized, provides anything like a comprehensive examination of Brook Farm. The
"standard" treatment is still Lindsay Swift's *Brook Farm: Its Members,
Scholars, and Visitors,* which was published more than a century ago.
Even more surprising was the amount of misleading, contradictory,
and flat-out incorrect information about the community found in
many of the sources—a good deal of it, surprisingly enough, in the
reminiscences of the Brook Farmers themselves. Brook Farm deserves
better than this, especially since there continues to be such an enduring fascination with the community—no doubt inspired partly by the
association with it of such prominent figures as Nathaniel Hawthorne,
Ralph Waldo Emerson, and Margaret Fuller.

Clarity is all the more essential because Brook Farm grew out of
the same cultural seedbed that gave rise to Transcendentalism, aboli-
tionism, the workingmen's movement, the women's rights movement,
and other manifestations of antebellum social reform in New England,
activities in which many of the Brook Farmers themselves participated. (Colorful New York labor organizer Mike Walsh, the leader of a
group of reformers known in the 1840s as the "Spartan Band," once
characterized the Brook Farmers as "pious professors and Infidels,
Fourierists, Abolitionists, Non-Resistants, etc., etc.") *Brook Farm: The
Dark Side of Utopia* takes note of some of these reform programs
along the way, but its real interest is in what early Brook Farmer
Nathaniel Hawthorne later characterized as "the inner truth and spirit
of the whole affair." Hawthorne hoped that Brook Farm's leaders—notably George Ripley, who founded the community and later achieved

great prominence in New York City's journalistic world, or Charles Anderson Dana, Ripley's second-in-command, who afterward became the powerful owner and editor of the New York *Sun*—would one day document the community's internal drama, but neither of them ever did. No doubt the story was too painful to record for posterity. *Brook Farm: The Dark Side of Utopia* is the first study to do so.

Since Brook Farm evolved out of the phenomenon known in New England in the 1830s as Transcendentalism, it might be expected that one of George Ripley's Unitarian brethren would naturally have played the role of biographer and documented the community's history. Several of them, after all, followed Ripley to the village of West Roxbury in 1841 to build anew the "city of God" on the 200-acre dairy farm that served as the site of the experiment. Others, like Theodore Parker and William Henry Channing, were intimately associated with the community at different stages of its six-year existence. Transcendentalists like Emerson, Orestes Brownson, Parker, and Channing, however, were never any more united in their support of Brook Farm than they had been in the religious and philosophical principles that they supposedly held in common in the 1830s. Brook Farm may be "the best representation of the social aspect of transcendentalism" (as one commentator has put it), but given the inconsistent and wavering support of those Transcendentalists associated with the community, it's probably more accurate to say that Brook Farm is the best representation of the amorphous nature of Transcendentalism itself. A history of the community is in fact nothing less than a record of the demise of that remarkable American cultural phenomenon that we refer to today as the Transcendental "movement."

There is nothing amorphous of course about Brook Farm's enduring importance in the history of American communal and utopian societies. It is one of the most interesting chapters in the rich and extensive record of that tradition because the experiment occurred at the precise moment that it did. One hundred nineteen communal and utopian societies were established in the United States between 1800 and 1859, and more than half of them—sixty to be exact—were formed during the "frenetic forties," a decade marked by some of the most intense reform fervor that America has ever witnessed. Of the sixty utopian communities established during that decade, only five were located in New England—four of them in Massachusetts. Brook Farm was the first to be organized. One notable feature of the New England communities that distinguishes them from those established west of the Hudson River is that they were born of ethical imperative rather than economic necessity. Brook Farm thus represents one of the important episodes in the annals of antebellum New England culture.

There are yet other reasons, though, why a close examination of Brook Farm is so valuable today. There were powerful historical forces at work in the United States in the 1840s, and two of them directly influenced the community's destiny. One of these was known at the time as Fourierism, which was the name given to the popular utopian reform program of Charles Fourier, the early nineteenth-century French social scientist. Nearly thirty Fourierist communities were formed in the United States in the 1840s, and Brook Farm adopted several of Fourier's "industrial principles" halfway through its existence. It was, in fact, the only Fourierist experiment ever established in New England. Fourierism, though, was not the snake in the garden that destroyed the Transcendental Eden in West Roxbury. There were serious financial problems in the community long before the Brook Farmers embraced Charles Fourier's industrial principles in January 1844. The seeds of failure were sown right alongside the potato and rutabaga seeds planted in the early months of the community's existence in 1841. If anything, the seeds of financial failure were cultivated even more by a small group of New York City-based armchair communitarians whose commitment to Brook Farm never extended beyond limited support, which they reluctantly provided on their occasional visits to the West Roxbury community.

The second historical force that had a significant impact on the community was the Industrial Revolution, which began to gather a full head of steam in the United States in the 1840s. When George Ripley resigned his pulpit at the Purchase Street Church in south Boston in 1840, the thirty-eight-year-old minister was animated by a vision of a society that would "insure a more natural union between intellectual and manual labor," that would combine "agricultural and mechanic arts" in the same individual. Brook Farm began as an agrarian and pastoral experiment. Three years later it was transformed into a Fourierist Phalanx whose leaders were forced to confront the workingmen's movement, the steam engine, and the grinding economic realities of the marketplace. Ripley and his supporters were hardly qualified to do so. The efforts of Brook Farm's leaders to deal with the new industrial age is a local enactment of the larger drama that was unfolding in American society that pitted values and ideals against financial expediency and marketplace economy.

It was precisely those values and ideals that provide the dramatic backdrop for the most poignant feature of the Brook Farm story. On the eve of the Brook Farm experiment, Ralph Waldo Emerson remarked of his fellow Americans that "we are all a little wild here with numberless projects of social reform. Not a reading man but has the draft of a new community in his waistcoat pocket." It may be difficult for us today to understand, much less appreciate, the depth of faith in individual potential and perfectability that prompted thousands of people to commit themselves to one scheme or another in an effort to meliorate social, educational, economic, and political inequities and injustices. It is a striking fact of American life that when Brook Farm was established in 1841, such faith was widely held and demonstrably on display all around the United States. In June 1845, after four years of difficult and nearly unrelieved financial struggle, Ripley still managed to speak hopefully in the "Introductory Notice" of a new weekly paper that was being launched at the community: "We address ourselves to . . . those who cherish a living faith in the advancement of humanity, whose inner life consists not in doubting, questioning, and denying, but in believing; who, resolute to cast off conventional errors and prejudices, are hungering and thirsting for positive truth; and who, with reliance on the fulfilment of the prophetic voice in the heart of man, and on the Universal Providence of God, look forward to an order of society founded on the divine principles of justice and love, to a future age of happiness, harmony, and of great glory to be realized on earth."

By the time of the community's collapse just two years later, such faith among Americans had already begun to wane. Just a few years later it was forever compromised by the most divisive civil conflict ever to scar the nation. Brook Farm returns us to a time when people like George Ripley still believed that the "city of God" could be built anew, and were prepared to act on the strength of their convictions, even if that meant renouncing the security of a fourteen-year career as a Unitarian minister in respectable Boston for an uncertain existence on a rural dairy farm in West Roxbury, Massachusetts.

Brook Farm: The Dark Side of Utopia is written for both a specific and a general audience. It is fully documented and thus entirely accountable, I trust, to the scholarly community. The story of Brook Farm is so essentially a human one, though, that it also demanded to be told with the general reader in mind. The narrative is based on the sizable body of extant primary materials, which includes extensive correspondence, community labor records, minutes of community meetings, financial journals, contemporary books and pamphlets, and contemporary newspapers and periodicals. Letting the Brook Farmers tell the story in their own words is very much at the heart of this narrative. *Brook Farm: The Dark Side of Utopia* foregrounds half-a-dozen or more of the most important participants, such as George and Sophia Ripley, Hawthorne, Charles Anderson Dana, Mary Ann Dwight, George William Curtis, and Isaac Hecker, as well as several of the interested bystanders, such as Emerson, Fuller, Henry Thoreau, Bronson Alcott, Theodore Parker, Albert Brisbane, William Henry Channing, and Horace Greeley. The story of Brook Farm features many different "voices," yet not all of them, it is clear, were always listening to one another as carefully as they might have when the community's best interests were at stake.

Brook Farm

Prologue

When on March 28, 1841, the Rev. George Ripley climbed the steps of his Purchase Street pulpit for the last time, the sanctuary in the Unitarian church in southeast Boston across from Central Wharf was hushed and quiet. He was thirty-eight years old, a studious and gentle-looking man with gold wire-rimmed spectacles that complemented his clean-shaven face. Though his sermons were invariably thoughtful, they were rarely inspirational. He certainly never had the commanding pulpit presence of his colleague and friend, Ralph Waldo Emerson. He was, nonetheless, among the most widely respected and admired religious leaders in New England, and now he was about to deliver his farewell remarks to the congregation to whom he had served as minister ever since his ordination from the Harvard Divinity School in 1826.

Ripley had stood before his parishioners hundreds of times before, but he had never been able to proclaim, as he proudly would today, that he was "a peace man, a temperance man, an abolitionist, a transcendentalist, [and] a friend of radical reform in our social institutions." He had no quarrel with the members of the congregation. He would reassure them that "we part in peace. An honest difference in opinion need alienate no kind feelings."[1] Sophia Willard Dana, Ripley's wife, would recall a few weeks later that she saw "tears flowing all around us." Yet neither she nor her husband would shed so much as a single tear that day. "We could not feel," she remarked later, "as the kindest among them [the congregation] seemed to feel, that they were losing their all."[2] The Ripleys, in fact, felt that they were about to "gain their all." For them it was the dawn of a new beginning—of a new life.

George and Sophia Ripley weren't just moving on to a new congregation. Ripley's resignation from the Purchase Street Church was much more comprehensive: he was leaving the ministry altogether. His congregants had known for several months that he would bid them farewell at the end of March. They also knew that he and Sophia were about to launch an experimental "colony" in nearby West Roxbury, though none of them would ever have imagined—least of all the Ripleys themselves—that Brook Farm would subsequently become the most celebrated utopian community in America. The much-beloved minister had first notified the Proprietors of the Purchase Street Society nearly a year before, on May 21, 1840, that he would willingly resign his pastorate because the "pecuniary affairs of the church are not in a prosperous condition." Ripley thought that financial exigency seemed the easiest way to raise the matter of his nagging unhappiness ministering to a congregation whose views on the role of its chief spiritual leader differed so widely from his own.

For several years now Ripley had been a religious and social activist, yet his congregation had always been complacent and even indifferent to the theological and social questions that fired his soul. He had always believed that the essence of religion had to do with such things as spiritual equality among all people, a willingness to examine the received doctrines of the church, and an abiding awareness of the social imperative implicit in the biblical dictum "Inasmuch as ye have not done it unto one of the least of these, ye have not done it unto me." His congregation, however, had always expected him to be an authority figure who would plainly and simply reiterate the time-honored teachings of the past. The pulpit was not the place to raise controversial questions. "They wish for a priest & a spiritual guide, not to say dictator, rather than for a fraternal helper," Ripley complained to his friend and fellow Unitarian minister John Sullivan Dwight shortly after raising the possibility of his resignation. "They [the congregation] would rather be exhorted than enlightened."[3]

Ripley's vocational crisis was directly linked to a more pervasive crisis of faith that had been in the making for several years and was shared by others of his generation. That crisis was known in the 1830s as Transcendentalism. Transcendentalism in turn provided the seedbed for the growth of social reform efforts such as the one that the Ripleys were about to undertake at Brook Farm. During the 1830s Ripley had found himself part of an ever-widening group of like-minded Unitarian ministers in Boston and Cambridge that included, along with Dwight, Ralph Waldo Emerson, James Freeman Clarke, Frederic Henry Hedge, Orestes Brownson, William Henry Channing, Theodore Parker, Amos Bronson Alcott, and Christopher Pearse Cranch— all but Brownson and Alcott graduates of the Harvard Divinity School (then known as the Cambridge Divinity College) and all of them "second generation" Unitarian clergymen. They were all loosely identified as Transcendentalists because, among other things, they rejected the rationalist material philosophy of early Enlightenment thinker John Locke in favor of the transcendental idealism of Emanuel Kant, because they enthusiastically embraced the current literature and philosophy then coming out of England, France, and Germany, and because they believed that the divine authority of Christianity did not require literal acceptance of the miracles reported in the Bible.

This isn't to say that the younger generation of Unitarian ministers subscribed uniformly to a set of religious beliefs or philosophical principles. On the contrary. James Freeman Clarke's remark about the

Transcendental Club, an informal group that was organized in 1836 by Ripley and his colleagues to provide a forum to discuss theological and moral subjects, applies with equal force to all Transcendentalists. The members of the Club, Clarke said, were designated "the club of the like-minded" because "no two of us thought alike." Orestes Brownson made a similar point when he stated that Transcendentalists "differ widely in their opinions, and agree in little except in their common opposition to the old school [that is, early Unitarianism]." In his comprehensive letter to the Purchase Street Society in October 1840, Ripley himself stated that Transcendentalists "believe in an order of truths which transcends the sphere of the external sense. Their leading idea is the supremacy of mind over matter. Hence they maintain that the truth of religion does not depend on tradition, nor historical facts, but has an unerring witness in the soul. There is a light, they believe, which enlighteneth every man that cometh into the world; there is a faculty in all—the most degraded, the most ignorant, the most obscure—to perceive spiritual truth when distinctly presented; and the ultimate appeal on all moral questions is not to a jury of scholars, a hierarchy of divines, or the prescriptions of a creed, but to the common sense of the human race."[4]

The Transcendentalists themselves insisted throughout that there was never much unanimity of agreement in their separate and progressive views, but one commentator's observation about the younger generation of Unitarian ministers more accurately reflects the real situation. The "infidels," Perry Miller has noted, referring to the Transcendentalists, came "so spontaneously and vocally to their coincident persuasions, and their activities . . . seemed so to fit into a pattern, that outsiders could accuse them of being a 'movement,' in fact of being a conspiracy."[5]

The most crucial of these "coincident persuasions" proved to be the historicity of the biblical miracles, especially those reported in the New Testament. Ripley's remark above that the apprehension of religious truth does not depend on tradition or historical facts is a thinly veiled reference to the firestorm over the authority of miracles that forever separated the Transcendentalists from first-generation Unitarian divines like Andrews Norton. The battle came into the open in November 1836, when Ripley published a review of British theologian James Martineau's *The Rationale of Religious Enquiry* in the *Christian Examiner,* the organ of formal Unitarianism. There he charged church elders like Norton, Nathaniel L. Frothingham, and Francis Bowen with religious intolerance that he said was even more shameful than that exhibited earlier by their Calvinist counterparts. Whereas Calvinist clergymen relied on supernaturalism (the torments of hell and the eternal bliss of heaven) to tyrannize believers, Unitarians, in their insistence on the historicity of miracles, were similarly bludgeoning the faithful because they made literal acceptance of the miracles a requirement for membership in the church.

Norton, the so-called "hard-headed Unitarian Pope," was so enraged by Ripley's remarks that he took the unprecedented step of airing what until then had been a private and internal church conflict in an open letter to the *Boston Daily Advertiser* on November 5, pointedly charging Ripley with academic and professional incompetence. In his letter Norton stated that those who challenge the views of recognized authorities ought first to make certain that they are qualified to do so, adding that such writings should also be submitted to others qualified to judge them (Norton was obviously referring to himself) before they are published. "It may be laid down as a general principle," Norton wrote, "that he who controverts doctrine, which many, who have thought most concerning them, think of the highest importance to the happiness of man . . . should satisfy himself that he has ability to discuss the subject . . . Let him then publish [his views] in such a form . . . that they will first go into the hands only of those who are capable of judging their correctness."[6]

When Ripley replied to his former Divinity School teacher just four days later in the same paper, he minced no words. He made it clear first that he and Norton were members of very different schools of Unitarian thought: "You [Norton, and obviously other Unitarians of his stripe] are a disciple of the school which was founded by Locke . . . For that philosophy I have no respect. I believe it to be superficial, irreligious[,] and false in its primary elements." Then he expressed his surprise that Norton hadn't engaged him in reasoned discourse but substituted instead "an appeal to popular prejudice in the place of reason and argument." Ripley stated that he "would be far, sir, from impairing your legitimate influence in our theological circles, but when you so far forget the principles of our Protestant fathers, as to wish to place shackles upon the press and to drown the voice of discussion by the cry of alarm, I must take leave to say, that I regret to see you manifesting the spirit of a class of men, who are too well known in the annals of the Church, and with whom I would gladly hope that few among us have any thing in common."[7]

Norton's attempt to smack his former student's hand was not endorsed by his colleagues, but that didn't prevent him from going after other proponents of the "newness."[8] The former Dexter Professor of Sacred Literature at the Harvard Divinity School undoubtedly would have liked to lock horns with Orestes Brownson, if only because Brownson had always been the most outspoken and hardest-hitting of all the Transcendentalists.[9] But Brownson wasn't a Harvard man, and Norton wouldn't dignify him by engaging in discourse with a self-educated farm boy from rural Vermont. Instead, Norton attacked Emerson, who had published his seminal Transcendental pamphlet *Nature* in 1836, which he followed with his controversial "Divinity School Address" in July 1838, in which, among other things, the former Unitarian clergyman (Emerson had resigned his pastorate from the prestigious Second Church in Boston in 1832) told the newly ordained graduates that "if a man is at heart just, then in so far is he God," and then admonished his listeners to "go alone": "Yourself a newborn bard of the Holy Ghost, cast behind you all conformity, and acquaint men at first hand with Deity." If this wasn't blasphemy then nothing was.

Norton was barely able to contain himself. He managed to remain quiet for five full weeks, at which point his anger had reached white heat. He turned once again to the *Boston Daily Advertiser* where, on August 27, 1838, he lashed out at "The New School in Literature and Religion." This was more than a "mere insurrection of folly," Norton charged. "'Silly women,' it is said, and silly young men, it is to be feared, have been drawn away from their Christian faith, if not divorced from all that can properly be called religion." Norton followed the article with a more elaborate *Discourse on the Latest Form of Infidelity* (1839), which immediately brought Ripley charging to Emerson's—and, by virtue of their association together, his own—defense in a pamphlet on *"The Latest Form of Infidelity" Examined* (1839), which the Purchase Street minister followed with two others in 1840.[10]

A second important "coincident persuasion" that seemed to unite several of the Transcendentalists was the insistence "that Transcendental metaphysics led inescapably to a social philosophy and to a critique of existing institutions."[11] Orestes Brownson was the single most vocal proponent of this view, although it was Frederic Henry Hedge, who graduated from the Harvard Divinity School two years after Ripley did, who first began to give voice to the conviction in a review titled "Progress of Society" in the March 1834 number of the *Christian Examiner.* The theme was more sharply focused by Brownson, however, one year later in the same journal. Although Brownson borrowed Hedge's title to indicate that he was continuing the discussion from the year before, Brownson, unlike Hedge, applied the critique to that still amorphous group of American workers known as the laboring class: "He who is at ease himself, rich, enjoying ample leisure . . . will be prone to forget, or not to suspect, the vast amount of suffering that lies beyond him; and unless perchance he has learned something more of Christianity than its dogmas, he will be very liable to look upon the manual laborer, not as a fellow immortal, with rights, duties, interests, and feelings, sacred as his own, but as a mere instrument of his wealth or pleasure, made to be used for his service." By May 1836 Brownson was warning Unitarian ministers that "the real sentiment of our epoch is the sentiment of social progress. To this sentiment the clergy must attach themselves."[12]

The devastating Financial Panic of 1837, which resulted in numerous bank failures, many commercial and individual bankruptcies, and widespread unemployment, gave people like Brownson further reason to criticize existing social institutions, which he did, for instance, in *Babylon Is Falling* (1837), a sermon in which he predicted violent confrontation between the party of "privilege, inequality, and war" and the party of "liberty, equality, [and] peace."[13] Ripley's radicalism was not as extreme as Brownson's, but he couldn't remain quiet in the wake of the social misery caused by the Panic.

Ripley's sermon on *The Temptations of the Times* is an early formulation of his rapidly evolving social consciousness, which led to his resignation from the Purchase Street Church and the experiment at Brook Farm. Ripley stated in the May 1837 sermon that the "great danger of our country . . . is the inordinate pursuit, the extravagant worship of wealth," and he appealed to his congregation to "learn from what we are now going through, to cherish a deeper sense of our dependence upon one another."[14] Even the venerable Dr. William Ellery Channing, the widely admired Unitarian clergyman who was so revered in the 1820s and 1830s by the younger generation of Unitarian ministers as the "spiritual and intellectual leader of the Unitarian movement in early 19th century New England," addressed the growing plight of laborers in lectures such as the two that he delivered at the Mechanic Apprentices' Library Association in Boston in 1840 that were collected and published as *Lectures on the Elevation of the Laboring Portion of the Community* the same year.[15]

Other Transcendentalists were not as quick as Brownson, Ripley, and Channing to give expression to the social imperative that several of them believed was implicit in Transcendentalism, but what mattered most to Ripley is that Brownson and Channing were as outspoken as they were.[16] These two men exerted the most influence on the Purchase Street minister in the years right before Brook Farm. Ripley would tell Brownson in December 1842, for instance, that "we have truly sympathized as few men have done; you have always quickened my love for humanity," adding that, "if I had never known you, I should never have been engaged in this enterprise [Brook Farm]." Channing's influence on Ripley dates all the way back to the latter's Divinity School days. Ripley even referred to himself during those years as a "child of Channing." Like Brownson, Channing's influence also had a great deal to do with the organization of Brook Farm. Years after its collapse, Ripley told his lifelong friend William Henry Channing, Channing's nephew, "But for your uncle William's encouragement I should never have undertaken Brook Farm."[17]

In May 1840, however, when Ripley tendered his first offer of resignation, he certainly wasn't thinking about organizing a community. He was working on the second and third tracts in his pamphlet war with Andrews Norton over the "latest form of infidelity," even as he was preparing the resignation overture to the Proprietors at Purchase Street Church, which he forwarded at the end of the month. For a man who in the previous few years had been articulating his religious convictions with both precision and a kind of expansive candor, Ripley's May 1840 letter is surprisingly confusing and brief and indicates that he was not at all clear about his future course of action.

He begins the letter by noting "with regret that the pecuniary affairs of the church are not in a prosperous condition." Not until halfway through does he make clear why he is writing: "a sense of the kindness I have received at your hands . . . has prevented me from requesting to be discharged from your service." And in his closing, Ripley confuses his purpose even more when he says, "In making this communication, I trust too much to your candor to suppose that it will be ascribed to a weariness with my duties or a want of attachment to my society. I wish to consult the common good, without peculiar reference to myself." Ripley shouldn't have been at all surprised by the Proprietors' response: "we beg leave to assure you that we think the continuance of the society in Purchase Street mainly depends on your continuance as pastor."[18]

Ripley's letter obviously missed the mark, but the cathartic effect merely of sending it was rejuvenating. His friends noticed the difference immediately. Margaret Fuller, for example, met him on the street in Boston a few days after the letter was delivered. She reported to Emerson that Ripley "is most happy in the step he has taken. He seems," she said, "newborn." Emerson himself applauded Ripley's courage: "What a brave thing Mr. Ripley has done, he stands now at the head of the Church militant."[19] In the months following his tentative offer of resignation in May, it became perfectly clear to Ripley that he really had no choice but to leave the ministry altogether. In his next formal communication with the Proprietors he would make certain that there was no doubt about what he intended to do.

That communication turned out to be a lengthy 7,300-word *Letter Addressed to the Congregational Church in Purchase Street,* which details the fourteen years of his ministry and is thus a valuable account of the progress of liberal theology in Boston and Cambridge in the period between 1826–1840. Ripley delivered it on October 3, 1840. With courteous clarity the letter cites the specific causes of his disaffection with Unitarianism and, by extension, with institutional religion generally. In the past he did not have the strength, he said, "to resist the formality and coldness which are breathed from the atmosphere of our churches." He vowed that henceforth he would never speak again without complete candor and frankness, for he could not be a different man from what God had made him. Ripley recalled that when he began his ministry at the Purchase Street Church in 1826, the same year in which the Society itself was formed, "the Unitarian controversy was in the ascendant." It was an exciting time because "inquiries relating to personal religion were not infrequent" and "religion became a subject of vast and solemn import" throughout the Unitarian community. But then a backlash occurred. "Liberal churches began to fear liberality," and ministers like Ripley "who defended the progress as well as the freedom of thought were openly denounced as infidels; various unintelligible names were applied to them . . . The plainest expositions of Christian truth . . . were accused of heresy."

For Ripley many of those "expositions" had to do with the social inequities that were so glaringly evident in the city of Boston, even along Purchase Street itself.[20] This is the most pervasive theme in his detailed letter: the need to establish a "social worship," for "the purpose of Christianity," Ripley stated, "is to redeem society as well as the individual from all sin." As a Christian, Ripley "would aid in the overthrow of every form of slavery; I would free the mind from bondage and the body from chains; I could not feel that my duty was accomplished while there was one human being, within the sphere of my influence, held to unrequited labor at the will of another, destitute of the means of education, or doomed to penury, degradation, and vice by the misfortune of birth." The Purchase Street minister remarked elsewhere in the letter that he could not "witness the glaring inequalities of condition, the hollow pretension of pride, the scornful apathy with which many urge the prostration of man, the burning zeal with which they run the race of selfish competition, with no thought for the elevation of their brethren, without the sad conviction that the spirit of Christ has well-nigh disappeared from our churches, and that the fearful doom awaits us." The true followers of Jesus, Ripley said, "are a band of brothers . . . they attach no importance to the petty distinctions of birth, rank, wealth, and station." "The poor widow," he went on, "who leaves the daily toil by which a suffering family is kept from want to gather with the faithful in the house of worship" should be welcomed with as much sympathy and sincere affection and should be treated with as much respect as "they who are arrayed in costly robes, or who come from the heights of office or the abodes of luxury." Views such as these "have been near my heart; they are a part of my life; they seem to me to be the very essence of the religion which I was taught."[21]

Ripley knew when he submitted his second letter to the congregation in October 1840 that it could never accept the conditions for his continuation as its spiritual leader, but he also knew that he had spoken honestly about a host of matters that were foremost in his mind at this time, matters that were about to lead him to undertake a courageous and daring experiment on a nearby dairy farm in West Roxbury. On January 1, 1841, Ripley formally requested permission to resign his pastorate in three months. The congregants in Purchase Street still loved and admired him—they did not want him to leave—but there was really no alternative. On January 31, 1841, the Proprietors of the Society regretfully accepted Ripley's resignation, at the same time that they thanked their beloved minister for his devoted and faithful service, and recommended him "to the Christian world as a Christian Minister in every way worthy and every way qualified to preach the Gospels." The resolution was signed by two hundred of his parishioners.

On March 28, 1841, Ripley preached his farewell discourse. When it was completed, he and Sophia walked out of the Purchase Street

Church, the granite and mortar of south Boston visible everywhere, but all Ripley and his wife Sophia were thinking about now was lumber and Roxbury pudding stone—the kind used to construct the community buildings that would be needed to build the "city of God" anew.

1

"Fermenting and Effervescing"

George Ripley had no idea that the seeds he was planting in his May 1840 resignation letter to the Purchase Street Society would eventually be cultivated at Brook Farm. In no way was his letter prompted by the intention to organize a community. His determination to establish Brook Farm developed in the months following, the result of several converging forces that were not in and of themselves individually galvanizing but, taken collectively, inspired his decision the following October to leave the ministry and move to West Roxbury. His initial thought in May had been to continue preaching, but not as a Unitarian clergyman.

This is quite clear from his ordination sermon for his friend John Sullivan Dwight, and from the separate testimony of two other friends who spoke to Ripley just a few days after he delivered it. In the ordination sermon for Dwight, an 1836 graduate of the Harvard Divinity School, on the *Claims of the Age on the Work of the Evangelist* at the Second Congregational Church in Northampton on May 20, Ripley indicates that, if anything, he was considering the possibility of establishing a more independent pulpit than he knew could be enjoyed within the confines of the Unitarian Church. The central question that he raises in the sermon is whether, in light of the growing popularity of lyceums, universities, and common schools, the pulpit has outlived its usefulness. Ripley argues in the sermon that it definitely has not: the evangelist's "office may be modified, but it cannot be destroyed." The evangelist, he notes, "may discover new and more effective modes of discharging [his] duties; but the truth as it is in Jesus will still remain the instrument for the reformation of society, and the salvation of man."[1]

Christ announced the coming of the Kingdom of God on earth, Ripley says, because "a purer and more happy state of society was to be realized on earth." Force would give way to love; man "would cease to lift up his hand against his brother; each would eat of the fruit of his own vine and fig-tree; oppressions would cease; slavery would be destroyed; . . . mutual love would crown every dwelling." But where, Ripley asked Dwight's congregation, could the Kingdom of God be found? "Where is the community, in which the order of society, the general tone of morality, the every-day dealings between man and man, are based on the new commandment which the Redeemer gave to his disciples?"

Establishing the Kingdom of God here on earth had originally been "entrusted to the fidelity of the Church," said Ripley, but the Church had failed to "bring the religion of society into accordance with the religion of Christ." This was the important work that the evangelist was still the best qualified to perform, but he would never accomplish it, Ripley added—no doubt thinking of his own congregation—if "he [the evangelist] thinks that he must color his own views to suit the popular taste," or if he thinks that he "must exhibit truth, not as it appears to his own mind, but as it is supposed to appear to other minds." If the evangelist placed the congregation's expectations above his own integrity, then he would lose his independence; he would become a "time-server and a slave; and of all slaves, a slave in the pulpit is the most to be pitied."

Ripley left Northampton and returned to Boston the day after Dwight's ordination to deliver his first letter to the Purchase Street Society.[2] Immediately afterward he sought out his friend and fellow

Unitarian minister Ezra Stiles Gannett, a graduate of the Divinity School three years before Ripley, with whom he spent several hours discussing his ministry. Gannett, who was assistant to and then succeeded William Ellery Channing at the Federal Street Church in Boston, noted in his journal right after their meeting on May 28 that Ripley "is uncomfortable in his present situation, is dissatisfied with the present religious and social institutions, and contemplates a change in his own mode of action; would like to preach freely, as did [Orestes] Brownson, or rather as [George] Fox in London."[3]

Margaret Fuller also encountered Ripley just a few days after his talk with Gannett. Fuller was beginning to emerge in 1840 as one of America's most influential advocates for woman's rights; her feminist manifesto, *Woman in the Nineteenth Century,* would be published in 1845. She attended half-a-dozen meetings of the Transcendental Club in the late 1830s, but Fuller was more widely known around Boston for her celebrated "Conversations" for "well-educated and thinking women," which she first began conducting in 1839. Sophia Ripley was a participant, as were Emerson's wife Lidian, popular author Lydia Maria Child, and educator Elizabeth Palmer Peabody and her sisters Mary and Sophia (the latter would marry early Brook Farm shareholder and resident Nathaniel Hawthorne in 1842). Fuller had agreed to become the first editor of the new Transcendental quarterly known as the *Dial* after Ripley—who was looking for a religious not a secular forum in which to carry on his work as an evangelist—declined the offer in October 1839.

When Fuller saw Ripley in Boston at the very end of May, they had a frank discussion about his prospects. She especially had reservations about his future as a preacher since Ripley had never been known as an inspirational force in the pulpit. She told Ripley "what is thought of him as a preacher, and expressed doubts as to his being able to build up a church here." Fuller urged Ripley instead to "leave preaching" and "enter on some business." But Ripley told Fuller that he was not ready to stop preaching "without a trial" first. He knew that he had never distinguished himself as a preacher, but that was because he had never been on his "true ground." There was much that "he longed to say and was sure that in suitable relations he should be able to breathe out what was so living in him."[4] That was one of the qualities—the courage to "breathe out what was so living in him"—that Ripley always admired about his friend Orestes Brownson. And Brownson was very much on his mind these days too because Ripley had just prepared a review of "Brownson's Writings" for the first number of the *Dial*, evidently unaware (it wouldn't have mattered anyway; Ripley would never have wavered) that it would appear at the exact moment that Brownson's most explosive essay to date on "The Laboring Classes" was also going to press.

Ripley focused the praise in his essay on the *Boston Quarterly Review*, the periodical established by Brownson in 1838, which was a journal, Ripley said, that stood "alone in the history of periodical works" because "it was undertaken by a single individual, without the cooperation of friends, with no external patronage, supported by no sectarian interests, and called for by no motive but the inward promptings of the author's own soul." Ripley also praised the variety of topics found in the *Quarterly*'s pages, as well as the "vigor and boldness" with which Brownson treated them. Much of the journal's vitality, Ripley was quick to note, was "called forth by the struggle between the old and the new, between prescription and principle, between assertions of authority and the suggestions of reason." Ripley stated that the influence exerted by the *Quarterly* would be "permanent" because of its "vigorous tone of argument," its "fearless vindication of the rights of humanity," and "the depth and fervor of its religious spirit." The strength of Ripley's language in these excerpts— "vigorous tone of argument," "principle," "fearless vindication," "fervor of religious spirit"—was anything but random. It reflects the woof and warp of his determination to confront his own situation.

As noted, Brownson's controversial essay "The Laboring Classes" was published in the *Boston Quarterly Review* the very same month that he was being praised in the pages of the *Dial*. This alone would have been all the evidence needed to convince most people that if Transcendentalism wasn't indeed a "conspiracy," then it surely had to be, as Andrews Norton had charged, "the latest form of infidelity." Brownson had immersed himself in the 1830s in the work of European writers, particularly the early socialists, such as Saint-Simon, Charles Fourier, and Robert Owen. His readings made him realize that, unlike Europe, America had never had a feudal class. The circumstances therefore that had led to the devastating financial panic in 1837 were a result of a struggle not between an aristocracy and the laboring class, but between merchants and laborers. As Brownson noted in the first installment of the essay (the second installment appeared in October 1840), "And now commences the new struggle between the operative and his employer, between wealth and labor."[5] The resolution of this conflict would not be brought about until laborers triumphed over merchants.

Toward that end Brownson proposed to "abolish the system." "Why not," he challenged his readers, "abolish the priestly office," since the "authorized teachers of religion . . . are always a let and a hindrance to the spread of truth"? This accomplished, "Uncompromising hostility to the whole banking system should . . . be the motto of every working man, and of every friend of Humanity." "The [banking] system," Brownson declared, "must be destroyed." Following the destruction of the banks "must come that of all monopolies, of all PRIVILEGE." What Brownson specifically had in mind was the abolition of the hereditary descent of property. A man's "power over his property," he declared, "must cease with his life." Brownson recognized of course that "the rich, the business community, will never voluntarily consent" to this or to any of the other radical changes that he was proposing; such changes "will [n]ever be effected peaceably." They would be brought about, he warned by way of concluding the first installment of his critique, "only by the strong arm of physical force."

It's not likely that Ripley would have agreed with his friend that physical force might be necessary to bring about social change, but it wasn't clear to him yet how meaningful reform might best be achieved. He had a lot of time to think about it that summer, however, while he and Sophia spent July and August, as they had the summer before, at Charles and Maria Ellis's dairy farm in the village of West Roxbury. Located about eight miles southwest of the Ripleys' Bedford Street home in Boston, Ellis Farm had only two buildings. One was a large two-and-a-half story white clapboard house, of the kind that has always been synonymous with New England. There was also a good-sized barn with two-dozen stalls for horses and cattle. These were situated on 170 acres of rolling pastures, meadows, and woodlots along the west side of Dedham Road—or Baker Street, as it is now known— that connected Dedham and West Roxbury to the town of Newton just a few miles to the north. The Ripleys, Sophia reported to John Dwight, spent the summer in West Roxbury "leading a life of extreme self indulgence in the most positive retirement," which gave George lots of time to read new books, including possibly Albert Brisbane's recently published *Social Destiny of Man; or Association and Reorganization of Industry* (1840), the first detailed exposition in America of Frenchman Charles Fourier's utopian socialist theories.

Ripley's West Roxbury neighbor and dear friend Theodore Parker certainly read Brisbane's book that summer and noted in his journal that it "contains many excellent things. It points out the enormous miseries of our present society, & proposes to remedy them by bring-

ing men together in *phalanxes* of 300 or 400 familis [*sic*] to live combined with all the advantages of [concerted?] action." Parker thought
that the Phalanx "does n[o]t appear less natural to me than a City
would to Patriarch Abraham," and he remarked that he had "never
seen so excellent a portrait of the evils of society as it is" as were described in *Social Destiny of Man*. Brisbane had done a good job stating Fourier's "case boldly & strongly." Conversation this summer between Parker and Ripley about the Frenchman's utopian principles
must have been very lively.[6]

Parker lived with his wife Lydia Cabot just down the road from the
dairy farm—less than two miles as the crow flies. The couple had
been living in West Roxbury since 1837 when Parker was ordained at
the Second Church on Spring Street, Ripley providing the "right
hand of fellowship" for his fellow Unitarian minister. Though Ripley
was several years older than Parker, the two men had been introduced
by a Harvard classmate in the 1830s, and their liking for one another
was immediate. There was even a physical resemblance between the
two. Neither man was very tall; both wore wire-rimmed glasses; both
had broad shoulders and a full chest; both had a prominent forehead
due to receding hairlines (though Parker's baldness was more advanced than Ripley's); and both had a ready and engaging smile that
immediately put one at ease. Temperamentally, according to Octavius
Brooks Frothingham, who wrote separate biographies of each man,
the Unitarian ministers were very different: "One [Ripley] was en-
grossed in books; the other was full of action. One was contemplative,
quiet, thoughtful; the other was impetuous . . . One was cautious to
the verge of timidity; the other was bold to the verge of rashness."[7] In
light of Ripley's risky and courageous resignation from the Purchase
Street Church at the age of thirty-eight, and his subsequent determination to put his religious and social convictions to the fire in West
Roxbury, Frothingham's characterization seems to miss the mark en-

tirely. Perhaps he was describing Ripley's early years at Purchase Street. It certainly doesn't apply to the Brook Farm years.

On a hot and hazy Monday morning in August, Parker set out from the parsonage on Centre Street—just across from his church on Spring Street—and, cutting through familiar backyard gardens and across open fields dotted with mountain laurel and blue gentians, followed his usual shortcut and walked an easy mile to the Ellis Farm to meet his good friend. The two men were going to take "a little foot-journey," as Ripley would say, to the town of Groton, about thirty miles northwest of Boston, to attend a religious gathering called the "Christian Union Convention," which is known today more familiarly as the "Groton Convention." The Convention had been organized by two groups: Second Adventists—followers of the millennialist William Miller, a New York farmer who forecast the second advent of Jesus Christ and the Day of Judgment in 1843—and "Come-Outers"—a group of men and women from Cape Cod who, like many others during this period, had "come out" of their established churches in order to pursue their own religious convictions. (Ripley was about to be a "Come-Outer" himself.)

That Ripley was willing to leave the serenity of the Ellis Farm to walk more than sixty miles in the hot August sun to attend a meeting that was being convened "to protest against all creeds and sects" indicates just how keenly interested he was at this time in religious reform activity. The Convention turned out to be an enormously important moment, not only for George Ripley but for utopian reform efforts in New England as well. For in addition to Ripley, the organizers of the only other three utopian communities ever to be established in Massachusetts during the antebellum period were also present at the Groton Convention, namely Adin Ballou and his "Practical Christian" followers, who organized the "Hopedale Community" in 1841, the antislavery followers of William Lloyd Garrison, who formed the "North-

ampton Association" in 1842, and Bronson Alcott, who established
"Fruitlands" in 1843.[8]

Ripley, unfortunately, no longer maintained a private journal, so
there is no personal record of his reactions to or impressions of the
Groton Convention. It's clear, nevertheless, that the gathering proved
to be a defining moment for him. Parker, fortunately, did record the
excursion in his journal, so we know that the two friends set out with
a third companion named E. P. Clarke (a cashier at Boston's New
England Bank), and together the three men journeyed first to nearby
Newton, where they picked up a fourth religious pilgrim named
Christopher Pearse Cranch.[9] Cranch graduated from the Harvard Divinity School in 1835, just one year before John Dwight and Parker.
He had only recently returned from Cincinnati, Ohio, where, with a
small group of Harvard men that included James Freeman Clarke and
William Henry Channing—all of them considered to be Transcendentalists—he went right after his graduation to introduce Unitarianism to
the West. Together Ripley, Parker, Clarke, and Cranch proceeded to
the village of Concord, enjoying one another's company and conversation. They stopped often at farmhouses along the way to refresh
themselves with drafts of cool well-water. July had been unseasonably
hot; the temperature had been in the nineties every day. There was no
relief this early August, either, although the travelers agreed that they
were compensated by the beauty of the route they chose for the
twenty-mile trek to Concord, as well as by "talk of various kinds,"
Parker remarked in his journal, "[that] beguiled its length." No doubt
some of their "talk" had to do with Orestes Brownson's "Laboring
Classes" essay, which by then was rippling through Boston like the
tremors of an earthquake.[10]

When the travelers set out for Groton the next morning—having
spent, in Parker's view, a "wasted" social evening at Emerson's
home—Bronson Alcott, the gifted but controversial educator, decided

to accompany the group. It obviously didn't trouble him to leave his wife Abba—"but newly risen 'from child-bed taint,'" baby Abigail May having been born just two weeks earlier—alone with their four "little women." As it turned out, however, the self-styled Concord philosopher was disappointed with the Convention. There were few individuals among the 275 who attended the gathering with whom Alcott "had grateful discourse." He came expecting to hear appeals for religious unity, only to find that the majority of those present were "yet in bondage to Sectarianism." Parker himself was more encouraged, though he agreed with Alcott's point about sectarianism. He was surprised to find so much "illiberality" among the men who organized the Convention. Despite their separation from institutional religion, they were not "emancipated from the letter of the Bible, nor the formality of a church." Their condemnation of other sects was only to make room for their own, Parker observed, "which will probably be worse than its predecessors." But Parker was "enchanted" to have met the "Come-Outers" from Cape Cod, as well as many others in attendance whom he thought had "emancipated themselves from the shams of the [Christian] church" and could now worship God simply and directly, as Jesus had urged his followers to do.[11]

Ripley's reactions to the three-day proceedings are nowhere recorded, but it seems very likely that it was at the Groton Convention that he first began to give serious thought to organizing a community, stimulated, as he probably was, by Adin Ballou's plans for Hopedale. For several months before the Groton Convention, Ballou and his "Practical Christian" followers had been discussing the possibility of "purchasing a common farm, [and] settling upon and running it as a means of mutual physical self-support." The plan had grown "into the more ample one of a community," and Ballou was now putting the finishing touches to an article on "Communities" that he would publish in his paper *The Practical Christian* in the forthcoming number for

September 15, 1840.[12] Evidently Bronson Alcott was inspired right away by Ballou's plan because he returned home and immediately contacted Emerson to discuss plans for a new university in Concord.[13] Ripley was excited too. By the time that he met with some of his colleagues in early September for what turned out to be the final two meetings ever of the Transcendental Club, he had decided to renounce the ministry altogether and organize a community instead.

The Transcendental Club had been organized back in September 1836 after Frederic Hedge had written to Emerson proposing a "symposium" for "the free discussion of theological and moral subjects." The first meeting took place at George and Sophia Ripley's home in Boston on September 19, 1836. The "Club," or the "Hedge Club," as Emerson and others sometimes referred to it, had been meeting irregularly ever since at different locations, almost always when Hedge, an 1829 graduate of the Harvard Divinity School, came down to Boston from his pulpit at the Independent Congregational (Unitarian) Church in Bangor, Maine. It was Hedge, in fact, whom Ripley engaged in spirited debate at the last two meetings of the Club on the 2nd and 9th of September.[14] It would be very surprising if it wasn't Ripley who set the topic for discussion because it was one that had been steadily on his mind since May: the "organization of a new church."

Elizabeth Palmer Peabody, at whose Boston home the thirtieth and last meeting of the Transcendental Club took place on September 9, 1840 (the meeting on September 2 was held at Parker's home in West Roxbury), wrote several days later to John S. Dwight in Northampton describing both occasions. She would have written sooner, she said, but it "would have taken a dozen sheets of paper." Ripley had his say at both meetings, she reported, and "very admirably too," impressing upon those assembled "the reality of the evils he deplores."[15] His main complaint was that the "ministers & church are upheld in order to uphold a [church] society vicious in its foundations—but which the multitude desire should continue in its present conditions." Hedge, on the other side, "eloquently defended the church," noting the important historical role that the Catholic Church particularly had played by providing "a true culture to the Imagination" that inspired Gothic architecture and painting. Hedge yielded to Ripley, however, on the issue of the Church's failure to recognize, or even acknowledge, its social imperative. Hedge agreed that "the social principle was yet to be educated—the Church of Humanity yet to grow," but he insisted nonetheless that it was not necessary to destroy the present-day Church in order to build anew upon its ruins. The new Church, Hedge argued, could grow "as another branch from the same trunk." Theodore Parker, in the privacy of his journal, noted right after the first of the two final meetings that Hedge—as well as a few other members of the Club—seemed to be "wedded to the past." He, too, loved the past, he commented sardonically, but "would as soon wed my grandmother whom I love equally well."[16]

Emerson attended the September 2, 1840, meeting of the Club but was not able to attend what turned out to be the final one on September 9. He sent a brief note to Peabody on September 8 in response to one that, a few days earlier, she had sent him. Emerson's is the earliest surviving document that establishes that Ripley now intended to organize a new community. In his note Emerson bemoaned the perceived need "to be always laying the axe at the root of this or that vicious institution"—a direct reference to and extension of Hedge's metaphor at the first meeting—but he told Peabody that he would "honor what you tell me of Mr Ripleys purposes," adding that "I look at him with great curiosity, & hope." Emerson suggested nonetheless that such a radical step as the one Ripley had in mind really wasn't necessary. He thought that the "whole sequel would flow out easily, & instruct us in what should be the new world" if Ripley "were democratized & made kind & faithful in his heart," which is a comment that Theodore Parker, and even Emerson's good friend Bronson Alcott, would surely have assigned to the "Party of the Past." One can only imagine Ripley's response to that piece of advice had he ever heard it![17]

It's not at all coincidental that the Transcendental Club died that September 1840. The ties that bound its members had always been thin, but now the participants could no longer agree even to disagree. For all intents and purposes the collapse of the Club marked the end of the Transcendental "movement," such as it was, although it's doubtful that anyone recognized the poignancy of the moment. For the past five or six years men like Emerson, Hedge, Brownson, and Ripley had stood together, though not always comfortably, patiently working out and defending the different religious, philosophical, and social views that ostensibly united them as Transcendentalists. And for the past four years they had come together on thirty different occasions to discuss such uncommon matters—uncommon, at least, in antebellum America—as "American Genius," "Mysticism and Christianity," "Pantheism," "Esoteric and Exoteric Doctrine," and the "Nature of Poetry." But now in September 1840 it was clear that the inevitable development of their separate views would not permit them to meet any longer on common ground, leading some of the Transcendentalists to pursue, after Emerson, secular individualism; others, following Brownson, democratic socialism (and, later, Catholicism); still others, like Hedge, a slightly modified but essentially traditional Unitarianism; even others, such as Parker and James Freeman Clarke, a liberal and progressive Unitarian Christianity; and yet others, like Ripley, Dwight, and William Henry Channing, what might be called religious egalitarianism.

Ripley, at least, had no time that September to think about the Transcendental Club. He was putting the finishing touches to his lengthy letter to the Purchase Street Society, even as he was completing his portion of the "Record of the Months" for the October number of the *Dial.* He found time, though, to attend the "Second Annual Meeting of the New England Non-Resistance Society" at the Chardon Street Chapel in Cambridge on September 23 and 24, 1840. When James Freeman Clarke wrote to his wife the day after the meeting ended, he noted that social life in Boston was in a "precious state of fermentation. New ideas are flying, high and low." "The prevailing idea, however," he informed her, "just now seems to be of a community . . . Mr. Ripley appears fermenting and effervescing to a high degree with these new ideas."[18] This is obviously not the same Ripley described years later by biographer Octavius Brooks Frothingham as "contemplative, quiet, thoughtful . . . [and] cautious to the verge of timidity." Clarke's Ripley is practically on the verge of frenzy, "fermenting and effervescing to a high degree" of excited anticipation. And no wonder. One week later, on October 1, he submitted his 7,300-word letter of resignation to the Purchase Street Society.

Part of Ripley's excitement was a result of his anticipation of a meeting that he scheduled with Adin Ballou right after the gathering of the Non-Resistance Society to discuss specific plans to launch a new community. Butler Wilmarth, one of Ballou's followers, provides a brief narrative. Ripley and his associates "had resolved upon carrying their views into practical operation," Wilmarth later recalled.

> On learning, therefore, that some of us were moving in the matter, meeting us at a Non-Resistance Convention in Boston, they suggested that we have a mutual consultation of the two parties in reference to it; which we accordingly did, at Mr. Ripley's house. And there was such a unanimity of general feeling, principle and purpose then and there manifested, that the first purpose was, that we should combine together, and start a community some-

where in New England, with a Practical Christian Test of membership, Mr. Ripley himself, particularly, inclined to this; but some of his associates, thinking that such a Test would make the enterprise too narrow and exclusive, it was finally decided that each class would do better to stand by itself, and select different locations on which to experiment with their different views and plans.[19]

The sticking point between Ballou and Ripley, Wilmarth makes clear, was the formal requirement of a religious pledge for admission to the community. Ripley himself evidently had no problem with the sentiments expressed in the religious pledge, but he obviously was persuaded that the pledge shouldn't be a formal requirement for membership in the new community because it might make it "too narrow and exclusive."[20] The community that he and Sophia envisioned would be religious, not sectarian; it would be egalitarian, not exclusive. "We meet in the church on the broadest ground of spiritual equality," Ripley repeatedly emphasized in the letter that he had just turned over to the Purchase Street Society. A religious pledge would discourage individuals with different theological views from uniting together to form the new colony that he and Sophia intended to organize.[21]

We'll obviously never know how well Ripley might have fared working alongside Ballou at Hopedale. Margaret Fuller might have been more confident about Sophia and George's prospects had Ripley joined forces with Ballou. She told William Henry Channing at the end of October that she wished Ripley might have "a faithful friend in the beginning, the rather that his own mind, though that of a captain is not that of a conqueror."[22] Perhaps Ripley recognized as much himself, for he went directly to Concord right after the meeting with Ballou seeking Emerson's support for the new community that he and Sophia intended to establish. By doing so, he forced Emerson to make one of the most crucial decisions of his life.

Emerson had been agitated for weeks before the Ripleys came calling. Emerson biographer Robert D. Richardson, Jr., describes his state of mind in September and October 1840 this way: "Never had Emerson lived as much in the present, never had he been less settled in his plans, his home, or his marriage."[23] For one thing, all the talk about community was troubling him. It forced him to confront the problem of society versus solitude. Several of his journal entries at the end of September 1840 indicate just how upset he was: "Perhaps it is folly this scheming to bring the good & like minded together in families, into a colony. Better that they should disperse and so leaven the whole lump of society." Then, just two sentences later, he writes: "I will not be chidden out of my most trivial native habit by your distaste, O philosopher, by your preference for somewhat else. If Rhetoric has no charm for you[,] it has for me[;] and my words are as costly & admirable to me as your deeds to you." And again, just a few lines after this: "There will be no confusion in reputations. I acquiesce to be that I am. But I wish no man to be civil to me." And not too many lines after that assertive statement: "In like manner the reformers summon Conventions and vote & resolve in multitude. But not so, O friends! will the God deign to enter & inhabit you, but by a method precisely the reverse. It is only as a man detaches himself from all support & stands alone, that I see him to be strong and to prevail. He is weaker by every recruit to his banner. Is not a man better than a town?" And, finally, right before the entry for October 5, 1840, Emerson writes: "Lidian [Emerson's wife] gives the true doctrine of property when she says 'No one should take any more than his own share, let him be ever so rich.'"[24]

Ripley had reason to expect Emerson's support. It was Emerson, after all, who had just written in the "Introductory Notice" of the *Dial* in July 1840 that the new journal would embody the spirit of the times, a spirit that he characterized as forward-looking, democratic, and reformist in nature, that was openly at war with those who looked backward only, who asked "only such a future as the past," and who suspected all schemes that tried to reconcile the practical with the speculative. Ripley was deeply moved by Emerson's words, so much so that when he wrote in his capacity as the journal's business manager to tell him that the "Introductory Notice" had gone to the printer, he felt compelled to say also that his colleague had expressed the very "thoughts which have long made me restless—which forbid me to be happy without the attempt to realize them." Emerson's comments gave Ripley extreme pleasure, not only because they confirmed his own faith in the "objects for which I am just now living," but because it was good to know that these very same objects had "taken such strong hold of another mind." Ripley hoped that Emerson would yet see some of his visions "made substantial in the 'city of God' which we shall try to build."[25]

George and Sophia traveled to Concord and met with Margaret Fuller and Bronson Alcott at Emerson's home on October 18 to discuss the particulars of their plan. The weather in October had been unseasonably cold, even by New England standards. Sophia was especially sensitive to it. The cold was so severe, she told a friend two weeks later, that "it penetrated to the heart."[26] (She would know several weeks later after Emerson finally contacted her husband just how apt her metaphor was.) She described the evening at Emerson's, nonetheless, as "very pleasant." Ripley and Alcott were each other's "poles" as they discussed the details of the "colony." Occasionally the "puissant Margaret" encouraged George to defend "the divine rights of mud[,] pigs[,] & snakes." Alcott, for his part, was depressed by such talk. Emerson, all the while, sat "benignantly listening."

Emerson, however, was feeling anything but "benignant" about

Margaret Fuller (1810–1850). Fuller attended the 1840 meeting at which
the Ripleys tried to persuade Emerson to join them in their utopian
adventure. She visited Brook Farm often during the early years.

what he was hearing. The Ripleys brought the October chill into his Concord parlor. He confided the next day in his journal that he "wished to be convinced, to be thawed, to be made nobly mad by the kindlings before my eye of a new dawn of human piety, . . . but not once," he admitted, "could I be inflamed." Ripley spoke excitedly about organizing a community "of the friends of the new order." He would purchase a tract of land of perhaps 500 acres. Buildings would be constructed for lodging, lectures, and "conversations." Private cottages would be built for families. Everyone would work and live together harmoniously. To Emerson, though, it all sounded like "arithmetic & comfort." The community would be nothing more than "a room in the Astor House hired for the Transcendentalists." Moving there would only mean removing himself from his present prison to another a little larger. "Moreover," he remarked in the journal, "to join this body [group] would be to traverse all my long trumpeted theory . . . that one man is a counterpoise to a city,—that a man is stronger than a city, that his solitude is more prevalent & beneficent than the concert of crowds."[27]

But Emerson said none of these things that evening. He sat quiet and aloof, "benignantly" listening. Fuller told her friend Caroline Sturgis two days later that she thought "the Phalanx talk was useless" to all but herself. To her, the discussion "brought out their [Ripley and Emerson's] different ways of thinking in strong relief, and helped me to a judgment." She didn't say just what that judgment was, but Alcott probably spoke for her too when he stated in his own journal that he and Emerson wanted something simpler than the community envisioned by Ripley. Their own vision hadn't really changed from a few months earlier when the two men constructed a university "out of straw" to be located right in Concord. That kind of arrangement, Alcott thought, would "preserve sacred the individual and the family." And though, ironically, he would seem to forget this concern entirely in June 1843 after starting his own Fruitlands community in the nearby town of Harvard, Alcott stated now that "there must be no violation of the sacredness of Home."[28]

George and Sophia Ripley were so focused on the vision of their plan that they probably didn't notice the motes in Emerson's and Alcott's eyes. Three days after the meeting in Concord, Ripley went to the Boston Athenaeum and charged out *Lowe's Elements of Agriculture,* the first of many titles having to do with farming that he borrowed there. In the months before heading to the Ellis Farm in West Roxbury, where, it had been decided, the community would be located, he immersed himself in the pages of the *Farmer's Magazine, Laudon's Encyclopedia of Gardening,* and, the paper that he found most useful, the *New England Farmer and Horticultural Register.* He borrowed the weekly *New England Farmer* more often than any other paper, probably because in addition to the proceedings of local agricultural societies, it also contained produce market reports and regular news summaries.[29] In addition to his agricultural readings, immediately after the meeting at Emerson's Ripley began to visit nearby farms to see what sage advice he might harvest from the local farmers.

Margaret Fuller caught up with the Ripleys in Boston at the end of October. She recognized immediately that they were even more intent on community than they had been just two weeks earlier. She expressed her concern to William Henry Channing that the couple was moving too quickly, that they weren't taking enough time "to let things ripen." And she wasn't wrong, either—at least about the determination with which George and Sophia were forging ahead with plans to launch the new community. Sophia informed a friend just a few days after the encounter with Fuller that her husband would "dissolve his connection" with Purchase Street on April 1, 1841, that they both planned to "go into the country" on May 1, and that Ripley himself was so determined to begin the experiment that should unforseen circumstances hinder their departure, he would "take some land not far from Boston & begin farming on his own account."[30]

There was no word from Emerson by early November so Ripley wrote him a long letter on November 9, 1840 "to submit the plan [for the community] more distinctly to your judgment, that you may decide whether it is one that can have the benefit of your aid and cooperation." Ripley's letter to Emerson is important because it is the only one surviving that provides a statement of his personal expectations for the community. The "Articles of Agreement" and the two constitutions under which Brook Farm operated between 1841 and 1847 all include a "preamble," but none of them provides so clear and direct a statement of Ripley's own original purposes and intentions as this letter to Emerson:

> Our objects, as you know, are to insure a more natural union between intellectual and manual labor than now exists; to combine the thinker and the worker, as far as possible, in the same individual; to guarantee the highest mental freedom, by providing all with labor, adapted to their tastes and talents, and securing to them the fruits of their industry; to do away the necessity of menial services, by opening the benefits of education and the profits of labor to all; and thus to prepare a society of liberal, intelligent, and cultivated persons, whose relations with each other would permit a more simple and wholesome life, than can be led amidst the pressure of our competitive institutions.

Ripley went on to say that he had already been offered a "beautiful estate" on the borders of Newton, West Roxbury, and Dedham; that the community would be principally an agricultural enterprise, though it would also sponsor a "school or college"; that it would be conducted in the simplest manner possible, perhaps by just three or four families at the beginning; and that the community would develop gradually, requiring as much as two to three years before "we should be joined by all who mean to be with us." Financially speaking, the community could get underway, Ripley thought, with an initial investment of $30,000. That amount would be raised by subscription in a joint-stock company. All investments would be guaranteed a fixed interest annually, and all investments would be secured by the real estate.

One effect of the October meeting in Concord was that it forced Ripley to refine his plans for the community. When he wrote to Emerson on November 9 he provided a much more conservative and scaled-down plan than the one he had presented three weeks earlier at Emerson's home. There is no talk in the letter, as there had been at the meeting, for example, of locating the community on a sprawling 500-acre property. Ripley also substantially reduced the amount of the initial investment that he thought was necessary to put the community on a secure financial footing from $50,000 to $30,000. Moreover, Ripley now added, Emerson wouldn't have to live in the community. An investment would be enough to demonstrate his support. "We wish only to know," Ripley stated, "what can probably be relied on, provided always, that no pledge will be accepted until the articles of association are agreed on by all parties."[31]

Emerson knew immediately—at least in some profound sense—that he could never be part of a community like the one George Ripley was proposing. But to say simply that Emerson decided right away not to support Ripley would seriously misrepresent what really happened. There should be no mistake about it: Ripley's appeal was not easy to refuse. It took Emerson five full weeks to draft his final response to his colleague—to tell him that he had decided, after much thoughtful de-

liberation, not to join the proposed community, even though its design "appears to me so noble & humane, proceeding, as I plainly see,
from a manly & expanding heart & mind that it makes me & all men
its friends & debtors." Thus it was a decision that he had reached, he
said, "very slowly & I may almost say penitentially."

Throughout those five weeks Emerson was perplexed and confused. He didn't like the pressure that Ripley was putting on him by
attaching so much importance to his participation, yet he wondered at
the same time whether he should commit himself to the new venture.[32] His initial reactions were alternatingly playful and serious. For
example, he wrote on November 15 to his wife Lidian, who was in
Boston visiting, that she had better hurry back to Concord right away
if she didn't wish to have the "house sold over your head." The community question was "in full agitation"; "you must come," he said, "&
counsel your dangerous husband." He was much more serious a few
days before, though, when he wrote to his young protégée Caroline
Sturgis and devoted the entire letter to a wide range of thoughts about
the community that were obviously on his mind. Then he joked again
when he wrote to Margaret Fuller on November 24 and apologized for
not being a very good correspondent, but, he protested, "on the
shoulders of G[eorge] R[ipley]'s 'community' must lie many of my
sins of omission." He was once more serious in his December 1 letter
to Fuller when he acknowledged that he was giving Ripley's proposal
"some earnest attention and much talk," and that he had "not quite
decided not to go." The very next day he sent off a letter to his
brother William in New York in which he summarized all the particulars of Ripley's letter, and then told him that whether they should
remain in Concord or move to West Roxbury was "the very question
we now consider." It took him nearly five full weeks, but Emerson finally made up his mind. Margaret Fuller reported to William

Henry Channing that "today [December 13] Mr. E[merson] has been here . . . He has finally decided not to join Mr. R[ipley]."[33]

Emerson sent his letter to Ripley on December 15 and thus brought a kind of closure to one of the great, if quiet, crises in his life. It's clear from a comparison of the original drafts and the "finished" version that the letter had not been easy to write. Robert D. Richardson, Jr., notes that the letter "shows evidence of uncharacteristic indecision and more than usual painstaking revision."[34] It is, in fact, a somewhat rambling and loosely connected list of reasons why Emerson eventually decided not to participate in the new community.

For one thing, he told Ripley, he was already living quite happily in Concord, a town that he had "many reasons to love," in which he had many friends, and "which has respected my freedom." For another thing, he feared that his "health & habits," as well as those of Lidian and his mother, were not robust enough to enable them to contribute their fair share of the work necessary to ensure the community's prosperity. And neither, he went on, would the community find him "as profitable & pleasant an associate as I should wish to be" because it was his inclination to withdraw and hide his attempts and failures at self-improvement rather than "perplexing" others around him. And as far as the proposed school or college was concerned, it might, he agreed, provide many attractions, but he and Ripley already kept school "for all comers" according to their respective abilities. "In the community we shall utter not a word more—not a word less." However, of all the statements that Emerson provided to justify his decision not to support the community, the one that Ripley probably anticipated the most—and the one that would always affect future relations with his Concord friend—was buried in the middle of the letter: "I think that all I shall solidly do," Emerson said, "I must do alone."

Though neither Emerson nor Ripley probably ever knew it, Margaret Fuller, in that insightful way that she had, drew the measure of both men two days before Emerson sent his letter. On December 13, 1840, she wrote to William Henry Channing to say that "Mr E[merson] knows deepest what he wants, but not well how to get it. Mr R[ipley] has a better perception of means, less insight as to principles, but this plan [to organize a community] has done him a world of good." She was concerned, however, that Ripley wasn't allowing for the possibility of failure. "He will not say . . . that he considers his plan as a mere experiment, and is willing to fail, or can well bear to fail. I tell him that he is not ready till he can say that."[35] Failure, however, was not a word in the Ripleys' vocabulary at the end of 1840. George and Sophia were going to put the security and respectability of Purchase Street and Boston behind them in order to organize a new "colony" in nearby West Roxbury. When it came to building the "city of God," failure was simply not possible.

2

Beginnings

Once it was clear to George and Sophia Ripley that they would not be joining forces with Adin Ballou and his "Practical Christian" followers, the decision about where to locate the new "colony" was a simple one. The Ellis Farm in West Roxbury had plenty of room for development on its 170 acres, and it was located just eight miles from the center of Boston. A Brook Farm circular described the property as a "place of great natural beauty, combining a convenient nearness to the city with a degree of retirement and freedom from unfavorable influences unusual even in the country." No wonder both George and Sophia had only the happiest associations of their time spent summering there, Ripley lying "for hours on green banks, reading Burns, & whistling to the birds who sing to him," and Sophia "jogging along on my white pony for miles & miles through the green lanes & small roads which abound in our neighborhood." More than one of these roads led to the village a mile or so away and to Centre Street where good friends Theodore and Lydia Cabot Parker lived.[1]

What the Ripleys were about to do was virtually unprecedented in New England. Brook Farm was the first nineteenth-century secular utopian community to be established there. All the cliched metaphors about uncharted waters and *terra incognita* really did apply to the new venture. There were no blueprints to consult, and no models to turn to for example. There were ten Shaker settlements still in existence in New England by 1841, but all of them were religiously inspired communities that had been established before 1800.[2] Besides, Ripley felt only contempt for the Shaker communities. Referring to Shakerism in March 1842, for example, he remarked that Shakerism "is a detestable, miserly, barren aristocracy, without a grain of humanity about it. Enormous wealth is made at the expense of all manly pursuits and attainments." There were many successful religiously based communities outside of New England of course, most notably the three organized by George Rapp and his German Separatist followers, namely "Harmony" (1805–1814) in Butler County, Pennsylvania; "Harmonie" (1814–1825) in Posey County, Indiana; and "Economy" (1824–1905) in Beaver County, Pennsylvania. And there were secular communities that had also achieved notoriety, such as "New Harmony" (1825–1827), the Indiana settlement based on the social theories of British industrialist Robert Owen, who would later visit Brook Farm. But, again, none of these were located in New England.

Evidently the stony soil and harsh climate made that region appear less hospitable and more forbidding to all but the chosen few. Of the thirty-seven communal and utopian societies organized in the United States between 1800–1840, only two were located in New England, and both were religiously based. To make the challenge faced by George and Sophia Ripley even more difficult, the singleness of purpose that inspired the devoted in the religious communities was never a unifying feature of Brook Farm life.[3]

The decision to locate the colony at the Ellis Farm was made several months before the Ripleys arrived there at the end of March 1841. The Boston press had been taking note of the Ripleys' plans since January, but none of the announcements identified the location of the proposed experiment. The *New England Farmer, and Horticultural Register* reported on January 27, 1841, for example, that it was the intention of Ripley and a few supporters to establish a "Practical Institute of Agriculture and Education," the design of which was "to furnish the means of a liberal education to those who are not intended for the learned professions." The weekly paper also stated that the proposed association would include a "department for classical learning, in which pupils will be prepared for admission to any of the New England colleges." A few weeks later the *Christian Register* reprinted a letter from the *Boston Daily Advertiser* stating that it was the purpose of "this [proposed] Institution . . . to combine the cultivation of an estate with the management of a school."[4]

When Ripley appealed to Emerson in November 1840, he noted that the new "colony" would be located at the Ellis Farm where he and Sophia had spent the previous summer. The location of the experiment was certainly no secret. Boston abolitionist Edmund Quincy wrote to a colleague on January 30, 1841, for example, informing him that "Ripley is actually going to commence the *'New State & the New Church'* at Ellis' farm, where he was last summer [1840], in the spring [of 1841]." Quincy wrote again at the end of February from his home in Dedham to fellow abolitionist Maria Weston Chapman and reported that "Ripley is actually coming out here next month [to West Roxbury] to commence the Millennium at Elllis' farm."[5]

The Ellis Farm was located about one mile northwest of the center of West Roxbury. Baker Street, which connected Roxbury and Dedham to the village of Newton, formed the eastern boundary of the farm. The Charles River provided the western boundary. In between were 170 acres of open pastures, rolling meadows, scattered woodlots, and a mature pine forest that spread along the northern edge of the property. Also at the northern end of the farm was "Pulpit Rock," a twenty-to-thirty-foot granite boulder where, according to legend, Puritan divine John Eliot, "apostle to the Indians," preached to the local native Americans in the 1640s.[6] The beauty of the farm, however, be-

Brook Farm. Oil on panel by Josiah Wolcott, 1844. Wolcott was a
Brook Farm supporter, but not a member or resident of the community.
He painted at least one other panoramic view of Brook Farm, which is
presently under the stewardship of the Massachusetts Historical Society.

lied its sandy and gritty soil, which had never been suitable for cultivation. That's why the Ellis property, like so many other nearby farms,
had always operated principally as a dairy farm, supplying hay from
its fertile grass fields to the livery market locally and in Boston.

The entrance to the property was on Baker Street, as, in fact, it
continues to be today. It was marked by a break in a low stone wall
that the farm's earlier owners—Edward Ward, Jonathan Ward, John
Mathews, John Mayo, and, most recently, Mayo's daughter Maria and

her husband, Charles—had patiently constructed along the entire length of the eastern side of the farm. To the left inside the entrance ran Palmer Brook, which inspired the community's name after it was organized.[7] Nearby was a large wooden barn. There were stalls sufficient for five horses and eighteen cattle on the main floor. In the cellar were half-a-dozen more stalls, which opened out toward the brook to a large fenced yard and piggery.

To the right of the entrance sitting atop three tiered terraces surrounded by mulberry and spruce trees and a single tall elm sat a large two-and-a-half story white clapboard farmhouse. In characteristic fashion, a long ell extended from the rear of the house, which included a good-sized kitchen. Above the ell were a series of small rooms that the Brook Farmers had to convert almost immediately to sleeping quarters. To the right upon entering the farmhouse were a front and a rear room. These were a bit larger than the corresponding rooms on the left because the staircase to the second floor was located just to the left of the entry. Beyond the staircase was the dining area. A large hall ran down the center of the house. Since the farmhouse was the scene of so many activities in the community, it became known right away as the "Hive."

Ripley embraced his new way of life with the zealousness of a new convert, although fourteen years as a Unitarian minister obviously hadn't prepared him for the demanding physical work required to run a farm. Neither had the dozens of calculations with which he filled the pages of his journal the previous winter. He made estimates of the expenses and profits of planting one acre of Indian corn; calculated the number of days required to harvest the crop (nine days for drawing manure; six days for ploughing twice; six days for planting; ten for hoeing; four for topping the stalks; and ten for harvesting); played with crop rotation charts, figuring, for instance, how potatoes, corn, small grain, and clover might be alternated with Indian corn and roots; and copied quotations from the *New England Farmer,* now his favorite weekly paper even though there wasn't much time to read it. The *New England Farmer* appealed to the pedantic side of Ripley's nature—the side that had responded so patiently and unrelentingly to Andrews Norton in 1839 and 1840. It included detailed "formulas" for projecting such things as the amount of manure that a specific number of cattle would produce, just how far that manure could be spread over tillage land, and, once done, how many potatoes and how much corn, for example, would be produced over a five-year period.[8]

But for all the time that he devoted to preparations, Ripley arrived at the Ellis dairy farm at the end of March armed with only his good intentions and just one person who had any real farming experience.[9] Young William Allen, originally from Vermont, had been living in West Roxbury managing Theodore Parker's small farm. Francis (Frank) D. Farley, who also came to West Roxbury with Ripley, evidently had done some farming in the Midwest, but he was a mechanic by trade. In addition to Allen and Farley, Ripley was joined in the first two weeks by Sophia and a woman named Elise (or Eliza) Barker. Mrs. Barker was a "domestic" from Boston and may have been the person to whom Ripley referred in his letter to Emerson the previous November when he said that "I should like to have a good washerwoman in my parish admitted [to the proposed community]." (She may also have been the person whom Ripley had in mind when, a month earlier, he alluded in his resignation letter to the "poor widow" through whose earnest toil "a suffering family is kept from want.") The small group, according to Elizabeth Palmer Peabody, "cleaned the stable[,] arranged the house[,] ploughed & planted— going through the hardest & most disagreeable work they will ever have to do."

Ripley himself was feeling newborn. Sophia reported to John

Sullivan Dwight in Northampton that her husband did "a harder day's work each day than the last; and feels better than ever before," and she told her friend Anna Alvord a few days later that "George . . . is as happy as a prince & works as hard as any day laborer with constantly increasing strength and no suffering." Even Ripley couldn't refrain from boasting a bit. When Boston abolitionist Ann Weston paid a visit to the community in mid-May, she reported to friends that she liked George Ripley very much. "He really talked con amore [about the community] & disclosed he never went to bed in his life so little tired as now after working in the field all day."[10]

Notably missing from the small group of early arrivals were most of Ripley's original supporters—his "disciples," Sophia had called them in October. These included two of his Unitarian colleagues, Samuel D. Robbins and Lemuel Capen, and two teachers from Cambridge, David and Maria Mack. But Ripley's classmate at the Harvard Divinity School, Warren Burton, did arrive in April. So did Nathaniel Hawthorne, although he had never been one of Ripley's "supporters." He was there because he hoped that the new community would provide a home after he wed his fiancee, Sophia Peabody. Burton and Hawthorne were followed by George Bradford, another of Ripley's Divinity School classmates (Ripley and Burton both graduated in 1826, Bradford in 1828), and an eccentric young man from Providence, Rhode Island, named Charles King Newcomb, who was the first nonworking boarder to join the new colony. Also arriving early on were two unmarried sisters, Ellen and Lizzy Slade, Ripley's friend the Rev. Ezra Stiles Gannett's sixteen-year-old niece Ora, and three teenaged boys—one of them Margaret Fuller's troublesome brother, Lloyd—who were the first students to enroll in the community's school. Sophia Ripley told John Dwight in early May that "the number assembled around the table in our large middle kitchen is thirteen & will soon number sixteen."[11] This diverse little group of people—

Ripley's supporters, the boarders, and the students—would always make up the population at Brook Farm, although the supporters would always be vastly outnumbered by the boarders and students, as well as by an assorted and shifting group of seekers whose purpose for coming to the community had little or nothing to do with high ideals.

The early arrivals settled into a routine right away, the women and men immediately reverting to the traditional gender roles to which they had been accustomed away from the farm. Allen and Farley arose first in the morning and sounded a horn at 4:45. The women then made their way to the kitchen to prepare breakfast while the men and boys went to the barn where the boys fed the two horses and four pigs and the men milked the nine cows. Around six o'clock the men returned to one of the small parlors in the rear of the house and changed their clothes so they could present themselves at the breakfast table looking no "less neat & civilized," Sophia happily noted, "than if they were to dine at our table in town." Sophia was the one, it seems, who urged this transformation every morning. A visitor to the community in May noted that Mrs. Ripley was "anxious to insure her own mind that . . . the canons of gentility were not infringed upon and she was still more obvious to let all else know the fact." The fastidious George Bradford, at least, wasn't bothered at all by Sophia's expectations. He happily remarked to a friend that when the horn sounded for the midday meal, the men "doff [their] cowhide boots & frocks and appear at table dressed up quite in the fashion of the rest of the world and you would not imagine from the appearance of some that they had been engaging in anything but study or some [easier?] employment."[12]

By half past six, Sophia and Ellen and Lizzy Slade were serving everyone cakes and huge loaves of brown bread that had just finished baking in the Stimpson's range, along with pitchers of fresh milk that the men had brought in from the barn. After breakfast, the men spent the morning shoveling and carting manure, hoeing the newly planted crops, and cutting straw and hay for the cattle. "The way these literary characters appear in a barnyard shoveling," William Allen observed with droll Yankee humor, "is a perfect caution to all laboring men." The women spent the morning cleaning up from breakfast and then straightening each room before going outside to cultivate the flower and fruit beds that had just been planted. The unusual amount of snow and rain in April and May considerably delayed the preparation of the fields for planting. It was one of the gloomiest spring seasons, in fact, that anyone could remember.

Everyone stopped for dinner at half past twelve ("served up in fine style," Allen remarked), after which the men returned again to their shovels, hoes, and pitchforks and spent the afternoon pretty much as they had the morning. Before supper, the horses and pigs had to be fed again, and the cows needed to be milked. (The horse that the father of William Allen's fiancee Sylvia had sold to George Ripley was living "like a countess sure enough," Allen reported, "and that is the name which he [Ripley] has given her.") Evenings were spent sitting together in the Hive mostly reading and talking. If people weren't too tired there might be a game of charades. Ellen Slade and Frank Farley were among the first to entertain their fellow laborers with a series of dramatic tableaux, an activity that was always one of the most popular in the community. "The relation we sustain to each other," Sophia Ripley proudly informed her friend Anna Alvord in May, "has been from the first of the highest and pleasantest kind."[13]

Sophia was perfectly suited to direct the community's domestic operations. Sophia Willard Dana was a member of the distinguished and prominent Dana family of Cambridge. Among her ancestors were Richard Dana, an early arrival in America in 1640; the Honorable Francis Dana, chief justice of the Supreme Judicial Court of Massachusetts and the first American minister to Russia; and Joseph Willard, a Harvard College president. Temperamentally, however, Sophia Ripley was no Brahmin. A tall woman with light-colored hair and a fair complexion, she was, according to fellow Brook Farmer Annie Salisbury, a person "of burning enthusiasm, warm feeling, and passionate will." When she was younger she conducted a school with her mother and sister (the husband and father Francis Dana, Jr., an eminent Cambridge jurist, having abandoned the family when Sophia was very young) at Fay House, now a part of Radcliffe College, in the Oval Room where she married Ripley in 1827. She was a gifted conversationalist as well, and she participated regularly in Margaret Fuller's popular "Conversations" for women in 1839 and 1840 in Boston, which helped to inspire Sophia's essay on behalf of "Woman" that had just been published in the *Dial* in January 1841. Yet she never hesitated at Brook Farm to perform the most demanding domestic work, as her title "chief" of the washing and ironing departments indicates. She scrubbed floors, nursed the sick, washed clothes, and taught classes in history and foreign languages. Brook Farmer J. Homer Doucet later recalled that Sophia, "so refined and cultured, was working like a slave, often for ten hours a day, in the sloppy wash room or in the hot ironing-room, not only willingly, but even cheerfully, speaking a pleasant word to this one and that one as she directed them in their work."[14]

The fact that Sophia, "so refined and cultured," would work "like a slave" should not be mistaken for weakness, nor should her domestic behavior be considered hypocritical. Sophia Ripley was a pragmatist whose vision for Brook Farm was as lofty as that of her husband. (The community might have fared better had George Ripley been more of a hard-nosed pragmatist himself.) Sophia was prepared to do whatever was necessary to ensure the success of the community. Thus she could complain, as she had just done in her *Dial* essay on "Woman," that "in our present state of society woman possesses not; she is under possession," or argue that "woman is educated with the tacit understanding, that she is only half a being, and an appendage," all the while remaining resolutely up to her elbows in washing and ironing.[15]

Despite the rigor and sameness of their daily schedule, not to mention the physical demands placed on the "literary characters," most if not all the early participants found their new life in the community not only satisfying but downright invigorating. George Ripley's enthusiasm was of course to be expected. But Harvard-educated George Bradford and Bowdoin graduate Nathaniel Hawthorne were also feeling inspired. Bradford told a friend two weeks after his arrival, for example, that he was working very hard, hoeing, shoveling, and spreading manure. Despite suffering a bit from overwork, "I have a sense of vigor and robustness," he happily reported, "that I have scarce felt before for a long time."

Ora Gannett recollected many years after her Brook Farm experience that one of Bradford and Hawthorne's responsibilities in those early weeks and months of communal life was milking the cows. In mid-June Bradford wrote to Hannah Thomas, a former student of his in Plymouth, "You will laugh when I tell you that I am learning to milk: I find that I make some progress, though I am far from dexterous." Yet despite his self-consciousness and even embarrassment, he couldn't refrain from boasting a bit, like a young boy finally allowed to wield the axe to split firewood: "Yet I get three or four quarts from my cows at a milking," he told Hannah proudly. Bradford and Hawthorne even developed a special fondness for two of the cows that they named "Daisy" and "Dolly." Gannett recalled that both men insisted that Daisy and Dolly be put into adjoining stalls at night because they were always together in the pasture during the day.[16] Bradford remembered this particular summer many years later with considerable affection—those "pleasant days," he later described them, working alongside Ripley, Hawthorne, and the others in the peat meadow, paring and cutting and stacking the dark bricks that would be used in the coming months to bank the fires in the Hive to keep out the blue-black cold of the New England winter.

Even the normally taciturn Hawthorne was in particularly high spirits during the first three months of the six-and-a-half that he spent in the community. For one thing, he liked his room at the Hive. He occupied the front right room and thought it was the "best chamber in the house," although he wasn't happy to discover a colony of wasps there just after he moved in ("not one of the accursed crew escaped my righteous vengeance," he reported to fiancee Sophia Peabody).[17] The wasps were more than compensated for, however, by the location of the room: George Ripley had accumulated one of the largest personal libraries in all of New England, and the books were stacked along the wall right outside Hawthorne's bedroom door. He also liked the old couch nearby that was tucked underneath the staircase. Here he could combine society and solitude, browsing through the volumes of Ripley's library while he quietly observed—like the protagonist Miles Coverdale in Hawthorne's thinly disguised satiric novel in 1852 about communal life, *The Blithedale Romance*—the comings and goings of his housemates. Two of those were Ora Gannett and her roommate Ellen Slade, who managed to engage Hawthorne in a memorable pillow fight one spring evening after they discovered him sitting alone in the hall. Hawthorne had no difficulty deflecting the cushions aimed at him with a nearby broom. Neither girl managed to land a single hit. "As fast as we could throw them at him [the cushions] he returned them with effect, hitting us every time, while we could hit only the broom," Ora recalled years later. Not a word was spoken during the battle. "We laughed and his eyes shone and twinkled like stars."[18]

Hawthorne missed Sophia Peabody terribly, of course. His letters gush with declarations of love for her. But when he wasn't anguishing over their separation, Hawthorne tended to be surprisingly playful, joking affectionately about one aspect or another of communal life. He teased Sophia, for instance, about a "transcendental heifer" that belonged to Margaret Fuller.[19] The cow was very "fractious and apt to kick over the milk pail. Thou knowest best," Hawthorne told Sophia, "whether, in these traits of character, she resembles her mistress." He told Sophia on another occasion that when he went to chop hay for the cows, he did so with such a "'righteous vehemence' (as Mr. Ripley says)," that within ten minutes he had broken the tool that he was using. A few hours after this incident, Ripley handed him a "four-pronged instrument . . . which he gave me to understand was called a pitch-fork," and with which he, Ripley, and Frank Farley "commenced a gallant attack upon a heap of manure." When he wrote to Sophia later that day, Hawthorne closed his note with the caution that he hoped the letter retained "none of the fragrance with which the writer was imbued."

Hawthorne couldn't resist taking a poke or two now and then at the New England clergy as well. When Ripley and Allen purchased four black pigs in mid-April, Hawthorne told Sophia that he thought they must be "members of the clerical profession" due to "several of their prominent characteristics, as well as their black attire." And when Sophia referred in one of her letters to Ripley's Unitarian colleague Warren Burton as "Mr. Dismal View," Hawthorne playfully scolded Sophia for her characterization, noting himself sardonically that "he [Burton] is one of the best of the brotherhood, as far as cheerfulness goes; for, if he do not laugh himself, he makes the rest of us laugh continually." Given this Hawthorne, it's no wonder that Sophia Ripley was referring to him by mid-May as "our prince—prince in everything." He was a man, she said, "to reverence [and] to admire." Just a few days earlier, on May 3, Hawthorne wrote to his sister Louisa in Salem and paid a similar compliment to his fellow Brook Farmers, noting as well that "the whole fraternity eat together; and such a delectable way of life has never been seen on earth, since the days of the early Christians."[20]

Sophia Peabody thought so too. She visited the community at the end of May and was especially taken by its natural beauty. "My life—how beautiful is Brook Farm!" she wrote to Hawthorne a few days later. "I was enchanted with it and it far surpassed my expectations. Most joyfully could I dwell there for its own beauty's sake." The visit, however, only made her feel more urgently than before the need to be alone with Hawthorne, to provide "a home for you to come to, after associating with men at the Farm all day." For while Sophia thought that she had never seen "such a divine expression of sweetness and kindliness" as appeared on Hawthorne's face "during the various transactions and witticisms of the excellent fraternity [at the community]," she already knew her future husband quite well. She recognized that Hawthorne's look of "sweetness and kindliness" was really just "the expression of a witness and hearer, rather than of comradeship."[21]

Sophia Peabody was certainly not the only person to visit the new community. Possibly because of its status as New England's first secular community—though more likely because of its convenience to Boston—Brook Farm was from its earliest days always something of a Mecca for the hordes of friends, well-wishers, and the merely curious who showed up with often annoying frequency on the steps of the Hive, invariably expecting a welcome reception and perhaps a cup of tea as well. No other antebellum American community—and eighty-four were in existence, at one moment or another, during the 1840s—attracted so many visitors.

Brook Farmer John Codman claimed years later that a record book in the reception room of the Hive included "a list of four thousand names, registered in one year." He may not have been exaggerating. In the year between November 1844–October 1845, for example, the Brook Farm financial records (which have not survived before November 1844) list receipts from visitors totaling slightly more than $425. It's impossible to say exactly how many visitors this amount actually represents, but a conservative estimate would put the number around 1,150 people for the one-year period. This is based on an average charge of thirty-seven cents per visit per visitor (visitors were usually charged twenty-five cents for dinner, twelve cents for supper, and twenty-five cents for one night's lodging). This estimate of visitors seems all the more conservative considering that the majority were—of necessity, given space limitations in the community—"day-trippers," and that friends of associates were often not charged for lodging or board.[22]

Among the Ripleys' friends, Bronson Alcott came down from Concord right away in April, but not with his neighbor Emerson, who was not yet willing to visit the West Roxbury community. Margaret Fuller traveled over from Cambridgeport in early May to spend a few days "with the fledglings of [the] Community."[23] And many local reformers from Boston and elsewhere—such as abolitionists Edmund Quincy and Ann Weston, and prominent author and editor Lydia Maria Child—were quick to inspect the Ripleys' new colony. Members of the families of West Roxbury neighbors and supporters like the Theodore Parkers, Frank Shaws, and George Russells could always be found at the community.

Over the years the visitors were generally a colorful assortment of characters. John Codman characterized them this way: "some of the oddest of the odd; those who rode every conceivable hobby; some of all religions; bond and free; transcendental and occidental; antislavery and proslavery; come-outers; communists, fruitists and flutists; dreamers and schemers of all sorts."[24] The names of some of these people are still easily recognizable today: Henry James, Sr., artist and sculptor William Wetmore Story, Horace Greeley, owner and editor of the powerful New York *Tribune,* and Albert Brisbane, America's foremost expositor of Fourierism, visited from New York City; engraver John P. Sartain made his way to West Roxbury from Philadelphia; Emerson, the Bronson Alcott family, and Henry Thoreau came down from Concord; Elizabeth Palmer Peabody, Richard Henry Dana, Jr., and Transcendentalists James Freeman Clarke, Christopher Pearse Cranch, and Orestes Brownson made the short trip from Boston; Margaret Fuller, who lived nearby in Cambridgeport, stopped by often; even Robert Owen, the British reformer and industrialist whose social theory of the "communities of united interests" inspired several American communities, paid Brook Farm a visit.

By midsummer 1841 cracks were already beginning to show in the colony's new foundation. Frank Farley's bouts with depression had become more frequent and forced him to leave the community in August. And Warren Burton had abruptly done so as well a few weeks earlier, evidently because he wasn't happy with Brook Farm life. Nathaniel Hawthorne, too, was becoming impatient with the community.

Farley was one of the most likable of the community's early residents. William Allen described him to his fiancee in early May as "naturally active and wity," and added that Farley could adapt himself to any sort of company and "entertain them with novel stories and wity sayings." Sophia Ripley was also enthusiastic about Farley. She wrote to John Dwight around the same time and said that he was "beyond praise": he was "the hardest worker in the field, the irresistible wit at table—the refined gentleman in the parlour & everywhere." In short, he was "noble & high souled in all relations." Even Hawthorne took an immediate liking to Farley. He enjoyed his companionship enough that he invited his new friend to join him, for instance, on his first extended walk around the farm at the end of April to explore the meadows and pastures, something that the two men did together again just a few days later. But after returning to Brook Farm from a two-week stay at the seashore with Hawthorne, Farley awoke one night "quite out of his wits." He departed the community at the end of August. Hawthorne, at least, was relieved to see him go: "his unappeasable wretchedness," he told Sophia, "threw a gloom over everything." In order to "escape a parting scene with poor Mr. Farley," Hawthorne sheepishly spent the morning in the bean field.[25]

Warren Burton had already been gone for several weeks by the time Farley left the community. Just why the itinerant Unitarian minister left isn't known. Hawthorne would only say that "it is a subject not easily to be discussed," adding cryptically that "it is an unfortunate event, in all its aspects."[26] Burton's early departure effectively ended Unitarian support of Brook Farm. And while Burton himself was never considered to be a Transcendentalist, his departure had to be a reminder to Ripley that, less than four months into his bold new venture, he was also without the support of the Transcendental community, for men like Emerson, Orestes Brownson, Frederic Henry Hedge, James Freeman Clarke, and Theodore Parker never committed themselves to the West Roxbury Association.[27]

Hawthorne's situation was another matter. He didn't come to West Roxbury imbued with religious zeal or lofty social ideals. His decision to support Ripley's venture was a pragmatic one. He joined the community expecting to have the time and quietude to concentrate on his fiction, and he hoped that the new colony would provide a home for him and Sophia once they were married. By early June, however, Hawthorne was already feeling the strains of communal living. The physically demanding work and the disproportionate amount of time that had to be devoted to physical rather than intellectual labors were beginning to trouble him. He was especially disheartened by the mounds of manure—which Ripley kept cheerfully referring to as the "gold mine"—that needed to be continuously spread around the farm. When he wrote to Sophia at the beginning of the month, he angrily referred to the manure pile as "that abominable gold mine!" "Of all the hateful places," he complained, "that is the worst. It is my opinion, dearest, that a man's soul may be buried and perish under a dung-heap or in a furrow of the field, just as well as under a pile of money." This is obviously a very different Hawthorne from the one who proclaimed seven weeks earlier that he felt "the original Adam reviving within me."[28]

Sophia Peabody knew her future husband as well as anyone did, but she may not have read between the lines of her fiance's letter and recognized what was really bothering him. His frustration with the community didn't have to do only with its physical demands; it had to do with its financial prospects. He made this clear a few weeks later to David Mack, who, with his wife Maria, was among the earliest to pledge support to Ripley, though the Macks subsequently withdrew this pledge and threw their support instead to the Northampton Association.[29] Hawthorne wrote to Mack on July 18 to correct—at least partly—some "imperfect communications" about Brook Farm that were made when the two men met briefly in Salem the week before.

For one thing, the amount of physical labor required at the farm had nothing to do specifically with George Ripley. "I have never felt that I was called upon by *Mr. Ripley* to devote so much of my time to manual labor . . . Our constraint has been merely that of circumstances, which were as much beyond his control as our own."[30] Hawthorne added that there were "private and personal motives which . . . would still make me wish to bear all the drudgery of this one summer's labor, were it much more onerous than I have found it." Hawthorne's "private and personal motives," of course, were both romantic and financial in nature, a point that he seemingly failed to clarify on this occasion perhaps because, as Hawthorne apologized, "I have written this letter in great haste."

He further recalled that when he had met Mack in Salem he had spoken "very despondingly, or perhaps despairingly, of the [financial] prospects of the institution," about which, he now said, he was still not "very sanguine." What worried him particularly was "the improbability that adequate funds will be raised, or that any feasible plan can be suggested, for proceeding [with the community] without a very considerable capital." Because Mack wasn't aware that Hawthorne intended to move to Brook Farm after he married Sophia Peabody, or that he had invested $1,000 in the community to help secure their future together, Mack wouldn't have realized that these were the "private and personal motives" to which Hawthorne was referring in his letter. If the community did indeed fail, Hawthorne had to wonder, would he still be able to go ahead with his plans to marry Sophia? And if the community collapsed from financial instability, would he ever recover his $1,000 investment?

Hawthorne expressed his concerns to Ripley directly in July, but it's not likely that the former Unitarian minister would have considered either Warren Burton's departure or Hawthorne's growing disaffection early warning signs of trouble in the community. As Hawthorne himself noted at this time, Ripley's "zeal will not permit him to doubt of eventual success." Besides, Ripley's young protégé John Sullivan Dwight had just resigned his pulpit in Northampton—yet another casualty in the ranks of the Unitarian clergy—and was thinking about making his way to Brook Farm. Ripley had also just received a letter of inquiry from a young man named Charles Anderson Dana. Dana was a distant cousin of Sophia, and he was also friendly with John S. Brown, who was married to Ripley's cousin, Mary. Dana had completed two years at Harvard College, but had severely strained his eyesight "through overmuch study" during the spring 1841 term.[31] He wouldn't be returning in the fall. His intellectual sympathies were very much with Ripley's new community. Could a place be found there for him?

Dana had no farming or business experience, and he certainly had no financial resources, but Ripley decided to recruit him anyway. He needed young men with strong shoulders. Farley and Burton were gone. Bradford was in earnest, but he was not accustomed to the long days of demanding physical labor. And Hawthorne had just worked out a new arrangement whereby he would "cease laboring for my board, and begin to write" beginning September 1. It was also Ripley's heartfelt conviction, as he said to Dana when he wrote to him on August 4, 1841, that "it is from the young, the energetic, the pure-minded, the self-relying, who have given no hostages to society and who expect and ask but little of it, that the life-blood of our enterprise is to proceed." The Hive was already "completely filled," but Ripley managed to make room for the young man who almost immediately would become second-in-command in the West Roxbury Association.[32]

Two other notable arrivals that September were Minot Pratt and Georgiana Bruce. Pratt, a thirty-six-year-old printer with the *Christian Register,* was a sober, quiet, and hard-scrabbled New Englander who went about his business without fanfare and stayed with a task until it was properly completed. George Bradford described him as "a man of singular purity and uprightness of character and simplicity," which were qualities that later earned him the hard-won friendship of Henry Thoreau. Pratt quickly became one of George Ripley's most trusted associates. Pratt's family had already been living in the community since June: his wife Maria (a "good, homely, and sensible" woman, Hawthorne thought), and their three children—Frederick, who was ten years old; John, who had just turned eight and who would marry Anna Alcott, the eldest of the "little women," in 1860; and Caroline, just five years of age.[33]

Georgiana Bruce was a young "nursery governess" in the employ of the Rev. Ezra Stiles Gannett. Born in England, Bruce had come to America five years before at the age of nineteen. She wanted to become a teacher, and it was agreed that she should first be a student-boarder at Brook Farm, working there full-time in return for her board and education. When Bruce first visited the community a few months before, she received a memorable lesson in the kind of Christian egalitarianism that had everything to do with George Ripley's mission at Brook Farm. William Allen, the young farmer from New Hampshire, was going to the Boston market the next day. "Mr. Ripley said, as illustrating the spirit prevailing there . . . that nothing would give him, Mr. R[ipley], more pleasure than to black his [Allen's] boots before he left." This gesture was not intended as a criticism of Allen's boots, Bruce noted later in her reminiscences of the community, but that "Mr. R[ipley] had reached a point in brotherly love which had swept the class feeling entirely away." Such "facts" about Brook Farm, Bruce thought, "were almost incredible."[34]

Had Hawthorne overheard Bruce's remark, he probably would have agreed that Ripley was earnestly trying to practice at Brook Farm what before he had only been able to preach at Purchase Street. But the Salem-born writer would surely have added that he thought other facts about the West Roxbury community were even more "incredible," not least of them that after five full months of nearly backbreaking physical labor around the farm, the community still had no reliable source of income or, even more alarming, a "feasible [financial] plan" to sustain the Association's future operations.[35]

3

Organization

The July 1841 number of the *Dial* includes a "Letter from Zoar" by Sophia Ripley that is actually a report on the communistic society of "Separatists" in Zoar, Ohio, that the Ripleys visited briefly in 1838. The German-based community was established in 1817 and had since become quite prosperous. Sophia found the community very attractive, so much so that her departure after a two-day visit had her wishing "that we might pass a season in the midst of its rural pleasures and country fare." She was particularly impressed by the cleanliness, the unhurried pace with which everyone went about their tasks, and the overall contentment of the community members. Zoar (which continued until 1898) was not a community, however, that would ever inspire her or her husband's highest or lasting respect, for its aims were ephemeral and were focused only on satisfying the material needs of its members. Its leader, Joseph Baumeler, "is nothing of a philanthropist," Sophia noted, "and this lessens our interest in the community."[1]

It would be interesting to know how the Ripleys might have compared the early developments at Brook Farm in the spring and summer of 1841 with the general success and financial stability of the "Separatists" at Zoar. Brook Farm had been in operation now for five full months and its financial footing was still not firm. Moreover, Ripley had still done nothing to bring the community to the attention of the public. He was not yet ready, for instance, to provide a statement of his aims and purposes. He knew that his friend Adin Ballou and his followers had drafted a constitution months before for their proposed community in Milford, Massachusetts, despite the fact that the "Practical Christians" had still not moved to the site chosen for the experiment. Elizabeth Palmer Peabody, at least, was very frustrated by Ripley's failure to provide even a "prospectus," and urged him repeatedly to publish a statement by way of enlisting the support of those "with solid cash in their purses." She first expressed her disappointment to John Dwight in late April 1841, immediately after Brook Farm's organization. At the end of June 1841 she complained again to the Northampton minister that she couldn't see how Brook Farm was "to step out of its swaddling clothes—unless Mr. Ripley makes known in some regular way or allows some friend to do so the plan in detail & in connection with the Ideal."[2]

For such a statement of purpose Ripley might easily have revisited his November 9, 1840, letter to Emerson. There he had declared, for instance, that the community he envisioned would provide opportunities to "insure a more natural union between intellectual and manual labor" and "combine the thinker and the worker . . . in the same individual." What Ripley had in mind was a community in which "the most complete [educational] instruction shall be given, from the first rudiments to the highest culture," regardless of an individual's economic or social background. The new colony, he told Emerson at the time, "would be a place for improving the race of men that lived on it; thought would preside over the operations of labor, and labor would contribute to the expansion of thought; we should have industry without drudgery, and true equality without its vulgarity." As noted in Chapter 2, Ripley was so committed to a community based on egalitarian principles that he even hoped, he also told Emerson in November, to include a washerwoman and her two children from his Purchase Street congregation, along with a few farmers and mechanics who also might benefit educationally from the unique circumstances that the community would provide.[3]

The central idea that animated Ripley's vision was probably first inspired by his mentor, William Ellery Channing, who was influenced himself by a lawyer named Elisha Ticknor. Channing noted in his *Lectures on the Elevation of the Labouring Portion of the Community* (1840) that Ticknor, who with fellow lawyer James Savage had been instrumental in organizing the Provident Institution for Savings as well as the primary schools in Boston, discussed a plan with him "for teaching at once Agriculture and the Mechanic Arts." Ticknor "believed, that a boy might be made a thorough farmer, both in theory and practice, and might at the same time learn a trade, and that by being skilled in both vocations, he would be more useful, and would multiply his chances of comfortable subsistence." Channing states that he was interested in the plan right away, and "Mr. Ticknor's practical wisdom," he said, "led me to believe that it might be accomplished." Channing and Ripley of course had many opportunities to share ideas in 1840; they were, for instance, at John Sullivan Dwight's ordination in Northampton in May just one day before Ripley delivered his first letter of resignation to the Proprietors at Purchase Street.[4]

Actually, the Brook Farmers did have a set of "Articles of Agreement," but Ripley wasn't willing yet to make them public.[5] Actions would speak louder than words. He would let Elizabeth Palmer Peabody, though, quietly spread the word about the new community. So far there had been only a few brief notices of it in the *New England Farmer and Horticultural Register* in January 1841, and in the *Christian Register* in February 1841. In May 1841 the *Monthly Miscellany of Religion and Letters,* which was under the editorial control of Ripley's good friend Ezra Stiles Gannett, announced with "sincere regret, and with a sense of personal loss," that Ripley had resigned from the ministry. "His plans for the future," readers were informed, "are connected with the education of the young of both sexes." The *Monthly*, a moderate Unitarian journal, added supportively that "we can discover nothing chimerical or 'Transcendental' in [his] scheme." Then two months later, in August 1841, the *Monthly* printed a lengthy letter "written by a friend—not a member of the new [Brook Farm] community." That "friend" was almost certainly Elizabeth Palmer Peabody, and her letter on "The Community at West Roxbury, Mass." is the first notice of Brook Farm that provides detailed information about its operations.[6]

Peabody's letter in August 1841 is, with two exceptions, a narrative version of the "Articles of Agreement and Association between the Members of the [Brook Farm] Institute for Agriculture and Education," which had been serving as an informal constitution for Ripley and the Brook Farmers right from the start. Peabody's statement that "there are compensations . . . which this community [Brook Farm] provides by its constitution" is a reference to these first "Articles of Agreement."[7] The "Articles" represent the earliest attempt on the part of the Brook Farmers to define their purposes. Peabody's letter touches on virtually all the matters included in the sixteen Articles that make up that document, except for Article II, which states, in part, that "no religious test shall ever be required of any member of the association; no authority assumed over individual freedom of opinion by the association, nor by one member over another."[8]

Ripley and his followers included this Article guaranteeing religious freedom to all the members of the community in order to distinguish Brook Farm from more narrowly circumscribed religious associations like Adin Ballou's Hopedale Community and the dozen or so Shaker communities long since established in Massachusetts and New Hampshire. Peabody makes no reference to Article II in her letter al-

most certainly because she feared that the public would tar Brook
Farm by charging that its members were "Separatists" and "Come-
Outers" and thus opposed to institutional and traditional Christianity.
Ripley's pamphlet war with Andrews Norton on the "latest form of
infidelity," Peabody knew, was still fresh in the public's memory. The
title and focus of her second essay on Brook Farm in October 1841—
"A Glimpse of Christ's Idea of Society"—was obviously intended
to dispel any notions about subversive religious practices at the community.[9]

The second exception in her letter about "The Community at West
Roxbury" is the omission of any reference to the nearly two-hundred
word "preamble" to the "Articles of Agreement." There was no reason
for Peabody to focus on this important statement because the ideals
contained in it were implicit in everything else that she had to say
about the community in her letter. It is included here because it remained virtually unchanged in the six-plus years of the Association's
existence, despite substantive revisions to the "Articles" that later
became the bases of Brook Farm's two constitutions. Reform ideology
and priorities may have changed in the course of the community's development, but the preamble did not. It was obviously an important statement of purpose and principle to George Ripley and his
supporters:

> In order more effectually to promote the great purposes
> of human culture; to establish the external relations of life
> on a basis of wisdom & purity; to apply the principles of
> justice & love to our social organization in accordance
> with the laws of Divine Providence; to substitute a system
> of brotherly cooperation for one of selfish competition; to
> secure to our children & those who may be entrusted to
> our care the benefits of the highest physical, intellectual,

& moral education which in the present state of human knowledge the resources at our command will permit; to institute an attractive, efficient & productive system of industry; to prevent the exercise of worldly anxiety by the competent supply of our necessary wants; to diminish the desire of excessive accumulation, by making the acquisition of individual property subservient to upright & disinterested uses; to guarantee to each other forever the means of physical support & of spiritual progress; & thus to impart a greater freedom, simplicity, truthfulness, refinement & moral dignity to our mode of life;—We the undersigned do unite in a voluntary Association, & adopt & ordain the following Articles of Agreement & Association, to wit.[10]

What then might a person expect if they cast their fortunes to the wind and headed to Brook Farm? That is essentially what Elizabeth Palmer Peabody tries to explain (no doubt with Ripley's blessing) in the August letter in the *Monthly Miscellany,* as well as in her follow-up article, "Plan of the West Roxbury Community," for the *Dial* in January 1842. Prospective members would know first that the property of the Brook Farmers was held in joint-stock proprietorship, which meant that associates were allowed to retain some private property, "enough to be so far independent," Peabody noted, "that each one could leave the Association, if it were necessary or desirable, and not be cast penniless into the world."[11] In the community itself, members performed whatever type of work appealed to their individual natures. Men might, for instance, devote themselves partially or entirely to domestic chores, just as women might similarly busy themselves with agricultural pursuits. Since, Peabody stated, the Brook Farmers believed that all labor was sacred "when done for a common interest," men and

Dress of the Men at Brook Farm

Usual dress of the Women at Brook Farm.

Dress of Brook Farm men and women. Many Brook Farmers—including
Nathaniel Hawthorne—preferred comfortable work clothing such as that
depicted here, but there was never a dress code in the community.

women were paid identical wages, regardless of the work they performed. Each Brook Farmer was entitled to board (that is, room, food,
fuel, light, and washing) in proportion to the number of days worked
each year for the community: "one year's board for one year's labor;
one-half year's board for one half year's labor, and if no labor is done
the whole board shall be charged."[12]

Ripley and the Brook Farmers agreed that the length of the workday at Brook Farm would vary according to the season—but in neither

case would it be longer than ten hours. In the months between May and October, when there was plenty of light and much outdoor work that needed to be done around the farm, associates worked a sixty-hour week—ten hours a day, six days a week. In the months between November and April, when the days were short and the farm required less attention, the workday was cut back to just eight hours. (This put the Brook Farmers well ahead of New England's workingmen, who, in 1844 and 1845, made the ten-hour day the centerpiece of the labor movement.)

In addition to housing and board, members of the Association were entitled to certain "guarantees," including "medical attendance, nursing, education in all departments, amusements; and to all persons over seventy and under ten years of age, and to all persons who are sick, free board, unless their five per cent interest can support them." With respect to board, nonworking residents (such as Charles King Newcomb) were charged four dollars per week; children of associates over ten years of age paid half that rate. Students enrolled in the Brook Farm school were charged on the basis of gender and age. The price of board and tuition for boys over twelve years of age was four dollars a week; for girls, it was five dollars. (It was decided the following August 1842 to make the rates identical.) Children under twelve paid three-and-a-half dollars a week, regardless of gender. These rates were "exclusive of washing and separate fire."

A second set of Articles was approved on September 29, 1841. These were the "Articles of Association of the Subscribers to the Brook Farm Institute of Agriculture and Education." The "Articles of Association" were intended to complement the "Articles of Agreement"—not supersede them. They are different documents. The twelve "Articles of Association" deal principally with financial matters (which the word "Subscribers" in the title is intended to indicate); the seventeen "Articles of Agreement . . . between the Members" have to do mainly with administrative and ideological matters.

Both sets of "Articles" identify the community as the "Brook Farm Institute of Agriculture and Education," but the "Articles of Association" state, for example, that the Association's property will be vested in four trustees (elected annually), that no shareholder will be held individually responsible for contracts or debts incurred by the Association, that shareholders will be guaranteed 5-percent annual interest on their stock, that shareholders must provide one year's notice before redeeming stock, and that a shareholder "may receive the tuition of one pupil for every share held by him, instead of five per cent. interest . . . or tuition to an amount not exceeding twenty per cent. interest on his investment."[13] The "Articles of Agreement" note, on the other hand, that the administration of the Association, for instance, will be handled by four "Directions" (committees really—General, Financial, Educational, and Agricultural), and that the Association "shall provide such employment for all its members, as shall be adapted to their capacities, habits & tastes; & each member shall select & perform such operations of labor whether corporal or mental, as he shall deem best suited to his own endowments & the benefit of the association" (an Article that might have been inspired by Hawthorne's dissatisfaction with the community).[14]

The list of names at the end of each document identifies Brook Farm's early participants and financial supporters. There are fourteen names listed on the "Articles of Agreement." These individuals were the first to pledge support for the new community. In addition to George and Sophia Ripley, there were (listed in original order):

> Sam[ue]l D. Robbins
> D[avid] Mack
> Maria Mack

Marianne Ripley

Nath[aniel] Hawthorne

Lemuel Capen

Warren Burton

Minot Pratt

Maria T. Pratt

Geo[rge] C. Leach

Mary E. Robbins

Francis D. Farley[15]

By the time that the "Articles of Association" were ready to be approved on September 29, however, only seven of the original participants were willing to affirm their support of Brook Farm with a financial commitment to the community. In addition to the seven, William Allen, Ripley's niece Sarah F. Stearns, and a Charles O. Whitmore also agreed "to pay the sum attached to our names" (listed in original order):

Geo[rge] Ripley	$1,500
Nath[aniel] Hawthorne	1,000
Minot Pratt	1,500
Charles A. Dana	1,500
William B. Allen	1,500
Sophia W. Ripley	1,000
Maria T. Pratt	1,000
Sarah F. Stearns	1,000
Marianne Ripley	1,500
Charles O. Whitmore	500

Article XI of the "Articles of Association" indicates that the community's capital stock was $12,000, the amount derived from the pledges of the ten subscribers to purchase twenty-four shares of stock at $500 per share.[16] The $12,000 was therefore "good faith" money and not actual cash received. Probably only half the amount pledged, at best, was actually paid at this time. Neither William Allen nor Charles Dana, for instance, was in a financial position to contribute anything more than his hard work and good intentions to the Association. Dana's biographer notes that while the former Harvard student came to the community prepared to do whatever should be expected of him, "it will not be forgotten that he was entirely without means to pay his way elsewhere."[17] Dana, in fact, would be beset by financial woes from the beginning to the end of his five-year stay at Brook Farm, and he would struggle throughout his time there to purchase even one of the three shares to which he committed himself. It's very doubtful, too, that the Pratts, with their three children, had accumulated enough financial reserves to enable them to provide the full amount of their pledges. More likely, they put up no more than $1,000. As for Charles O. Whitmore, he seems never to have spent even a single day at Brook Farm. He must have immediately regretted his $500 investment, which, it appears, he never recovered. The community, in any case, was carried in the early months of its existence on the financial shoulders of the three Ripleys, Minot and Maria Pratt, and Hawthorne.[18]

Hawthorne undoubtedly had second thoughts about his purchase of Brook Farm stock even before the "Articles of Association" were approved at the end of September. He returned to West Roxbury on September 20 from a visit to his family's home in Salem no more certain about his future in the community than he had been when he left it three weeks before. What he did know is that he wanted to wed Sophia Peabody. He was also sure that he wouldn't stay at Brook Farm through the winter. "I cannot and will not spend the winter here," he told Sophia on September 25, just four days before the "Articles" were approved and his financial entanglement with Brook Farm was complicated further. "The time would be absolutely thrown

away," he added, "so far as regards any literary labor to be performed."
Yet he had not ruled out the possibility that the Farm might still be
the place to begin his marriage to Sophia.

Aware of Hawthorne's disaffection with the community, Ripley
cleverly arranged to have him appointed chairman of the newly created "Direction of Finance" (Allen and Dana were also appointed to
this committee), which automatically made him one of Brook Farm's
four trustees (Ripley, Allen, and Dana were the other three).[19] Ripley
hoped that Hawthorne's involvement in Brook Farm's affairs might
eventually also wed him to the community. Hawthorne was quite
flattered and more than a little flabbergasted by his newly acquired
status, especially his position on the Finance Committee. He playfully
scolded Sophia the same day: "Now dost thou not blush to have
formed so much lower an opinion of my business talents, than is en-
tertained by other discerning people?"[20]

Despite Brook Farm's limited financial resources, George Ripley decided to purchase the Ellis Farm right away rather than wait a while
longer to see whether those resources might be placed on a firmer
foundation. Less than two weeks after the approval of the "Articles of
Association," Ripley, Allen, Dana, and Hawthorne, acting as trustees
on behalf of the "Brook Farm Institute of Agriculture and Education,"
purchased Charles and Maria Mayo Ellis's dairy farm for $10,500.
The deed states that "said farm contains about one hundred and seventy acres." The purchase on October 11, 1841, included "also a certain other lot of land known as the Keith lot, consisting altogether of a
farm with dwelling house, barn, and outbuildings thereon situated."[21]
Since the Keith lot was approximately twenty-two acres in size, a total
of 192 acres was included in the purchase. The Keith lot was an especially important feature of the purchase because it held a farmhouse—
which the Brook Farmers immediately began calling "The Nest"—

that was already being used for classrooms and living quarters for the community's fledgling school.[22]

It would appear that the purchase of the farm was one of Ripley's most successful financial transactions at Brook Farm because he secured two mortgages on the property, one for $6,000, the other for $5,000, thereby generating an additional five hundred dollars over the purchase price for use in the community. The extra five hundred dollars came from Mrs. Lucy Cabot, Theodore Parker's mother-in-law, who was living with the Parkers at the parsonage in West Roxbury. Parker himself must have had great confidence in Brook Farm's eventual success or else he would presumably have discouraged his wife's mother from making the investment. The $6,000 mortgage was provided by Josiah Quincy, Jr., and David Wilder, both of whom were commissioners of the sinking fund of the Western Railroad Corporation. The $4,500 mortgage was held by three of Brook Farm's West Roxbury friends and neighbors, namely Francis G. Shaw, George R. Russell—whose families were old Boston merchants—and Shaw's brother-in-law, Henry P. Sturgis.[23] The Shaws and Russells lived next door to Theodore and Lydia Parker and Lucy Cabot, with a path behind the Parkers' house leading to the Shaw and Russell homes. The families were all very friendly, not only with each other, but with George and Sophia Ripley and other Brook Farmers as well. George Russell had married Frank Shaw's sister, Sarah Parkman, several years before, and two of Sarah and Frank Shaw's brothers were married to Henry Sturgis's sisters. There's no doubt that without the ongoing financial support of Frank Shaw and George Russell, Brook Farm would have collapsed sooner than it did.[24]

Nathaniel Hawthorne obviously stayed around long enough to participate in the purchase of the Ellis Farm, but he departed the community for good just a few weeks later, the second major defection (Ripley's colleague Warren Burton was the first) since July. Hawthorne spent the month of October taking long walks and writing in his journal. Although a few of the entries found their way into *The Blithedale Romance* ten years later, it was not a productive month for the Salem writer. Though generally undisturbed by activities in the community that September and October, Hawthorne was simply marking time there. For all intents and purposes, he did no writing at all during his final five weeks in West Roxbury. The last entry in his journal from Brook Farm is dated October 27: "Fringed gentians, found the last probably, that will be seen this year, growing on the margin of the brook."[25]

Hawthorne's final quiet days at Brook Farm stand in dramatic contrast to George Ripley's that October. It was decided at the beginning of the month to construct a new house at the Farm because the twenty or so people living in the community had already filled the rooms in the Hive and the Nest to capacity. Rather than cutting back on the number of residents in the community, or waiting until the following spring to see whether the usually severe New England winter would chill the ardor of any of the faithful, ground was broken on the highest point of the Farm, with Ripley superintending the work. Confidence that autumn in the community's future prospects is reflected in a remark by Sophia Ripley at the end of September. "I must tell you how well we are satisfied (I trust without fanaticism) with the success of our experiment," she wrote to Margaret Fuller on the 23rd. "We have all learned a great deal—more perhaps than in any six months of our life."[26]

Ripley himself was particularly looking forward to the first formal meeting of the Brook Farm Association on October 30. There was important business at hand. First, "the Institution recently carried on by George Ripley" and "the establishment recently carried on by Marianne Ripley [the Brook Farm school]" needed to be formally transferred to the "Brook Farm Institute of Agriculture and Education" from and after November 1, 1841. Then a few practical regulations had to be set down for the general operation of the Association until both sets of "Articles" could be combined into a more formal constitution.[27]

The year 1841 was easily one of the most momentous of George Ripley's life. Mistakes were inevitable. How could anyone have expected otherwise when faced with the daunting challenge of building—as Ripley had characterized it the year before in his November 9, 1840, letter to Emerson—the "city of God"? But there was already much to show for the arduous work that he and Sophia and the handful of his supporters had invested. The nearly two-hundred-acre Ellis dairy farm now belonged to the "Brook Farm Institute of Agriculture and Education"; "Articles of Agreement," "Articles of Association," and some general regulations were formally approved; and the Brook Farm school was continuing to attract more students. The school notwithstanding, the community was still without a reliable source of income. The time seemed right for another appeal to one of the men that Ripley initially hoped would stand shoulder to shoulder with him in building the new world. He wrote once again to Emerson on December 17, 1841, to ask for his support, although not this time as a participant but as an investor in the community.

It wasn't Ripley's style to boast, but he and the Brook Farmers were "full of joy and hope" at year's end. He was writing "to request some of those who have faith in us and in our enterprise, not to endow us, or to portion us, but to invest in our stock." He felt "so sure of [Emerson's] sympathy in the ideas which our little company are trying to illustrate, that I do not hesitate to bespeak your attention to our prospects." The little group gathered at Brook Farm was entirely devoted to its new way of life: "we feel the deepest inward convictions that for us our mode of life is the true one"—here Ripley could not help underscoring the difference between the Brook Farmers and their Concord neighbor—"and no attraction would tempt any one of us to exchange it for that which we have quitted lately." There was reason to be encouraged about the community's financial prospects too, Ripley claimed. In addition to a "ten per cent. net gain on the value of the estate" from their farming endeavors, "our personal resources are sufficient . . . for the immediate improvements we contemplate." Still, Ripley acknowledged, "without larger means than are now at our command, we must labor to great disadvantage, and perhaps retard and seriously injure our enterprise." Ripley hoped that Emerson might "seek the ownership of one or more of our shares [of stock] . . . in this time of our infant struggle and hope."[28]

When Ripley wrote to Emerson first on November 9, 1840, it took New England's most notable spokesman for the culture of self-reform five full weeks before he finally responded in a letter that showed "evidence of uncharacteristic indecision and more than usual painstaking revision."[29] This time Emerson didn't respond at all—not even in the privacy of his own journals. Either it was never received, or, more likely, Ripley's second letter made Emerson squirm even more in light of Brook Farm's apparent early success. Ripley wouldn't realize for many weeks, however, that his appeal had fallen on deaf ears. What filled the former Unitarian minister with a fervent sense of hope and promise for the future as the year 1841 came to an end was his belief that "a rare Providence seems to have smiled on us in the materials which have been drawn together on this spot; and so many powers are at work with us and for us, that I cannot doubt we are destined to succeed in giving visible expression to some of the laws of social life, that as yet have been kept in the background." Just how Ripley intended to bring about the new social order without a specific financial plan or adequate sources of income, however, remained to be seen.[30]

4

The Seeds of Fourierism

The single most persistent circumstance of Brook Farm life in 1842 was financial necessity—that factor made itself felt in virtually everything of consequence that took place in the community that year. Nathaniel Hawthorne had been the first to speak "despondingly, or perhaps despairingly," about Brook Farm's financial prospects the previous July 1841, and his anxiety at that time about whether "adequate funds will be raised," or "any feasible plan can be suggested, for proceeding" with the West Roxbury Association, was entirely justified. Brook Farm had an organizational plan, but, although the community had already been in existence for nine full months at the beginning of 1842, there was still no financial plan. Had there in fact been one, it would not have been necessary to proceed so hastily in the new year.

For one thing, Ripley might have been more careful about controlling the community's swelling population. For another, he probably would have been more cautious in proceeding with the Association's physical expansion. And for yet another, Ripley likely would have listened more warily to what was being said by three men from New York City—one of them the editor of the recently established New York *Tribune,* another a young man who was destined to become the foremost American apostle of the French social scientist, Charles Fourier, and the third a forty-five-year-old shoemaker who joined Brook

Farm at the end of the year. All three men were to exert considerable influence on Brook Farm. That influence might have been less consequential were it not for the community's vulnerability due to its uncertain financial prospects.

When Ripley wrote to Emerson in December 1841 seeking his financial support, there were about twenty people living in the community. By May 1842 there were already fifty. In July ten more people moved into the Association. Just one month later, Brook Farm's population was up to seventy people. The majority of them were boarders and students whom Ripley indiscriminately welcomed into the Association because they represented its only steady source of regular income.[1] One important consequence of having so many boarders and students is that they outnumbered associates fifty-five to fifteen by August, the effect of which was to compromise and distort the original aims for which Ripley and his supporters had come to West Roxbury in the first place. Another significant consequence is that Brook Farm's leaders felt compelled to undertake a premature building program in order to accommodate the large number of people who were steadily flocking to the community, thereby immediately and dramatically increasing the Association's indebtedness.

The community's first new building was hurriedly completed in March 1842. Construction had begun the previous November, and work on it continued right through the winter. The Brook Farmers decided to locate the thirty-five-to-forty-square-foot house on the highest point at the Farm, which was several hundred yards behind and northwest of the Hive. It was immediately christened the "Eyrey," although Ripley joked that "there are no eagles there, only doves and such poultry."[2] The location provided scenic views all around. The house was built on top of several very large rocks—boulders, really— which provided the foundation for the new building as well as a fairly spacious, if not very high, storage cellar (both still noticeable today).

Ripley's extensive library was moved from the Hive to the Eyrie (as everyone else except Ripley would spell it). The parlor opposite the new library immediately was designated a music room. Behind the two front rooms were six smaller ones (altogether, four very small rooms on each side of a center hallway), where several students were moved right away from the Nest, which was located on the Keith lot diagonally across from the Farm's entrance on Baker Street. On the second floor of the tall, square, flat-roofed, and "fawn-colored" wooden building were eight small bedrooms for sleeping. George and Sophia moved into one of the front rooms, and Georgiana Bruce and Ripley's niece Sarah Stearns shared a room immediately behind them. Charles Newcomb occupied one of the rooms across the hall.

Construction of the Eyrie was very careless: the walls were so thin that even the softest whispers managed to echo like public announcements throughout the building. If there were any concessions to aesthetics (not including a cornice that ran around the house just below the roof line), it would have been the large, floor-to-ceiling French windows on the first floor. They offered front views that spread out over a small orchard and several terraced slopes and extended all the way to the Charles River along the western side of the Farm. The windows in the rear of the Eyrie looked out over the densely wooded pine grove in which the Brook Farmers loved to walk and to picnic, and where, some two hundred years before, as legend has it, John Eliot, the English-born missionary, preached to local native Americans in their own tongue standing atop the large boulder that is still referred to today as "Pulpit Rock."[3]

The purpose of moving several of the students from the Nest to the Eyrie was mainly practical, but Ripley and his associates would not have been unmindful of the symbolism associated with relocating several of the educational activities to the center of the community.[4] The school was Brook Farm's principal source of income in 1842, and Ripley and his associates were obviously aware of its importance. Ripley stated in the *United States Magazine and Democratic Review* in November 1842 that "every community should have its leading purpose, some one main object to which it directs its energies. We are a company of teachers. The branch of industry which we pursue as our primary object, and chief means of support, is teaching."[5] That statement is perfectly consistent of course with Ripley's original intentions for organizing Brook Farm. His later actions, however, show that he allowed himself to be distracted by other concerns that ultimately undermined the community's educational program. Time would show just how unfortunate that was because, apart from its financial potential, the Brook Farm school was quite special—even unique in antebellum America.

From its faculty to its curriculum, and even to its students, the school was exceptional. It was really a prototype for the private boarding academies that were later established in Massachusetts and elsewhere in New England, except that it differed from them by not restricting education just to the wealthy and privileged. Where else were teachers assembled, for example, the likes of George Ripley, George Bradford, and John Sullivan Dwight, all three men graduates of both Harvard College and the Harvard Divinity School?[6] Even Charles Dana had managed to complete two years at Harvard College before coming to Brook Farm the previous summer. These men were joined by a versatile group of women that included the three Ripleys— Sophia, Ripley's sister Marianne, and his cousin Hannah—as well as Georgiana Bruce and Abby Morton, the last of whom later made her mark some years afterward as the author of the popular "William Henry" series of books for children.

These individuals comprised the "Faculty of the Embryo University"—to use Elizabeth Palmer Peabody's unusual characterization in the *Dial* that January—who provided instruction to the nearly thirty students enrolled in the school in 1842, among them Margaret Fuller's youngest brother Lloyd, Emerson's nephew Frank Brown (the son of Lidian Emerson's sister Mary), Orestes Brownson's son Orestes, Jr., Theodore Parker's ward George Colburn, Charles Sumner's younger brother Horace, George Bancroft's two sons, and Francis G. Shaw's son Robert Gould Shaw, who later headed the celebrated but tragically fated Fifty-fourth Massachusetts (Black) Infantry in the Civil War. James P. Sturgis, West Roxbury neighbor Francis G. Shaw's brother-in-law, introduced an international dimension to the Brook Farm school when he brought several Spanish-speaking students to the community in 1842. Two of these were brothers from Manila named Jose (or Hosea) and Lucas Corrales. A third student was Manuel Diaz, from Cuba, who was elected to membership in the Association on October 3, 1842, and later married Abby Morton.[7] Not all students, however, were children. There were adult learners too, among them Burrill and George Curtis. George reported to his father in October that he had "commenced" German, agricultural chemistry, and music. Minot Pratt, another of the "adult learners," attended George Ripley's algebra class that winter.

The Brook Farm school was divided into three programs. The "infant program," for which Georgiana Bruce and Abby Morton were mainly responsible, was for children below the age of six. The "primary program," headed by Marianne Ripley, was for children between the ages of six and ten. The "preparatory program" was a six-year course of study for young men and women who were "fitting" themselves for college. (In 1844 a day nursery was also organized, which, if it was not the first in America, was one of the very first to be established in the United States.) Ripley, Dana, and Dwight devoted most of their time to the college prep program; Sophia Ripley moved between the primary and preparatory programs. Ripley himself offered

Intellectual and Natural Philosophy and mathematics; Sophia was responsible for history and modern languages; Dwight handled Latin and music; Dana taught Greek and German. Hannah Ripley provided instruction in drawing.

When Hannah's brother-in-law, John Brown, settled in the community in the summer of 1842, he taught Theosophical and Practical Agriculture. The Ripleys' good friend Amelia Russell drew on her earlier travels in Europe to provide instruction in French and in dancing. (She choreographed the children's dance performance at the Christmas party that December.) And during the periods when George Bradford stayed at the Farm, he was responsible for "Belles Lettres." At any given time, he might direct an examination of Dante's great work in the original (Sophia Ripley, among others, was one of those who followed Bradford into the infernal regions), teach a class in astronomy, or guide his students through Homer's *Iliad* or Virgil's *Aenead*. (Minot and Maria Pratt's son Frederick recalled years later that "I learned easier and faster with him [Bradford] than any other teacher I was ever under.")[8] The educational program at Brook Farm was so highly regarded locally that Harvard endorsed it for students "fitting for college."

Ripley himself especially enjoyed the evening classes that attracted many of the "adult learners" in the community. Brook Farm also served as the prototype for the evening adult educational programs that are found today in virtually every American town in which there is a high school. No other antebellum American community—and that certainly includes those run by the Shakers—provided such an interesting or diversified evening educational program to so many of its members.

Such "adult learners" as the Curtis brothers, Minot Pratt, and Sophia Ripley have already been mentioned. There was also a large group of single women at Brook Farm that included Ripley's cousin

Sarah Stearns, Georgiana Bruce, Abby Morton, Ora Gannett, Caddy Stodder, and Emerson's friend Caroline Sturgis, who were all in their early twenties (or younger), as well as another slightly older group of women, such as Marianne Ripley, Hannah Ripley, Anna Alvord, and Amelia Russell, who were in their late thirties and early forties. The attractive Almira Penniman Barlow, from Brookline, should also be added to this latter group, even though she was still married to former Unitarian minister, David Hatch Barlow. The couple had separated, however, in 1840.[9] Almira retained custody of their three sons, with whom she arrived at the community in the spring of 1842.

These were the likes of the Brook Farm women in 1842. As a group, they weren't to be found at any other antebellum New England community, and probably not, for that matter, at any antebellum community in America. Brook Farm's women, at least in the early years of the community's existence, were well-bred and genteel, independent and intelligent, and socially conscious and reform-minded. George Ripley's characterization of those of Sophia's qualities that originally attracted him may also be used to describe many of Brook Farm's women. Ripley reportedly said that his marriage was "founded not upon any romantic or sudden passion" but rather "upon great respect for [Sophia's] intellectual power, moral worth, deep and true Christian piety and peculiar refinement and dignity of character." It isn't known whether it was these particular qualities or simply the sheer number of so many attractive single women at Brook Farm that prompted Margaret Fuller's friend Marcus Spring to remark to a friend in September 1842 that "if I were a single man I should certainly go to Ripley's [i.e., Brook Farm]."[10]

Several young and single men had in fact already followed Marcus Spring's suggestion. In addition to Charles Dana, who was twenty-three years old that August, and John Sullivan Dwight, who was twenty-nine and would have his romantic advances rebuffed by

Almira Barlow, there were, among others, James Bryant Hill, a farmer in his twenties, Charles Salisbury, a twenty-three-year-old trunkmaker and occasional farmer, and Charles Newcomb, Brook Farm's eccentric twenty-three-year-old vegetarian boarder. Also in the community in 1842 were the Curtis brothers—James Burrill, twenty years old, and George William, just eighteen—who arrived at the Farm in early May. Ripley and Dana had actively recruited the two natives of Providence, Rhode Island, who had recently been living with their father, a wealthy banker, in New York City. Ripley excitedly announced the young men's arrival: "Now we're going to have two young Greek gods among us," he proclaimed. Ora Gannett's first encounter with the two men lived up to Ripley's boast. She was walking from the Eyrie down to the Hive when she encountered Charles Dana in the company of two "strange young men." She realized immediately that Dana's companions had to be the "Greek gods" to whom Ripley had referred. Her first impression of them was very distinct: "They stood disclosed by their beauty and bearing. Burrill Curtis was at that time the more beautiful. He had a Greek face, of great purity of expression, and curling hair. George too was very handsome,—not so remarkably as in later life, but already with a man's virile expression."[11]

It was the younger George William Curtis, though, who later achieved notoriety as one of America's most respected "liberal reformers," largely because of the influence he exerted as editor of *Harper's Weekly*, a position he came to in 1863, and through which he championed such causes as antislavery, women's rights, and industrial reform. He and Burrill arrived at Brook Farm as young men in 1842 because Burrill, especially, had "fallen . . . under the influence of the New England 'Transcendental Movement'" as an undergraduate at Brown College. Both had been much inspired by, among other things, a series of lectures given by Emerson at the Franklin Lyceum in Providence in 1840. Burrill even acknowledged that for him, at least, "my enthusiastic admiration of [Emerson] and his writings soon amounted to a high and intense 'hero-worship.'" Thus it was "probably something of a relief to our father that . . . George and I proposed nothing worse than to become boarders . . . with the Community at Brook Farm."[12]

That spring in the privacy of his journal, Emerson took a swipe at George and Sophia Ripley, including a poke at "this eager crowd of men & women," so many of whom were being drawn to the West Roxbury community. "I cannot help feeling a profound compassion for G[eorge]. R[ipley]. & S[ophia]. R[ipley].," Emerson wrote, "who by their position are or must be inevitably, one would say, transformed into charlatans, by the endeavor continually to meet the expectation & admiration of all this eager crowd of men & women seeking they know not what who flock to them."[13] Many of these young "seekers after they know not what"—the single women especially—likely would have protested that they knew exactly what they were looking for at Brook Farm: they sought freedom from restrictive and repressive domestic and intellectual expectations, as well as opportunities for personal growth and development—for "Amplitude" and "Awe," as Emily Dickinson, New England's most renowned single woman, expressed it in one of her poems a few years later.[14]

It's this quality of Brook Farm life that James Burrill Curtis had in mind when he told his father in July that Emerson's young protégée Caroline Sturgis "likes no place better than the Community [Brook Farm]" because "Carrie, of course, as most *true* young persons do, stands in her house *in affectionate strife.*" This essence of Brook Farm's community life is also distinctly evoked in Georgiana Bruce's memory, years after her residence there, of George Ripley's class on moral philosophy in the winter of 1842: "The evenings spent in that class were delightful and inspiring," Bruce remembered. "He [Ripley] led us into wide fields of thought hitherto undreamed of." It explains as well why Charles Dana had no trouble leading a determined group of devoted Brook Farmers that same winter through several very difficult German texts—among them, Schiller's *Song of the Bell* and Goethe's *Faust* and his *Hermann und Dorothea*—despite the fact that "dictionaries were scarce, oil lamps dull, hours too short, and the students often over-weary from labor." And it is captured in Ora Gannett's recollection, years after Brook Farm's demise, of the many evenings that George Bradford "showed us the constellations, quietly talking of all this beauty in a way that inspired love and reverence in us."[15]

Early Brook Farm biographer Lindsay Swift was right when he said that "enjoyment was almost from the first a serious pursuit of the community."[16] Surviving reminiscences are filled with happy recollections of moonlit walks to the pine grove, picnics, dances, and evenings devoted to dramatic tableaux. But Swift fails to make an important distinction when he forgets to add that the "enjoyment" that is invariably recalled with a kind of "reverence"—to use Gannett's word—in many of the reminiscences of the Brook Farmers is not physical but cerebral and even spiritual in nature. It was the enjoyment inspired by George Bradford when he read passages from Racine and Moliere's plays in the original, when John Dwight performed pieces by Beethoven on the pianoforte, or when the Brook Farm glee club joined voices to sing Mozart's and Haydn's psalms and masses.

There were other voices being heard in the Association in 1842, however. Ripley particularly was listening to two of them, and they weren't those of his fellow Brook Farmers. On March 1, 1842, a new column was launched in Horace Greeley's New York *Tribune* by a man who was bound to exert enormous influence not only on Brook Farm but on nearly thirty other utopian communities and dozens of other local Associative unions in the United States in the 1840s. The author of the daily front-page feature, "Association; or, Principles of a True Organization," was a widely traveled thirty-two-year-old New Yorker named Albert Brisbane, the son of a wealthy land-investor from upstate Batavia and one of the first Americans to pursue his education in European universities. He began a six-year sojourn abroad in 1828, studying first at the Sorbonne with the celebrated French eclectic philosopher, Victor Cousin (whom several of the Transcendentalists so admired), and then, a year later, at the University of Berlin, where he was a student of the prominent social philosopher, Georg Wilhelm Friedrich Hegel. His travels in western Europe enabled him to meet the likes of Goethe, Felix Mendelssohn, Franz Liszt, and Heinrich Heine, men known at the time only to Americans like Ripley, Emerson, Fuller, Parker, and a few others, and to them only by their published writings. Brisbane's wanderlust eventually led him to Vienna, Trieste, and Constantinople, as well as to other faraway destinations, such as Turkey, Greece, and Ireland, where he was deeply affected by the poverty and generally poor social conditions in those countries.

Brisbane embraced the ideas of French social scientist Charles Fourier after reading his *Traite de l'association domestique-agricole* (1821–1822) when he returned to Berlin. ("I was carried away," he later said, "into a world of new conceptions.")[17] Seeking out Fourier in Paris, Brisbane managed to convince the master himself to instruct him in his social theory, which Fourier agreed to do twice a week over a six-week period, charging the young American five francs an hour for the privilege. Having returned to the United States in 1834, six years passed before Brisbane finally published his *Social Destiny of Man; or, Association and Reorganization of Industry* in September 1840, a work in which Brisbane yoked together his own views with his translations of various passages from a few of Fourier's voluminous writings. The book was the definitive American exposition of Fourierism throughout the decade in 1840.

ALBERT BRISBANE.

Albert Brisbane at the age of thirty. America's foremost apostle of French
social scientist Charles Fourier, Brisbane single-handedly ignited the wave
of Fourierist fervor that swept across the United States in the 1840s.

Brisbane's timing in the New York *Tribune* was inspired. Horace Greeley, whose interest in social reform activities was already well known, had begun publishing the popular daily paper just the year before, in April 1841, but his readership had increased dramatically in that short time. He told Emerson on May 26, 1842, that "we now print some 10,000 Daily and 9,000 Weekly copies of the *Tribune*." Brisbane was therefore able to reach a much larger audience than would have been possible had he limited his propagandistic efforts to disseminate Fourier's utopian views to the lecture platform or the publication of small tracts and pamphlets. Among the *Tribune*'s readers were George Ripley and the Brook Farmers. Greeley had been sending copies of the *Tribune* to the West Roxbury community at least since January 1842, although not, perhaps, without ulterior motive. His wife, Mary, was suffering from a visual impairment, and Greeley hoped that the Brook Farmers might find a place for her in the community, where "her recovery to health and vision will be sure and rapid." Whatever the actual reason for sending the *Tribune* to Ripley, the Brook Farmers were delighted to receive it. Ripley told Dana in early April that he was "glad to get the *Tribune* every week, as we do from Mr. Greeley: it is as pleasant an avenue as we could have wherewith to communicate with the Babel world it comes from."[18]

Ripley would have recognized Brisbane's name right away of course even without the *Tribune*. For one thing, *Social Destiny of Man* had been reviewed in the *Dial* the previous October 1840, possibly by Ripley himself.[19] For another, Theodore Parker read the work when it was first published in the summer of 1840 and would undoubtedly have discussed it with his good friend and neighbor. It's not likely, in any case, that Brook Farm's leader would have missed Brisbane's four-part series of articles in the *United States Magazine and Democratic Review,* the first two installments of which appeared in January and February 1842 and the third in April. Ripley was very familiar

with the *Democratic Review,* which was in its heyday in 1842 under
the editorship of John L. O'Sullivan, and was one of the most vigorous literary and political journals of the period. However, the fourth
and final article in June 1842, in which Brisbane addressed the interesting question of the necessary conditions for a practical trial in "Association," would have been the most interesting to Ripley.

Brisbane had already broached this subject in his March 26, 1842,
New York *Tribune* column, but he knew that an experimental community on the scale envisioned by Charles Fourier was entirely unrealistic in the United States, so the New Yorker had been carefully avoid-
ing any discussion of particulars. His readers, however, kept pressing
the subject. In his May 3, 1842, *Tribune* column, Brisbane noted that
"we are in constant receipt of letters, inquiring when a first Association will be commenced, and where it will be located"; he decided to
discuss the subject at some length in the final installment of his *Democratic Review* articles.

Charles Fourier's leading American apostle recognized that an Association of 2,000 persons living and working together in a 6,000-acre
community (approximately three square miles in size) was not likely
to be realized any day soon in the United States, even with the country's still vast open spaces. So Brisbane quickly modified the Frenchman's "requirements" by suggesting that a practical trial might be
possible with just 400 persons cultivating a 1,500-acre tract of land:
these, he cautioned, are "the smallest number[s] with which Association can succeed."[20] Ripley and his associates obviously knew that
Brook Farm didn't fulfill either of those requirements, but they must
have been struck by some of Brisbane's other "conditions." One was
that a practical experiment in Association should be located near a
large city because of the importance of easy access to convenient markets for the sale of goods produced in the community. Brook Farm

was, in fact, just eight miles southwest of the center of Boston. A second was that the Association should be operated administratively by a
"Council of Industry," the members of which, elected annually, would
oversee, according to their various skills and expertise, the agricultural, mechanical, and cultural life of the Association. Brook Farm's
original "Articles of Agreement" already stipulated that "the General
Direction shall oversee & arrange the affairs of the Association,"
working in conjunction with members of the "Direction of Industry,"
the "Direction of Education," the "Direction of Finance," and the
"Direction of Domestic Economy." A third condition for an experimental community in America, Brisbane said, was that the Association should be organized as a joint-stock company rather than one
requiring community of property. "We condemn Community of Property entirely," Brisbane had noted in an earlier *Tribune* column on
March 15, 1842; "we consider it as the most false of principles and as
the grave of individual liberty." Here again it must have seemed as
if Brisbane was speaking to the Brook Farmers, for Article III of
the "Articles of Agreement" stated that "the members of this association shall own & manage such real & personal estate, in joint-stock
proprietorship."

If Brisbane had a mission in life after 1840 it was to convince people
that many more benefits would someday be realized in the "Phalanx"—Fourier's word for his ideal community—than had ever been
achieved under existing social arrangements. And he missed very few
opportunities to propagandize the cause that had become so undeviatingly the center of his life. The *Tribune* column and the four-part series in the *Democratic Review* allowed him to spread his message to a
large audience, but no audience was too small when there was an opportunity to proselytize for Associationism. In March 1842 Brisbane
arranged to have Greeley introduce him to Ralph Waldo Emerson,
who was in New York City delivering a series of six lectures on "The

Times," despite the death of his beloved five-year-old son Waldo just a few weeks earlier. Brisbane persuaded Emerson to give him some space in the *Dial*. Ripley and the Brook Farmers would certainly have caught Brisbane's article on the "Means of Effecting a Final Reconciliation between Religion and Science" in the July 1842 number, if for no other reason than they would have been anxious to see Charles Dana's poem, "Eternity," in the same number, and probably even more eager to read the strange "tale" that Charles Newcomb had reluctantly sent along to the Transcendental periodical.[21]

Emerson, whose editorship of the *Dial* had begun with the July 1842 number, found himself working very hard to fill the pages of the journal. Once he decided in March 1842 to take over the editorial responsibilities of the periodical from Margaret Fuller (he agreed to be in charge for at least one year), he immediately began soliciting contributions. Margaret promised an article highlighting "Entertainments of the Past Winter" in Boston, Henry Thoreau said he would provide a piece on the "Natural History of Massachusetts," and Caroline Sturgis told her friend that he could "select anything that suits my [Emerson's] purposes" from poems that she had written the previous summer (Emerson chose "Outward Bound"). It was easy to get several poems from Ellery Channing, especially now that he was living in Concord. Transcendental mystic Jones Very also sent along an "indifferent" poem (though Emerson printed two). Henry Hedge continued to be a reluctant supporter of the journal, but Emerson managed to solicit a translation from him of a poem by the German poet, Johann Ludwig Uhland ("The Castle by the Sea"). Theodore Parker was too preoccupied by his ongoing quarrel with the Unitarian community to contribute anything to the July number. (His article on the "Hollis Street Council" in the next number continued to rock the Unitarian establishment.) Despite these contributions, Emerson still had to provide nearly half the content himself for the July 1842 number.

He was very deft, however, in handling Albert Brisbane. Emerson admired the New Yorker's energy and zeal, but he was always wary of single-issue reformers. Although he needed material for the July number, he was not about to turn its pages over to this "indefatigable apostle" of Charles Fourier for a disquisition on Associationism. (Emerson had already been treated to one himself in March during the lecture series in New York City.) In fact, Emerson returned a version of Brisbane's article in late March because it was too long. Besides, Brisbane's continued prodding about supporting the Associative reform program was not only presumptuous; it was also becoming annoying. When Brisbane notified Emerson at the end of May 1842 that he was still revising his article but would forward it in a few weeks, he closed by asking the new editor of the *Dial:* "When shall we see you the advocate of Social Harmony and Unity, and of the devotion of the whole human race to the standard of the *true Man?*"[22] Perhaps still uneasy about George Ripley's most recent appeal for support the previous December 1841 (which he never acknowledged), and evidently bothered now by Brisbane's proddings, Emerson decided that it was time to say a word or two himself about "Fourierism and the Socialists." His remarks are important because he was among the earliest and few Americans who could speak knowledgeably about the growing influence of the phenomenon that would immediately become known in the United States as Fourierism.

Emerson "lifted" his prefatory remarks to Brisbane's article nearly verbatim from his journal.[23] Essentially they were reactions to his meetings with Greeley and Brisbane in New York City in March. There's an obvious "tongue-in-cheek" quality in Emerson's summary of the world of Phalanxes and Phalansteries as envisioned by Charles Fourier, a world made so sublime and perfect by mechanical contrivance that mere language was inadequate to describe it: "Aladdin and his magician, or the beautiful Scheherazade, can alone in these prosaic times, before the sight, describe the material splendors collected there."[24] And imagine, Emerson told the *Dial*'s readers, "the earth planted with fifties and hundreds of these phalanxes side by side,— what tillage, what architecture, what refectories, what dormitories, what reading rooms, what concerts, what lectures, what gardens, what baths!" Emerson agreed that one could not help feeling anything but great pleasure having such "gay and magnificent" pictures described. The great merit of Fourier's scheme was that it was a "system; that it had not the partiality and hint-and-fragment character of most popular schemes, but was coherent and comprehensive of facts to a wonderful degree." Moreover, the earnestness of Fourier's advocates, combined with the comprehensiveness of the Frenchman's plan and the directness of proceeding to the end to be achieved, "commanded our attention and respect."

Yet despite the assurances from Fourier's proponents that his scheme was different from "all other plans for the regeneration of society," Emerson could not exempt it from "the criticism which we apply to so many projects for reform with which the brain of the age teems." Fourier, Emerson thought, "had skipped no fact but one, namely, Life." He treated man as a plastic thing, something to be shaped and molded, "ripened or retarded," made into a solid, gas, or fluid at the will of the leader. What Fourier forgot was the "faculty of Life, which spawns and scorns system and system-makers, which eludes all conditions, which makes or supplants a thousand phalanxes and New Harmonies with each pulsation." For these reasons, Emerson would never embrace Fourier or Associationism, though he was prepared to acknowledge that "in a day of small, sour, and fierce schemes, one is admonished and cheered by a project of such friendly aims, and of such bold and generous proportion."

George Ripley, of course, had all along been listening to what Bris-

bane and Emerson were saying. It was time now to speak. He forwarded a letter to Horace Greeley on August 3, which the New York
editor proceeded to publish in the *Tribune*—evidently with Ripley's
permission—in the number for August 13, 1842. The letter isn't attributed but it had to have been written by Ripley, or possibly by Dana.
The *Tribune* notes that it is "a private letter from a gentleman who is a
member" of the Brook Farm community. If it was written by Dana,
then he drafted it under Ripley's watchful eye. In either case, the letter
marks the first direct communication to the public from the leaders
themselves of the West Roxbury Association.

The letter is cautious about Fourierism. Ripley wasn't yet ready to
jump on Brisbane's bandwagon. But neither was he seeking to initiate
a protracted public discourse with Brisbane as he had done two years
before with Andrews Norton. So far, he liked what he had been hearing about Associationism. Whatever made Ripley decide at this moment to bring Brook Farm to the attention of the *Tribune*'s extensive
readership, it's clear that financial need had something to do with the
decision. "The greatest difficulty we find [at Brook Farm] is, what you
would expect, the want of money," Ripley acknowledged in the letter.
"This limits us in every way," he added. The community was still
without a shoemaker, a blacksmith, and a carpenter, which meant that
"large sums" had to be paid to outsiders for these services.

The Brook Farmers were happy, however, that "our organization is
not fixed and finished," and that is why "an Association on Fourier's
system might suffer.—That system seems to leave little to be done by
circumstances, but starts with definite rules for every possible case,"
Ripley said, echoing one of Emerson's criticisms in the *Dial*. At the
same time, he added, the Brook Farmers were aware of the "immense
practical wisdom embodied in Fourier's plan." Ripley recognized especially the advantages of a single large building over separate dwell-
ings to centralize an Association's operations. In fact, he now an-

nounced, such a building was already being planned for the West Roxbury community. He cautioned, nevertheless, that he would "not willingly give up the simple beauties of cottage architecture for the palace of a Phalanx."[25]

Ripley was being quite earnest when he referred to the "simple beauties of cottage architecture." For several weeks that summer the Brook Farmers had discussed the details of a cottage that would be built just to the south of the Eyrie. Sophia Ripley's recently widowed friend Anna Alvord, who had been boarding at the community for several months, decided that she wanted a more permanent arrangement, so she offered to loan Ripley the necessary funds to construct a small cottage, with the understanding that space would be set aside for her when it was completed. The "Cottage" was finished in the autumn of 1842. Like the Eyrie, it was also situated on a prominent and grassy knoll that provided open views of much of the Farm, although they weren't as expansive as those seen from the Eyrie. The simple design of the two-story building was in the shape of a Maltese cross, with four gables. On the first floor were two large rooms and two small ones, as well as a washroom, a storeroom, a cistern, and a privy. There were four bedrooms on the second floor. Alvord, who loaned the community nearly $1,600 to construct the building, took over one of the first-floor parlors for her living quarters. The second parlor was shared by the other occupants of the house, among whom this autumn and early winter were Charles Dana, who was given a reprieve from his cell-like room in the Hive, and Amelia Russell, Brook Farm's "mistress of the revels," who would soon purchase several shares of Brook Farm stock.

Hammers and saws could be heard all around the farm this autumn. There was yet another building underway, although the Pilgrim House, as it became known right away, wasn't instigated by Ripley and the Brook Farmers. The circumstances related to its construction nonetheless should have troubled Ripley and his associates. Brook Farm's third new building in less than a year was financed by Ichabod Morton, a "plain man," according to Emerson, who was a successful merchant from the coastal town of Plymouth, which accounts for the name of the new building. Morton had visited the community several times during the spring and summer with his daughter, Abby, and his two sons and was immediately taken with its natural beauty and the warm geniality of the Brook Farmers. He decided almost immediately to build a double-house, each half mirroring the other, for his and his brother Edwin's families. The site agreed upon was at the end of the long knoll on which the Cottage and the Eyrie were situated.

Architecturally, the Pilgrim House was two-and-a-half stories high and combined the basic design of a Georgian-style home with several second-story dormers, which were becoming more common in the 1840s in New England and would eventually be identified with both Greek Revival (ca. 1820s–1850s) and Gothic Revival (ca. 1840–1880s) styles of architecture. An ell extended off the rear of the house. On the first floor of the double-house were, altogether, four large rooms and two kitchens, a washroom with a large cistern under it (which could hold up to 5,000 gallons of water), a bakery, a workshop, and a privy. On the second floor there were nine bedrooms, and the attic provided four more. Like the Eyrie and the Cottage, the new house also contained a cellar with a furnace. The cost of the Pilgrim House was nearly $5,000.

In mid-1842 Brook Farm's financial resources were still so unsteady that it's hard to imagine that supporters like Francis G. Shaw, George Russell, or Horace Greeley wouldn't have cautioned Ripley and his associates that the decision to go ahead with two major building projects representing an additional $6,300 of indebtedness on top of the existing $11,000 in mortgages made no financial sense whatsoever.[26]

Evidently Ripley didn't consult them. Nathaniel Hawthorne, however, did "consult" with Ripley. He came down from Concord in early October to inform Brook Farm's leader that he wanted the remainder of his original investment in the community returned.

Hawthorne and Sophia Peabody had just been wed in July 1842. Despite their marital bliss living together in Concord at the Old Manse, the newlywed couple had no regular income. Ripley was perfectly aware that there was no money to pay his former associate, but he may have expected that there soon might be because he managed to persuade the former Brook Farmer to convert his stock certificate into a promissory note, payable on demand in thirty days. On October 7, 1842, Ripley and Dana, acting as trustees for the Brook Farm Association, signed the note for $524.05 (some interest was evidently also included). Hawthorne was satisfied with this arrangement—at least for the moment. He had no way of knowing that Brook Farms's indebtedness was steadily mounting, as his letter to Charles Dana ten days later makes clear. When he wrote on October 17 tendering his resignation "as an associate of the Brook Farm Institute," Hawthorne said that he probably should have done so sooner, "but I have been unwilling to feel myself entirely disconnected with you." He added that he would always take "the warmest interest in your progress, and shall heartily rejoice at your success—of which I can see no reasonable doubt."[27]

Horace Greeley was much less sanguine about Brook Farm's eventual success than Hawthorne claimed to be. He had written to Dana at the end of August to thank the Brook Farmers for arranging to have his wife in the community, which gave him the opportunity to say that he disagreed with their "plan for a community of which every member shall be actuated solely by a true Christianity or a genuine manfulness—a disposition to bear others' burdens, and to count it happiness to do and suffer for the indolent and unthankful." Greeley thought such expectations were wholly unrealistic, for what would happen to the Association if "there shall be two or three who cherish a disposition to *enjoy* and not *earn*—to be helped by others and not help others. What then?" Greeley was acquainted with such persons himself, he said, which is why he was worried about Brook Farm: "it is adapted only to angelic natures," he stated; the "entrance of one serpent would be as fatal as in Eden of old."[28] Fourier's system "avoids this danger, by having a rampart of exact justice behind that of philanthropy," the *Tribune* editor added. Greeley closed his letter with sobering—and, to the Brook Farmers, perhaps very surprising—words of caution: "I hear awful predictions of your overthrow, at which I trust *you* smile, but which to a distant friend may well cause some little anxiety."

In October Greeley picked up the theme again of Brook Farm's "tendency to exclusivism" in a letter that must have reached Ripley and Dana just a few days after their meeting with Hawthorne.[29] The "cant of exclusivism," Greeley warned, is "the curse of our friend Brisbane" and was the reason why his New York *Tribune* column was less effective than it might be. Brisbane wouldn't allow Associationism to progress "in harmony with other Reforms, . . . it must be pitted *against* them all—something diverse, original, antagonistic." Greeley prayed that the Brook Farmers wouldn't allow this to happen in the West Roxbury community. He was for democratizing the Association; he thought there should be tradesmen there like Louis Ryckman, "a strong, robust, intelligent man, of 45,—a man of ideas, who knows the world—a Shoemaker by trade," whom Greeley was now recommending to the Brook Farmers. Ripley, Dana, and the other community leaders didn't need to be reminded that Brook Farm still didn't have a shoemaker—or a carpenter, a blacksmith, or even a tailor, for that matter—which meant that a great deal of the work at the Farm had to be contracted to "civilizees," as the Brook Farmers affectionately referred to people living in "conventional" society. If there's a single image that epitomizes the confused state of the Association's financial affairs at this point in the community's development, however, it's not that of Brook Farm without a single tradesman, powerful as that is: it's Charles Dana helping to broker the financial arrangement with Hawthorne.

Dana had been at Brook Farm a little more than a year, but there is no evidence whatsoever that he had yet paid even a fraction of his pledge for the three shares of stock to which he had committed himself after settling there in 1841.[30] The former Harvard student wrote to Hannah Ripley (George's cousin) on September 22, 1842—less than three weeks before the meeting with Hawthorne—because he was "to confess the truth rather blue" about personal matters. He was out of sorts, he complained, because the relocation that he had been anticipating from the cramped confines of the Hive to a larger room in the soon-to-be completed "Cottage" would not, it now appeared, take place. But what was really tormenting him, he told Hannah, were his "perpetual debts," which stood before him "as ugly & burdensome as [a] nightmare." "Every dollar I owe," he complained, "jeers & gibbers at me like a little devil." How could there be any pleasure shaking hands with a man, knowing "that you owe him a hundred dollars or when you say good morning to another that he holds your note for ten"? Dana told Hannah that he didn't usually dwell on these kind of matters, but he felt "bullied" when he was reminded of them. The weight of his indebtedness was so pressing, he said, that it might even "drive me away from the community."[31] (Dana obviously "signed away" that possibility a few weeks later when he added his signature to Hawthorne's promissory note.)

Ripley, too, was anxious enough in early November 1842 that he contacted his friend Adin Ballou about the possibility of uniting Brook Farm and Hopedale, and he even considered joining forces with Bronson Alcott, whose "Fruitlands" experiment the following year turned out to be one of the most abysmal failures of the sixty communities that were organized in the United States in the 1840s. Adin Ballou's patience with the Hopedale Community provides an interesting contrast to Ripley's sense of hurry at Brook Farm. Ballou and his "Practical Christian" followers had agreed back in September 1840 on "the desirability of establishing a colony," and they began to organize Hopedale in earnest at the end of January 1841, two months before Brook Farm was established. They did not take "full possession" of their community home, however, until April 1842. In the intervening months, Ballou and his people met many times to formalize a constitution, to discuss the location of the proposed community, to go over the financial details related to the purchase of a property, to draft by-laws and other regulations, to review administrative procedures, and to consider potential sources of revenue to sustain the community's operations. Only after much thoughtful deliberation did Ballou's followers slowly begin to make their way to Milford, Massachusetts, the site of the Hopedale Community. One family moved to the single dwelling on the site in October 1841. A second family took up residence there in December. As they were doing so, the Brook Farmers were already breaking ground for the Association's third new building.

Ballou brought Ripley's proposition to his fellow "Practical Christians" and had "a full consultation with them," Ballou wrote on November 3, 1842. The "temptation [to unite the communities] is strong to severe," Ballou went on, but the brethren had decided against it: "We are unanimous in the solemn conviction that we could not enlist for the formation of a community not based on the distinguishing principles of the standard of Practical Christianity [the pledge required of prospective members of Hopedale] so called, especially *non-resistance*, etc." The members of the Hopedale Community,

Ballou said, had only the deepest affection for Ripley and his follow-ers at West Roxbury: "We love you all, and shall be happy to see you go on and prosper," but it would not be with the Practical Chris-tians.[32]

Meanwhile, Alcott paid the Brook Farmers a visit on November 4. He had just returned from a five-month trip to England (financed by his friend, Waldo Emerson), bringing home with him two of his Eng-lish supporters, Charles Lane, who arrived with his son, and Henry Gardner Wright. They brought with them a 1,000-volume library and a plan for a new community, a "New Eden," as Lane referred to it. No sooner had the men settled in Concord at the Alcott family's already crowded house than they set about finding a location for the pro-posed community while lecturing and conversing about their plan for the new utopia wherever an audience could be found. Emerson re-marked jokingly to Margaret Fuller that Alcott, Lane, and Wright "cannot chat, or so much as open the mouth on aught less than a new Solar System & the prospective Education in the Nebulae. All day and all night they hold perpetual Parliament."[33]

When they visited Brook Farm in November, Alcott, Lane, and Wright spent the day looking around the West Roxbury community. In the evening they discussed their plans with the Brook Farmers. Burrill Curtis, for one, was not impressed. Despite his youth, he was already a fairly shrewd judge of character. Curtis had no doubt that Lane and Wright were "men of some virtues," but "they have many great faults," he wrote to his father the day after the visit, among them "exclusiveness, spiritual pride, egotism, and a certain supercilious su-pervising peeping" that the Brook Farmer resented (Curtis had been elected a member of the Association on August 4, 1842; brother George continued simply to be a boarder). He respected Alcott's in-tellectual abilities, but he also thought that the Concord philosopher's "knowledge of the actual is not so large as his faith in the possible ideal." On that last point, at least, Alcott and Ripley shared philosophical kinship.

After the meeting at Brook Farm, Emerson decided to open his doors to the visionaries and invited a group of friends to Concord to hear more about Alcott's proposed community on November 10. "George Ripley & all Brook Farm came in strength," Emerson noted in his journal. Although they were also invited, neither Orestes Brownson nor Theodore Parker attended the meeting. Nathaniel Hawthorne did attend, but not because he harbored any fantasies about joining another community.[34] He was there to remind Ripley about the promissory note owed him, which had been due in full three days before the meeting at Emerson's house. Ripley must have anticipated that he would encounter Hawthorne in Concord because just the day before the meeting he quietly approached Burrill Curtis to see if the young enthusiast would purchase a share or two of Brook Farm stock, which would have enabled Ripley to repay at least a portion of the debt to Hawthorne. "It has been proposed to me to put my name to two shares in the Brook Farm stock," Burrill told his father on November 9. Burrill decided not to.[35]

While Ripley was angling for ways that autumn to get Brook Farm on a more secure financial footing, the Brook Farmers were completing the fall harvest. They had a masquerade picnic similar to a memorable one held the previous September to celebrate the harvest. The picnic the year before was so colorful that it "left a fantastic impression" in Hawthorne's mind that inspired "The Masqueraders" chapter in *The Blithedale Romance.*[36] While he was walking and talking with George Bradford, Emerson, and Margaret Fuller, who had come for an afternoon visit, Hawthorne was struck on the hand by an arrow from the bow of the goddess Diana. Hawthorne was already familiar with the antics of Ellen Slade and Ora Gannett from their pillow fight at the

Hive during the early days of his residence in the community. Ellen and Ora were incarnated at the picnic as the goddess Diana and a gypsy fortune-teller, and they were just two of the many "wild and fabulous" characters participating in the masquerade birthday party for Sophia Ripley's six-year-old nephew, Frank Dana. (The young boy died in 1843.)

Hawthorne was particularly impressed by all the contrasts at the picnic, and it was these that afterward found their way into his satiric novel. The contrast between Diana and the gypsy fortune-teller immediately appealed to his imagination, Ellen Slade being "blonde, fair, quiet, with a moderate composure; and the gypsy (Ora Gannett) a bright, vivacious, dark-haired, rich-complexioned damsel." He was also impressed by the overall contrast provided by so many of his Brook Farm acquaintances appearing before him now in the forms of an Indian chief (complete with blanket, feathers, and paint), an Indian squaw, "a negro of the Jim Crow order," a Swiss girl, "one or two foresters; and several people in Christian attire." Even a neighborhood farmer named Thomas Orange, "a thickset, sturdy figure, in his blue frock," struck Hawthorne's fancy because, despite his apparent enjoyment and participation in the festivities, Orange remained aloof and apart, "with a shrewd Yankee observation of the scene" that Hawthorne appreciated. In "The Masqueraders" chapter, Silas Foster, the head farmer of the Blithedale community, as he "leaned against a tree . . . in his customary blue frock . . . did more to disenchant the scene [of the novel's picnic party], with his look of shrewd, acrid, Yankee observation, than twenty witches and necromancers could have done."

The masquerade picnic this year featured many of the same "characters" that Hawthorne originally preserved in his journal and then transferred to his novel. The goddess Diana was there again, and so was the gypsy fortune-teller, impersonated once more by Ora

Gannett, still the "bright, vivacious, dark-haired, [and] rich-complexioned damsel" that captivated the former Brook Farmer the year before. Other familiar figures were backwoodsmen, Africans, and an Indian squaw (impersonated this October by Georgiana Bruce). New to
the festivities was "Fanny Elssler," the celebrated Austrian dancer
whose recent performances in Boston were being enthusiastically applauded. Impersonating Elssler at the masquerade was George William Curtis, who, dressed "in a low-necked, short-sleeved, book-muslin dress and a tiny ruffled apron," arrived at the picnic "making
curtsies and pirouetting down the path." His appearance threw the
Brook Farmers "into convulsions of laughter."[37]

Margaret Fuller must have found the picnic in 1841 memorable, too,
because she made a point of returning to Brook Farm this September
and October. There had been a killing frost at the end of September,
but then the early October days immediately gave way to a beautiful
Indian summer. The Farm was ablaze with color. The maple and elm
trees and the barberry bushes were still rich with shades of orange
and red and yellow. For the previous few weeks, nearly everyone in the
community participated in the harvest, digging potatoes, husking corn
and hay, and preparing fruits and vegetables for canning. Even Fuller
leant a hand. She spent several days at Brook Farm in late September
and then returned for a week in mid-October, walking and reading
during the day, and holding conversations in the evening. ("There is
no end to her talk," one young man remarked to a friend.) One evening she joined a group of men, women, and children for a husking in
the barn—"a most picturesque scene," she wrote in her journal—
where she "helped about half an hour, then took a long walk beneath
the stars."[38]

By December 1842 finishing touches were being put on the Pilgrim
House. The Brook Farmers nearly lost the new building before they
even had a chance to occupy it. Three or four men had been sent over

to the house to sweep up the last of the remaining wood shavings in order, ironically, to prevent an accident from fire. The men were burning the shavings in the fireplace when cinders ignited a section of the surrounding wooden floor. In their haste to exterminate the fire, one of the men threw a pail of what he thought was water on the flames. The pail, it turned out, was filled with turpentine. Nearby beams immediately caught flame, and buckets of water had to be run down all the way from the Eyrie because the cistern near the Pilgrim House was already frozen, as was the nearest water pump at the Cottage. Fortunately, one of the men had sense enough to cut away the burning section of beam with his axe. The episode ended with Ripley providing a sound scolding of the men for their carelessness, followed by "a thanking of stars" all around that the recently finished house had not been destroyed.[39] This would not be the only fire in the community; a far more costly one would occur just a few years later.

The community celebrated its good fortune by decorating a large evergreen tree at Christmastime, which was placed in the Hive with small candles, candy "horns of plenty," sugar plums, and blown eggs. Every Brook Farm child received a present. The new year was welcomed with a fancy-dress masquerade ball in the parlors of the Pilgrim House. Several of Brook Farm's neighbors joined the festivities. Theodore and Lydia Parker came over, though not in costume. Some members of the Frank Shaw and George Russell families came dressed as priests and dervishes. The Brook Farmers were in costume as Spanish bolero dancers, Little Nell and her grandfather, and several characters from classical Greece. Even "an Indian left his native forests for our amusement." George Curtis exchanged the short-sleeved, book-muslin Fanny Elssler dress that he wore for the October costume picnic for the "sad and solemn 'reverence'" of Hamlet, attired this New Year's day in black cloak and black plume head-cover, a glittering rapier at his side.[40]

As had the October costume picnic, the Christmas festivities and the fancy-dress ball at the end of 1842 belied a more incessant and urgent reality for George Ripley and his Brook Farm associates. Just nine months earlier, Ripley thought that Brook Farm was in such a "prosperous state" that he could say to Dana that "I almost dread the effect of being allowed not to struggle with poverty and hardship." If there was one thing that Ripley had learned in the intervening months, it was this: the "purely democratic, Christian principles" on which he had established the community, though seeming at first, as he remarked to Dana in March, "seed-corn for the nations," wouldn't provide even a single meal for seventy Brook Farmers living on a dairy farm in West Roxbury, Massachusetts.[41] Ripley had to be feeling very uncertain in late 1842 about the community's future direction. He needn't have worried. There would be plenty of advice in the weeks ahead from well-intentioned friends. Horace Greeley contacted the Brook Farmers in mid-December to warn them again, as he had in August and October, against "exclusivism": "Don't become a sect," he urged them. "Don't build up a wall, and think yourselves better than your neighbors."[42] Greeley had one other piece of advice in December that Ripley and Dana must have found even more sobering than the prediction Greeley reportedly had heard the previous summer about Brook Farm's "overthrow." "Your *dependence* on your pupils is a fetter which you ought not to wear another season," he exhorted. "You *must* not."

Greeley wasn't the only New Yorker, however, who was urging the Brook Farmers at the end of 1842 to adopt a more radical and progressive approach in order to assure the community's future welfare. They were also getting advice from Louis Ryckman, "a whole man," Greeley had noted by way of recommending the New York shoemaker in October, "not a dreamer, not a fanatic, but one who knows life." Ryckman arrived with his wife Jane and daughter Jean in mid-November right after the meeting at Emerson's home in Concord. On December 30, he offered some interesting year-end observations about the community by way of a letter to Albert Brisbane and the readers of his New York *Tribune* column. He and his wife were very happy at Brook Farm, Ryckman said. They were surrounded by "persons whose education, accomplishments and manners are such as would win approbation and esteem anywhere." No one living in the community could have the slightest doubt about "the devotion of each for the welfare of all, or of the friendship of all for each of the members of this Community." With regard to Charles Fourier's social reform program—about which Brisbane and his readers were obviously anxious to hear—the Brook Farmers were "not pledged to advocate or support his [Fourier's] or any other man's theories." There was, nonetheless, a "prevailing opinion" in the community that "we [the Brook Farmers] are fortunate in being so situated that all or any of his [Fourier's] plans may be adopted or rejected, as to the Society may seem fit; and if true, *they will* become a part of our system."[43] Ryckman's emphasis on *"they will"* underscored his own expectation that Brook Farm would eventually embrace Fourierism. And on that subject the New Yorker had much to share with his new friends at Brook Farm: he may have been living in West Roxbury, Massachusetts, but he was still the Second Vice President of the New York Fourier Society.

5

The Winds of Change

Instead of taking an immediate and hard look at the community's financial prospects, George Ripley and the other newly elected officers of the Brook Farm Institute began 1843 reactively rather than pro-actively. Although the members of the Association (still numbering only about fifteen or sixteen actual associates) met on February 7 to "consider the state of the . . . [community's] financial difficulties" and to "propose several methods of retrenchment," the early weeks of the new year were devoted to a series of unproductive and time-consuming administrative exercises—as if the clamor of motion would somehow muffle the sound of the proverbial wolf rapping ever more loudly at the door of the Hive.[1] The community's administrative and financial assignments in January and February indicate that Ripley and the directors were still more preoccupied by the method than by the means of running the Association, a tendency, it should be added, that predisposed them to the detailed mathematical computations inherent in Charles Fourier's system of "Groups" and "Series."

On January 7, 1843, for instance, the directors voted that "the members of the Association deliver to the Secretary [James Burrill Curtis had just been elected to the office] a written statement of the mode in which their time is employed." At the same meeting the "Direction of Education" was given a charge "to prepare a statement of the recitations of the different pupils," and the "General Direction" was told to "bring before the next meeting of this board a statement of the time employed by the boys in labor." After Burrill Curtis presented a labor report the following week, he was subsequently ordered to tabulate the information according to "time employed & kind of labor performed for the Association by Associates." Likewise, each teacher in the Brook Farm school was directed "to return weekly to the *Direction of Education* an account of the attendance of each pupil in his charge."

When George Ripley presented the report on the work of Brook Farm's children on January 21, it was agreed that the General Direction, which he headed, should "ascertain every week the time employed in labor by each of the minors under its charge." When Curtis presented the tabulated statement on January 28 of the time and kind of labor being performed by associates, he was "ordered . . . [to] draw up in addition a similar tabular statement of the Labor of persons employed by the Association, and make an estimate of the amount of labor in each department." None of these various efforts, in fact, resulted in any discernible changes in the Association's operations, and they certainly did nothing noticeably to improve the community's balance sheet. (The Brook Farmers' penchant for bureaucratic overlay occasionally manifested itself unwittingly in humorous ways, as when in the spring of 1843 George Ripley was elected "Superintendent of Fodder," and James Bryant Hill, a farmer, was appointed "Superintendent of Tools.")

Brook Farm's economic difficulties were too chronic, however, to be avoided very long, and it was decided in February that retrenchment measures were necessary in order to tighten the community's belt. As chairman of the "Direction of Finance," Charles Dana presented "a verbal statement of the financial difficulties" confronting the community at a general meeting on February 7. Following his report, three proposals were adopted: "1. No purchases shall be made on credit[;] 2. No purchases shall be made without the approval of the *Direction of Finance*[;] 3. The expenditures & receipts of every week shall be reported at the weekly meeting of the Directors." Either Dana or Ripley approached Burrill Curtis *sotto voce* just a day or so later because Curtis reported to his father on February 9 that "I have been asked to loan the Community $100."[2] Two immediate casualties of the informal retrenchment program were "Carrie," one of the Association's horses, which was sold on February 11, and a Mr. Dudley, the local milkman, with whom the community terminated its contract on March 18. The arrangement with Dudley is an important reminder that even for so fundamental a staple as milk, the Brook Farmers found it necessary to contract with "civilizees" to supply the community's needs. Ripley was too intelligent not to have recognized the irony of having to purchase milk for a community that was situated on a property that, until the Brook Farmers took it over, had always been successfully operated as a dairy farm.

It was Louis Ryckman who introduced the first "industry" at Brook Farm. Although he and his wife Jane had only arrived in West Roxbury the previous November, the forty-seven-year-old New York shoemaker wasted no time working out a tentative arrangement with a Boston shoe merchant named Timothy Kimball to manufacture women's shoes from precut materials that Kimball would provide, and for which he would pay the Brook Farmers twenty-eight cents a pair for their assembly. Ryckman's proposal was approved on February 19, and thus was born the first of the four main "industries" upon which the Brook Farmers would rely over the next four years to supplement the income from the school, boarders, and the community's modest farming endeavors.[3] Ryckman immediately struck a second deal on March 5 with another local shoe merchant named Henry L. Daggett, who agreed to take twenty-five pairs of shoes for his shop on Washington Street in Boston. Over the next few years, the Brook Farmers dealt regularly with Daggett, and with another retail shoe shop also on Washington Street known as "Newell & Neibuhr." Ryckman, in other words, seems to have done more to stimulate Brook Farm's financial resources in just the three months since his arrival in West Roxbury than Ripley, Dana, and the community's other leaders had managed to accomplish in the nearly two years of the Association's existence.

Ryckman's efforts notwithstanding, it was going to take a lot more than one or two contracts with local shoe merchants to stop the community's financial bleeding, as events on April 6, 1843, made dramatically clear. On that day, Ripley and the trustees took a third mortgage on the community. In his capacity as guardian of George Colburn (his wife's nephew), Theodore Parker loaned the Association $1,000—at 5-percent annual interest. The third mortgage increased the Brook Farmers' legal indebtedness to $12,000. To complicate matters further, Ichabod Morton, to whom the Brook Farmers already owed nearly $5,000 for his good faith loan for the construction of the Pilgrim House, decided that he was not suited to communal life and resigned from the Association on the same day that the third mortgage was executed. The mortgages and personal loans, now amounting to more than $18,000, must have made Nathaniel Hawthorne's promissory note for $524.05, which had been due the previous November 1842 and had still not been paid, seem relatively inconsequential.[4]

The financial drama that pretty much occupied center stage at Brook Farm that spring was occasionally offset by some of the melodrama going on, so to speak, in the wings—although one situation, involving a young woman named Marianne (or Mary Ann) Williams, a seamstress and domestic servant occasionally in the employ of the Emerson family, has a larger significance as well. Emerson wrote to his brother William in New York in January 1843, telling him that during a recent visit he had been unable to pick up medicine for "the lame girl [Williams] who came to N[ew] Y[ork] to be healed," and requesting that it be sent to Concord. Emerson then wrote in April 1843 to his good friend George Bradford, who had just returned to Brook Farm to live, asking if a place might be found in the community for the young woman. Bradford responded on April 16, saying in the very same letter that, no, it didn't seem likely that Williams could be accommodated at the Farm, then adding in a postscript that, yes, "I am directed by the proper authorities to say that it is quite probable that they may wish to receive your applicant." Eleven days later, Bradford informed Emerson that Williams could not be received by the community, explaining that "in the present state of affairs . . . it is necessary to make the most rigid inquisition into the extent to which applicants can be of use." On May 25, however, Bradford wrote to Emerson again, this time telling him that some changes had occurred at Brook Farm, and that "the community would like to have [Williams] come as soon as possible"—for a one-month trial!⁵

Although the Marianne Williams situation appears to be nothing more than a somewhat comic episode of Brook Farm life, it's really an indication of the changes that were beginning to occur in the community. The language in Bradford's letters to Emerson is important. Whenever he refers to Williams's admission to the community, the genial Bradford uses phrases like "rigid inquisition," "proper authorities," "bureau of internal affairs," and "commissioned by the powers that be." The formality and stiffness of such phrases are one of the earliest indications that life in the West Roxbury Association had begun to change in the early months of 1843. If at one time there had ever been anything distinctively "Transcendental" about the community, there wasn't any longer. The effects of the austerity program were increasingly more noticeable as Ripley and the Brook Farmers moved ever more steadily toward the embrace of Fourierism.⁶

A more sensitive situation than the one involving Marianne Williams concerned Ichabod Morton's daughter Abby and Manuel Diaz, one of Brook Farm's three Spanish-speaking students. Morton and Diaz's affection for one another had evidently become uncomfortably "public" because the directors asked Georgiana Bruce on April 29 "to ascertain from Manuel Diaz and Abby Morton their intentions with respect to farther residence at the Farm."[7] It's possible of course that Ichabod Morton's departure from the community in early April was connected to his daughter's budding romance.

Almira Barlow, Brook Farm's so-called *femme fatale,* had already made *her* intentions toward John Dwight quite clear a few months before. The twenty-nine-year-old Dwight had become smitten with the older Barlow—she was thirty-five—who arrived at Brook Farm with her three sons the previous spring. Dwight wanted romance; Barlow desired friendship. She wrote to him on January 6, 1843, to say that she had "felt for some time that, whether consciously or not, you were getting too much attached to me." She was unsure "how to keep the friend and reject the lover" because she enjoyed Dwight's companionship: "There is much in our congeniality of tastes and similarity of opinions to bring us together in various pleasant interchange." Barlow hoped that just because they could not have "intimate communion," she and Dwight might still manage to enjoy "genial trustful friendship."[8]

Barlow also cast her spell on another young man living in the community in 1843. Isaac Hecker came to Brook Farm in January for what would turn out to be a seven-month stay in the community. Like so many other young people in the 1840s (not the least of them the Transcendentalists themselves), Hecker was on a spiritual quest, one that would later inspire him to establish the religious order known today as the Paulist Fathers. In 1843, however, Hecker was just an inexperienced twenty-three-year-old who found the charms of an older woman like Barlow difficult to resist. He spent Saturday afternoon, April 15, walking with her in the Pine Woods behind the Eyrie, after which he recorded his rapture in a rambling stream-of-consciousness passage in the privacy of his diary. "After having said a lesson in French I went with ["Mrs. Barlow" is crossed out] a walking in the woods[.] My time was spent very pleasantly[,] the scenery was beautiful[,] the gothic formed woods which was very striking[,] the beautiful green pine trees and the moss of various tints covering the ground[,] the heavens with the clouds[,] the sun bursting through them at intervals[,] with the silence and shadey mystery of the woods[,] above all a soul susceptible of love and beauty gave to all such enchantement [*sic*] and [word canceled] my heart filled with love that I felt guilty of enjoyment."[9] Although he was obviously quite attracted to Barlow, Hecker managed finally to resist her lure because he was even more agitated about his own spiritual state.

Hecker's spiritual crisis was occasioned, in part, by his readings in German philosophy. Orestes Brownson, with whom the Hecker family had become quite friendly in 1842, recommended the works of Emanuel Kant, Johann Fichte, and Georg Wilhelm Hegel to his young friend (Brownson was sixteen years Hecker's senior). It was Brownson, in fact, who urged Hecker in January 1843 to board at Brook Farm for a while, where the controversial author of "The Laboring Classes" thought that the young seeker would find an atmosphere conducive to both contemplation and reflection, as well as one that would provide stimulating intellectual companionship. He certainly had plenty of the latter. In addition to attending classes that ranged from agriculture to botany to Kant, Hecker became friendly right away with Charles Dana, Burrill and George Curtis, and John Dwight. Dana and he were exactly the same age, and the Curtis brothers were just a few years younger. Dwight was only a few years older. Dana especially enjoyed conversing in German with his new friend, whose parents had emigrated earlier to America. (Dana's facility with the language was even better than Hecker's.) Despite the fact that their later journeys in life took them in very different directions, the five men developed a friendship at Brook Farm that endured throughout their lifetimes.

However disheartened George Ripley may have been at this time (Ripley always wore a brave face) by the Association's financial difficulties, Brook Farm's leader must have felt a sense of renewed affirmation by Isaac Hecker's presence in the community. It was just such a person as the earnest and spiritual Hecker that Ripley had in mind when he wrote to Emerson back in early November 1840: "Our objects, as you know, are to insure a more natural union between intellectual and manual labor than now exists; to combine the thinker and the worker, as far as possible, in the same individual." Hecker hadn't been in the community more than two weeks when he wrote to his brothers in New York City to report that "the bread baking has fallen into my hands. I take whole charge of the bread for the community, in which there are 90 persons, consuming about 50 to 60 lbs. of bread a day."[10] Hecker may have been on a spiritual quest, but he was prepared to do his share of the physical work too.

Ripley also must have been encouraged by recent developments in the rapidly expanding communitarian movement in the United States. Community-building—as Albert Brisbane would so often state in his newspaper columns—was very much the "aspiration of the age." Just in the past two years alone, since Brook Farm's inception in April 1841, seventeen had come into existence. No wonder Emerson had quipped to Thomas Carlyle that "we are all a little wild here with numberless projects of social reform. Not a reading man but has a draft of a new community in his waistcoat pocket." These utopian experiments ranged from the Hopedale Community and the Northampton Association in Massachusetts, to the Jefferson County Industrial Association in Cold Creek, New York, to the Teutonia, or McKean County Association, in Monroe County, Pennsylvania, to the Marlborough Association in Marlboro Township, Ohio.[11] Now in June 1843 there were two more. The North American Phalanx, near Red Bank, New Jersey, was in the early stages of its organization, and Bronson Alcott and his English friend Charles Lane finally packed up family and belongings on the first of June and moved fourteen miles west of the Alcott "Cottage" in Concord to the small town of Harvard to begin the fourth and last antebellum communal experiment in Massachusetts, which they named "Fruitlands"—ironically, as it turned out, because not a single fruit tree ever provided even an ounce of nourishment for the small group who gathered there.

When Albert Brisbane launched his front-page column in the New York *Tribune* on March 1, 1842, it was inevitable that a North American Phalanx based on Charles Fourier's utopian socialist principles would be organized. The new community in New Jersey was mainly instigated by readers of Brisbane's column, who kept inquiring when a practical experiment in Fourierism would be tried. Brisbane announced in his *Tribune* column at the end of October 1842 that the "books" would soon be opened for subscription of capital stock for the organization of an Association in the vicinity of New York City. By the end of January 1843 those books were still closed, but Brisbane did publish a set of "Articles of Association of the North American Phalanx," and he announced that he and Horace Greeley were ready to receive subscriptions to stock, which they hoped would amount to $200,000—that amount based on "two hundred persons who can invest each upon an average of a thousand dollars." (When he saw those numbers it's a wonder that Ripley didn't walk straight to New York to assure Brisbane that it would take a whole lot less than $200,000 to secure an already tested Brook Farm its financial future.) In April 1843 a small group of Fourierists from Albany, New York, met and drafted a set of rules of organization, and named themselves "The Albany Branch of the North American Phalanx."[12] A location still needed to be determined.

Much closer to West Roxbury and Brook Farm, Bronson Alcott and his wife Abba and their four daughters—the "little women," Anna, now twelve, Louisa May, ten, Lizzie, almost eight, and the baby, Abba, nearly two—set off from Concord with Charles Lane and his son William for the nearby town of Harvard and the ninety-acre Wyman Farm that Lane had just purchased for their communal experiment.[13] Alcott and Lane's ideas about social reform were very different from those of George Ripley and the Brook Farmers. Apart from obvious contrasts between the two communities (Fruitlands, for instance, never attracted more than twenty participants during the six months of its brief existence), the main ideological difference between them lay in conceptions about, and the appropriate circumstances for, what Transcendentalists then and now refer to as "self-culture," that is, the "progressive unfolding and development of the spiritual and intellectual potential of the individual."[14]

For Alcott and Lane, as well as for Emerson and Henry Thoreau, radical social change began with the individual; for George Ripley, and for other Transcendentalists such as Orestes Brownson, Theodore Parker, and William Henry Channing, reform began with institutions. In his explosive essay on "The Laboring Classes" in the July 1840 number of the *Boston Quarterly Review,* Brownson had noted that reformers of Alcott and Emerson's stripe "tell us that we want not external changes, but internal; and therefore instead of declaiming against society and seeking to disturb existing social arrangements, we should confine ourselves to the individual reason and conscience . . . Self-culture is a good thing, but it cannot abolish inequality, nor restore men to their rights." This was precisely George Ripley's point when, just a few months after Brownson, he submitted his lengthy resignation letter, noting along the way that "the attention of some good men is directed chiefly to individual evils; they wish to improve private character without attacking social principles which obstruct all improvement; while the attention of other good men is directed to the evils of society; they think that private character suffers from public sins, and that, as we are placed in society by Providence, the advancement of society is our principal duty."[15] Not until institutions were changed and competition thereby significantly diminished would individuals be truly free to live in "all the faculties of the soul," as Elizabeth Palmer Peabody expressed it in her January 1842 article in the *Dial* on the "Plan of the West Roxbury Community."

Because the reformation of the individual was central to Alcott and Lane's utopian vision, they placed a great deal of emphasis on diet, regimen, and health; they believed that spiritual regeneration was ultimately linked to physical purification. The belief that "outward abstinence is a sign of inward fullness," however, led to some extreme practices at Fruitlands. Each day began with a purging cold-water shower, and members of the community adhered to a strict vegetarian diet. (A young and exuberant Louisa May Alcott exclaimed in her journal, "I love cold water!") Not only were all stimulants such as coffee, tea, and alcohol avoided, but clothing made from cotton, wool, or leather was not permitted because its production required the exploitation of slaves and animals. That's why Alcott and Lane decided in June not to use horses or oxen to till the eleven or so acres of arable land on the farm. No matter that they were already more than a month behind the planting schedule when they arrived at the Wyman Farm.[16]

It's true that the Brook Farmers had voted in October 1842 "not . . . to furnish wine or ardent spirits to any associates on any occasion," and usually only the simplest fare was found at the tables in the Hive, but life in West Roxbury would hardly have been characterized as austere. The decision in September 1843 to discontinue the use of coffee was prompted by ongoing retrenchment efforts and not ideological commitment. So it's not surprising that Lane sneered at the Brook Farmers when he and Alcott journeyed down from Harvard one evening at the end of July 1843, just a few weeks after settling in the small farmhouse at the Wyman Farm. His West Roxbury neighbors, he thought, were "playing away their youth and day-time in a miserably joyous frivolous manner." (Lane should only have seen the community's balance sheet.) He reported to a British journal with obvious disgust that the Brook Farmers had "no less than sixteen cows, besides four oxen, a herd of swine, [and] a horse or two." As if this weren't awful enough, the Brook Farmers were purchasing butter "to the extent of 500 dollars a year."[17]

Isaac Hecker wouldn't have exactly agreed with such a cranky assessment, but for a while now he thought that something was missing in the West Roxbury community. Fruitlands, Hecker knew, was an ascetic community. Alcott and Lane had stimulated his curiosity with their talk of simplicity in manners and diet on the way to a more thoroughly spiritual existence. He decided to spend a few days at Fruitlands in June. The difficulty, Hecker was already aware, was only partially Brook Farm. The real problem was more personal. Five months at the West Roxbury community hadn't diminished his nagging sense of psychic anxiety, which was more acute now than ever before. Hecker was even more troubled in June than he had been just a few months before in February when he wrote to his parents that he felt as if he were "tossed about on a sea without a rudder of my own." Exactly where he was, he didn't know. "I have no power over my present," he wrote then, "and do not even know what my present is." Partly to blame was the entanglement with Almira Barlow, who was still living in the community that summer despite a retrenchment decision by Brook Farm's directors in April to have her and her three sons vacate their rooms at the Hive so renovations there to enlarge the dining area could get under way.[18]

Hecker's three-day trial visit to Fruitlands in June made at least one thing clear to him: "There is a deeper [spiritual] life there [at Fruitlands] than there is here [at Brook Farm]," he wrote in his diary right after returning from Harvard. But he had also come to love many of his companions at Brook Farm; they were "delightful[,] fine[,] beautiful[,] cultivated people." It was this aspect of life in the West Roxbury Association that made his decision to leave the community so difficult. He told one of his brothers in May that the "company" at Brook Farm "could not I imagine be more congenial . . . The tone and social feeling they treat each other here is all that your heart can de- sire. In a word, they love each other and the reception I receive ex- pands and warms my feelings towards them." But life itself at Brook Farm was not demanding enough, not self-denying or self-sacrificing enough, "not Christlike enough" for the anguished young man.[19] He didn't know whether Fruitlands could fulfill his psychic needs, but he had to find out. On July 11, Hecker departed West Roxbury for an ex- tended visit to the new community. He was fairly certain that he wouldn't return again to Brook Farm to live.

It's not likely that George Ripley was at all aware of the real source of Hecker's dissatisfaction with Brook Farm, but even if he were, he might not have responded to it anyway. For one thing, he was too busy dealing with the more mundane demands of running a large commu- nity. He didn't have much time to examine his interior life. For an- other, while it's obviously true that during the years that he served as a Unitarian minister the spiritual health of his congregants had been one of his regular concerns, Ripley himself had never been a deeply spiritual person in the sense, say, that Henry Thoreau or Bronson Alcott were. His wife Sophia probably would have better understood the crisis that Isaac Hecker was experiencing in 1843, especially since that summer she was gripped by a similar one herself.

On July 5 Sophia wrote an unusual letter to Waldo Emerson that indicates that she was feeling enervated, even depressed, by her life at Brook Farm. The letter may have been inspired by the most recent number of the *Dial*. Emerson visited the community at the end of June, probably bringing along a copy or two of the Transcendental journal because it had just been published, and it included a poem by Charles Dana on "Manhood," and another by George Curtis titled "Song of Death." But it wasn't these contributions that prompted Sophia to exclaim in the letter that "I cannot but tell you how rich & strong & faithful to its early intentions this last no [number] seems to me. It is really the first Dial we have had."[20] She was impressed by Ellery Channing's poems and letters, Samuel Ward's "Notes on Art and Architecture," and Margaret Fuller's lengthy appeal on behalf of women, "The Great Lawsuit. Man *versus* Men. Woman *versus* Women" (soon to be revised and published in 1845 as *Woman in the Nineteenth Century*—one of the most important feminist tracts of the antebellum period).

These contributions were so vigorous and robust that Sophia couldn't help thinking about the scarcity of these vital qualities at Brook Farm itself. George Curtis's poem was "graceful, a specimen of the best our young men can now produce, while they refuse themselves," she added sharply, "to deep experience, & in place thereof indulge in sentiment." Sophia was discouraged by the pervasive narcissism that she thought characterized the lives of so many of the Brook Farmers. Emerson had remarked during his visit to West Roxbury that there was "great wealth of nature" at Brook Farm, and Sophia agreed that the community provided a "free and vigorous atmosphere for it to unfold in," but she "mourned . . . the prodigality with which it is wasted away. I see everywhere around me those who might prophesy of the next age to the present, . . . prophesying only of themselves, casting their horoscopes, impertinently prying into their own emotions, or intoxicating themselves with the excited emotions of others." The lives of the best people at Brook Farm, Sophia said, "are narrow & dreary, or overheated . . . The movement of many here through the hours & days emits no fragrance, kind hearted as they are, so wrapped and swathed in selfism are they."

It must have genuinely surprised Emerson to hear the wife of the organizer of the community that he had refused to join, or in any way support, telling him, "What joy I feel that in the small circle of your nearest the craving heart may find such scholars & such workers as we need." Sophia's mood was only slightly more conciliatory when she wrote again to Emerson on July 29: "I do not wish or need stronger persons about me here [Brook Farm] than elsewhere, & am grateful for all the ornamental groups or solitary figures [of those living in the community] reposing in the shade at noon, or gazing on the setting sun; but why do they not with clear, strong vision meet his meridian glance & challenge him as a coworker to run his race with them? Why not live & move with head erect under the [word unclear] of his rays, instead of waiting for the reflection of the last upon some flower or lake?"[21]

Sophia Ripley's surprising letter to Emerson isn't the only such correspondence that has survived from July 1843. Two other letters are equally valuable because they provide considerably different perspectives from which to view the Brook Farm landscape of mid-1843. One is from Minot Pratt, who, with his wife Maria, was among the Association's hardest-working and most devoted members. He was writing to inform George Ripley that he was considering permanently withdrawing himself and his family from the community—as early as that summer. The other letter is from a young correspondent named Sophia Eastman, a rural farm girl from Franklin, New Hampshire, who arrived at Brook Farm at the beginning of July.

Like Sophia, Pratt was also discouraged about his life at Brook Farm but not for the same reasons that prompted Sophia's complaints to Emerson. Pratt was upset because after two years of sacrifice and hardship, he still felt no closer to the goals on which Brook Farm had originally been established. He was also disturbed by the difficulty of raising young children in the community, as well as by the crowded and inconvenient domestic conditions for a family living in the Hive (made worse now by the renovations begun there in June to extend the dining room by eliminating one of the two parlors).

George Ripley was immediately sympathetic. "I cannot look without daily admiration," he wrote to his good friend at the end of July, "on the patient toil & perpetual sacrifice, which you in common with other Associates, so faithfully endure in our common cause."[22] Ripley acknowledged that because of the community's financial difficulties, "our daily life is not the expression of our aspiration, and only a hopeful life in the future can cheer us amidst present embarrassments." (Even Ripley's reply to Pratt was delayed because, Brook Farm's leader said, "I have been so perplexed with pecuniary cares the past week.") For his own part, however, Ripley told Pratt that despite the enormity of the difficulties facing them, he had not lost faith in the ideal with which the community was begun. "I believe," he said, that "there is sufficient power & love in the spirit of man to carry it through." Besides, he added, he could never imagine returning to the "artificial forms of society." Such a move would be "little better than death."

Ripley, himself childless, was less understanding about the difficulties of raising children in a community. He recognized that the Pratt children—Frederick, now twelve, John, eleven, Caroline, just six, and Theodore Parker Pratt, who had just been born the previous summer of 1842—were "under a two-fold influence, that of the parent, & that of the Association," but he may not have really appreciated why the Pratts were so concerned about the influence other children in the community were exerting on their sons and daughter, which often undermined their own. Ripley was only able to say that he was sorry that Frederick and John had not shown much interest in school, but this, he thought, had less to do with Brook Farm than with the boys' "peculiar" temperaments. "I am not sure," he wrote, "that they would do any better, at the common city or village schools." Ripley himself was perfectly satisfied with the educational arrangement for young boys at Brook Farm: "I certainly never had any intercourse with boys, who called forth such deep attachment, or gave me so much real pleasure, as those I have instructed here."

Ripley was more responsive to Pratt's complaint about living conditions at the Hive, probably the "most unfavorable" location in the community for a family with children. The restricted accommodations and the general confusion and disorder of arrangements there would be difficult enough for a single person, much less a family of six. Ripley regretted that the Pratts hadn't taken advantage of earlier opportunities to move to one of the community's other buildings. (He probably had in mind the recently completed Pilgrim House, which, much more than the Cottage, was constructed with a view toward the comfort of families.) Disruptive living arrangements, Ripley said, were just another of the unfortunate inconveniences caused by the community's limited financial resources.

Above all, however, Ripley wanted Pratt to know that his departure from the community would be a source of "pain & regret" to all the associates, but especially to himself. He valued his friend's devotion, his patient and wise counsel, and his perseverance. It would be difficult, if not impossible, to replace him. But Ripley was in no position to predict the future. He couldn't say when conditions would improve, though he continued to believe that "comparatively, a small sum of money would place us at ease in pecuniary matters & enable us to improve our outward life." Ripley acknowledged, however, that "the want of that small sum, may prove a serious, perhaps fatal obstacle to our progress."

Perhaps it was the well water, or the homegrown rutabagas, that explains the grumbling and discontent in the community that summer. Even the young Sophia Eastman had a number of complaints to make soon after her arrival in the community in early July. She recorded them in a letter home in the form of "first impressions." Nearly all of them had to do with the kind of people in the Association rather than with specific individuals.[23] "There is an aristocracy prevailing here," the seventeen- or eighteen-year-old told her family right away, and "many complain of being neglected." And even though the "community speaks of receiving no individuals unless capable of refinement, a great taste for literature, and possessed of superior abilities . . . I assure you there are a great many of the reverse. The fact is they are rather dull and backward in there [*sic*] studies, and I am inclined to think will always remain so." One of these backward types was Eastman's roommate, an orphan from Ireland who was "a very good girl but rather ignorant [and] not such a person as I should wish to have for a friend."

The New Hampshire farm girl knew that her parents would be anxious to hear about Brook Farm's religious principles: "I regret to say that many have no principles at all. But very few attend church on the Sabbath, and it is a fact they do knit and sew." A carriage was provided for those who wished to attend religious services in West Roxbury, the student-boarder noted, but many stayed at the Farm instead and listened to Sophia Ripley read "gipsy stories" in the Pine Woods. Eastman added that there were four Unitarian ministers at Brook Farm who "have renounced these sentiments and become Transcendentalists. They seldom attend Church on the Sabbath." She couldn't resist providing one other tidbit before closing her letter: "It is nothing uncommon for people to get married and then part from there [sic] husbands. There are three who board here and there [sic] husbands have left them." If her brother James ever "tired of [his wife] Sarah," Eastman advised, "he must come and live here."

Had George Ripley ever seen Sophia Eastman's letter he probably would have dismissed it as a willfully exaggerated report from a teenager who was anxious to alarm her parents now that she was beyond the pale of their authority, and who enjoyed the sense of helplessness that she imagined they would feel being unable to protect their daughter from the iniquitous influences of Transcendentalists, lapsed Unitarian ministers, and married women cavorting around without their husbands. (Eastman was effectively dismissed from the community in November.)[24] Ripley didn't need to see Eastman's letter, however—or his wife Sophia's to Emerson, for that matter—to know that the community that was so undeviatingly the center of his life was not meeting the needs of some of its most important members. He would have known that from Louis Ryckman's decision in May to take an extended leave of absence from Brook Farm in order to visit the newly formed Sylvania Association in Pennsylvania, in which shoemaking was to be one of the principal industries. He obviously also knew that Minot Pratt was prepared to leave the community for good. The earnest Isaac Hecker's visit to Fruitlands was another reminder that Brook Farm couldn't be all things to all people, but Ripley possibly didn't yet know that the young seeker's impending departure from West Roxbury would be permanent. And Ripley's two "Greek gods," Burrill and George Curtis, agreed that Brook Farm wasn't Mount Olympus after all and announced that they would leave the community in August.[25] Ripley knew that he had to take more decisive action to stanch the hemorrhaging of the community's lifeblood. He decided to test the waters that were beginning to swirl about the rapidly expanding Associationist movement. In early August 1843 Ripley participated in a "Convention" at the Albany Exchange in Albany, New

York, to help delegates from Catskill, Troy, and Albany draft a constitution and formulate a "covenant to invest in the capital stock" of the North American Phalanx, the location of which, it had by then been decided, would be Red Bank, New Jersey. Ripley's participation in the Albany Convention marks the beginning of an entirely new direction for the Brook Farm community.

Ripley's role at the Convention was consultative. He was there in an advisory capacity to help with language, answer organizational questions, and clarify procedural matters, all of which he was obviously well qualified to do. What's really significant about Ripley's presence at the Albany Convention, however, is that it marks the first time that he publically identified himself with the expanding community of American Fourierists.[26] He evidently liked what he heard at the meeting. When he returned to West Roxbury in mid-August, he was not alone: with him was none other than the leading apostle of Fourierism in the United States, Albert Brisbane.

Brisbane came to Boston because he had arranged to deliver two lectures on the social reform program that he had been so vigorously promoting in his New York *Tribune* column since March 1842. He was anxious now to extend the campaign to New England. Always a shrewd propagandist, Brisbane hoped to capitalize on the interest that his recently published eighty-page pamphlet on *Association; or, A Concise Exposition of the Practical Part of Fourier's Social Science* had been generating. New England was as yet a new frontier since, as Brisbane noted in his column for August 30, 1843, right after the visit to Boston, "The doctrine of Association has been but little spread there." He was determined to change that because he thought that New Englanders combined "liberality and breadth of thought with energy of action," and they were prepared "for the great and profound idea of a Social Reform by the various intellectual movements which have already been agitated [there]." These were Brisbane's views. As for New Englanders themselves, most would happily have agreed with Brisbane's first point, but would prove him almost entirely wrong on the second point. As Orestes Brownson astutely observed to Isaac Hecker right after Brisbane made his New England debut, "Fourierism will not take with us [New Englanders].[27]

Brisbane gave his first talk on Wednesday evening, August 23, 1843, at the Chapel on Marlborough Street in Boston. The New Yorker estimated the attendance to be about 300 people. (Dana thought that it was actually more like 400.) Brisbane lectured on the scientific foundation of the Associative doctrine, which gave him the opportunity to discuss "the triple destiny of man upon earth, and [to] show how the Social Order, which we advocate, will direct mankind in fulfilling their destiny." His second talk two evenings later filled the large hall of the Chapel. This lecture was "exclusively practical." It focused on "the mechanism and principles of Association—its system of property, education and commerce; the organization of industry, the mode of living, its architecture, and the means of spreading and rendering the system universal." Immediately following the second lecture, a special meeting was held to organize a committee to investigate Fourier's social reform principles more thoroughly. This committee's investigation, it was hoped, would lead to "the establishment of a regular Society for the propagation of [Fourier's] doctrine" in New England.[28] The person selected to serve as chairman of the new committee was George Ripley.

The Boston lectures also gave Brisbane the chance to make his first visit to Brook Farm. The New Yorker immediately recognized Brook Farm's usefulness in the effort to widen the propaganda campaign on behalf of Fourierism. He stated in his *Tribune* column on August 30 that there was a "nucleus" at West Roxbury such as he knew of nowhere else. "A fine spirit of friendship, union, confidence and brotherhood reigns there," he said, "and . . . Mr. Ripley is admirably adapted to the position which he holds; for he combines, beside the advantages of a polished education, great activity, practical talent and high benevolence."

Brisbane encouraged those among his readers who were blacksmiths, carpenters, machinists, and shoemakers to consider joining the West Roxbury Association, which he presumably did with Ripley's blessing. Brook Farm, Brisbane said, was anxious to add an "industrial" basis to its operations, which is not, certainly, what the former Unitarian minister envisioned when he first came to West Roxbury in 1841 to build anew the "city of God."[29] Ripley probably recognized that for Brisbane, Brook Farm's chief attraction was that it represented a New England base from which to proselytize for Associationism and Fourierism. From Ripley's perspective, Brisbane represented influence and an important potential source of financial support. There was no sudden rush on the part of either man to embrace the other's vision.

The Convention of Associationists in Albany and Brisbane's visit to West Roxbury were, in any case, like tonic to George Ripley. They rejuvenated his spirit. They renewed the ardor of his commitment to the new world, which, surprisingly, the struggles of the previous two years had not noticeably diminished. Brisbane's reassurances in the *Tribune* were testimony that his and Sophia's labors in West Roxbury had not been without important consequence. The Association was still without adequate sources of income, but it would take relatively only a small amount of money, Ripley thought, to relieve the financial pressures on the community. It might be expected that the Brook Farm leader would have contacted someone like Horace Greeley once he decided to seek investors in the New York City area (it was still too soon to approach Brisbane), but oddly enough he turned instead to the one person in that great metropolis who was, temperamentally, probably the most ill-suited in the entire state to solicit financial support for the West Roxbury Association.

If words were wings then Ripley's letter to Isaac Hecker in mid-September would have soared to his former associate, who was in New York City living with his family. The Brook Farmer's appeal to Hecker is infused with evangelical fervor. Ripley hoped that Hecker's aspirations had not been "quenched" by the "evils of a city environment."[30] Ripley himself didn't think that he could return to "common society. I should pine like an imprisoned bird, & I fear, I should grow blind to the visions of loveliness and glory which the future promises to humanity. I long for action which shall realize the prophesies, fulfill the Apocalypse, bring the New Jerusalem down from Heaven to earth, and collect the faithful into a true and holy brotherhood." Some of those faithful were already gathered at Brook Farm. "All here, that is, all our old central members," Ripley told Hecker, "feel more and more the spirit of devotedness, the thirst to do or die for the cause we have at heart." They would willingly "traverse the wilderness for forty years; we ask no grapes of Eshcol for ourselves; we do not claim a fair abode in the promised land." But with "raiment waxing old and shoes bursting on our feet," the journey of the faithful who were congregated in West Roxbury would be mired in the sloughs until the weight of the financial millstone around the community's neck was lifted. "The want of $2 or 3,000 fetters us and may kill us," Ripley stated. If such a comparatively small amount could be raised, it "would free us from pecuniary embarrassments . . . Are there not 5 men in N[ew]. Y[ork]. city," Ripley asked, "who would dare to venture $200 each in the cause of social reform?"[31]

While Ripley was waiting to hear from Hecker, his spirits must have been further bolstered by the appearance of a new reform-minded journal called *The Present*. When on September 15, 1843, he published the first number of the monthly, Ripley's old friend and fellow Unitarian minister William Henry Channing added his voice to the growing number of others now calling in increasingly more urgent tones for a new millennium based on Associationist principles. The charismatic nephew of the widely esteemed and recently deceased Unitarian divine, William Ellery Channing, would, in the months to come, devote important attention to Charles Fourier's utopian socialist views in the pages of his New York-based periodical, the special aim of which, Channing told his readers in the "Introduction," would be "to show the grounds of reconciliation between the sects and parties, native and foreign, the controversies, theological and political, the social reformers and prudent conservatives, the philosophers and poets, prophets and doubters, which divide these United States."[32]

In addition to the lengthy "Introduction," the first number contained, among other items, a review of his cousin William Ellery Channing's (not to be confused with his more famous uncle) recently published *Poems,* and a page and a half of remarks about Charles Fourier. In the comments about Fourier, Channing made it clear that he was not yet prepared to endorse the French social scientist without first examining some important qualifications. He hoped, nonetheless, that the pages of the new monthly journal would serve as a forum for discussion of such matters as the Frenchman's system of "passional harmonies" and his theory of "attractive industry," and that members of the new communities established during the previous two years would not hesitate to report their experiences in the pages of *The Present.*

Less than three weeks after the appearance of *The Present,* a second new reform journal was launched in New York City, this one devoted unabashedly and exclusively to the cause of Fourierism and the Associationist movement. Its founder and editor was Albert Brisbane. The journal was called *The Phalanx.* Brisbane may have found the demand of providing several columns a week for the *Tribune*—as fellow New Yorker Parke Godwin had just discovered with his own recently collapsed paper, *The Pathfinder*—to be too time-consuming and difficult, especially since he was now in great demand himself as a speaker at various Fourierist conventions and gatherings around the country. *The Phalanx* would appear as a monthly. If and when it attracted a thousand or so subscribers, Brisbane might convert the paper to a weekly.

The first number of *The Phalanx* appeared on October 5, 1843, and Brisbane immediately filled its sixteen pages with all manner of matter relating to Fourierism and Associationism. These ranged from translations of Fourier's writings, to summaries of the proceedings of Fourierist conventions, to news of Fourierist activities in France and England, to articles by Brisbane himself elucidating Fourierist doctrine, to reports of developments concerning the many new Associations around the country. Although Brook Farm had yet made no formal commitment whatsoever to Fourierism, Brisbane included a brief description of the West Roxbury community in the very first number of *The Phalanx,* right alongside reports of three avowedly Fourierist communities—the Sylvania Association in Pennsylvania, the North American Phalanx in New Jersey, and the Jefferson County Industrial Association in New York, all three of which had recently been established.

It's not hard to imagine the effect that the two new journals might have had at this critical time on George Ripley and his supporters (not to mention, obviously, on communitarians around the country). To readers of *The Present* and *The Phalanx*—with their regular publication of article after article on Charles Fourier and Fourierism, and notices of and reports on gatherings and other Associationist activities in New York, Pennsylvania, Ohio, and elsewhere—it must have seemed that "Association" was the watchword of the day. Channing's series of detailed articles that autumn titled "Call of the Present" ("Social Reorganization," "The Science of Unity," and "Oneness of God and Man"), combined with Brisbane's barrage of correspondence, reports on Fourierist conventions around the country, and translations from the writings of leading French Associationists, also must have helped assuage whatever reservations Ripley and others had about the efficacy of Charles Fourier's social reform program, which was actively being discussed at Brook Farm at that time.

After lamenting that "the money does not come," Sophia Ripley reported to Margaret Fuller that meetings were being held every week in the community, at which "the men out of the association [that is, residents who hadn't formally become associates] are present . . . They are very united, & are attempting to make an arrangement by which our mechanical departments may be increased & the support of the establishment thrown in a great measure upon them." Ripley himself had still not definitely decided in late November "what course it is best for us to take with regard to the great movement [Associationism] now agitating the country." There can be little doubt, however, that he would have considered auspicious Louis Ryckman's return from the Sylvania Association earlier in the month, and Minot Pratt's decision to remain for the time being at Brook Farm.[33]

Even Waldo Emerson's iconoclastic neighbor and protégé Henry David Thoreau was agitated enough by all the talk about Associationism and Fourierism that he decided to visit Brook Farm in December 1843 to find out for himself whether communal life might be something that he should reconsider. He had been in Staten Island, New York, since May tutoring Emerson's brother William's children. He returned to Concord on November 23 to deliver a lecture at the Lyceum on the "Ancient Poets." Thoreau was certainly no friend of community. His reaction to an invitation to join Brook Farm in early 1841 was quite sharp. He wrote in his journal for March 3, 1841: "As for these communities, I think I had rather keep bachelor's hall in hell than go to board in heaven." But now at the end of 1843 Thoreau was casting about for direction. The return to Concord reminded him just how much he missed the New England town that had been, and would always be, so essential a part of his life. Frankly, he was homesick. He was also aware, as biographer Walter Harding notes, that the Staten Island experiment "on the whole had to be written off as a failure."[34] When he left Concord on December 3, 1843, to gather up his possessions in Staten Island, Thoreau unexpectedly veered south and headed straight to West Roxbury.

Although he was without any attractive prospects for the future, the brief visit to Brook Farm made Thoreau more determined than ever not to compromise his independence for the purported conveniences of Associative life. (Just a little more than a year after his visit, Thoreau would begin preparations for his own experiment in alternative living at Walden Pond.) He also engaged the Brook Farmers on these matters; as George Bradford told Emerson in a letter on December 12, "We [the Brook Farmers] were quite indebted to Henry for his brave defence of his thought which gained him much favor in the eyes of some of the friends here who are of the like faith."[35]

That remark is particularly interesting in light of the fact that George Ripley and a few others were getting ready for a "Convention of Friends of Social Reform" in Boston at the end of the month. The community was still abuzz with talk about Associationism and Fourierism, but not everyone, as Thoreau's visit indicates, was in agreement. Several of the "old central members," as Ripley had characterized them to Hecker in September, who were ready then "to do or die for the cause," were not so certain now that they would even remain much longer at Brook Farm. For Ripley and his supporters, the upcoming Convention would turn out to be another of those defining "moments" in the community's troubled history. The Brook Farmers who participated in the Convention returned to West Roxbury more certain than ever that the time had come to reorganize the community according to the industrial principles of Charles Fourier.

6

Reorganization

The "Convention of Friends of Social Reform in New England" was held in Boston over a four-day period from December 26 to 29, 1843. It effectively marks the end of the so-called Transcendental period of Brook Farm's existence and the beginning of its experiment with Fourierism. A call for the meeting had gone out earlier in the month in both *The Present* and *The Phalanx,* as well as in William Lloyd Garrison's popular antislavery weekly, *The Liberator.* The purpose of the meeting was to gather together those who were committed to social reorganization and reform, although the "Call" listed the following as one of the Convention objects: "To cheer our hearts by a united contemplation of the wonderful progress in our own and other countries of the great TRUTHS of Social Science, discovered by Charles Fourier." The account of the Convention in Horace Greeley's New York *Tribune* noted that the object of the gathering was, more broadly, "to afford men of different views to meet each other in free and earnest discussion, rather than to sanction any particular scheme of Association."[1] The names of a few of the participants make it clear that advocates of several different plans for social reorganization did indeed attend the meeting.

Adin Ballou and a few of his "Practical Christian" followers represented the Hopedale Community, David Mack and George W. Benson were there to speak for the Northampton Association, and John Collins, the former general agent of the Massachusetts Anti-Slavery Society, represented the Skaneateles Community that he had recently organized in Skaneateles, New York. George Ripley, Charles Dana, Louis Ryckman, and John Dwight were there for Brook Farm. Reformers from Boston and elsewhere also attended the meeting, including such recognizable New Englanders as William Lloyd Garrison, Bronson Alcott, and Orestes Brownson, as well as New York-based proponents like Albert Brisbane, William Henry Channing, and Parke Godwin. Abigail Folsom was also present. A familiar figure at reform conventions, Folsom was known for her long and usually disruptive harangues. Another recognizable local "character" was an unnamed reformer with a long flowing beard, which was "venerably white—as was also his hair—& . . . [who was] dressed in garments of undyed cloth."[2] A more impressive participant was Frederick Douglass, the fugitive slave whose powerful *Narrative of Frederick Douglass, An American Slave* would be published in 1845.

Several other current or soon-to-become Brook Farmers attended the meeting, including John Allen, who, with David Hatch Barlow (Almira Barlow's estranged husband), had just finished a lecture tour in New England to spread the gospel of Fourierism; Jonathan Butterfield, a Boston printer; Frederick S. Cabot, also from Boston and an active member of the Massachusetts Anti-Slavery Society; Christopher List, a lawyer who had just moved to Brook Farm two months before on a "trial" basis; and Ephraim Capen, a pewterer who would soon establish the Britannia-ware "industry" at the community. There were probably as many future Brook Farmers in attendance, in fact, as there were current associates in the West Roxbury Association, of whom the number continued to be still only about fifteen. Ripley was elected one of the Vice Presidents of the Convention, and Dana one of its Secretaries. Ripley joined Channing, Douglass, Collins, and representatives from Hopedale and Northampton to form a "Committee of

Business," whose responsibility it was to draft resolutions for the Convention participants.

The Convention was held at the popular Tremont Temple, with meetings and discussions lasting each day until nearly midnight. Eight resolutions were discussed by the Convention participants, and three were eventually adopted. One reaffirmed the participants' faith in "Christian Brotherhood" and in "Peaceful Reform," at the same time that it condemned, among other things,

> the inefficacy of all modes of Public Charity to relieve or prevent *Pauperism* . . .; the injustice of our common system of *Wages;* the tediousness, oppressiveness, and unhealthiness of our habits of *Labor;* the unequal distribution of means and opportunities for *Culture, Refinement, Recreation* and *Social Pleasures;* the imperfect character and degree of *Popular Education,* both for children and adults; the unnatural subservience of *Woman;* the distinctions of *Caste* based upon outward and artificial circumstances; [and] the universal war of *Competition.*

Another resolution recommended the establishment of local societies "of the friends of this cause [Associationism]" for the purpose of "disseminating their principles by Lectures, Tracts, Conventions or otherwise." It was the third resolution, however, that must have most pleased Ripley and his supporters. That resolution—which Ripley had a hand in drafting—called for a "thorough test" of Fourier's principles in an Association, in the same breath that it commended "to the efficient encouragement and aid of all the friends of Human Progress, the various Associations for Social Reform already partially established."[3]

Even Margaret Fuller found herself invigorated by the renewed spirit of determination that Ripley and the others brought back from the Boston Convention. She decided to welcome the new year in West Roxbury in order to spend some time near her dear friend William Henry Channing, who, along with the New York Fourierist Parke Godwin, was staying at Brook Farm for a few days after the Social Reform Convention in order to assist Albert Brisbane with a course of five or six lectures on "Association" at Boston's Amory Hall.[4] Fuller was perfectly happy whether her time in West Roxbury was spent alone with Channing or in the company of "these many of different ages, tempers, and relationships with us, for all seemed bound in our thought this happy day."

Channing addressed the entire community on the morning of New Year's Eve on the "destiny of the Earth," and then Fuller—anxious to extend the mood inspired by her friend's remarks—read a lofty twenty-four-line poem written by her brother-in-law Ellery Channing on "The Earth" ("The forests and the mountains high, / The foaming ocean and its springs, / Thy plains,— O pleasant company, / My voice through all your anthems rings"). That evening, with the moon "nearly full" and shining brightly "in an unclouded sky" over the snow-covered meadows and pastures around the Farm, Fuller admired the beauty and serenity of the night from the window in her old friend Charles Newcomb's room at the Cottage. Afterwards, she and a few others walked up to the Eyrie and settled for a while in George and Sophia Ripley's room for some end-of-the-year reflections. Later still, back in the absent Newcomb's room, and filled with a mixture of feelings brought about by the events of the previous days (she evidently had attended at least part of the Convention), Fuller was moved to write a forty-four-line poem, the thoughts of which, she acknowledged, "relate more to what had passed at the Fourier Convention [that is, the Social Reform Convention], and to the talk we had been having in Mrs. R[ipley]'s room than to the deeper occupation of my mind" ("Yes! sound again the horn, of Hope the golden horn; / Answer it, flutes and pipes, from valleys still and lorn, / Wardens from your high towers with trumps of silver scorn, / And harps in maidens' bowers with strings from deep heart torn / All answer to the horn, of Hope the golden horn.").[5]

The "Convention of the Friends of Social Reform in New England" made it clear—at least to George Ripley—what action needed to be taken before Brook Farm collapsed from the weight of its mounting indebtedness: the community had to be reorganized in such a way that Albert Brisbane, Horace Greeley, and other leading Fourierists in New York City and around the country might support it financially. Brook Farm needed to be positioned more centrally in the Associationist movement. Ripley called the members of the community together in the Hive on January 2, 1844, to discuss future prospects. Charles Dana, it was agreed, would attend a follow-up meeting in Boston the very next day sponsored "by the friends of Asso[ciation] & make some statement of the present condition of [the] Brook Farm Asso[ciation]," and Ripley, Dana, and Louis Ryckman would "be a Committee to revise the Constitution [that is, the original Articles] of the B[rook] F[arm] I[nstitute]."[6]

Marianne Ripley reported afterward that the follow-up meeting in Boston—at which Charles Fourier's social and industrial principles were discussed—was "very fully attended," and that "about twenty gave in their names . . . who were desirous of becoming members of the Association under the amended Constitution." Much more important, she said, "three thousand dollars were subscribed" in anticipation of the community's reorganization, though she might have reminded her correspondent that a pledge of subscription did not represent actual cash.[7] Charles Dana, after all, had also "subscribed" to three shares of Brook Farm stock, but, now more than two years later, had still not managed to purchase even one of them.

The decision to cast Brook Farm's fortunes onto Associative waters was not supported by everyone. In fact, it caused a serious rift between Ripley, Dana, and Georgiana Bruce, on one side, and several unidentified Brook Farmers on the other. Sophia Ripley's letter to Margaret Fuller describing the particulars of the disagreement isn't as detailed or as specific as it might have been, but it does provide a clear outline of what happened.[8]

Evidently, while Ripley, Dana, Ryckman, and the other Brook Farmers were in Boston attending the Convention, those who remained in West Roxbury must have been grumbling about the prospect of the community being absorbed into the national Associative movement. Georgiana Bruce must have been one of those who stayed behind and listened to the grousing because "there would have been no manly calling to account of any of us," Sophia said, "if Georgy's truthfulness, had not forced persons into it." A confrontation took place in January sometime after the community meeting at the beginning of the month. It did nothing, Sophia thought, to mend "the tie that had been ruptured," which, she claimed, did not discourage her because her "heart was not deeply wounded, for it had never been deeply attached to the persons concerned." The affinity of her nature, like that of the people who supported her husband, wasn't naturally drawn to those who were unable to recognize that "the only legitimate union is found in oneness of purpose," which Sophia now said she had discovered in Associationism, "& to Association," she stated, "I purpose to devote my life."

The future at Brook Farm was very uncertain, but Sophia felt neither solicitous nor sad about it. Her husband was "suffering from these things more" than she. "He has less varied ties than I," she remarked, adding that he was still "nobly supported here by two or three & I trust will be carried through."[9] She would continue to be steadfast and practical, for "in these days we must take our life in our own hands, be ready to dwell no where, to encamp any where, & give to our work that devoted loyal love, which we have hitherto given to our localities, friends & environments."

Louis Ryckman and Charles Dana were definitely two of the supporters to whom Sophia alluded in her letter (John Dwight was probably the third, though it could also have been Minot Pratt), although the fervor of Dana's idealism more closely resembled Ripley's than it did Ryckman's. The New York shoemaker was a card-carrying Fourierist (he was still the Vice President of the New York Fourier Society) for whom Fourierism was an end in itself. What interested him primarily was the melioration of social and economic conditions that affected tradesmen and workingmen like himself. Ryckman's views, compared to those of Ripley and Dana, were narrow and partial. Ripley and Dana were animated by a nobler spirit. Fourierism was a means to a more glorious end, which would be nothing less than the arrival of the era of Universal Harmony in which all partial reforms would finally be reconciled.

Louis Ryckman would never have said, as Charles Dana did early that January of 1844, "To the attainment of this end [the era of Universal Harmony] I devote myself; not as a sectarian,—not as a disciple of any special school,—but as far as my weakness will permit,—as the pupil and servant of the Divine Ideas." That didn't mean that the former Harvard student had anything less than the highest regard for Charles Fourier. Dana may have thought that Albert Brisbane "was not a man of sufficient depth of intellect to interpret the profound things of the great Frenchman," but he was already certain that Fourier was, along with eighteenth-century Swedish scientist and theologian Emanuel Swedenborg, the "profoundest thinker of these modern times."[10]

Reorganization of the Brook Farm community took place formally on January 7, 1844, when Ripley, Dana, and Ryckman presented a revised and amended copy of the "Articles of Agreement" and the "Articles of

Association" to the members of the community, "which was read and with some amendments accepted." On January 18, the new "Constitution of the Brook Farm Association for Industry and Education" was published.[11] It incorporates virtually all the main features of both sets of the 1841 "Articles," including the nearly two-hundred-word "Preamble" found in the "Articles of Agreement." The new constitution is more efficiently organized, however, than the earlier documents. It contains six Articles and twenty subsections—each Article having at least two but no more than six subsections. The original documents combined had contained a total of twenty-eight Articles (and no subsections).

The new constitution provides for a slightly modified administrative structure from the one that the Brook Farmers had been relying on since 1841. Instead of five "Directions," there would now be four: a "General Direction," a "Direction of Education," a "Direction of Finance," and a "Direction of Industry." The earlier "Direction of Agriculture" and the "Direction of Domestic Economy," the latter of which had been established in February 1842, would now become "Series" in the new Fourierist regime under the authority of the "Direction of Industry." Stockholders would continue to earn 5 percent interest on their investments, and the "Guarantees" (housing, food, education, and the like) remained the same in 1844 as they had always been.

In addition to these similarities, there are four important differences between the new constitution and the earlier Articles. One is the change of the Association's name; two others are the "Introductory Statement" and a set of "By-Laws," neither of which were included in the earlier Articles; and the fourth is the actual publication of the constitution.

Until now the Association had been known as the "Brook Farm Institute of Agriculture and Education." Hereafter it would be called the

Charles Fourier. Brook Farm adopted many of the utopian industrial
principles of French social scientist Charles Fourier in 1844. Fourier's
theories inspired dozens of other communities and organizations in the
United States in the 1840s.

"Brook Farm Association of Industry and Education." The shift to "Association" and "Industry" indicated the intended future emphasis on mechanical industries, but, more important, it quietly signaled the community's new commitment to Charles Fourier. This new allegiance is directly referred to in both the "Introductory Statement" and the "By-Laws." Ripley, Dana, and Ryckman acknowledged "emphatically" at the beginning of the lengthy "Introductory" that "while on the one hand we yield an unqualified assent to that doctrine of universal unity which Fourier teaches, so on the other, our whole observation has shown us the truth of the practical arrangements which he deduces therefrom. [Fourier's] law of groups and series is, as we are convinced, the law of human nature." The fourth Article of the nine new By-Laws, in fact, is devoted to "Groups and Series." It contains nine short subsections that briefly describe the administrative operation of Groups and Series, around which all labor activity in the community would now be organized.[12]

In his *Association; or, A Concise Exposition of the Practical Part of Fourier's Social Science* (1843), Albert Brisbane defined a Group as "a body of persons united from a taste for any occupation, whether of Industry, Art or Science, and who combine for the purpose of prosecuting it . . . Series are composed of a number of Groups, as Groups are composed of individuals and operate upon Groups as Groups upon individuals."[13] Brook Farm's new constitution states that "the department of Industry shall . . . consist of three primary series; to wit, Agricultural, Mechanical, and Domestic Industry." (An "Educational Series" was quickly added to the mix.) In the "Agricultural Series," there was a Ploughing Group, a Planting Group, a Weeding Group, a Hoeing Group, a Milking Group, and so on. The "Domestic Series" included several related Groups, among them a Dormitory Group, a Washing, Ironing, and Mending Group, a Refectory Group, and a Consistory Group. George Ripley was elected chief of the "Agricultural Series," and Sophia was appointed the first chief of the "Domestic Series." The Association's minutes don't indicate who took charge initially of the "Mechanical Series," but most likely it was either Charles Dana or Minot Pratt. The number of hours that probationers and associates devoted to each Series was dutifully logged into the Series Account book every month.

Without minimizing the sincerity of Ripley's interest in Charles Fourier's industrial and social doctrines and theories, the most urgent reason why Brook Farm's leader thought that the community needed to be identified with the expanding Associationist movement was financial necessity rather than zealous enthusiasm for Fourierist ideology. That's not to say that Ripley didn't find Fourier's plans for industrial reform attractive. For one thing, the intricate record-keeping that they required would have appealed to the pedantic side of his personality, just as, it will be recalled, the *New England Farmer* had done a few years before when, on the eve of Brook Farm's organization, it inspired one calculation after another in Ripley's journal about such matters as planting, harvesting, crop rotation, the amount of manure that a specific number of cattle would produce, how many acres of tillage land the manure would cover, how many crops the land would yield, and so forth.[14]

Much more important, however, Ripley would have recognized that Fourier's plans for industrial reorganization were prompted by a view of human nature that resembled one fundamental to Transcendentalist thought, at least as that had been articulated by Ripley's mentor, William Ellery Channing. The Frenchman's theories about "attractive industry," "Groups and Series," and "passional attraction" (see Chapter 7) were based on Fourier's belief in human potentiality—a potentiality that was subverted by and would never reach fruition under existing industrial arrangements. Fourier was no Calvinist. He "denied the doctrine of the essential depravity of human nature and the conclusion based thereon that men must be disciplined and enslaved by an alien industrial power," Norman Ware noted in his study, *The Industrial Worker 1840–1860.* Fourier "claimed that men were not necessarily lazy and of no account, but had impulses of a creative character that modern industry was especially adapted to destroy. He proposed the reorganization of industry on the basis of these creative impulses to permit their free expression, believing that in this way industry could be made attractive and efficient rather than repulsive and wasteful."[15]

It didn't require a great leap to see that, at the very heart of it, there was an essential similarity between Fourier's views about the individual in the workplace and Transcendental notions about what Dr. Channing had referred to in his 1838 lecture of the same title as "Self-Culture," a lecture, David M. Robinson has noted, that "indicates his [Channing's] growing orientation toward social ethics." Even before his 1819 sermon on "Unitarian Christianity," Channing had been patiently working out the concepts of the movement among liberal Christians that came to be known in antebellum America as Unitarianism. In Channing's hands, those concepts became increasingly more socially oriented in the 1830s. In 1828 he had preached an ordination sermon on "Likeness to God" in which he argued that the "great work of religion is to conform ourselves to God, or to unfold the divine likeness within us." Formation of character through "right and vigorous exertion" was thus an individual's greatest responsibility. "Likeness to God," Channing went on to say, did not "consist in extraordinary or marvelous gifts, in supernatural additions to the soul, or in anything foreign to our original constitution; but in our essential faculties, unfolded by vigorous and conscientious exertion in the ordinary circumstances assigned by God." (It would obviously be difficult to unfold those "essential faculties" if one had to spend twelve to fourteen hours a day, six days a week, engaged in tedious or even mindless labor that had little or nothing to do with the wellsprings of one's true nature.)

By 1838 Channing had recast his religious imperative into the arena of social reform: "[Channing's] 1838 lecture 'Self-Culture' proposed a life of strenuous effort at constant self-improvement, offering self-culture as both a spiritual goal and a social good," Robinson observes. Channing himself directed his energies to a wide variety of social reforms, as the titles of some of his sermons and lectures in the 1830s indicate: *The Ministry for the Poor* (1835), *An Address on Temperance* (1837), and *Remarks on the Slavery Question* (1839). The point to make, however, is that Ripley, who once characterized himself as a "child of Channing," would certainly have found Fourier's plans for industrial reform quite compatible with the brand of Transcendentalism that had been nurtured in him by the great Unitarian divine. After all, that's what organizing Brook Farm had been about in the first place. Five months before launching the West Roxbury community, Ripley summarized his goals this way:

> to insure a more natural union between intellectual and manual labor than now exists; to combine the thinker and the worker, as far as possible, in the same individual; to guarantee the highest mental freedom, by providing all with labor, adapted to their tastes and talents, and securing to them the fruits of their industry; to do away [with] the necessity of menial services, by opening the benefits of education and the profits of labor to all; and thus to prepare a society of liberal, intelligent, and cultivated persons, whose relations with each other would permit a more simple and wholesome life, than can be led amidst the pressure of our competitive institutions.[16]

Ripley's decision now to reorganize Brook Farm along Fourierist lines was, in any case, as necessary as it was practical. It was also smart. It was no secret at the West Roxbury community in late 1843 that the Association's future prospects didn't inspire much confidence. Even the quiet and unobtrusive Amelia Russell, whose administrative role at Brook Farm was limited to serving as "mistress of the revels," was aware of that fact. The reorganization, she recalled years later, "was no doubt influenced in a great degree by the absolute necessity there was of some bold effort to enable us to exist, and there seemed no other alternative than either to adopt this course [Fourierism] or to dissolve the association."[17]

What Ripley really hoped was that Brook Farm would be designated the "Model Phalanx" in the United States and, as noted earlier, would thereby receive financial support from the growing number of Associationists in New York City and elsewhere around the country. He obviously knew that the North American Phalanx had just been organized in Red Bank, New Jersey, but he felt that Brook Farm had many advantages not available there or at the other five recently organized Fourierist communities. He was also aware from reports in *The Present* and *The Phalanx* that many new Fourierist Associations were being planned. Typical of the reports in *The Phalanx* was a letter by a T. C. Leland from Rochester, New York, that appeared in the number for April 1, 1844: "*Nine* Associations are now contemplated within fifty miles of this City [Rochester] . . . I have no hesitation in saying that 20,000 persons west of the longitude of Rochester in this State is a low estimate of those who are now ready, and willing, nay anxious to take their place in Associative Unity." Ripley wanted Brook Farm to be at the front of the wave that was beginning to roll across the country.[18] That's really why he decided to publish the new constitution, something he had not done with the original Articles.

Ripley himself noted in the "Introductory Statement" of the constitution that Brook Farm "has hitherto worn, for the most part, the character of a private experiment, and has avoided rather than sought, the notice of the public." Until now, Ripley had judged it better "to publish no statements of . . . purposes or methods, to make no promises or declarations, but quietly and sincerely to realize, as far as might be possible, the great ideas which gave the central impulse to their [the Brook Farmers'] movement." Now, however, Ripley wanted "to bring Brook Farm before the public, as a location offering at least as great advantages for a thorough experiment [in Associationism] as can be found in the vicinity of Boston." The public everywhere was clamoring for Association. If a practical experiment were to be undertaken, it should be at the West Roxbury community.

Among the farm's advantages were its location, just "three miles from the depot of the Dedham Branch Railroad, and about eight miles from Boston"; its natural beauty—"the whole landscape is so rich and various as to attract the notice even of casual visitors"; its two hundred acres of land, "of as good quality as any land in the neighborhood of Boston"; and the value of its property, "now . . . worth nearly or quite thirty thousand dollars."[19] These were important reasons "why Brook Farm should be chosen as the scene of that practical trial of association which the public feeling calls for in this immediate vicinity." The most important consideration, however, was that Brook Farm had now been in operation for nearly three years, which was more than enough time for the community to experience "all the misfortunes and mistakes incident to an undertaking so new and so little understood." These, Ripley concluded, have "prepared us to assist in the safe conduct of an extensive and complete Association."

When the new constitution was published on January 18, 1844, Brook Farm, for all intents and purposes, became a Fourierist community (even though it didn't formally declare itself a Phalanx until May 1845).[20] Not coincidentally, just three days earlier the "New England

Fourier Society" was formally established, and Ripley elected its first president. As Charles Dana excitedly reminded former Brook Farmer Isaac Hecker a few weeks later, "You will remember our conversation in the back-parlor in your house concerning a change of Brook Farm into a 'Fourier' association.—That change my dear Isaac, has really taken place,—the words 'group, series, phalanx,'—are all in our mouths."[21] Since the conversation to which Dana refers took place in New York City in early November 1843, Ripley and the Brook Farmers, as was noted in the previous chapter, were obviously contemplating the conversion to Fourierism many weeks before delegates attended the "Convention of Friends of Social Reform" in Boston at the end of December 1843. Just as obviously, the decision to draft a new constitution in early January was not as spontaneous or sudden as it might at first appear to have been.

The "change" to which Dana refers in his letter to Hecker, in any case, was much less dramatic than his words make it sound—at least to "civilizees." When Emerson visited Brook Farm at the end of January 1844, for instance, he made no mention of the "conversion" at all. Neither did Bronson and Abba Alcott when they stayed overnight at the community just a week or so after Emerson's visit.

Emerson stopped at the community sometime between the 20th and 26th of January 1844, despite a particularly demanding winter lecture schedule that had him delivering as many as twelve talks that month alone in Concord, in nearby Dorchester and Cambridge, and as far away as Salem and Plymouth, Massachusetts, and Providence, Rhode Island. He wasn't happy with the schedule, either. "I waste much time from graver work in the last two months in reading lectures to Lyceums far & near," he told one correspondent on January 31, "for there is now a 'lyceum' so-called, in almost every town in New England, & if I would accept every invitation I might read a lecture every night." It's therefore surprising that Emerson didn't politely refuse an appeal for a talk from Sophia Ripley, who wrote on January 17, 1844, to tell him, in the newly adopted language of Charles Fourier, that "there is . . . a 'passional attraction' for your written and spoken word, at Brook Farm" because "a large number of our friends" had been prevented that very same day from hearing Emerson speak at the Cambridge Lyceum due to a hard-driving rain storm. She hoped that he would be moved by their disappointment and would "pass a night here in the course of the season, & deliver whatever lecture of yours seems best adapted to the atmosphere of our place."[22]

Though there is no direct mention of it in his journals or correspondence, Emerson came to West Roxbury right away—possibly because he wanted to take the measure himself of Brook Farm's conversion to Fourierism, about which he certainly must have received reports from Henry Thoreau, who had just been there in December, and from George Bradford, who was preparing to leave the community for good in February. No doubt Emerson's upcoming lecture on "New England Reformers" scheduled for March 3 at Amory Hall in Boston was on his mind. According to Linck Johnson, it would be "his firmest reply to the communitarians, who had steadily sought to enlist him in their cause."[23]

Emerson picked one of the coldest weeks of the winter to go to Brook Farm. The average daily temperature for the entire week was less than fourteen degrees. (It dropped to just two degrees daily the following week.) Emerson was apparently warmed by his reception at the community, however, because, according to one Brook Farmer, "he seemed very much gratified" with the evening, and he told those who gathered at the Hive to hear his talk that "it would be very agreeable to him to come often." Emerson himself noted in his journal just a few days after the visit, "'And fools rush in where angels fear to tread.' So say I of Brook Farm. Let it live. Its merit is that it is a new

life—why should we have only two or three ways of life, and not thousands and millions?"[24]

As for the Alcotts, after just six months of communal but not always
very cooperative living on the ninety-acre Wyman Farm in the town of
Harvard, Bronson and Charles Lane's Fruitlands community came to
a sudden end that January of 1844 (for Abba, upon whom had fallen
nearly all the domestic responsibilities, the end probably couldn't
have come soon enough). The Alcotts decided to visit Brook Farm,
the Hopedale Community, and the Northampton Association with
a view toward possibly spending part of the year at each of these
communities. (Lane—upset with the Alcotts over the breakup of
Fruitlands—wrote bitterly to Isaac Hecker on January 16, 1844, and
told him that Bronson's "notion of passing 3 months at Brook Farm, 3
mos. at Northampton, & so on, appears to have died away and been
buried in the same grave of flowery rhetoric where so many other [of
his] notions have been buried.") Abba, in any case, noted in her journal that at Brook Farm "there was more neatness, order, beauty, and
life than in either of the other places [Hopedale and Northampton]."
But she was hardly converted. "I could find no advance on the old
world," she remarked. She thought that "education at Brook Farm is
of a higher and more elaborate kind, but no better than our schools afford," and, she concluded in her journal, "I see but little gained in the
association in labor."[25] There's not a single mention of Fourier, Fourierism, or Associationism.

Emerson may have told the Brook Farmers upon his departure from
West Roxbury that it "would be very agreeable to him to come often,"
but come often he did not. In fact, he never came again at all after his
January 1844 visit. Although from all accounts his evening was a
pleasant one, he would not support a community (or any organization, for that matter, such as the various antislavery and temperance

societies) that had chosen a patron, just as, a year and a half later, he would not, for the same reason, provide a single word for a new Fourierist weekly called *The Harbinger* launched at Brook Farm in June 1845. Several of the early participants in the community were similarly disaffected by Brook Farm's new allegiance, as the warm reception accorded Henry Thoreau in early December and the confrontation lamented by Sophia Ripley in January indicate. The popular George Bradford made arrangements for his departure from the community in late February. He wrote to Emerson on the 27th to report that "I have turned my back this morning on B[rook] F[arm], and it seems a fitting time to end my life there with the old dispensation [that is, before the adoption of Fourierism]. Many of my friends also are leaving or have left." One of them was Georgiana Bruce, who had been in the community for two years but felt now that she also had to leave. She would later say that "it was plain that there could be no congeniality between the newcomers [that is, tradesmen, such as carpenters and shoemakers] and those who had been so united under the first dispensation." Even mild-mannered Amelia Russell afterward would note that "busy as we were, we found time to feel many regrets for the old regime; for if we gained many pleasant additions, we also lost many of those who gave its greatest charm to Brook Farm. One by one they dropped away, the new organization being distasteful to them, and the aesthetic view of life which was their one bright vision having resolved itself into the Dutchman's wooden leg, a compound of clockwork and steam."[26]

Bradford, Bruce, and Russell would have included Burrill and George William Curtis and Isaac Hecker among those of the "first," or earlier, "dispensation." Their departure from the community the previous August had nothing to do, however, with Charles Fourier, although George Curtis told Dwight in early March of 1844 that he thought that Fourier "seems to me to have postponed his life, in finding out how to live."[27] More recently, the engaging Ora Gannett, one of Brook Farm's earliest and most likable residents, and George Ripley's outspoken niece Sarah Stearns defected from the community, evidently because they weren't happy about Brook Farm's future direction. This seems also to have been the reason that James Bryant Hill departed the community around this time. Hill had arrived at Brook Farm back in the spring of 1842 and subsequently became a devoted member of the community, serving throughout 1843 as head of the "Direction of Agriculture" and as "Inspector of Tools." As recently as November 1843 he had been appointed to a committee with Minot Pratt and Louis Ryckman to "make an estimate of the improvements which have been made on the place during the last year," but he may have been one of those who resisted Ripley after the December Convention. There's no record that he ever served on the committee, and he definitely didn't sign the revised constitution in January 1844, which associates were expected to do.[28]

John Brown, the husband of George Ripley's cousin Mary, also left Brook Farm in late October 1843, but his departure seems to have been primarily motivated by a religious "calling" rather than the prospect of Fourierism. Ripley wrote to Brown on November 6, 1843, acknowledging that "we must needs have a hard struggle this winter," and he appealed to his friend by repeating "still more distinctly than I did before, that whatever temporary arrangements you may make . . . it is my fervent wish, that you will not relinquish your hold on the Community as the final home for yourself and your children."[29] But Brown had still not returned by February of 1844, and now it really didn't matter anyway because his wife Mary and her sister Hannah Ripley had decided to leave Brook Farm, neither of them happy about the Association's new allegiance.

About eighteen miles away in the village of Concord, Henry Thoreau was settled once again in his home. Both he and Waldo Emerson were putting finishing touches to their talks, respectively, on "The Conservative and the Reformer" and "New England Reformers" for the lecture series on reform that winter in Amory Hall. What Thoreau and Emerson had to say would not be at all sympathetic to Associationism. Assaults on Charles Fourier and his American proponents, as George Ripley and the Brook Farmers were about to discover, were only just beginning to intensify, and they would soon be heard in the very same place where, just a few weeks before, Brisbane, Godwin, Ripley, and others had met to discuss the virtues of Associationism.[30]

7

The Second Dispensation

If ever there was a time when deliberation and restraint should have been the watchwords at Brook Farm, that time was the period immediately following the publication of the new constitution in January 1844. The Brook Farmers were still living pretty much hand-to-mouth because the school continued to be the community's only source of steady income. That in itself should have made George Ripley and his associates cautious. As they had done several times before, however, the Brook Farmers let their zeal outrun their patience in the reorganization of the West Roxbury Association from an agricultural to an industrial enterprise.

Charles Dana confidently reported to Isaac Hecker in March that "we are moving with as much vigor as prudence will permit in making our final enlargements. We are talking seriously of building a shop 60 feet by 28, for a group of cabinet makers, carpenters, copper smiths, wheelwrights, & Block tin workers." Dana didn't mention that plans were also being discussed for a large three-story unitary dwelling—what Charles Fourier called a "Phalanstery"—which would accommodate all the members of the community and be located about one hundred yards below the Eyrie, right at the center of the Farm. These decisions were made even as the community was struggling to keep its creditors at the door. At an Association meeting on February 29, Brook Farm's leaders were authorized to raise a hefty $3,200 "for the liquidation of all outstanding debts," pledging "that no debt hereafter shall be contracted on behalf of the Association"—a pledge that was somewhat akin to locking the proverbial barn door after the horses had escaped.[1] How then did the Brook Farmers expect to pay for the Workshop and the Phalanstery? They would be financed by the new "industries" that it was expected would soon be established by the dozens of workers who were flocking to West Roxbury in the early months of 1844.

In the six months after the publication of its constitution, eighty-seven applicants were admitted to the community. By July 31, fifty-eight of them had formally been elected members of the Association or were completing the two-month probationary period required by the constitution. Most of the thirty-two men who became associates were skilled or semiskilled workers. (Many of them were also active in the larger social reform community around Boston as members or supporters of the antislavery and nonresistance societies, and as advocates of the movement to abolish the death penalty in Massachusetts.)[2] Among them were seven shoemakers, five carpenters, a cabinetmaker, and two printers. There was also a pewterer, Ephraim Capen, from the nearby town of Dorchester; Porter Holland, a tallow chandler, from Belfast, Maine; and thirty-eight-year-old Peter Baldwin, a baker from Boston. Buckley Hastings, a grocer from Franklin, Massachusetts, became Brook Farm's purveyor of all things large and small. Only two of the applicants during the six-month period identified themselves as farmers, which is really not surprising considering the new emphasis at the Farm on industries. Included among the twenty-six women who became associates at this time were Charles Dana's sister Maria, and John Sullivan Dwight's mother, Mary, and both of his sisters, Mary Ann and Frances (Fanny). Like Maria, Mary Ann, and Fanny, thirteen of the other women who joined the Association in 1844 were unmarried, thereby continuing a pattern that marked the early days of Brook Farm's existence: no other ante-bellum New England community attracted so many single women.[3]

Brook Farm was entirely hospitable to families as well. John Codman (not to be confused with the author of the same name whose narrative *Sailors' Life and Sailors' Yarns* appeared in 1847) and his wife Rebecca arrived at the community in April 1844 with their children Charles, John T., and Sarah Rebecca, just a few days after Dwight's parents and sisters had settled there. There were other pairs of sisters besides Mary Ann and Fanny Dwight—Harriet and Mary Bacon, for instance; groups of brothers—shoemakers Castalio, Charles, and Granville Hosmer; combinations of mothers and daughters—among them, Mary Macdaniel and her daughters Frances and Eunice; and sister/brother pairs—Dolly and John Hosmer and Charles and Maria Dana, to mention just two. Of the 127 associates and probationers whose names are listed on the "Brook Farm Labor Record" for the period May 1844–April 1845, seventy-seven have the same surname as at least one other Brook Farmer.[4]

In April Ripley traveled to New York City with Charles Dana, Louis Ryckman, and a recently elected associate named Christopher List, an attorney, for a three-day "General Convention of the Friends of Association in the United States," which concluded with a birthday celebration for Charles Fourier at the Apollo Saloon on the 7th of that month. It was a good opportunity to raise some of the $3,200 to pay off creditors (among them, still, Nathaniel Hawthorne), and to showcase the community to other "friends of the cause" who had only heard about the West Roxbury Association. The Convention attracted delegates from Massachusetts, Maine, western New York, Pennsylvania, and Virginia. New York City residents Albert Brisbane, Horace Greeley, William Henry Channing, and Parke Godwin attended, as did Osborne Macdaniel, whose two sisters Frances (Fanny) and

Eunice were participants at the Convention. Originally from the Georgetown area of Washington, D.C., Fanny, Eunice, and their mother Mary decided to board at Brook Farm right after the Convention; the sisters were to sign its constitution eight months later on December 29, 1844.[5] Although she didn't yet know it, Eunice's future husband was part of the Brook Farm delegation to the Convention.

The high esteem with which George Ripley was already regarded among American Associationists is obvious from his immediate appointment as president of the Convention. Dana was elected one of the six vice presidents. Ripley added himself, Dana, and Louis Ryckman to the other nine men selected for the Business Committee, whose job it always was at gatherings like these to draft resolutions reflecting the will and sentiments of those assembled. The resolutions on this occasion numbered nine. Most were quite detailed and entirely predictable both in rhetoric and content, except for the sixth resolution, which clearly indicates how anxious Charles Fourier's American proponents were to distance themselves from the more controversial aspects of the Frenchman's social science.

The sixth resolution states that "we desire always to be publically designated [as] THE ASSOCIATIONISTS OF THE UNITED STATES OF AMERICA. We do not call ourselves *Fourierists*." There were two reasons for this, the resolution states. One, because Fourier himself was opposed to identifying what he considered to be the universal and eternal laws of social science with the name of any individual. The second reason, however, refers to a matter that would increasingly hound American Associationists. This had to do with the "conjectural" parts of Fourier's theories, especially his views about sexual relations between men and women. "We do not receive all the parts of his theories," the resolution states, "because Fourier gives them as speculations—because we do not in all respects understand his meaning—and because there are parts which individually we reject."[6]

Ripley had Charles Dana make the pitch to Convention delegates on behalf of Brook Farm. It was a particularly opportune moment to do so because national interest in organizing a "model" Association was steadily mounting. At the reform convention in Boston in December 1843, in which Ripley and the Brook Farmers participated, a resolution was approved stating that "we desire to see a thorough test of the actual working of [Fourier's] principles in an Association, organized upon them as a basis." And more recently, on March 13, at a "Convention of the Friends of Social Reform and Associated Industry" in Batavia, New York, a resolution calling for the establishment of an Association based on Fourier's social principles was unanimously adopted. The very next day, at the "Second Convention of the Friends of Association at Cincinnati," stock books were opened "for an Association, called the Cincinnati Phalanx, to be located . . . on the Free States side of the Ohio River." And on March 20, the Genessee Valley Association met for the purpose of establishing a community near Dansville, New York. Also in March, Solyman Brown, the general agent for the recently formed Leraysville Phalanx in Pennsylvania, sent a letter to Brisbane claiming that "the location at Leraysville, has many advantages rarely attainable by any Association."[7]

Ripley and his supporters must have found these expressions of proposed commitment to the Associative reform program simultaneously encouraging and discouraging. Such widespread interest and enthusiasm in Associationism were reassuring signs that the Brook Farmers themselves were on the right track, but the formation of so many new communities might easily divert support away from the West Roxbury community as the ideal location for a "model" Association. The April 1844 meeting in New York City was thus a good opportunity to make a few comments about the successes that the Brook Farmers had met with so far.

Dana's remarks are particularly interesting to students of Brook Farm today because they provide the only surviving assessment of what its leaders considered to be the community's "achievements" in the three years since it had been established. There were essentially three. "In the first place," Dana said, "we have abolished Domestic Servitude. In the second place, we have secured thorough education for all. And in the third place, we have established justice to the laborer, and ennobled Industry." Dana wanted it to be perfectly clear to those assembled that what he had to say was based on facts.[8] He would not exaggerate; he would not waste time describing hopeful plans or indefinite schemes, such as those being proposed at the numerous gatherings of Associationists around the country. "This is not a dream which we propose [at Brook Farm]," Dana said, "but something which has actually been done." Dana would give those assembled at the General Convention "some simple, plain truths, without any exaggeration—simple facts."

Dana noted that one of the "first impulses" behind Brook Farm's original organization was to change the attitude toward menial labor. "Inasmuch as ye have not done it unto the least of these, ye have not done it unto me," Ripley had characterized the impulse in his resignation letter to the Purchase Street Society back in October 1840. For the past three years, efforts to abolish domestic servitude at Brook Farm were similarly "actuated by religious sentiments." Domestic servitude was "a deadly sin—a thing to be escaped from." Dana was proud to say to those gathered in New York that "we have now for three years lived at Brookfarm, and have carried on all the business of life without [domestic servitude]." All at Brook Farm were the servants of each other. No single person was "master." Every duty in the community—no matter how mean or degrading—was embraced freely and happily by the members. "The man who discharges one of these duties," Dana stated, "he who digs a ditch or discharges any other repulsive duty, is not at the foot of the social scale—he is at the head of it."[9]

The Brook Farmers had also managed to incorporate this same

egalitarian principle in the community's school by making education available to anyone who desired it. At Brook Farm a formal education was not restricted to the wealthy and privileged in society. An "integral education," Dana said, using Charles Fourier's term, was the birthright of every human being—"a right conferred upon him by the very fact of his humanity." The system of education at Brook Farm did justice to everyone; it paid no attention whatsoever to considerations of wealth, gender, or social standing. "Here," too, Dana modestly boasted, "we claim to have made an advance upon civilized society."

He would also brag, Dana continued, about Brook Farm's system of labor—how its rewards were directly proportionate to the amount of work expended by the laborer. In this area as well Brook Farm could "humbly claim that we have gained somewhat upon civilized society." Rarely in society did the laborer ever receive a "just reward." Everywhere "the gain is to the pocket of the employer. He makes the money. The laborer toils for him." At Brook Farm, however, not only was all labor honorable, but the community was organized on a system that enabled it to "distribute the results and advantages which accrue from labor in a joint ratio" to the members of the Association. Dana's last point about labor, he might also have pointed out to Convention delegates, was one important reason why the adoption of Fourierism at Brook Farm was relatively so simple. The "system" of labor at the community was nearly identical—in principle, at least—to the one prescribed by Charles Fourier. (Albert Brisbane had himself pointed out back in the October 5, 1843, number of *The Phalanx* that the Brook Farmers already "accept some of [Fourier's] fundamental practical principles, such as joint stock property . . ., unity of interests, and united domestic arrangements.")

Charles Dana delivered his remarks to those gathered in New York City at the very moment that labor activities at Brook Farm were being reorganized into "Groups" and "Series." At the heart of Fourier's uto-pian program to reorganize existing social arrangements in order to create a system of "attractive industry" was the Frenchman's theory of "passional attraction." Fourier believed that each person possessed twelve active "passions," which Brisbane characterized as "spiritual or moral impulses, springs of action or moving powers" in the human soul.[10] These passions have been variously termed sentiments, in-stincts, and feelings. In addition to the five senses, there were four "af-fective passions" (friendship, love, ambition, and paternity), and three "distributive" passions (the cabalist, or love of intrigue; the butterfly, or love of variety; and the composite, which brings about the union of opposites, such as material and intellectual, and physical and spiri-tual).

Collectively, the tendency of the twelve passions is to what Fourier termed "Unityism," or universal unity, if, that is, the passions were al-lowed free and full development. Then there would be universal har-mony in society. "But in our present societies," Fourier thought, "so far from being developed and satisfied, they [the twelve passions] are suppressed and outraged in every way." The goal therefore was noth-ing less than the complete reorganization of existing social arrange-ments, particularly industrial relations, to "allow and elicit," to quote Brisbane again, "a free and full expansion and development of all the true and noble passions . . . in the Soul, which seek restlessly some means of manifestation and satisfaction."

The best way to give expression to this development, Fourier be-lieved, was to reorganize labor into Groups and Series.[11] Through Groups and Series, attractive rather than repugnant industry would be realized. As Brisbane had pointed out in his recent eighty-page pamphlet on *Association; or, A Concise Exposition of the Practical Part of Fourier's Social Science* (1843), "the *Repugnance* of Industry does not arise from the *Labor* which is connected with industry, but solely from the *manner* in which it is prosecuted, and the *circumstances* attendant upon it." Members of the Association were therefore both encouraged and expected to participate in as many different Groups and Series as their "passional attraction" might draw them to.

At first, the Brook Farmers divided labor into four primary Series: "Agricultural," "Mechanical," "Domestic," and "Educational." In September 1844 a "Second Mechanical Series" was added, and in November 1844 a "Waiters Series" was included in the new organization. Two other Series in the community were known as the "Functional" and the "Miscellaneous." Each Series included several related Groups. In the Agricultural Series, for example, there were Groups for ploughing, for planting, for weeding, for harvesting, for haying, and so forth. The Mechanical Series included the shoemaking industry, as well as the manufacture of Britannia ware and sashes, windows, and blinds. In the Domestic Series there was a "Refectory Group," a "Dormitory Group," a "Consistory Group," and a "Washing, Ironing, and Mending Group," among others. Until the Second Mechanical Series was established in September, women doing "fancy work" were credited for their labor in the Miscellaneous Series. The organization of the Second Mechanical Series was an acknowledgment of the important contribution that women were making to the Association. It really should have been called the "Women's Series" because the top fifteen Brook Farmers who contributed the most labor to it—at least during the year between May 1844–April 1845—were all women. In fact, of the ten hardest-working members in the entire community for this one-year period—in terms of total number of hours worked—nine were women.

These women were Ripley's sister, Marianne (3,057 hours), followed by Mrs. Mary Ann Cheswell (2,866 hours), who, as "Chief" of the Washing Group, devoted 2,113 of her total hours to the Domestic Series; and Louis Ryckman's wife, Jane (2,828), half of whose total hours were spent in the Domestic Series, although she devoted the other half of her time to the Mechanical Series (403 hours), the Miscellaneous Series (294 hours), the Educational Series (193), the Second Mechanical Series (102), and the Waiters Series (35). Like Jane Ryckman, Fanny Dwight (2,823), John Sullivan Dwight's sister, also devoted nearly half of her time to series other than the Domestic, logging 653 hours of her time in the Educational Series, 282 hours in the Second Mechanical Series, 160 hours in the Waiters Series, 156 hours in the Mechanical Series, and 61 hours in the Miscellaneous Series. She was followed by Charles Dana's sister, Maria (2,795), two-thirds of whose time was credited to the Domestic Series; Mrs. Mary Dwight (2,750), John and Fanny's mother, who spent half of her time in the Agricultural, the Mechanical, and the Second Mechanical Series, and the other half in the Domestic Series; and Mrs. Rebecca Codman (2,697), who logged 2,280 of her total hours in the Domestic Series. Mrs. Codman was followed by her daughter Sarah Rebecca (2,682), whose work patterns were virtually identical to those of her mother, except for the 228 hours that she spent in the Waiters Series; and Mrs. Maria Pratt (2,670), nearly all of whose hours were spent in the Domestic Series.[12]

The one man among the ten hardest-working Brook Farmers for the one-year period was Peter Baldwin (2,813), nearly all of whose hours were credited to the Domestic Series because he did the baking for the community. George Ripley (2,502) was the twelfth-hardest-working Brook Farmer for the period May 1844–April 1845; Charles Dana (2,449) ranked fourteenth. Ripley spread his time out in the Educational Series (578 hours), the Functional Series (570), the Agricultural Series (308 hours), and the Miscellaneous Series (1,010), the last of which probably reflects his administrative efforts on behalf of the community. Ripley spent only thirty-four hours in the Domestic Series, just fifteen in the Mechanical Series, and none at all in the Waiters Series.

As for Charles Dana, his "passional attraction" drew him literally to every series. Surprisingly enough, he devoted the most time—591 hours—to the Agricultural Series, but he was also credited with 585 hours in the Miscellaneous Series, 514 hours in the Educational Series, 335 hours in the Functional Series, 241 hours in the Waiters Series, 176 hours in the Domestic Series, just four hours in the Mechanical Series, and only three hours in the Second Mechanical Series. In the sheer variety of his work patterns, Dana epitomizes the real advantage of Charles Fourier's industrial scheme, although it's also obvious from the above numbers that many other Brook Farmers took advantage of the opportunity to engage in a range of work activities.

Certainly that was true for a new probationer named Mary Ann Dwight. It was much too soon to say in April 1844 whether she would have agreed with Charles Dana's claims at the New York Convention about abolishing domestic servitude at Brook Farm, but she could speak with some authority herself on the matter of work in the Association. She had done plenty of it already, even though she had only been at Brook Farm for a few days. Fortunately, Dwight also managed to find time to become Brook Farm's most prolific letter writer; much of what we know today about day-to-day life in the community during the "second dispensation" of its existence—the Fourierist years—is owing to her frequent and chatty letters to her brother, Frank, and to her close friend, Anna Q.T. Parsons.

Dwight had moved to Brook Farm on April 2 with her sister, Fanny, and her mother, Mary, just one day before Ripley's departure with his colleagues for New York City. Her other brother John, of course, had already been a devoted member of the community for the past two-and-a-half years, although he didn't formally become an associate until February of 1844. However, another brother, Frank (Benjamin Franklin Dwight), her correspondent, was not yet willing to leave his position in an architect's firm in Boston for the utopian life. Mary

MARIANNE DWIGHT
Who wrote the letters.

Mary Ann Dwight. Dwight's detailed and gossipy letters provide valuable information about day-to-day life at Brook Farm during the second half of the community's existence.

Ann's father, John, Sr., did spend considerable time at Brook Farm, but his work as a physician prevented him from living there on a regular basis. Whatever time he devoted to the Farm that spring must have been very welcome because there were several serious cases of scarlatina in April and May. Carry Pratt, Minot and Maria's seven-year-old-daughter, and Allie Kay, Philadelphia supporter James Kay's only son, developed "pretty severe cases," and Lucas Corrales, one of the two Spanish-speaking brothers from Manila, "came near dying" in May.[13]

On the day of the Dwights' arrival, Mary Ann, Fanny, and their mother were welcomed at the Hive, where all the "bees," as the Brook Farmers sometimes referred to themselves, were sharing the midday meal. Brother John, Charles Dana, Horace Sumner, Dora Wilder, and the other associates were eager to serve the new residents. In the afternoon Mary Ann and Fanny acquainted themselves with their room at the Pilgrim House, where Marianne Ripley was also now living with a few of her students. Mary Dwight went immediately to the Eyrie to be near George and Sophia Ripley, Louis and Jane Ryckman, and other "older" members of the Association. That evening everyone gathered in the parlor there and listened to flute and piano music. "And oh! What a magnificent evening," Mary Ann wrote right away to Anna Parsons.

The following day, as Ripley, Dana, Ryckman, and List were readying themselves for the Convention in New York, Mary Ann and Fanny unpacked clothing and books, and arranged the bed, bureau, and washstand in the small room that they would be sharing. Before his departure, Ripley found time to tease them a bit, telling them "in a very amusing way" how "pleasant it was to him to see *Christian people* about (alluding to us [Mary Ann and Fanny]) and *proper, grown up,* well *behaved* young women, free from all the vices of the *world,* and *filled with all the virtues of association.*" The very next morning

Dwight began her first day of work in the community, Sophia Ripley having asked her to spend the morning with the Nursery Group, and then to join the Refectory Group in the afternoon.

Mary Ann Dwight's routine as a probationer provides a nice illustration of Brook Farm's determination to incorporate Fourier's program of Groups and Series. On April 14, less than two weeks after settling in the community, she described her schedule to brother Frank:

> my business is as follows (but perhaps liable to frequent change): I wait on the breakfast table (½ hour), help M. A. Ripley clear away breakfast things, etc. (1½ hours), go into the dormitory group till eleven o'clock,—dress for dinner—then over to the Eyrie and sew till dinner time,—half past twelve. Then from half past one or two o'clock until ½ past five, I teach drawing in Pilgrim Hall and sew in the Eyrie. At ½ past five [I] go down to the Hive to help set the tea table, and afterwards I wash tea cups, etc. till about ½ past seven. Thus I make out a long day of it, but alternation of work and pleasant company and chats make it pleasant.

As Dwight's last remark indicates, the days may have been long, but they weren't unpleasant. It's true that she didn't find her first assignment in the nursery particularly satisfying, but by mid-September she was happily reporting to Parsons "that the feeling of maternity has taken full possession of me . . . I have two boys, one eight, the other eleven years old confided to my care." And earlier in the month she joked with Parsons about the three new babies who had recently been born in the community—shoemaker Nathaniel Colson and wife Hannah's son, Charles Fourier Colson; grocer/purveyor Buckley Hastings and wife Cynthia's daughter; and carpenter Flavel Patterson and wife Caroline's baby girl. As these were, after all, Brook Farm babies, they were naturally very intelligent and would, Dwight boasted to her friend, "no doubt soon be able to utter their first words,—which of course we expect will be 'groups and series' and 'association.'"

Dwight did complain to brother Frank just a few days after her arrival at Brook Farm, however, that "we need more leisure, or rather, we should like it." And she worked so hard through her first months in the community that "for one week I have indulged my passional attraction," she told Anna Parsons on August 30, "and painted to my heart's content." Otherwise Dwight's correspondence right through the summer generally speaks enthusiastically about life in the community. As early as the end of April, for instance, she enthused to Parsons, "Oh! It is so pleasant here, even with all the work." Just a few weeks later, in her May 11 letter to Parsons, she noted: "we love Brook Farm more and more,—like its arrangement better and better,—and tho' we find fault (sometimes perhaps unreasonably) are patient with its imperfections and wait for the perfect day." After attending a concert in Boston at the end of the month to hear the celebrated Norwegian violinist "Ole Bull," Dwight decided to stay overnight at the Parsons home for fear that one more person in the Brook Farm wagon heading back to West Roxbury would kill the overworked horse. "I enjoyed my visit to Anna's very much," she told brother Frank on May 29, "yet was truly glad to get home here—and right welcome and cheerful was the first glimpse I caught of the Eyrie, as I was walking from Dedham."

As summer drew to a close a few months later, however, she occasionally became impatient with Fourierism. In her September 5, 1844, letter to her brother, for example, Dwight complained: "Oh! How the men, and women too, do talk '*groups and series*' here. It is as bad as politics." Less than two weeks later she wrote again to Frank, remarking that "there is a sense in which all is not right [at Brook Farm]." She quickly added, however, in this same September 19 letter that "for myself, I would not exchange this life for any I have ever led . . . I enjoy here more than I have ever enjoyed . . . Life is so full and rich here, that I feel as if my experience were valuable, and I were *growing* somewhat faster than when I lived in Boston."

Interestingly enough, some former Brook Farmers stopped in West Roxbury that spring and summer to visit, but their perspective on the community differed quite a bit from that of Mary Ann Dwight. Ora Gannett contacted Isaac Hecker in May 1844, having heard from former Brook Farmer Georgiana Bruce that Hecker had recently spent a day at Brook Farm. Gannett told Hecker that she had considered returning to the community that spring to live, but now after a visit there she had no desire to do so. What was Hecker's reaction to Brook Farm, she wondered? "Does it seem as pleasant as it used to?" she asked. "It does not to me[.] I really felt bad last time I was there to see no familiar faces—I doubt much too if many of the new persons are the right ones for 'Association.'"

George William Curtis had a similar reaction when he visited the community at the end of June 1844. He and his brother Burrill were living now in Concord (where other former Brook Farmers had gravitated, including Hawthorne, George Bradford, and Almira Barlow and her three sons), so Ida Russell invited Curtis and about twenty other of her Brook Farm neighbors to the annual strawberry festival at her home in West Roxbury. Curtis came down a day early and stayed at the Farm. He enjoyed singing at the Eyrie that evening, entertaining the new associates and probationers with his melodious Irish tenor voice. At least that hadn't changed: "The Eyrie parlor was full as it used to be," he wrote to Isaac Hecker on June 27, 1844; "the floor, & doors & windows each had their company." Less pleasing were the renovations to the Hive, two rooms of which (formerly Almira Barlow's and her sons) had been converted the previous autumn to enlarge the dining room. Curtis thought that "that long, narrow room [the dining room] ill compensates for the delightful inconvenience of Entry & small front room" (the latter room the one Hawthorne had occupied). It was, in all, a "sad, sweet day. All sorts of memories haunted me like shadowy forms . . . The place was so familiar & yet so changed. The persons so different, the tone so different."

Curtis told Hecker that he admired the "order" that the conversion to Fourierism had brought about, but, he added nostalgically, "the wild, loitering, busy leisure of old times was far finer to my mind." It turned out to be a very emotional visit for Curtis. But he was not sorry to leave. "Concord was very beautiful to me when I returned & received me as a weary child," he ended his letter to the friend with whom he first became acquainted during their days together before Brook Farm embraced Fourierism.[14]

Had Mary Ann Dwight spoken to either Ora Gannett or George William Curtis during their visits to West Roxbury she would have explained that her own enthusiasm for the community had much to do with a Group that she and several other Brook Farm women had formed. Dwight joined forces with, among others, her mother, Mary; Sophia Ripley; longtime resident Amelia Russell; Caroline Clapp, a seamstress whose brother James was a bricklayer in the community; Catharine M. Sloan, a seamstress and tailor; and a recent arrival, Julia Whitehouse. These were the "new" Brook Farm women who had joined Sophia and Amelia after the conversion to Fourierism, and who effectively replaced the likes of Georgiana Bruce, Abby Morton, Anna Alvord, and Ora Gannett from the earlier period of the community's existence. The women of the second dispensation were less genteel and reform-minded than their predecessors, but they were, like those before them, independent, intelligent, and uncomplaining. Nor were they strangers to hard work, as was noted above in the roster of the ten hardest-working Brook Farmers for the one-year period from May 1844–April 1845, nine of them women.

Together these women quickly established a "Fancy Group" to make caps, cap-tabs, collars, capes, under-sleeves, and other similar articles for sale in Boston. James Kay, an active Philadelphia Associationist who spent the summer of 1844 at the community with his two daughters so they all could be near son and brother Allie, became the group's patron and loaned the women $25 so they could purchase start-up materials. The women arranged to market their articles locally through "Houghton's Shop," and in Boston through "Holmes and Hutchinson's," near King Street. Dwight reported to Anna Parsons on July 7 that "our manufacture is quite workmanlike. I assure you, we realize considerable money (!) from this." Dwight thought this was very important because "women must make money and earn their support independently of man." If women could gain financial equality with men, then "what intellectual developments may we not expect?" She herself earned up to $1 for a painted lampshade, and $1.50 for a painted fan.

On February 27, 1845, Dwight informed Parsons that "I keep very busy, painting six or seven hours a day . . . I have more demands for lampshades and other painted fancy things than I can at present supply. I seem to have got myself into business at present." Two weeks later Dwight complained, again to Parsons, that "I'm so busy at my painting that I scarcely see anyone." She quickly added, however, that "I assure you I feel very happy to have such profitable work to do." Dwight's success with her painting was so profitable to the community, in fact, that the Council of Science, one of the four central administrative committees created right after Brook Farm formally became a Fourierist Phalanx in 1845, invited her at the end of May 1845 "to be present at all their readings, discussions and business meetings."

However, life in the community in the summer of 1844 consisted of a good deal more than deciding which Groups and Series best satisfied one's "passional attraction." The population may have changed between the so-called first and second dispensations—the Transcendental and Fourierist periods of Brook Farm's existence—but the penchant for fun among the community's many mechanics and tradesmen was just as lively as it had been in the period before their arrival. In addition to picnics and rowboat rides on the Charles River, which ran along the western side of the Farm, there were frequent evening walks in the cool Pine Woods that lined the northern side of the community. Many evenings of the week were taken up with piano-playing and singing in the Eyrie's parlor. (There were two pianofortes at the Eyrie, the second having arrived along with the Dwight women.) Much informal socializing also took place at the Eyrie, where associates often browsed through George Ripley's extensive library. A few hundred yards below the Eyrie at the Pilgrim House there were coffee parties and informal get-togethers in the rooms of individual associates. Marianne Ripley, Mary Ann and Fanny Dwight, Amelia Russell, Dora Wilder, and Mary Ann Williams were all living at the Pilgrim House that summer, as were Fred Cabot and Martin Cushing, two attractive young men who had taken over Horace Sumner's small room after his departure from Brook Farm in April.[15] Whenever there was a community dance—as there had been on May Day that year and again after the community's festivities on the Fourth of July—it was usually held at the Pilgrim House.

Mealtimes at the Hive were also regular occasions for merriment and fun, despite the retrenchment programs that associates often had to endure. Rebecca Codman, for instance, remembered years later that mealtimes were a "pleasant social time; all joined in making the time spent at our meals the pleasantest part of the day's intercourse." Likewise, Amelia Russell, who was now one of just a few Brook Farmers who'd been around since the early days of the community's existence, afterward recalled that "our meals were very pleasant, and there was often much conversation mingled with merriment and jokes." The members of the Waiters Series were often the instigators of the foolery. One evening, for instance, a Vermont farmer named John Orvis, who arrived at Brook Farm several weeks after Mary Ann Dwight, fresh from his participation on the Business Committee (with Frederick Douglass and a few others) at the recent meeting of the Massachusetts Anti-Slavery Convention in Boston, picked up a piece of watermelon rind left over from dessert and began an oration "On this Melon Collar occasion" as he placed the rind around the neck of a surprised Frederick Pratt. Orvis's combination prank/pun produced fits of laughter in the dining area of the Hive.[16]

One other activity that particularly interested the Brook Farmers (not to mention many New Englanders generally, including Waldo Emerson) was "reading" a person's character by holding a piece of writing by the "subject" against one's forehead and then "dictating" the received impressions à la a stream-of-consciousness utterance while someone made notes. Mary Ann Dwight's friend Anna Parsons was considered to possess this special "impressibility." So did John Orvis. Even the normally reserved James Kay couldn't resist the opportunity to "read" Fred Cabot's character one evening in August, as did Parsons and Orvis. Charles Newcomb wasn't happy, however, when he learned that Parsons had read his character from a poem of his that Mary Ann Dwight had passed along to her friend, but he was quickly mollified by the beauty of Parsons' description of him, so much so that he sent her notes to his friend Waldo Emerson, which Newcomb then later shared with Margaret Fuller as well.

A few weeks later, Dwight and Rebecca Codman discovered Newcomb by the shed behind the washroom at the rear of the Hive. He was reading stories to a group of boys who were hard at work scrubbing and peeling potatoes for supper that evening. Noticing that Dwight and Codman were spying on him, Newcomb fired a volley of potatoes at the two women to chase them away. He soon returned to the reading, but not without heaving a potato every few minutes in the direction where Dwight and Codman had been standing—his eyes never for a moment leaving the pages of his book. Obviously it was all in good fun, the incident illustrating the mood of spirited playfulness that was often found in the community.

As there had been in the earlier period, plenty of cerebral pleasures were also available to those who found their way to the community during the so-called second dispensation. Whenever friends like Isaac Hecker, William Henry Channing, or Bronson Alcott came to visit, as they all did that summer, there was always lots of lively discussion to be enjoyed.[17] More organized discussions were held at the weekly Fourierist meetings on Sunday evenings. And in September, George Ripley began conducting a Fourier class on Monday and Thursday evenings to study the master's works. "Countless other classes" were formed at this time as well, enough, Dwight told Parsons on September 18, "to make one's brain whirl."

Associates also attended the quarterly meetings of the New England Fourier Society in Boston. The first quarterly meeting of the recently organized society took place on March 28, and Mary Ann Dwight reported that the second quarterly meeting, on June 3, was just "grand." Those Brook Farmers who attended "are in high spirits about it," she told Parsons the next day. Brook Farm's proximity to Boston made it fairly easy to take advantage of the numerous cultural activities there. Ole Bull's first Boston concert at the Melodeon at the end of May has already been mentioned. Many of the Brook Farmers also visited the exhibition of Washington Allston's celebrated last painting, "Belshazzar's Feast," which was displayed that summer at the Corinthian Gallery. And the Boston Athenaeum opened its doors to the public in May, as it had been doing every year, for its annual exhibition of paintings and sculptures.

It wasn't necessary to travel to Boston, however, to enjoy artistic representations. They were available at the community any evening when dramatic tableaux were presented. From the earliest days of the community's organization, dramatic tableaux were one of the most popular forms of entertainment at Brook Farm, and they usually featured full-dress costumes, props, and suitable makeup. In the summer of 1844, for instance, one Saturday evening was devoted to the presentation of six different scenes, including a sequence depicting the four seasons. Charles Dana and his sister Maria represented Summer; George Ripley and Fanny Macdaniel depicted Autumn; Minot Pratt and Mary Ann Dwight, Winter; and Abby Foord and Popelston Booth, Spring. Another dramatic tableau featured "Childhood," and it involved several of the community's boarding students, among them Anna Page and Anna Foord, Theodore Parker's ward George Colburn, Allie Kay, and Mary Ann Dwight's friend, Anna Parsons. With so many attractive participants, this scene turned out to be one of the most successful of the evening, although Fanny Dwight was most impressed with George Ripley, who "looked beautiful" in the Autumn tableau. Ripley's partner, Fanny Macdaniel, wore a thin black dress embroidered with golden ears of wheat, the costume complementing her rich black hair. Because she was quite tall, she made an impressive figure standing next to Ripley, who held a large sheaf of wheat in his hands.[18]

Of all the activities in which the Brook Farmers engaged that summer, however, the one that associates likely remembered the most, though probably not happily, was the community meeting. There were thirty-seven of them altogether in the five months between May and September. These meetings were held for a variety of purposes. There were meetings to elect delegates for a conference at the Hopedale Community in May (George Ripley and Ephraim Capen represented Brook Farm), as well as for another gathering at the Northampton Association in July (Louis Ryckman attended). There were meetings to discuss the financial report for the six months since the beginning of the new fiscal year on November 1, 1843. There were meetings to appoint committees—one committee to consider a more "regular organization" of the Groups and Series, another to discuss improvements in the washing and ironing departments, and another "to make arrangements relative to the work of the boys"—to name just a few.[19] There were meetings to consider what was to be done about all the visitors—"civilizees," as the Brook Farmers referred to "outsiders"—who kept showing up in large numbers on the doorstep of the Hive. And there were meetings to decide on plans for the construction of a Phalanstery, which involved selecting a site, choosing a foreman to oversee the construction (a "civilizee," Benjamin Rogers, was settled on), and appointing a building committee with whom the superintendent would confer during construction. Most of all, however, the meetings of the "Brook Farm Association of Industry and Education" were devoted that summer to applications from prospective probationers, or from current probationers who, having completed the necessary two-month trial period, now wished to become members of the Association.

The minutes of the community's meetings show that in the five months between May 1 and September 30, 1844, for example, the Association received more than one hundred such applications. Twenty-five were "indefinitely postponed," which was a convenient euphemism for rejecting an application outright. These numbers indicate that not only was there lively interest in the community in the months following the adoption of Fourierism, but that the Brook Farmers (every associate participated in the review process) were trying to be selective about who was admitted to the Association (as the roughly 25 percent rejection rate suggests). Reasons for "indefinitely postponing" an application were almost never cited. Neither were they given for those applicants invited to Brook Farm as probationers. It's easier to speculate about this latter group, however, because many of them eventually became members of the community and subsequently listed their previous occupation when they signed the new constitution. The men invariably were skilled or semiskilled workers who, it was expected, would contribute to one of the community's new industrial enterprises.

During the second dispensation, associates bumped heads a lot more often than they ever had during the "Transcendental" period, which was probably to be expected since the people living in the community now came from more diverse backgrounds.[20] One perplexing disagreement—for the circumstances behind each man's actions are not entirely certain—occurred in April, for example, between Christopher List, an attorney, and Fred Cabot, a clerk. A week and a half after he returned from the Convention in New York City, List noticed one evening that someone had tacked a notice on the dining-room wall in the Hive announcing an upcoming meeting of Associationists at Theodore Parker's church in West Roxbury. List confronted Cabot, who had come to Brook Farm in the early months of 1844 and was known for his participation in various reform activities, and asked whether he had put the notice on the wall. Cabot said that he had not (although he may in fact have done so). List subsequently removed the notice from the wall, which prompted Cabot to pin it back up again (the pins being happily supplied by Sophia Ripley, Mary Ann Dwight, and a few others who witnessed the incident while they were washing dishes after the evening meal). Cabot later confronted List, telling him that he would raise the matter with the Association if List removed the notice again, which List, obviously undaunted, proceeded immediately to do.

Why List was so disgruntled isn't known. It's possible that he didn't find it congenial living in the community with so many mechanics and tradesmen, which may explain why he departed Brook Farm for good in December 1844, although his interest and involvement in the Associative movement continued for some time afterward. List was involved in another incident in September 1844. He and Jeremiah Reynolds, an unmarried carpenter who had become a member of the Association the previous April, were "expelled" by the Group with whom they had been working on the Phalanstery. There is no reference to this incident in the community minutes, but Mary Ann Dwight noted it in a September 19, 1844, letter to her brother Frank. She didn't say what the cause of the problem was, but she does note that List and Reynolds immediately appealed to the General Direction for new work. Dwight, at least, found it appropriately ironic that the men were sent back to work on a portion of the Phalanstery foundation that was smack in the midst of the very Group from which they had originally been expelled. Ironic, too, was George Ripley's remark to an unnamed correspondent just a few days before (of which Dwight wouldn't have been aware), who inquired about Brook Farm's experience with practical Association: "Our experience has been thus far," he wrote, "cheering in the highest degree."[21]

There were yet more misunderstandings to come. One of them again had to do with the new Phalanstery. Judging from the fact that its construction was discussed at four separate meetings between June 4 and July 26, 1844, evidently not everyone agreed that a new three-story, $175' \times 40'$ building was necessary at that time. The minutes of these meetings are characteristically formal and businesslike and don't provide any specific information. By contrast, there were no disagreements about the decision on March 23, 1844, to construct a $60' \times 28'$ Workshop behind the Hive.

With respect to the Phalanstery, most if not all associates would have agreed that more living space was needed at the farm for families and for married couples. Mary Ann Dwight notes in her September

18, 1844, letter to Anna Parsons that "there is some excitement here just now . . . about the people who want to be married and have 'spoken for rooms' large enough for two, and [who] are mad and vexed, because in our present crowded state, they can't have them." The problem affected new applicants as well. At a community meeting just a few weeks later on October 6, it was "voted that Thomas Treadwell [a printer] and Wife be received as Applicants, with the Condition that they be not received into the Association until Spring [1845]." (Thomas and Elizabeth Treadwell and their two sons patiently waited and were eventually admitted.) So the disagreement over the Phalanstery probably wasn't about the need for more space. Much more likely it had to do with financial considerations, since it's reasonable to expect that some members of the Association would have questioned how a community that had already accrued substantial indebtedness could undertake such an ambitious building project. Ripley and his supporters had their way in the end because the Phalanstery cellar was dug in July 1844.

Aside from the conflicts at Brook Farm, there were also troubling signs in 1844 that the national movement to promote Fourierism and Associationism was already beginning to founder. The Sylvania Association in Greeley, Pennsylvania—about which there had been so much fanfare when its books were opened for stock subscriptions in 1843—halted operations in August 1844 because of "its inability," according to one report, "to contend successfully against an ungrateful soil and ungenial climate." Just a few months earlier, William Henry Channing announced in April—"Notwithstanding the urgent request of friends"–that he would immediately halt publication of *The Present* because of the "near and sacred duty" of preparing a memoir of his uncle, William Ellery Channing, the recently deceased and widely admired Unitarian divine who had exerted such important influence on

George Ripley. And the temporary editors of *The Phalanx,* Albert Brisbane's New York-based monthly that had begun to be published as a bimonthly in the spring of 1844 with the expectation that it would soon be a weekly, were forced to announce in September that the paper would become a monthly again because of dwindling financial support.

As for Brisbane himself, he departed for France in April 1844, having embarked on a special mission right after the "General Convention of the Friends of Association" finished its business in New York City. He intended to copy more of Fourier's manuscripts and establish new relations with leading French Associationists in Paris. He expected to return to the United States in the autumn, but he quickly realized soon after his arrival that he had greatly underestimated the time necessary to complete the mission. He informed his American supporters by letter from Paris in July that he might have to remain abroad for as long as a year. Evidently it never occurred to Brisbane that his extended absence would produce a serious void in the national campaign on behalf of Fourierism now that the American Associationist movement was without its most active and vocal leader.[22]

The always feisty Orestes Brownson wasted no time taking advantage of Brisbane's absence—not that he wouldn't have relished a head-to-head confrontation with the New Yorker. He pounced on the Fourierists right away with a series of three articles in the April, July, and October 1844 numbers of his journal, *Brownson's Quarterly Review,* which "demonstrate conclusively," he claimed, "that Fourierism is repugnant to Christianity." Even his old friends at Brook Farm didn't escape his condemnation, though at least he didn't express it publically in the pages of his journal. He went to the community on September 22 to preach a discourse on the virtues of Catholicism, the religion to which he had himself just converted, and, while he was pleased that as a result of his talk "two or three [Brook Farmers] will become Catholics," he told his protegee Isaac Hecker two days after the visit that "the atmosphere of the place [Brook Farm] is horrible." As for his old friend George Ripley, Brownson added, he "is worse than an infidel," a characterization that Ripley would surely have found both amusing and ironic had he ever heard it, coming from a man who had himself been similarly tarred just a few years before by reactionary Unitarians like Andrews Norton and other conservative members of the Unitarian establishment.[23]

Brownson's articles, in any case, hit their mark, and Ripley, Dana, and other Fourierist supporters knew that more time would have to be devoted in the coming months to addressing the charge of "infidelity."[24] That autumn, however, Ripley and Dana were focusing their attention on a forthcoming meeting of Associationists in Rochester, New York, in early October, as well as the first organized convention ever of New England workingmen scheduled a few weeks later in Boston. Dana would carry Brook Farm's banner to Rochester and promote the community to Associationists there. There were high hopes as well for the workingmen's convention in Boston, in which Ripley, shoemaker Louis Ryckman, and a few other Brook Farmers intended to participate. As Dana prematurely and foolishly boasted to Parke Godwin at the end of October ("though this expectation is not *to be spoken of*"), "I think we can hardly fail to have it [the workingmen's movement] in our hands."[25]

8

From Association to Phalanx

In the very same month that the Brook Farmers confidently reported to the public that "our capital has been enlarged by the subscription of about ten thousand dollars," Charles Dana had to ask fellow Associationist Parke Godwin for a twenty-dollar loan so he could attend a Fourierist convention in Rochester, New York. As it had done so often before, the "Brook Farm Association of Industry and Education" showed two very different faces during the autumn months of 1844—one to the public and another to those living in or nearby the West Roxbury community.

To the public, the "Notice to the Second Edition" of the community's constitution, published that October, confidently proclaimed that "the situation of the [Brook Farm] Association is highly encouraging." Many new skilled workers had joined the Association's ranks, and Brook Farm's organization had "acquired a more systematic form" since the new constitution was originally printed in January 1844. Two new buildings were among several improvements at the Farm. A 60' × 28' workshop was being used by "mechanics of several trades" (the building had already needed to be "underpinned"), and a wing of the 175' × 40' Phalanstery, located just below the Eyrie, was nearly finished. Just a few weeks after these encouraging words were published, however, Dana had to write again privately to Parke Godwin on October 30 with an even more urgent appeal: "We are in want of ready money & three or five hundred dollars would do us more good than twice as much at some other periods," he said. "Unless we get it we shall suffer sadly."[1] There's no record that the Brook Farmers were ever given the "three or five hundred dollars," and they certainly never received the $10,000. Dana did, however, receive the twenty-dollar loan for the convention.

It's good that he did, too, because Dana wound up on a business committee that, without his presence, could easily have set plans in motion for the organization of a national union of Associations, with many of the leaders of the "western" New York Associations installed in positions of authority. Except for Dana and Parke Godwin, the other delegates at the Rochester convention in October were all from western New York communities, including the Sodus Bay Phalanx; the Jefferson Industrial Union (Cold Creek); the Port Richmond Association; the Bloomfield Association (Honeoye Creek); and the Ontario Union (Littleville). Albert Brisbane's extended stay in France had left the Associationist movement at home without a center of influence; in his absence, Godwin was assuming more of a leadership role in the movement. He was one of the three other men on the committee who decided "not to form such a union [of Associations]" because "the present state of the Associative movement in the United States and the condition of the several Phalanxes that have already been formed do not seem to demand an intimate confederacy between them."[2] Neither Dana nor Godwin would likely have ever favored a national organization without a strong infusion of Associationists from the Northeast. It is fair to say that the New Englander and the New Yorker sandbagged the Rochester convention, although neither probably did so consciously or in collusion, and most likely did so for very different reasons.

Dana and the Brook Farmers were quite aware that their hope of having the West Roxbury community designated the "Model Pha-

lanx" nationally would require the influence and financial backing of
New York City-based Fourierists. But securing that support was not
turning out to be so easy. Godwin, for his part, though he respected
the abilities of men like Dana and George Ripley—and John Dwight
and Louis Ryckman too—was an armchair communitarian who harbored a profound antipathy for New Englanders generally. Moreover,
he had no personal interest in or commitment to Brook Farm at all.
Godwin may have said to Dana in May 1844 that "there is no establishment in this country, to which I look with so much faith as that in
which you are engaged," but Brook Farm's importance to the New
Yorker was its potential usefulness in advancing the Associative cause.
What really appealed to the son-in-law of William Cullen Bryant was
the intellectual stimulation provided by certain aspects of Fourier's
utopian social thought, especially, at this time, the Frenchman's ideas
about the "Law of the Series." The challenge of understanding the
"Law of the Series" wasn't likely to be advanced very much, Godwin
would have thought, by colleagues living on the western fringes of
New York State. As for Brook Farm (or even the nearby North American Phalanx in New Jersey), he would admire it from afar. He would
certainly never live there.[3] (Godwin would even beg off attending an
informal but important strategy meeting at Brook Farm in January
1845, pleading a recent injury.)

The Brook Farmers and New York Fourierists stood on more common ground with respect to efforts to capture the support of New
England's workingmen. For their part, the New York Fourierists were
anxious to extend their influence into New England. Brook Farm was
the only Fourierist Association east of the Hudson River (as it always
remained). But the Brook Farmers, too, wanted to see the spread of
Associationism into the growing and increasingly more vocal ranks of
New England's workingmen, mainly because men like Ripley, Dana,
and Louis Ryckman believed in and were sincerely committed to

Charles Fourier's plans for industrial reform—an issue all the more of interest now that the Brook Farm community was filled with so many mechanics, carpenters, and other skilled and semiskilled workers.

So it's not surprising that the Brook Farmers were early participants in the rapidly developing workingmen's movement. As Charles Dana pointed out to Parke Godwin at the end of October 1844, "Let the [laborers] be awakened to a knowledge of their real rights and a demand for them and the work will be very near its accomplishment." That, Dana said, "will be a new day in history," one that he thought would "astonish demagogues of all parties,—when the *Right to labor* becomes the rallying cry of the masses and legislators are compelled to take a step into new regions." Dana and Ripley and other Brook Farmers like Ryckman believed that New England was ready for such a day. "I think," Dana told Godwin, "we shall see it."[4]

It was the Fall River (Massachusetts) mechanics who first issued a "call" in June 1844 for a convention to bring together workingmen throughout New England to address their mutual grievances and goals. Principally, there were two: a ten-hour working day (rather than the standard twelve- to fourteen-hour day) and a national workers union. Throughout the summer pro-workingmen's newspapers such as the Fall River *Mechanic,* the Lynn (Massachusetts) *Awl,* the Boston *Investigator,* and the New York *Workingmen's Advocate* urged workingmen forward as they gathered in local Massachusetts communities like Newton, Upper Falls, South Weymouth, Taunton, Woburn, and Worcester to form labor associations. At Brook Farm, associates devoted an entire Sunday evening meeting on September 22 to a discussion of possible remedies "to be offered to the Working Men for the existing evils of Society."[5]

By all accounts, the workingmen's convention in Boston on October 16 and 17 was a great success. It was attended by more than 200 delegates from recently formed labor associations throughout New

England, including Massachusetts, New Hampshire, Rhode Island, and Connecticut. Large delegations arrived from Fall River, Lynn, and Lowell, which were particularly conspicuous because they marched into historic Faneuil Hall in procession waving large banners with slogans such as "We Know and Claim Our Rights" and "Union is Strength" stitched on them in gold letters—thanks to the handy-work of the workingmen's mothers, wives, and sisters. The meeting also attracted numerous other interested persons, including several editors of newspapers and journals sympathetic to the workingmen's cause, and John Collins, the founder of the Skaneateles Community in New York. Brook Farm was represented by as many as a dozen of its associates.

It was George Ripley, though, who attracted some of the most prominent attention among those in attendance. On the first day of the convention, both Ripley and Louis Ryckman participated in a lively discussion about the need for a ten-hour workday—something that had been the standard at Brook Farm virtually since the community's original organization in April 1841. When the issue was brought to the delegates in the form of a resolution at the end of the second day, it was approved by a margin of 75 to 22.[6] The two-day convention also featured several rousing speeches supporting the cause of workingmen. Only Ripley and one other speaker, however, were specifically singled out for praise by the *Workingman's Advocate* for their "eloquent" remarks. The Boston *Investigator* also devoted a full paragraph to Ripley, noting that he was "a delegate from the Brook Farm Association, who was formerly a clergyman, but who is now a practical working man [and who] made a most eloquent speech, and as radical as it was eloquent. His remarks produced a deep impression, and from the great applause with which they were received, we have no doubt . . . that what the pulpit lost when Mr. Ripley left it, humanity has gained." Ripley was also singled out by the *New England Opera-*

tive among those the paper considered "the most able speakers" at the convention.

In addition to Ripley, the paper also applauded Brook Farmers Christopher List and Louis Ryckman, along with popular labor organizer Mike Walsh, the colorful and controversial leader of a group of New York reformers known as the "Spartan Band." Walsh visited Brook Farm right after the convention ended. He was "highly pleased" with the people that he met there (he characterized them as "pious professors and Infidels, Fourierists, Abolitionists, Non-Resistants, etc., etc.") because the Brook Farm associates confirmed for the Irish labor leader the "full perfectability of Man when freed from the contaminating influences of a corrupt and spurious state of society."[7]

In an effort to sustain the momentum generated by the convention, Ripley immediately accepted invitations to speak at a number of mechanics' associations, where he lectured on various aspects of the labor issue. Dana reported to Parke Godwin at the end of October 1844 that Ripley was "received with the greatest satisfaction" at these gatherings, and Brook Farm's leader planned to speak at more such meetings in November. "I think we can hardly fail to have it [the workingmen's movement] in our hands," Dana confided to Godwin. "We are in fact the only men who can really point out their course for them & they can hardly help looking to us for their advisors." Godwin heartily agreed. "The working classes are ready for us—and absolutely ask for instruction and guidance," he wrote back to Dana on November 8.[8]

Ripley's influence with the New England workingmen forced prominent Associationists that autumn to look ever more seriously at Brook Farm as the operational center for propagandizing the national cause. Not only was the West Roxbury Association the only avowedly Fourierist community in New England, but Ripley's impact on workingmen in that region made Brook Farm all the more important in the estimation of influential Associationists like Horace Greeley, Osborne

Macdaniel, and Philadelphia supporter James Kay, whose son, Allie, continued his long-term residency at Brook Farm as a student in the community's school. Also of growing importance to many of these Associationists was the fact that Brook Farm's leaders—particularly Ripley, Dana, and John Dwight—were among the most literate and cultured men in the country, something that could not be said, it was becoming increasingly more evident, about the leaders of other Fourierist communities around the country.[9]

This factor was especially significant to New York City Associationists because they hoped to launch a new paper or journal to propagandize for Associationism and Fourierism. Godwin and Macdaniel had been sharing editorial duties managing *The Phalanx* since Albert Brisbane's departure to Europe in April 1844, but *The Phalanx* was now on the verge of collapse. Its subscription lists continued to dwindle during the summer, forcing Godwin and Macdaniel to issue it as a monthly again in September (it had appeared bimonthly between April 20 and September 7). No number was published at all in November 1844, and Godwin acknowledged to Dana in his November 8 letter that the paper was "sickly" and that it "may be compelled to stop." Godwin therefore proposed a change in the paper's format. It might even be better, he thought, to start a new paper under some such title as "Young America." He wondered, in any case, whether Dana and Ripley could be relied on for regular contributions.

Ripley was immediately enthusiastic about the possibility of publishing a new paper at Brook Farm. Dana wrote back to Godwin on November 20, 1844, telling the New Yorker that "your plan strikes both Mr. Ripley & myself very favorably." Godwin might rely on the Brook Farmers, Dana said, for "notices of important events in Boston, & New England generally." Dwight might be able to provide reviews of musical performances, Ripley could handle notices of reform movements, and Dana himself might "try [his] hand at the literary &

philosophical apparitions which the teeming matrix of this region will certainly produce." These, however, were just "hypothetical" possibilities, Dana cautioned Godwin: "we cannot be bound" to anything specific because "we are so much occupied with business of various kinds that we cannot easily make any positive promises." What did Godwin think of the possibility of altogether transferring *The Phalanx* "to our hands," Dana inquired? John Allen, a former Universalist minister and prominent Boston reform activist, was anxious to transfer his own paper, *The Social Reformer,* to Brook Farm. "Should this be done," Dana advised Godwin, "& should the stoppage of the Phalanx become necessary, it would obviously be better to mask its failure under a similar transfer."[10]

For their part, the Brook Farmers found the prospect of transferring *The Phalanx* and *The Social Reformer* to the community very appealing for at least three reasons. One is that Brook Farm was home to four printers—Minot Pratt, Jonathan Butterfield, George Houghton, and Thomas Blake—so there was already a skilled and underutilized "Printers Group" at the Farm. Another is that the publication of the "official" organ of Associationism and Fourierism in the United States would demonstrably affirm Brook Farm's central importance in the national reform movement, which, in turn, might attract more outside financial support for the community until the Farm's new industries began to generate a steady flow of income. Mary Ann Dwight encouragingly noted in a letter to Anna Parsons on December 14, 1844, that the "Friends of Association in New York and else where are beginning to see the need of concentrating their efforts in some one undertaking, and it is to Brook Farm that they look."[11] A third reason why the transfer would be welcome is that the publication of *The Phalanx* and *The Social Reformer* at Brook Farm under a single new title might provide a much-needed source of permanent regular income for the financially troubled community, which still could not depend on the meager income from the manufacture of Britannia ware, shoes, fancy goods, and sashes and blinds that had only recently been established in the Association.

While Ripley, Dana, and Ryckman were off at mechanics' conventions devoting their attention to matters outside the community in the autumn of 1844, troubles were fomenting right at home. The usually quiet and devoted John Dwight, for example, could not refrain from making "some dismal and discouraging remarks about the state of feeling here [at Brook Farm]" that October, which may have been exactly what Orestes Brownson had sensed when he noted after his visit to Brook Farm just a few days before Dwight's "discouraging remarks" that "the atmosphere of the place [Brook Farm] is horrible." It was also obvious to Margaret Fuller, who stopped in West Roxbury in mid-October and noted that not all was well in the community. "The wheels seemed to turn easily," she reported to former Brook Farmer Georgiana Bruce on October 20, "but there was a good deal of sound to the machinery."[12]

Shortly after Fuller's visit, the Brook Farmers adopted a vigorous retrenchment plan after a committee consisting of Buckley Hastings, a grocer and purveyor, Marianne Ripley, Mrs. Rebecca Codman, Mrs. Julia Whitehouse, and Ephraim Capen recommended that such regular staples as meat, tea, coffee, and butter be discontinued at table. This arrangement proved almost immediately unsatisfactory to Brook Farm's boarders and students, however, and it was agreed on December 8, 1844, that a separate table "furnished with meat" be made available to these residents, as well as to "such members of the Association as shall receive permission by a vote to sit at it." Several associates wasted no time requesting permission. The very same evening that it was agreed to provide a separate meat table, Mary Hosmer, Cynthia Hastings, William and Mary Ann Cheswell, Job Tirrell, and

Augustina Kleinstrup all requested and received permission to sit at the separate table. Louis Ryckman's wife Jane was given permission to drink tea, and Mary Dwight "to use tea and butter."

The resolve of several other associates wasn't much firmer. Just one week later—at the very next scheduled meeting of the Association—Sophia Ripley, Peter Kleinstrup, Amelia Russell, Jeremiah Reynolds, and James Clapp requested and received special permission to sit at the meat table. Not surprisingly, the rapid defection of so many associates from the original retrenchment plan upset other Brook Farmers, and so on December 22 it was "voted that those members of the Association who sit at the meat table shall be charged extra for their board, the amount of which charges shall be deducted from their annual dividend." A number of other associates were happy to pay the additional charges, especially since they weren't required immediately to do so.[13]

Mary Ann Dwight, at least, wasn't as upset as some of her fellow Brook Farmers because there happened to be "a *few associates* who feel that their *health* requires (!) the use of meat, tea, etc." In a letter to Anna Parsons on December 14, Dwight noted that "this 'retrenchment' has afforded us no little amusement," but, ever the optimist, she thought nonetheless that "much good will come out of it," though she didn't say just what she thought that would be. Besides, there were plenty of good things to eat at the retrenchment table, Dwight noted, including potatoes, turnips, squashes, puddings, and, of course, lots of freshly baked ginger and Boston brown bread. "At our breakfast table," Dwight told Parsons, "I counted nine different articles this morning," one of which must surely have been "brewis," the simple combination of Boston brown bread and milk that the Brook Farmers found so tasty and that is recalled more than any other food item in various reminiscences of the community.

Nor was Dwight upset with the behavior of Brook Farm's perennial boarder Charles Newcomb, who was taking his meals at the retrenchment table but "is excepted from the general rule and allowed to have tea and butter brought to him."[14] Evidently Newcomb's tenure in the community since its earliest days (he began his residence at the farm in 1841 and didn't make his final departure until December 1845) conferred on him a special status that wasn't questioned by the "new" associates, nearly all of whom had joined the community after the conversion to Fourierism in January 1844.

The retrenchment program at the Farm, nevertheless, was really just another sign of more profound troubles in the community at that time. Despite Ripley, Dana, and Ryckman's initial successes in October and November 1844 with New England's workingmen, John Dwight's "dismal and discouraging remarks about the state of feeling" at the Farm continued to characterize the mood at Brook Farm right through the autumn months. There was a growing sense among some of the associates that the community's priorities were skewed, that Brook Farm was being mismanaged both financially and administratively. Although he was surely aware of the undercurrents swirling about the Farm, Charles Dana understandably made no reference at all to any difficulties in his letters to Parke Godwin that autumn. Surprisingly enough, it's the invariably reserved and formal minutes of the community's regular meetings that reveal the disquieting mood at Brook Farm.

The minutes for November 24, 1844, for instance, note that a committee was appointed to confer with Laura Hosmer—who had just become an applicant at the end of July—"respecting her [evidently subversive] views on Association." At the very same meeting, another committee was chosen to confer with cabinetmaker Robert Westacott "and to investigate certain charges alleged against him," having to do, it seems, with missing tools. A few weeks later Charles Dana presented the annual financial report for the fiscal year ending October 31, 1844. The report, however, was not accepted by the associates. Instead, it was "voted that a Committee of five be appointed for the examination of the Financial Report," an action that was unprecedented in the community.[15]

The most telling entry in the minutes, however, appears on January 12, 1845, just one week after the meeting to elect officers for the new year. At the earlier meeting George Ripley was chosen once again to head the General Direction, and Charles Dana and Louis Ryckman were elected to serve with him on this most important of the community's three administrative committees. Dana was elected chairman of both of the other committees—the Direction of Finance and the Direction of Education—effectively concentrating all administrative power at Brook Farm in the hands of the two men. (Sophia Ripley and John Dwight were elected to serve with Dana on the Direction of Education; John Sawyer, a broker who had just achieved associate status only two weeks before the elections and thus had no real clout in the community, and Jonathan Butterfield, secretary of the New England Fourier Society, would work alongside Dana on the Direction of Finance.) Conspicuously missing among Brook Farm's officers in 1845 was Minot Pratt, an original shareholder and an officer of the community from its very beginning in 1841, whose absence to inquire about living arrangements in Concord was yet another reminder of the "troubled state of feeling" at Brook Farm.[16] That the elections were not widely supported by all the members of the Association is indicated by the decision at this Sunday evening meeting on January 12 to have the General Direction, along with two other associates, serve as a committee "to confer with certain members of the Association, who have expressed dissatisfaction with the management and officers of the Institution [Brook Farm]."

Mary Ann Dwight quickly dismissed these disgruntled associates as "discordant spirits" who numbered only "about five or six individuals." Evidently, neither Ripley nor Dana took them any more seriously, although Minot Pratt's extended absence from the community since December should have reminded Brook Farm's leaders that the "dissatisfaction with the management and officers of the Institution" was possibly more profound than it might at first have appeared. But in January 1845 Ripley and Dana still had their eyes focused beyond the community's snow-covered meadows and pastures. Many of New England's workingmen seemed on the verge of embracing Associationism; efforts to capture this movement needed to be concentrated and continued. The prospect of the transfer of Albert Brisbane's *The Phalanx* and John Allen's *The Social Reformer* to the community was also greatly anticipated. A new paper under Brook Farm's banner would further establish the community's importance in the national reform movement. Of more immediate moment, however, was the annual meeting of the New England Fourier Society, which was scheduled to begin on January 15 in Boston—just three days after the meeting at the Farm at which the community's "discordant spirits" were making themselves heard. Ripley, Dana, and Ryckman intended to take advantage of the local gathering in Boston. Although they would be preaching to the converted, they would repeat more emphatically what had been stated in October in the "Notice to the Second Edition" of the Farm's constitution: that Brook Farm was a harmonious and prosperous community, and "that the situation of the Association is highly encouraging."

The January 1845 meeting of the New England Fourier Society marked the beginning of a six-month period that was, in some respects, one of the most promising in Brook Farm's entire history. For George Ripley personally it may have been, with one important exception, the most satisfying. It began with a large gathering of the faithful in January, increasing presence in the workingmen's movement in March, a new constitution and the Association's incorporation as a Fourierist Phalanx in May, and the publication at the Farm of the first number of a new Associationist paper called *The Harbinger* in June. And despite the internal grumblings in the Association in the previous autumn and early winter, there was even a renewed sense of confidence about the future because of the ongoing progress on the Phalanstery, and the installation of a new steam engine in the Workshop to support the community's mechanical enterprises. The industrial age was about to assert itself at Brook Farm.

The Fourier Society meeting in Boston, marking the occasion of the first anniversary of its formation, attracted a mixed group of participants, among them the thoroughly committed, those less zealous but still sympathetic to the cause, and the "merely curious." Local Bostonians attended as did residents from such nearby towns as Lynn, Northhampton, Dighton, and Watertown. The ranks of the "merely curious," according to *The Phalanx*, were thinner than at the Social Reform Convention in Boston the previous December 1843, but the "character of the audience" this time was "higher—the assemblage consisting of earnest and intelligent converts to the faith." Among them were many Brook Farmers, who attended the meeting "in full force."[17] George Ripley and Charles Dana and their sisters, Marianne and Maria, were there, as were Amelia Russell, John Dwight, Louis Ryckman, John Orvis, and Eunice Macdaniel. Many of Brook Farm's new corps of workers also attended the meeting. Dressmakers Elmira Daniels and Maria Clapp came, as did shoemaker Granville Hosmer, carpenters Robert Westacott and William Davis (the former evidently vindicated of the earlier charges against him), and printer Thomas Blake.

Anna Q. T. Parsons, Mary Ann Dwight's friend and correspondent, was there too. ("It was the most harmonious Convention," Parsons reported right away, "the most beautiful spirit breathed around—it was the purest moral atmosphere I ever breathed.")[18] Certainly the person who traveled the farthest, however, was the itinerant Albert Brisbane, who, after spending eight months tramping around France gathering and transcribing copies of Charles Fourier's voluminous manuscripts and meeting with French Associationist leaders, finally had returned to the United States on December 21. When he arrived at the port in Boston, America's most prominent Fourierist headed straight to Brook Farm, where he pretty much settled in for the next four months.

Brisbane arrived in West Roxbury the evening before Marianne Williams died, hers being the first and only death at Brook Farm in the six-plus years of the community's existence. Williams was the seamstress and domestic servant whose admission to the community in June 1843, it will be recalled, was due to the persistence of Waldo and Lidian Emerson. She was already quite sickly when she arrived in West Roxbury, but that didn't prevent her from being a productive member of the community, mainly through her domestic and agricultural labors. She was "released from her severe sufferings" on December 22, 1844, the morning after Brisbane's arrival. She was thirty-eight years old. Carpenters William Cheswell and Job Tirell quickly constructed a coffin, and Williams was buried "on a lovely knoll" behind the Pilgrim House (where she had lived with Mary Ann Dwight, Fanny and Eunice Macdaniel, Fred Cabot, John Orvis, and others), amid a "beautiful grove of cypress trees." The day of Williams's funeral was dark and misty, and Amelia Russell, who watched the solemn affair from her room in the Cottage because she was ill, later likened the mourners and Williams's coffin being transported on the shoulders of her fellow Brook Farmers to a "weird procession seen on Scottish hills." Soon after the burial, Peter Kleinstrup, now in charge of Brook Farm's new greenhouse, planted evergreens and flowering shrubs by Williams's gravesite.

Mary Ann Dwight, for one, considered Williams's final days to be testimony of the beautiful humanity of "Association." "Nowhere else," she wrote to Parsons, "could this poor woman, who has no near relatives and no property, have fared so well. Here is one of the pleasantest blessings of Association." A fellow Brook Farmer expressed similar sentiments in an extended notice of Williams's death that was printed in *The Phalanx:* "No rude Undertaker was permitted to hustle her body into the grave—but brethren, who seemed to vie with sisters in gentleness, did the last sad office of giving her coffin to the earth." Half a century later, John T. Codman still remembered the occasion distinctly, though "I could scarcely be called acquainted with [Williams]." In his reminiscence of the community, Codman recalled that "there was no pomp or rivalry of show, no gaudy deckings . . . but all was done decently, lovingly, peacefully and well."[19]

Brisbane spent several days in West Roxbury describing his travels in France to the Brook Farmers before heading down to New York City at the very end of December to organize his affairs. He returned with Osborne Macdaniel and William Henry Channing on January 12, at the very moment that the newly formed committee was being charged to determine why certain members had expressed "dissatisfaction with the management and officers" of the Association. Perhaps it was the presence of the visitors that prompted the committee to confront the community's half dozen or so "discordant spirits" right away and give them an ultimatum before the Fourier Society meeting: "the *few* intriguing, caballing, mean, troublesome, people, have been very plainly dealt with," Mary Ann Dwight happily reported to Anna Parsons, "and told that if they don't go, or come into harmony,— wholly cease their caballing and their slander, they will be expelled!"

Right after their arrival the New Yorkers enjoyed an oyster supper in Amelia Russell's room at the Cottage. Russell had one of the largest rooms in the Cottage, but its walls were pushed to the limit by the three guests from New York, George and Sophia Ripley, Charles and

B R O O K   F A R M

200

Maria Dana, Osborne Macdaniel's mother and two sisters, and John
Dwight and both of his sisters and their mother. Also included at the
festive meal were Fred Cabot and John Orvis, both men currently the
objects of Mary Ann Dwight's romantic attention. Had Brisbane,
Macdaniel, and Channing arrived at the Farm a few days earlier, they
would have also enjoyed some of the community's "home-bound" activities, caused this early winter by a heavy snow that began falling
right after Christmas day. The snow was so deep that a "shoveling
group" had to be formed to clear paths through the five-feet-high
snowdrifts in order for the Brook Farmers to move between the buildings for a performance of *Pizarro* at the Hive (complete with "splendid" costumes); card-playing, coffee, and hot-chocolate parties at the
Pilgrim House; a reading of Shakespeare and a variety of musical performances at the Eyrie; and a community dance—the women in calico
gowns and aprons—in the dining room of the Hive to celebrate
Rebecca Codman's twentieth birthday. The dance gave Brook Farm's
men the chance to demonstrate what they had learned in a new class
organized by Amelia Russell in early December 1844 "teaching grown
men to dance"—twelve men took the lessons. Outdoors the heavy
snow meant sledding and coasting on the hills at the Farm, which
many Brook Farmers particularly enjoyed on moonlit evenings, when
it was easier to admire the "glittering coral branches that border our
paths, and the trees of crystal, of silver and diamonds, that make magnificent this fairy place."[20]

Brisbane, Macdaniel, and Channing all participated actively during
the two days of meetings of the New England Fourier Society on January 15 and 16. Fellow New York Associationist Parke Godwin was
unable to attend because of an "accidental injury." Horace Greeley
couldn't be there either because of a severe winter cold. The Society,
in any case, was really nothing more than Brook Farm speaking with a

different voice. It's true that none of the four vice presidents were Brook Farmers, although one of them, Francis G. Shaw, might just as well have been. But being a "Vice President" was nothing more than an honorific title anyway. Real authority for the operation of the Society was wielded by the president, the recording secretary, the corresponding secretary, and the treasurer, and all these positions were held by Brook Farmers.

George Ripley had served as the Society's first president in 1844, and was immediately reelected to the position again on the first day of the convention. Joining him in 1845 were Jonathan Butterfield, a twenty-six-year-old printer who was elected recording secretary of the Society, and John Sawyer, a broker, the Fourier Society's treasurer. John Allen, the corresponding secretary for 1845, was preparing to move to Brook Farm with his wife just a few weeks after the Fourier Society meeting. These three men had served on the Society's eleven-person Executive Committee in 1844, along with Brook Farmers Rebecca Codman, Henry P. Trask, and Fred Cabot. For 1845, Sawyer, Allen, and Cabot were reelected to the Executive Committee, which also included John Sullivan Dwight and George C. Leach. (Leach, a hotelkeeper in West Roxbury, was one of Ripley's earliest supporters.) Ripley devoted his welcoming remarks to the emergence of the Associative movement in New England, describing it as the "inevitable result" of the various theological and philosophical controversies that had burned at white heat just a few years before in and around Cambridge and Boston. Ripley also acknowledged the importance of the burgeoning workingmen's movement, and expressed his sympathy with its goals. The very next day, he and Louis Ryckman, along with John Allen and S. C. Hewitt, a labor organizer from Fall River, engaged in a lively discussion about the movement.

John Dwight also provided a talk on "the educational processes by which industry and teaching may be made supplementary and instrumental to each other" (probably a reworked version of his "Lecture on Association, in Its Connection with Education" delivered to the New England Fourier Society the year before). John Orvis described how "balance of character" could be achieved by an "Attractive system of Industry." And William Henry Channing—who, it was noted in *The Phalanx*, may be "classed" with the Brook Farmers—spoke "eloquently" on behalf of the reform work underway at the West Roxbury community, as he did about Associative reform activities generally. If anyone monopolized the floor, however, it was Charles Dana. He occupied the platform virtually the entire second evening, taking nearly three hours to deliver a report to convention attendees from the Society's Executive Committee.[21]

That didn't prevent Albert Brisbane, however, from describing his recent European experiences to those assembled. He pointed out that Associationists in the United States enjoyed important advantages over their European brethren. In America there was no class of "degraded peasantry and operatives so ignorant . . . that they cannot read." In America there was an "intelligent, aspiring, self-respecting and respected body of farmers and working class."[22] Even Europe's leading intellects—Brisbane particularly singled out Thomas Carlyle—were without hope for the future. In Carlyle's case, Brisbane thought, "his disbelief that any essential amelioration can take place in the condition of mankind, at least for ages to come, grows out of his peculiar melancholy temperament."

Nevertheless, it was Osborne Macdaniel's remarks that must have most pleased the Brook Farmers. On the first day of the convention he called for national support of the community among Associationists across the country. Macdaniel, whose sisters had just been formally elected members of the Association on December 22, expressed "the deepest solicitude" for the success of all the "infant communities in existence" that hoped to realize "practically the idea of Association" (nineteen Fourierist communities were in existence in the United States in January 1845—all but Brook Farm located west of the Hudson River), and he hoped that they all would be able to overcome the obstacles that stood in the way of eventual success. He even extended his sympathy to those communities "which do not recognize the system of Charles Fourier" (thirty-nine non-Fourierist American utopian communities were in operation in 1844). Macdaniel wanted convention delegates to recommend specifically, however, that Associationists throughout the United States "concentrate and direct their efforts, and apply their means and energies to the building up of the Brook Farm Association," because it was this community more than any other that "presents a bright promise of success and affords a healthy germ of that Divine Social Order that is soon to replace the societies of discord and suffering now existing on earth." The quickest way of achieving this transformation was to establish a successful Phalanx in the United States. Brook Farm, he stated, should be the model.

The convention's approval of Macdaniel's resolution was an important endorsement for the West Roxbury community—despite the number of Brook Farmers who dominated the Fourier Society—because it appeared to indicate that New York Associationists were prepared to extend financial support to Brook Farm. Ripley, Dana, Ryckman, and their fellow associates returned to the community on January 16 understandably encouraged by the convention proceedings. Brisbane and Macdaniel spent the next ten days there—Brisbane occasionally providing a "sermon" on Association (Mary Ann Dwight's characterization), which he usually illustrated with impressive views of a Phalanx that showed the extensive buildings and grounds envisioned by Charles Fourier.[23]

The high spirits swirling about the Farm at the end of January 1845 were especially in abundance once again in Amelia Russell's room at the Cottage the evening before Albert Brisbane and Osborne Macdaniel's departure for New York City.[24] The group that happily crammed themselves into her room was essentially the same one that had enjoyed the oyster supper there two weeks before. Here again were Brisbane and Macdaniel and both of Macdaniel's sisters, Eunice and Fanny, as well as George and Marianne Ripley (Sophia didn't join in the festivities this time), Charles and Maria Dana, John, Mary Ann, and Fanny Dwight, John Orvis and Fred Cabot, and Sarah Whitehouse, one of the unmarried women who came to the community the previous spring. The evening was filled with a variety of toasts, informal speeches, and much good humor. Ripley toasted Brisbane—the "first apostle of Fourierism in our country"—and Dana, with great feeling, toasted his absent friend, Parke Godwin, whereupon Fred Cabot supplied the evening's first pun: "*God wins* always in the end." Toasts were also extended to others not present—to Fourier, of course, to William Henry Channing ("the priest and poet of Association"), and to Horace Greeley, all of which were prefaced with generous and enthusiastic remarks.

Dana recalled the meeting in New York City in April 1844 when, at its conclusion, all the participants stood up and clasped hands to demonstrate their solidarity to one another and to the cause of Association. He asked everyone gathered in Russell's room now to rise and join hands, which everyone did while, together, they vowed "truth to the cause of God and humanity." It was, Mary Ann Dwight told her brother Frank the next day, "a solemn moment, one never to be forgotten."

Such high seriousness prompted George Ripley to wish that Brook Farm might eventually be filled with so many devoted members to the cause that they could all join hands and encircle Cow Island, the section of land near the Charles River on the western side of the Farm that was a popular destination for Sunday afternoon picnics. Brisbane said that he would have the circle extend entirely around the globe. John Dwight then lightened the mood considerably by toasting the coffee pot: "Our patient friend," he said. "'Tho' drained of its *contents,* it has not lost its patience,—if it is not *spiritual,* it certainly is not *material*' (is immaterial)." Ripley, Mary Ann Dwight noted, jumped a foot at such a good pun. Others in Russell's room began punning on John Orvis's last name, Dwight remarking, "God bless the sun and also Orpheus. God bless the moon and also Morpheus." And so it went throughout the evening—all the way to midnight, in fact.

At the end, Brisbane struck a more serious note again, saying that he was returning to New York to propagate the Associationist doctrine there—a city of duplicity and fraud—which prompted Fred Cabot to observe that he hoped that the New Yorker might "go his proper gait (propagate)," and that the greatest fraud that the metropolis could impose on the Brook Farmers would be depriving them of his regular presence in the community.[25] "You see our entertainment was a regular series," Mary Ann Dwight summarized the evening in good Fourierist fashion, "ascending gradually from a few jokes to the highest spiritual emotions, and then gradually descending again." Altogether it was an evening filled with reverence, true eloquence, "deep earnestness and sacred solemnity."

Dwight's words would never be used to describe the often boisterous proceedings of the second workingmen's convention in the town of Lowell on March 18, 1845, but when the noise subsided, Louis Ryckman had been elected president of the newly formed "New England Workingmen's Association," and George Ripley was appointed to the Executive Committee. This gain was offset, however, by a much more serious loss just a few weeks later. Minot and Maria Pratt, upon whom Ripley and the Brook Farmers had relied so steadily since the earliest days of the community's existence, decided to withdraw from the Association in April and move with their children to the village of Concord (where a small group of Brook Farmers had already settled themselves).[26] Pratt had expressed a desire to leave West Roxbury nearly two years before, in July 1843, but Ripley managed to persuade him to remain at Brook Farm, despite Minot and Maria's concern that their children were not always reaping all that they had sown while living in the community. There was no rancor or ill will as the Pratts made their departure. On the contrary, Pratt said in a letter to Ripley on April 3, 1845, that he continued to have "a very deep interest, in the success of the cause in which I have in my humble way labored with you for the last few years." Pratt also wanted to express, "but could not do it, to say to you and others how much I love and esteem you, and how painful it is for me to leave those to whom I am so much indebted for personal kindnesses."[27]

The Pratts had always been among the hardest-working members of the community. Their departure must have been very difficult both for practical as well as personal reasons, especially to George, Sophia, and Marianne Ripley. The Pratts, after all, were the last remaining members of the so-called "first dispensation"—those associates whose residence at Brook Farm dated back—as now only the Ripleys' still did—to the very beginning of the community's existence in 1841. Ripley remarked that the Pratts were leaving the community to found "a little colony of their own" in Concord. He expressed his sorrow for their departure, and he recalled the years that they had all labored together at the Farm. After extending his and the Brook Farmers' hopes for the Pratts' present and future welfare, Ripley, who always managed to wear a brave face, tried to relieve the awkwardness of the moment with an informal toast: "The late Chief of the Farming Series, Minot Pratt and his family—they cannot remain long in *Concord* without returning to *harmony*."[28]

Exactly one month to the day after Minot Pratt handed George Ripley his farewell letter, Brook Farm legally became "a corporation by the name of the Brook Farm Phalanx." The change had been in the works for several months. Revisions to the existing constitution began in late December 1844 with the appointment of a five-person committee consisting of Ripley, Dana, Ryckman, Fanny Macdaniel, and John Sawyer. The revised constitution was formally adopted by the Association on March 20, 1845, which was the very same day that the Massachusetts Legislature approved the Association's petition for incorporation. Incorporation, however, did not take effect until May 1.[29] The hope engendered by Brook Farm's conversion to a Fourierist Phalanx prompted George and Sophia Ripley to purchase an additional ten shares of stock in the Association, thereby increasing the total of their cash investment in the community to $3,447.50. Marianne Ripley put up $1,950 for nineteen and a half more shares to go along with the twenty that she already owned.[30]

The most obvious difference between the constitutions of January 1844 and May 1845 are the length and arrangement of the Articles in the two documents. The 1844 constitution contains six Articles and twenty subsections; the 1845 constitution has eight Articles and a whopping forty-nine subsections. This difference alone suggests the kind of bureaucratic "fat" that Brook Farm had gradually acquired since shifting its allegiance to Fourierism in January 1844. The organization of the Articles in the May 1845 constitution also clearly indicates not only the community's new priorities, but the considerable attention that the Brook Farmers were paying to procedural details in the Association's daily operations. A summary comparison of the two documents indicates the new priorities:

JANUARY 1844 CONSTITUTION	MAY 1845 CONSTITUTION
Article I: "Name & Membership" (Two sections)	Article I: "Name & Membership" (Two sections)
Article II: "Capital Stock" (Four sections)	Article II: "Government" (Seventeen sections)
Article III: "Guarantees" (Four sections)	Article III: "Capital Stock" (Eight sections)
Article IV: "Distribution of Profits" (Two sections)	Article IV: "Guarantees" (Five sections)
Article V: "Government" (Six sections)	Article V: "Organization of Labor" (Six sections)
Article VI: "Miscellaneous" (Two sections)	Article VI: "Division of Profits" (Six sections)
	Article VII: "Membership" (Six sections)
	Article VIII: "Amendments to Constitution" (No sections)

The significance of repositioning Article V on "Government" in the January 1844 constitution so it could be more prominently featured in the May 1845 constitution as Article II, and of the increase in the number of subsections in this Article from six to seventeen, is obvious enough. Not surprisingly, the new constitution pays considerable attention to Charles Fourier. The very first Article notes that the organization of industry at Brook Farm shall be "in accordance with the system of Association and the laws of Universal Unity as discovered by Charles Fourier." There are throughout the May 1845 constitution many such references—both direct and indirect—to Fourier and Fourierism that are not found in the January 1844 constitution.

The public had been informed in October in the "Notice to the Second Edition" of the 1844 constitution that the location of Brook Farm's new industries was "a work-shop sixty feet by twenty-eight, for mechanics of several trades."[31] The Workshop had been constructed during the summer of 1844 behind and to the north of the Hive to accommodate the many different tradesmen who were then flocking to the community. The Carpenters' Shop occupied the entire first floor, while the second floor was home to the Britannia-Ware Shop, the Shoemakers' Shop, and the printing office of a new Associationist paper called *The Harbinger*. The Workshop also contained a basement and an attic, the latter providing a small dormitory for the men and boys whose regular work was on one of the floors below. By November 1844 the building had already needed to be underpinned (a recurring oversight at Brook Farm—the fireplace in the Cottage caved in because Charles Dana hadn't realized when he constructed it that the chimney required a supporting foundation).

Arrangements were already underway in the summer of 1845 for the installation of a new steam engine—at a cost of more than $1,000—to replace the horse mill in the basement that was used to drive the community's industries. If Brook Farm's industries were to be competitive, such a costly capital expenditure seemed necessary. The installation of the steam engine, like the Pratt family's departure, is another powerful reminder that Brook Farm had broken irrevocably with the past when it was principally an agrarian and romantic retreat whose prosperity, Ripley then thought, would be assured by the piles and piles of rich manure (the "gold mine," he called the fertilizer) that were spread around the farm. The past was now forgotten amid calculations of caloric and the clangor echoing from the Workshop in the new Fourierist Phalanx.

And just what were the new "industries" about which the Brook Farmers had such high hopes? Mainly there were three—pewterware, shoes, and sashes and blinds. The community, however, always kept an eye open for any activity that might serve as a source of income.[32] Brook Farm's venture into Britannia ware—the manufacture of pewterware—was inspired by Ephraim Capen, the "Parson," as he was affectionately known to his fellow Associationists because he had at one time prepared for the ministry until he realized, as Ripley himself had, that he would never be comfortable preaching the kind of hellfire and brimstone sermons expected by parishioners. (John Dwight had also similarly disappointed his Northampton, Massachusetts, congregation before coming to Brook Farm in November 1841.) Capen came to the Association during the hectic six months following the conversion to Fourierism in January 1844. He signed the Brook Farm constitution on May 12, 1844, the only person ever to describe himself on that document as a "pewterer." Capen probably worked alone at Brook Farm, though he may have had occasional assistance from George W. Pierce, a mechanic who became a member of the Association three-and-a-half months after Capen did. Their names sometimes appear together in the financial records.

Most likely Capen was producing whale-oil lamps and teapots at the Farm in the months before and after he formally joined the Association in May 1844, but the only surviving financial records do not begin until November 1, 1844, so information about his "industrial" labors in the community is limited mostly to the period after that date. There are surviving "Brook Farm Labor Records" for the one-year period from May 1844 to April 1845, however, and they indicate that Capen logged nearly all his hours during this one-year period in the "Mechanical Series," under which the manufacture of Britannia ware would have been one of the "Groups." The financial records, in any case, show very clearly that the production of Britannia ware was one of the main enterprises at Brook Farm in 1845, although Capen seems to have concentrated more on pewter whale-oil lamps than on teapots.

Pewter whale-oil lamp and Brook Farm "mark." Britannia ware such as
this, manufactured at Brook Farm during the Fourierist period, is one of
the few surviving relics of community life in West Roxbury.

There is an occasional reference or two to the latter in the financial records, but there are a great many more to whale-oil lamps. Because
they were intended to be functional rather than decorative, the design
of these lamps had few variations. Some were manufactured with a
"dish" or saucer-like base (as in the lamp shown in the illustration);
others were produced with a simple stand. There was slight variation
in the length of the shaft. Most of the Brook Farm lamps seem to have
had an "acorn"-shaped font to hold the oil, and each was stamped
with a simple "Brook Farm" marking underneath the base.

Brook Farm's financial records for the fiscal year November 1,
1844–October 31, 1845 indicate that income from the production of
Britannia ware was slightly more than $500. Nearly an equal amount
is listed for expenses, but those expenses include not only the cost of
materials, such as block tin, but several indirect costs as well. Capen's

shop was charged, for instance, more than seven dollars in March 1845 for the "use of horse & power." Once the new steam engine became fully operational by the end of the year, the shop was debited nearly thirty dollars in October 1845 for the use of power.

Income and expenses may also have been skewed by other factors. To settle an outstanding bill with Boston crockeryware merchant John Collamore, Jr., in April 1845, the Brook Farmers provided his shop on Washington Street with more than forty pairs of lamps. At roughly seventy-five cents a pair, the lamps would have brought in thirty dollars of income.[33] Unfortunately for the Association, the sale of Britannia-ware lamps and teapots, as Brook Farmer John T. Codman later noted, was "limited, the market being dull or glutted," which accounts for their slim profit at Brook Farm. In March 1845 that was $65; in October 1845, it was about $55. Ironically, Capen's whale-oil lamps and teapots became very popular after he moved to New York City in 1848 and joined forces with another pewterer named George Molineux. According to one leading authority on American pewter, "Capen & Molineux appear to have been the leading specialists in pewter lamps" between 1848–1853.[34]

No other wares from Brook Farm have survived the ravages of time—certainly not any of the hundreds and even thousands of pairs of shoes and boots that were manufactured there. During the "great migration" to the community in the spring and summer of 1844, there were nine shoemakers at Brook Farm. Now, one year later, there were still seven: Nathaniel Colson, Charles Fuller, Castalio Hosmer, Jr., and his brothers Charles and Granville, William Teel, and Louis Ryckman, the man who first organized the shoemaking industry in the community. But shoemaking proved to be nearly as disappointing as the production of Britannia ware. These seven men spent most of their time taking care of the needs of their fellow Brook Farmers, who managed during the year November 1, 1844–October 31, 1845 to accrue nearly $900 in personal charges from the Shoemakers Shop. Although Brook Farm did business with two shoe merchants in Boston—"Henry L. Daggett" and "Newell & Neibuhr," both of which were on Washington Street—income from these sources amounted to little more than $400 for the year. Expenses for the same one-year period were just over fifty dollars, because, first, there was very little overhead involved, and, second, most of the raw materials for shoes and boots were supplied by the Boston merchants.

Net profit to the community, nevertheless, was still quite small because the nearly $900 of charges incurred by the associates were debited to their individual accounts to be settled at the end of the year. That obviously left the community without a substantial amount of "earned" income. Worse, many associates left Brook Farm before these annual accountings, thereby leaving the Association with a considerable amount of bad debt.[35] It's hard to imagine why the General Direction or the Direction of Finance—the former comprised in 1845 of Ripley (committee head), Dana, and Ryckman, the latter of Charles Dana (committee head), John Sawyer, and Jonathan Butterfield—did not address such an inherent and ultimately critical weakness in the community's financial structure, especially since associates obviously accrued charges not just for shoemaking but for virtually all their regular needs, such as tailoring, extras at table, sundry supplies, and postage, to mention only a few.

A similar problem occurred with Brook Farm's carpenters, whose services were in demand from one end of the community to the other. Renovations were needed in the Workshop in order to accommodate the industries there; repairs on the Hive and other community buildings routinely had to be made; blinds for the many windows in the Cottage, Eyrie, Pilgrim House, and Hive had to be constructed in an ongoing and mostly futile effort to insulate those drafty buildings; special sewing blocks for the "Fancy Group," bulletin boards for the school, and knifeboards for the Refectory needed to be made; farm equipment had to be repaired; and flower stands, bureaus, bookcases, and a slew of other items required by associates were regularly in demand. None of this work produced any income.[36]

Even more serious, however, was the failure to turn the carpenters' skills to good profit in the "sash and blind" industry. This enterprise, which was just getting underway in June 1845, turned out to be the most costly and least profitable—not to say the most space-consuming and inconvenient—of all of Brook Farm's industrial activities. The decision to include it, nonetheless, is understandable. Seven carpenters came to the Farm between April and June 1844 right after the untimely decision in March 1844 to construct a Phalanstery. Now, more than a year later, five were still living in the community, including William Cheswell and his wife Mary Ann; Peter Kleinstrup and wife Augustina, and their daughter Louisa; Jeremiah Reynolds, who had been expelled from the Carpenters' Group the previous September 1844, but who, for the time being at least, had apparently seen the error of his ways and had come into the harmony of Association; Job Tirrell; and Robert Westacott.

The sash-and-blind industry at Brook Farm highlights two of the most serious problems that persistently undermined the community's financial endeavors throughout its six-and-a-half-year history: bad financial judgment and poor location. An example of the former was the decision that year to purchase a steam engine for the Workshop at the very substantial cost of one thousand dollars. As noted earlier, before the new steam engine became fully operational in September 1845, power for Brook Farm's industries had been supplied by a horse mill in the basement of the Workshop. Each of the industries in the building was charged accordingly. In June 1845, for instance, the Carpenters' Shop was debited only seventeen dollars for "horses in power and teaming." Four months later, however, with the steam engine up and running, the Shop was charged a hefty $180 for power.

Materials and labor were expensive too. In July 1845, for example, nearly $300 was debited in the account book for these items; in August, approximately $200 was. By October 1845, when the sash-and-blind industry was fully underway, these expenses cost more than $600. Total expenditures for sash-and-blind manufacturing for the fiscal year ending October 31, 1845, amounted to nearly $1,200. Income from this venture for the same period turned out to be only about $870. Brook Farmer John Codman understood that the failure of this industry resulted from its being undercapitalized: "I believe that this business [sashes, blinds, and doors] could have been made profitable, but here again the inevitable want was capital." Lindsay Swift made the same point in his study of Brook Farm: the "sash and blind industry [at Brook Farm] ought to have been remunerative . . . but lack of capital was particularly disastrous to this industry."[37]

Inadequate capital was always a persistent problem at the community, but there was another crucial factor: the kind of bad financial judgment that would organize such a cost-intensive industry as the manufacture of sashes, blinds, and doors at a time when the community not only was already deeply in debt, but when a large cash outlay was also required for the purchase of the steam engine. When the expense of the steam engine is added to the related costs of its operation for the last three months of the fiscal year ending October 31, 1845 (which was a whopping $950), it's no surprise that the Brook Farmers had to turn once again to West Roxbury friend and neighbor Frank Shaw for financial relief. On August 20, 1845, a fourth mortgage was placed on the Brook Farm Phalanx for $2,500 (plus interest), payable annually for five years.

Brook Farm's distance from the Boston markets only exacerbated the community's industrial endeavors. J. Homer Doucet, who arrived at Brook Farm at the beginning of the Fourierist fervor in the spring of 1844, noted particularly in his reminiscence of the community that "there was no railroad. The lumber [for the manufacture of sashes, blinds, and doors] had to be hauled from the yards of Boston with horses. Then the bulky finished products had to be transported to market by the same means." Lindsay Swift makes this point too: "A formidable obstacle to prosperity was the distance of the farm from its market. It was nine miles from Boston and four from the nearest railroad station . . . and all the stock for manufacturing purposes, as well as family stores, coal, and manure, had to be transported by teams, while the manufactured goods and farm produce must go back over the same ground to be sold."

In the case of the sash-and-blind industry, there was an additional problem. John Codman observed that "in order to make these articles of good quality [sashes, blinds, and doors], it is of the first importance that the stock in them shall be well seasoned, for if it is not, changes of temperature will produce shrinkage and warping. The wood should be either kiln-dried—a novelty then—or dried by long keeping in sheds, and it was important to buy largely when there was a good chance, and store for future use. These things the Brook Farmers could not do, and consequently some of the doors and sashes shrank, much to the disgust of everybody."[38]

Hindsight, the saying goes, is always twenty-twenty, and Doucet, Swift, and Codman's observations benefit from the perspective and distance of several decades following Brook Farm's eventual collapse. It was not yet evident to the Brook Farmers themselves in the summer of 1845, however, that the Association's industries would collectively fail to produce even enough income to meet the expenses of running them. Instead, Ripley, Dana, John Dwight, and the community's corps of printers were thinking about the transfer of Albert Brisbane's *The Phalanx* and John Allen's *The Social Reformer* in June 1845. The prospect of additional income from a new Fourierist newspaper to be published at the community enabled the Brook Farmers, for the moment, to discount, once again, whatever anxieties they may have felt about the Association's future financial prospects.

9

The Harbinger

The Harbinger (1845–1849) was the immediate successor to Albert Brisbane's *The Phalanx* (1843–1845), as well as to John Allen's *The Social Reformer and Herald of Universal Health* (1844–1845). The first number was published at Brook Farm on June 14, 1845, where it continued to be printed weekly until October 1847 (Volumes 1–5), at which time it was transferred to New York City (Volumes 6–8). While it was under the editorial control of George Ripley, Charles Dana, and the Brook Farmers, the paper was marked by a liveliness and high-mindedness that are conspicuously absent in the New York version of the paper. The final number of *The Harbinger* appeared on February 10, 1849.

The decision to publish the paper at Brook Farm was made in January 1845, right after the first annual meeting of the New England Fourier Society. Ripley and the Brook Farmers returned to West Roxbury accompanied by Albert Brisbane, Osborne Macdaniel, and William Henry Channing, all of whom had come up from New York City for the Fourier Society meeting in Boston. Brisbane had only just returned to the United States a few weeks earlier after an eight-month sojourn through France gathering many of Charles Fourier's unpublished manuscripts, and meeting with prominent French Associationists. For Macdaniel and Channing, the trip to New England meant time with family. For Macdaniel, who with Parke Godwin had been editing *The Phalanx* in Brisbane's absence, the Boston meeting provided an opportunity to visit his mother and two sisters at Brook Farm. Eunice and Fanny Macdaniel had been formally elected members of the Association in December 1844. (Their mother, Mary, never formally became a Brook Farm associate.) For Channing, a graduate of Harvard College in 1829 and the Harvard Divinity School in 1833, his roots had always been in Boston, despite his recent prolonged absences the previous few years in Ohio and New York. He was always one of the Brook Farmers' most-welcome friends. Ripley and Dana had hoped that Godwin also would be present at the Boston meeting, but the New York Associationist begged off, protesting the effects of an "accidental injury."

Ripley and Dana planned on a "quiet assembly" at Brook Farm following the public meeting of the Fourier Society—"quiet" because there really wasn't much to cheer about in January 1845. *The Phalanx,* the unofficial organ of Associationism in the United States, was about to fold; several Associations in western New York had recently collapsed; and Brook Farm, the only Fourierist Association in New England, was still struggling to establish dependable and profitable industries at the community. "Our practical operations," Dana acknowledged to Godwin in November 1844, referring to both Brook Farm and the Associationist movement nationally, "have not been successful enough to justify any loud jubilations." Perhaps an informal meeting at the Farm among a few "friends of the cause" might manage to produce a "lasting effect." One important way to do that, Ripley and Dana thought, would be to "establish a central School speaking authoritatively upon doctrinal questions." Dana urged the New Yorkers to come to Brook Farm in January 1845 to see whether "we cannot do something towards the organization of a School whose office shall be the propagation & defense of the [Associationist] doctrine."[1]

The Brook Farmers' appeal for greater organization and unity among Associationists, however, fell on deaf New York ears. It was decided instead to propagandize the cause in a new Associationist paper that would be published at the West Roxbury community. Ripley and Dana still didn't recognize that the depth of commitment among New York Associationists was nowhere near that of Brook Farm's leaders. The sincerity of purpose that always characterized the activities of Ripley, Dana, and John Dwight, and a few other Brook Farmers, was not now, and never would begin to be, matched by New York Associationists such as Godwin, Macdaniel, and Horace Greeley. Parke Godwin's barely concealed antipathy toward his fellow New York Associationist Albert Brisbane is just one illustration of the problem.

Godwin's contempt for Brisbane, it should first be said, was equaled by his general disdain for New Englanders. Even now, in the early months of 1845, as discussions about the transfer of *The Phalanx* became more urgent, Godwin couldn't resist taking a swipe or two at New Englanders. One of his longest and most acidulous tirades came in a letter to Dana sometime in late winter or early spring 1845.[2] Dana had written in February 1845 requesting assurances from Godwin that the New Yorker would provide regular contributions to the new paper if the Brook Farmers agreed to take charge of its publication. Godwin replied that he would be willing to provide occasional articles on political matters, but he wanted Dana and Ripley to know that he would require "considerable freedom" to say whatever he would.

"On Texas and such matters," Godwin wrote,

> I could write nothing to suit the pestiferous philanthropy
> of New England,—whose people by the way never see
> more than their own noses and only one side of those.
> The Texas question [whether Texas would ultimately be-

come slave-holding territory or remain a free state] is the only political question of any vitality now before us, and the New England view of it is the narrowest, meanest, and most despicable that a conceited and bigoted intellect could take of it. I believe, by the Lord, that if the Deity should consult New England about making a new world, they would advise that it should be made of the size of Massachusetts, have no city but Boston, and insist that its moral code should consist in making an occasional donation to a charitable institution and uttering shallow puling anti-slavery sentiments.

His outburst inspired Godwin to take a poke at his friend Horace Greeley as well—"who is in so many respects," Godwin allowed, "one of the best men in existence." But the New York Associationist was sorry that "our friend Greeley . . . should allow his Eastern origin to warp his benevolent and just mind on so many important questions. His talks on Texas are [as] miserable stuff, as one ever saw."

Godwin's eruptions over Albert Brisbane in early 1845 were occasioned by the demise of *The Phalanx* and the decision to locate its successor at Brook Farm. Although *The Phalanx* would not cease publication until May 1845, it had been limping along for many months, appearing monthly, then bimonthly, and then not for several months, under the joint editorship of Godwin and Osborne Macdaniel. Part of Ripley and Dana's plan to organize a "central School" in the United States included publication of a regular newspaper that would propagate and defend Associationist doctrines. The Brook Farmers were certainly interested in publishing the new paper, but they were "somewhat afraid of it" too.

There were many unanswered questions. Ripley was hesitant about announcing himself the central editor because of the additional responsibility that came with the position. Moreover, who would fill the paper's columns? "For myself," Dana told Godwin on February 20, 1845, "I must for the most part religiously abstain from much writing" because of pressing duties at the Farm. And how many paying subscribers could be expected from the transfer of the subscription lists of *The Phalanx?* Five hundred or so, Godwin thought. And what should the new paper be called? Godwin was much more certain about this. Since at least the previous November 1844 he had been anticipating the demise of *The Phalanx* and the creation of a new paper. For months now he had been casually referring to the new publication as "Young America," a title, however, that was immediately rejected by the Brook Farmers because it had already been adopted by the National Reform Association, and any connection with that organization might suggest that the new paper was being conducted by "unbalanced & headstrong youths aiming at rash innovations." Godwin then offered *The Pathfinder,* the name of his own short-lived weekly paper that he had published in 1843.[3] The Brook Farmers weren't happy with that title either. Ripley favored retaining the present name of the paper, *The Phalanx,* or calling it "The Brook Farm Phalanx." Dana acknowledged that he didn't like the latter title so well, but, he quickly added in his February 20, 1845, letter to Godwin, "I think it is of great importance that the paper should be explicitly connected with Brook Farm. It will thus have a life and interest," Dana sensibly pointed out, "which it could not have if published from any other place. Its doctrines will in this way possess something of the vitality & charm which belong to [the] truth of personal experience."

Godwin, unfortunately, didn't agree with the Brook Farmers at all, for if he had the editors of *The Harbinger* might have devoted more regular attention to the West Roxbury Association in the pages of the new paper, thereby creating the kind of expanded interest in the community that might have enabled it to survive a series of crises that were about to occur in the autumn of 1845 and the winter of 1846. But the New York Associationist thought that the Brook Farmers were "already separated from the world enough." "Your paper must come down into the world itself," Godwin admonished Dana on March 21, 1845, "and fight things as they are." As for the idea of retaining the paper's present title, Godwin said that he wouldn't work for the new paper if it were titled *The Phalanx*, "for it would [be] like working for a dead horse." He therefore begged the Brook Farmers to consider any other name—just not *The Phalanx*.

> Call it the Pilot, the Harbinger, the Halycon, the Harmonist, the Unitarian, The Worker, the Architect, The Zodiac, The Pleiad, the Iris, the Examiner, The Aurora, the Crown, the Imperial, the Independent, the Synthesist, the Light, the Truth, the Hope, the Teacher, the Reconciler, the Wedge, the Pirate, the Seer, the Indicator, the Tailor, the Babe in the Manger, the Universe, the Apocalypse, the Red Dragon, the Plant, Beelzebub—the Devil or anything rather than the meaningless Phalanx.

The Brook Farmers agreed right away on *The Harbinger*.

Much of Godwin's vehemence about retaining *The Phalanx* as the title for the new paper was its connection with founder and still controlling editor, Albert Brisbane. *The Phalanx*, Godwin wrote to Dana on March 17, 1845, "heretofore, has been little more than a vehicle for Brisbane's vanity." Brisbane's extended absence in France in 1844, Godwin told Dana a month earlier on February 14, had improved him somewhat, "but his personal habits and his modes of thought are so disagreeable to me that his presence is a sort of moral torture." "He annoys me more than I dare confess," Godwin complained. "I utterly detest the rude steam-engine like hardness with which he treads upon all the more delicate and beautiful graces of the soul." Dana didn't disagree with this particular criticism. The Brook Farmers liked Brisbane well enough, and his visit during January had been pleasant. But Dana acknowledged to his New York friend on February 20 that he was quite annoyed by Brisbane's "conscience-less way of handling subjects" that ought to be treated "in the most revered manner," though he didn't specify just what those "subjects" were. Even worse, Dana added, "I abominate more than I can express his manner towards women."

Brisbane's character aside, there were plenty of reasons why the Brook Farmers might understandably have refused the opportunity to publish the new Associationist paper at the Farm. Ironically, the most urgent of these was probably the very one that ultimately prompted Ripley and Dana to undertake the responsibility of publishing the new paper: financial exigency. Brook Farm could ill afford another drain on its chronically depleted financial resources, but there were reasons to think that the new publication would benefit the community financially and otherwise.

For one thing, there was already a small corps of printers in the community in the persons of Jonathan Butterfield, Charles Codman, and Edgar Palisse (to the ranks of which Ripley was encouraging one more prospective probationer in late March 1845).[4] For another, Ripley was negotiating a barter with John Allen. In return for the press used to print *The Social Reformer,* Allen would receive $400 worth of Brook Farm stock. Additionally, Ripley obviously expected that the new paper would provide an important source of income for the Association. If the 500 paying subscribers to *The Phalanx,* and a handful more from John Allen's *Social Reformer,* could be transferred to *The Harbinger* at $2 per subscription—the rate per annum for *The Phalanx* and the one decided upon for the new paper—this would provide important income to the community. There was every reason to think, too, that the subscription list might be easily increased, what with the literary abilities of men like Ripley, Dana, and John Dwight, and the contributions that might be provided by Transcendentalist "friends" like Waldo Emerson, Theodore Parker, William Henry Channing, Christopher Pearse Cranch, and Frederic Henry Hedge.

But neither Emerson nor Parker, it turned out, would ever contribute so much as a single line to *The Harbinger*. More surprisingly, even avowed "friends" of the Associative cause—most notably, Parke Godwin and Horace Greeley among them—didn't offer much support either, which is oddly ironic since, when it came to Brook Farm, their words always spoke louder than their actions. Ripley, Dana, and John Dwight, in any case, wound up writing nearly three-fourths of all the original material in the five volumes printed at Brook Farm.[5] Even Dana, whose departure from Brook Farm was more imminent than he knew, only contributed a mere three reviews and one article for the fourth volume, and nothing at all for the fifth. The former Harvard student, however, was the single most prolific contributor to each of the first three volumes of *The Harbinger*, despite his protest in February 1845 to Godwin that he would have to "religiously abstain from much writing" for the new paper. For the first volume, Dana provided fifty-three articles and reviews. He was even inspired to write three poems. Altogether he contributed a combination of sixty articles and reviews for Volume 2, and forty-nine for Volume 3.

Ripley and Dwight's contributions to the first three volumes were also very considerable, Ripley managing thirty-four, thirty-five, and thirty-seven items, respectively, and Dwight contributing thirty-four, twenty-eight, and forty-seven. For Volumes 4 and 5, Ripley provided forty-seven and sixty items, respectively, and Dwight, fifty-four and fifty-one.[6] By contrast, Parke Godwin only contributed one article (on "The Oregon Question") to the first volume, just three items to the second, none at all to the third, again only one to the fourth volume, and nothing at all to the fifth.[7] Horace Greeley's only contribution to *The Harbinger* appeared in the first volume. Ironically enough, it was titled "Duty of Associationists to the Cause." Brisbane, Channing, and Macdaniel were much more supportive than Godwin and Greeley. Alhough their contributions didn't begin to match those of Ripley, Dana, and Dwight, the three New York-based Associationists easily provided more material than any of the other eighteen individuals who eventually contributed at least one item to the five volumes published at Brook Farm.

John Dwight was given the job of soliciting a contribution or two from Waldo Emerson, but the Brook Farmers shouldn't have been very sanguine about his support: Concord's most celebrated resident had not visited the Association since way back in January 1844, which is when the community first expressed its allegiance to Charles Fourier with the publication of the first constitution. If there had been any doubt before, Emerson made it perfectly clear in his response to Dwight's request in June 1845 why he would never contribute a single word to the new paper: "Though I should heartily rejoice to aid in an uncommitted journal,—not limited by the name of any man [that is, Charles Fourier],—I will not promise a line," he wrote in June 1845, "to any which has chosen a patron." Emerson decided that this was a good opportunity to tell the Brook Farmers that he thought that the French social scientist was just "another French soldier or rather mathematician, such as France is always turning out." He also expressed his sadness that scholars and philosophers had no literary organ that was not "desperately sectarian." (The *Dial* had collapsed in April 1844.) As long as *The Harbinger* remains "sectarian, I shall respect it at a distance," Emerson closed his letter to Dwight. "If it should become catholic, I shall be found suing for a place in it."[8]

Emerson was entirely right of course, and that's almost certainly why other friends not particularly sympathetic to the Associationist cause were reluctant to contribute to *The Harbinger,* especially Ripley's former Transcendentalist colleagues. Ripley would certainly have solicited a contribution or two from his dear friend and West Roxbury neighbor Theodore Parker, but Parker never provided a single line to the weekly paper. Frederic Henry Hedge could only be persuaded to send along a single poem, and James Freeman Clarke contributed just one review. Christopher Pearse Cranch, one of the few Transcendentalists who ever visited the Farm both before and after its conversion to Fourierism, was more supportive. He sent along half-a-dozen poems and three articles for the first three volumes of the paper. None of Bronson Alcott's work, however, appeared in *The Harbinger,* almost certainly because, like his friend Emerson, he had little sympathy with Charles Fourier's social theories. That's definitely true of Orestes Brownson, who in 1844 emphatically punctuated his social, religious, and philosophical break with all the Transcendentalists by his conversion to Catholicism.

All of these men with the exception of Brownson—that is, Ripley, Dana, Dwight, William Henry Channing, Hedge, Clarke, Cranch, and Alcott—had earlier been contributors to the *Dial* (1840–1844), as was William Ellery Channing (the younger), who provided a single poem for the third volume of *The Harbinger.* Other than similar contributors, however, the *Dial* and *The Harbinger* had very little in common. If the publication of the *Dial* made it appear that the phenomenon known as Transcendentalism was a unified movement, then the publication of *The Harbinger* made it perfectly clear that the sympathies that once bound men like Ripley, Emerson, Hedge, and Brownson together no longer existed.[9]

With the collapse of *The Phalanx* and Emerson's charge of sectarianism fresh on their minds, Ripley and the Brook Farmers launched *The Harbinger* on June 14, 1845. From the start they were very aware of the importance of producing an attractive literary paper (something that *The Phalanx* never was), but one that, at the same time, espoused and advanced the cause of Associationism in America. To achieve these mutually important goals, *The Harbinger,* Ripley stated in the "Introductory Notice," would regularly include such features as occasional poetry (most of it reprinted because original verse proved nearly impossible to find), a column of literary reviews (one of the most prominent features), and another devoted to "Fine Arts" (particularly music), in addition to articles and other matter having to do with Associationism and the Associationist movement both in America and in France.

"We mean to discuss all questions of public interest," Ripley promised in the first number of the new weekly paper, which carried two mottoes, both of which appeared in every issue thereafter. The first— "All Things, At The Present Day, Stand Provided And Prepared, And Await The Light"—was a quotation from the eighteenth-century Swedish philosopher, scientist, and theologian Emanuel Swedenborg—and appears directly below the masthead of the paper. The second heads *The Harbinger*'s editorial column. It was Ripley's way of paying public tribute to his mentor, Dr. William Ellery Channing, whose name is featured at the end of the quotation: "Of modern civilization, the natural fruits are, contempt for others' rights, fraud, oppression, a gambling spirit in trade, reckless adventure, and commercial convulsions all tending to impoverish the laborer and to render every condition insecure. Relief is to come, and can only come from the new applications of Christian principles, of Universal justice and Universal love, to social institutions, to commerce, to business, to active life."

In his seminal study of *The Periodicals of Transcendentalism,* Clarence Gohdes remarked that in *The Harbinger,* such features as the literary review, musical criticism, verse, and fiction were merely "a sauce for the weighty editorials dealing with various aspects of socialism, the translations from Fourier, and other French believers in 'Unity,' and the essays by American advocates of the cause."[10] Gohdes was obviously right about *The Harbinger*'s avowed commitment to Associationism and Fourierism, but his metaphor is somewhat misleading because it suggests that subjects other than those having to do with the Associative reform program did not receive serious attention in the paper. That simply was not the case. The more than 350 literary reviews and 100 musical and art reviews suggest by their sheer numbers alone that matters such as these were taken very seriously. The serialization of controversial French novelist George Sand is a good example of Ripley's and the Brook Farmers' commitment to publishing a lively and engaging paper. The first English translations in the United States of the allegedly immoral French writer's two novels, *Consuelo* and *The Countess of Rudolstadt,* appeared in *The Harbinger.*

Francis G. Shaw provided copyrighted translations of both Sand's *Consuelo* (originally published in France in 1845) and her *Countess of Rudolstadt* (1846). These two novels, the only fiction ever published in *The Harbinger,* were serialized in the first four volumes of the Associationist paper, *Consuelo* appearing in twenty-five of the twenty-six numbers of the first volume, all twenty-six numbers of the second volume, and in three numbers of the third volume. With its completion, the Brook Farmers began running *The Countess of Rudolstadt.* It was serialized over twenty-three numbers in the third volume and fifteen in the fourth volume. The decision to publish the novels in *The Harbinger* was both daring and courageous, considering the general hostility of the American audience toward French fiction in the 1840s. "*The Harbinger* stands out in the [eighteen] forties as the staunchest defender of [the] French novel," one commentator has remarked, "and in particular of George Sand, who was by far the most controversial French literary figure of the time."[11]

THE HARBINGER,

DEVOTED TO SOCIAL AND POLITICAL PROGRESS.

ALL THINGS, AT THE PRESENT DAY, STAND PROVIDED AND PREPARED, AND AWAIT THE LIGHT.

BURGESS, STRINGER, AND COMPANY, No. 222 BROADWAY, NEW YORK.   •PUBLISHED BY THE BROOK FARM PHALANX.   REDDING AND COMPANY, No. 8 STATE STREET, BOSTON.

VOLUME III.   SATURDAY, NOVEMBER 7, 1846.   NUMBER 22.

MISCELLANY.

THE COUNTESS OF RUDOLSTADT,

SEQUEL TO

CONSUELO.

FROM THE FRENCH OF GEORGE SAND.

Translated for the Harbinger.

XXI.

The Porporina, judging that her companion was determined not to exchange a single word with her, thought she could not do better than respect the singular vow he seemed to observe, after the manner of the ancient knights-errant. In order to escape the gloomy images and the sad reflections which Karl's recital suggested to her, she compelled herself to think only of the unknown future which opened before her, and by degrees she fell into a revery full of charms. Only a few privileged organizations have the gift of commanding their thoughts in a state of contemplative idleness. Consuelo had often, and most frequently in the three months of isolation she had just passed at Spandaw, had occasion to exercise this faculty, granted moreover less to the happy of this world than to those who contend for life in the midst of labor, of persecutions and of dangers. For we must, indeed, recognize the providential mystery of *circumstantial grace*, without which the strength and serenity of certain unfortunates would appear impossible to those who have never known misfortune.

Our fugitive found herself, moreover, in a situation strange enough to give rise to many castles-in-the-air. That mystery which enveloped her as with a cloud, that fatality which drew her into a supernatural world, that kind of paternal love which surrounded her with miracles, was quite enough to charm a young imagination rich in poetry. She recalled those words of Scripture which in her days of captivity she had set to music:

* Entered according to Act of Congress, in the year 1846, by FRANCIS G. SHAW, in the Clerk's office of the District Court of Massachusetts.

" I will send one of my angels to thee, and in his arms he shall bear thee up, lest thou dash thy foot against a stone.''

" I walk in the darkness, and I feel no fear — because the Lord is with me.''

These words had henceforth a clearer and more divine sense for her. In an age when men no longer believe in direct revelations, and when the outward manifestation of the Divinity, the protection and assistance of Heaven, are translated under the form of assistance, affection and devotedness on the part of our fellow-mortals, there is something so sweet in abandoning the direction of our own destiny to those that love us, and in feeling ourselves, as it were, borne by another! It is a happiness so great that it would soon corrupt us, if we did not struggle with ourselves not to abuse it. It is the happiness of a child, whose golden dreams upon the maternal breast are not troubled by any apprehensions of real life.

These thoughts, which presented themselves as a dream to Consuelo, at her sudden and unexpected escape from so cruel an existence, soothed her in a holy delight, until sleep came to drown and to confound them in that kind of repose of body and soul which may be called a conscious and prolonged annihilation. She had entirely forgotten the presence of the mute companion of her journey, when she woke quite close to him, with her head resting on his shoulder. At first she did not think of moving; she had dreamed that she was travelling in a cart with her mother, and the arm which supported her seemed that of the Zingara. A more complete awakening made her feel the confusion of her mistake; but the arm of the unknown seemed to have become a magic charm. She secretly made vain attempts to free herself from it; the unknown appeared to be himself asleep, and to have mechanically received his companion in his arms when fatigue and the motion of the carriage had made her fall into them. He had clasped his hands together about Consuelo's waist, as if to prevent his letting her fall at his

feet while he slept. But his slumber had not relaxed the strength of his interlocked fingers, and it would have been necessary to wake him completely in attempting to disengage them. Consuelo did not dare to do it. She hoped that he would himself restore her to liberty without knowing it, and that she could return to her place without appearing to have positively remarked all these delicate circumstances of their tête-à-tête.

But while waiting for the unknown to sleep more soundly, Consuelo herself, whom the calmness of his breathing and the immobility of his repose had reassured, again fell asleep, overpowered by the exhaustion which succeeds violent agitations. When she awoke once more, the head of her companion was bent upon her own, his mask was unfastened, their cheeks touched, their breaths intermingled. She made a quick motion to draw back, without thinking to look at the features of the unknown, which, moreover, would have been quite useless, on account of the darkness that prevailed without and especially within the carriage. The unknown pressed Consuelo to his bosom, the warmth of which magnetically enkindled hers, and took away from her the strength and the desire to withdraw. Still there was nothing violent or brutal in the gentle and burning embrace of this man. Her chastity did not feel terrified or stained by his caresses, and Consuelo, as if a charm had been cast upon her, forgetting the reserve, we might even say the virgin coldness, from which she had never been tempted to depart, even in the arms of the fiery Anzoleto, returned to the unknown the enthusiastic and penetrating kiss he sought upon her lips.

As all was strange and unusual in that mysterious being, Consuelo's involuntary transport neither appeared to surprise, nor to embolden, nor to intoxicate him. He again pressed her slowly to his heart, and though this was with an extraordinary force, she did not feel the pain which a violent pressure always occasions

It took another kind of courage to withhold most of the unpublished Fourier manuscripts that Albert Brisbane unloaded on the Brook Farmers late in December 1845 (acquired during his travels in France the year before). If the aim was merely to fill the pages of the paper with "weighty" translations such as these, then they surely would have been included, especially since finding material every week for *The Harbinger*'s columns routinely presented difficulties for Ripley, Dana, and Dwight, who served together, for all intents and purposes, as co-editors while the paper was published at the Farm. But only four of Fourier's works in translation ever appeared in the Associationist paper (although translations of works by other French Associationists, such as Victor Considerant, Victor Hannequin, and Matthew Briancourt, occasionally were included).

Given the difficulty of filling *The Harbinger*'s pages—especially with original material—it's a bit surprising that more attention wasn't devoted locally to the activities of New England's workingmen. It will be recalled that Ripley, Dana, and Louis Ryckman all participated actively in the workingmen's convention in Boston in October 1844, and that Ripley afterward visited several nearby mechanics' associations where he spoke to receptive audiences on different aspects of labor reform. In the "Introductory Notice" to the first number of *The Harbinger,* Brook Farm's leader reassured readers that "every pulsation of our being vibrates in sympathy with the wrongs of the toiling millions, and every wise effort for their speedy enfranchisement will find in us resolute and indomitable advocates." One year later he was still reaffirming support of the New England workingmen. In "The Working Men's Movement [in New England]" in the June 20, 1846, number of the Associationist paper, Ripley noted that "we are devotedly attached to the movement ourselves. We would labor, night and day, summer and winter, by word and by deed, for the realization of its objects."

Despite such claims of support, however, relatively few articles hav-

ing to do with labor conditions in New England appeared in the
five volumes of *The Harbinger* that were published at the Farm. For
instance, in the first volume all but a few of the labor-related items
were reprinted from a number of different sources, such as Horace
Greeley's New York *Tribune,* the French Associationist paper *La
Democratic Pacifique,* and the *Chambers Edinburg Journal.* As the titles of these papers suggest, the reprinted articles didn't even deal
with labor issues that were of any immediate importance to the New
England workingmen. The same is true in the second and third volumes, which include, for example, a series of articles reprinted from
Greeley's paper on the "Circumstances, Conditions, and Rewards" of
labor in New York City, and essays on "American Labor" by Ripley,
"Industrial Feudalism" by Charles Dana, and "Industrial Reform" by
Albert Brisbane, none of which have anything to do with labor reform
in New England. By the beginning of 1847, with the Brook Farmers'
proverbial back already broken from the accumulated weight of their
long-endured financial difficulties, Ripley and his associates managed
to include just two labor-related articles (one a reprint) in Volume 4,
and only one in Volume 5 before the paper was transferred to New
York City in November 1847.

In fairness to Ripley and Dana, however, both men would immediately, and rightly, have pointed out that it was never their aim to propagandize exclusively on behalf of New England workingmen for specific reforms, such as a ten-hour working day or the establishment of
mechanics' associations (cooperative organizations, that is, not communities).[12] Their aim was to proselytize for Associationism and Fourierism, which together provided a comprehensive social and industrial reform program that included provisions for the melioration of
conditions affecting workers everywhere—not just in New England.
Ripley was thus understandably pleased to report in the February 21,
1846, number of *The Harbinger* that following recent talks on the vir-

tues of Associationism and Fourierism by Brook Farm lecturers John Allen and John Orvis to "those who are devoted to manual labor" in Lowell, Massachusetts—"a city where industrial pursuits are so prominent"—the "Lowell Fourier Society" was organized. Ripley joined Allen and Orvis when they later traveled to Manchester, New Hampshire, and Rockport and Gloucester, Massachusetts. In each of those towns Ripley found "staunch and true friends of Association" who were "devoting themselves earnestly and steadfastly, to the promotion of the Associative cause."

Similarly, when Charles Dana took to the field a few months later with Albert Brisbane and William Henry Channing, Brisbane lectured to audiences in Lowell and Worcester, Massachusetts, on the "Organization of Labor," but Dana and Channing themselves provided talks on such central Associative matters as the "tenure of property," the "distribution of wealth," the "right to education," and the "principle of mutual insurance."[13] So it would be wrong to say that the Brook Farmers failed to galvanize New England's workingmen. That may have been Louis Ryckman or John Allen's purpose, but it was never specifically Ripley or Dana's. Their devotion was to Associationism and Fourierism. If anything may be said to have failed in New England in the mid-1840s, it wasn't so much the efforts of men like Ripley and Dana as it was the Fourierist movement itself—just as Orestes Brownson, in 1844, predicted it would.

One feature to which Ripley and Dana devoted a lot more attention than they ever did to the New England workingmen was the literary review column, which is today among the more interesting in the paper—particularly when works by "friends" like Nathaniel Hawthorne, Ralph Waldo Emerson, Margaret Fuller, and Theodore Parker were under consideration. Even though the paper only survived for two years and a few months at Brook Farm, *The Harbinger*'s reviewers also managed to discuss a surprising number of works by popular British, German, and American authors, thereby providing an interesting window on the contemporary American reception of such important writers as Dickens, Charlotte Bronte, and Shelley; Goethe, Fichte, and Schlegel, whose works were so deeply felt by early Transcendentalists like Ripley, Emerson, and Frederic Henry Hedge; and Longfellow, Poe, and Melville, to name just a few of the writers reviewed. Not surprisingly, assessments were based as often as not on extraliterary rather than strictly literary considerations, the Associationist biases of the reviewers usually manifesting themselves in the assessments. Reviews nonetheless were frequently balanced and perceptive, for men like Ripley, Dana, and Dwight—who wrote most of them—were well educated, high-minded, and as well informed about native and foreign literary matters as anyone in the country. The treatment of Hawthorne and Emerson, for instance, is representative.[14]

The only work of former Brook Farmer Nathaniel Hawthorne to appear while *The Harbinger* was published at the community was *Mosses from an Old Manse* (1846), which collected seventeen tales and sketches, including "The Birthmark," "Young Goodman Brown," and "The Celestial Railroad," the last a satire on Transcendentalism. (Hawthorne saved the satiric barbs that he would hurl at Brook Farm for his 1852 novel, *The Blithedale Romance*.) William Henry Channing provided the review for the third volume, and it turned out to be one of the most perceptive ever to appear in the Associationist paper. Four years before Herman Melville's adulatory review of "Hawthorne and His Mosses" in *The Literary World* (August 17 and 24, 1850), in which he discussed Hawthorne's "great power of blackness," Channing recognized that, more than any other contemporary American writer, the Salem-born author "had been baptized in the deep waters of *Tragedy*." That was why the light on his pages was always a "serene brightness," Channing said, the kind that seldom cheered because it was never clear or brilliant. It was like "dusky twi-light." It resembled the light of evening deepening into night, or the light of noontime obliquely piercing through the heavy shadows of the forest.

In Hawthorne's fiction, Channing noted, sadness was never occasional or transient: it was found in every page. Yet despite the gloom, Hawthorne never allowed his tragic awareness to overcome him. He was neither morbid nor extravagant, Channing remarked, for one of the exceptional things about the writer was the fact that, given his ability to penetrate appearances and detect frightening realities, he had not allowed his awareness of life's superficialities to degenerate into cynicism. "He has been endowed with a truly awful power of insight," Channing concluded his review. "No masks deceive him. And most plainly, the mockeries of life have cost him sleep-less nights and lonely days."[15]

Whatever resentment the Brook Farmers harbored for Waldo Emerson because of his refusal to support the new paper (or the Association, for that matter) didn't find its way into the pages of *The Harbinger*. For the second volume, New York Associationist William Wetmore Story provided an extended summary of Emerson's course of lectures on "Representative Men" given at the Boston Lyceum; Charles Dana reviewed *Professor [George] Bush's Reply to Ralph Waldo Emerson on Swedenborg* (1846) two months later for the same volume; and John Dwight devoted several columns of remarks to the publication of Emerson's *Poems* (1846) for the fourth volume.[16]

Dana and Dwight, however, didn't let the opportunity pass without taking a swipe at Emerson in their reviews, Dana noting in his that "we desired to see the primary errors of Mr. Emerson's speculative thinking called into court [by Professor Bush] and convicted," and Dwight remarking that the poems of the author of "Self-Reliance" "yield no warmth . . . they shine aloft, serene, august, resplendent like

Orion on a frosty night, and like him cold and distant; they counsel loneliness, and call that true life." Dana acknowledged nonetheless that Dr. Bush's failure to point out the errors of Emerson's thinking was hardly the professor's fault. "He [Professor Bush] might perhaps as well have grasped at the Aurora Borealis as to have attempted with the uninitiated understanding to apprehend the nimble ideas of that gentleman's [Emerson's] beautiful and poetic rhetoric." Dwight, too, had to acknowledge—his criticisms of individual poems notwith-standing—that "it cannot be denied that Mr. Emerson is a consummate artist in expression," and that "what he writes emanates from fresh depths that lie below the surface of life; it is living waters; it has the miraculous charm."

William Wetmore Story had earlier established *The Harbinger*'s tone toward Emerson when he stated in his own review that, say what one would about any of the individual lectures in the "Representative Men" series, "one thing is certain, that a man stands behind his [Emerson's] words, and that he is never idle in his speech, but sincere and strong." Story thought that all the lectures in the course "abounded in fine analysis and vigorous thought. They were characterized by more definiteness and purpose than any previous course we have ever heard from Mr. Emerson, and were more clear and concise in their language."

It turned out to be the "Musical Review" column, however, that immediately distinguished *The Harbinger* from all other journals and papers of the day—as it continues to distinguish the Associationist weekly even today. At a time when musical matters were rarely even mentioned, much less discussed, in contemporary American journals and newspapers, *The Harbinger* featured a regular music column in its pages nearly every week. John Sullivan Dwight managed it almost single-handedly during the two-and-a-half years that the paper was published at Brook Farm. He wrote eighteen of the twenty columns for Volume 1; fifteen of twenty for Volume 2; and seventeen of eighteen for Volume 3. For the fourth and fifth volumes, he contributed all the material in the column, which amounted to more than forty items. The column was expanded somewhat after the paper's transfer to New York City in November 1847 to include articles on art and theater.

When *The Harbinger* was launched in June 1845, Dwight noted in the first number that there had been in America "no composers; no great performances in our churches; no well-endowed and thorough academies to train the artist, or to educate the public taste by frequent hearings of the finest compositions, except in a very limited degree." By the time of the paper's demise in February 1849, Dwight had written a total of 110 essays, critiques, and reviews on subjects ranging from Beethoven to Leopold de Meyer, from the Boston Philharmonic Society to the New York Philharmonic Society, from the "traditional" school of music to the "new" virtuoso school, and from Italian opera in New England and New York to the music teachers' conventions in Boston. If anyone raised the American public's awareness of music in the 1840s, it was Brook Farmer John Sullivan Dwight.

Not that *The Harbinger*'s circulation was ever very extensive. Just one month after the paper was launched at Brook Farm, Ripley happily reported in the number for July 12, 1845, that "we have now a circulation of over one thousand, and new names coming in every day." Ripley's optimism was premature because the subscription rolls to *The Harbinger* never significantly exceeded this number—if they even reached it in the first place—but the Associationist weekly managed nonetheless to become widely respected by its journalistic competitors, at least during the time it was published at the West Roxbury community. Even the usually acidulous Edgar Allan Poe had a good word for the paper.

Poe himself was noticed twice in *The Harbinger*. Charles Dana reviewed *Tales* for the July 15, 1845 number of the paper, and John Dwight reviewed *The Raven and Other Poems* on December 6, 1845, so both men would have been aware of Poe's earlier and ongoing literary battles and the *ad hominem* attacks on his fiction and verse. Neither Dana nor Dwight, however, make any reference to Poe's troubled literary life.[17] Dana criticized his tales for their generally melodramatic quality, and he also thought that they were "clumsily contrived, unnatural, and every way in bad taste." The Brook Farmer recognized nonetheless that "a peculiar order of genius is apparent" in the tales, although their power, he thought, derived from "disease" rather than "health": the tales "are like the vagaries of an opium eater," he said.

Likewise, Dwight, too, acknowledged that Poe's poems "have a great deal of power, a great deal of beauty (of thought frequently, and always of rhythm and diction), originality and dramatic effect." There was, however, "a wild unearthliness, and unheavenliness, in the tone of all his pictures, a strange unreality in all his thoughts," which of course was precisely the atmosphere—though Dwight wouldn't have understood why—that Poe was anxious to create in his poetry especially. Dwight, however, did praise the poem that "has won the author some renown." He thought that "The Raven" expressed the "true grief of a lover"; it was marked by the "power of strange, sad melody, which there is no resisting. So there is in all his poems." But Poe's verse ultimately repelled the reader, Dwight had to conclude, because of his "morbid egotism": Edgar Poe did not write for humanity.

Poe evidently respected Dana and Dwight's critical assessments, for just one week after the latter's review he had occasion to remark in the *Broadway Journal* for December 13, 1845, that "'The Harbinger,' edited by 'The Brook Farm Phalanx,' is, beyond doubt, the most reputable organ of the Crazyites. We sincerely respect it—odd as this assertion may appear. It is conducted by an assemblage of well-read persons who mean no harm—and who, perhaps, can do less. Their objects are honorable and so forth—all that anybody can understand of them." Poe took another playful swipe at the Brook Farmers at the end of his column when he said that he hoped in the future that "'The Snook-Farm Phalanx' will never have any opinion of us at all."[18]

These brief remarks constitute high praise coming from Edgar Allan Poe, and he wasn't alone in his regard for the Associationist paper. Despite *The Harbinger*'s particular ideological bent, *Hunt's Merchants' Magazine,* a popular New York City weekly, thought that it was "one of the most ably conducted and most readable weekly journals that comes to our office."[19] The Boston *Atlas,* a daily newspaper, stated that while it could not "sympathize with the tenets of its conductors," it could not "but admire the kind and catholic spirit of brotherly love with which this journal is, for the most part, conducted." The *National Era,* an antislavery paper published in Washington, D.C., observed that *The Harbinger* was "an able periodical, liberal in tone, courteous in the style of its discussions, and comprehensive in its views." *Nineteenth Century,* a Philadelphia magazine, remarked that the Associationist paper was "distinguished by its critical character, its elevated and serious tone, and its deep faith in the future perfection of the race." The Chicago *Daily Tribune* said that it spoke with confidence when it stated that "there is not a single newspaper in the Union which maintains so high a standard of literary taste." And the Cincinnati *Herald* noted that "there is no periodical which we read with more pleasure or profit, and none to which we recommend the subscription of our readers with more satisfaction than the Harbinger."

None of this support had anything to do with Brook Farm itself, however, because the community was rarely referred to in the pages of the Associationist paper. George Ripley and Charles Dana's unwillingness to feature Brook Farm in *The Harbinger* ("We are the humblest of pioneers in the mightiest of works," Ripley would say) represents, in fact, yet another serious failure of understanding by the community's leaders, for what was always lacking in the American Associationist movement—as Ripley and Dana were particularly aware months before *The Harbinger* was launched—was what Ripley himself characterized as a "centre of influence."[20] Brook Farm might easily have managed to become that "centre" after the paper was established at the Farm, even without the support of New York Associationists, which had always been unreliable anyway. Considering how anxious the Brook Farmers were to have the West Roxbury Association designated the "Model Phalanx" in the national reform movement, it's obviously ironic that Ripley and Dana didn't take advantage of such a perfect opportunity to showcase Brook Farm in *The Harbinger*. It is referred to just six times in the two-and-a-half years that the paper was under Ripley's editorial control.[21]

Had he and Dana assumed a more active leadership role for Brook Farm in the national Fourierist movement, who's to say that Associationists around the country wouldn't have embraced the community by providing a measure of financial support?[22] But after the adoption of Fourierism at the West Roxbury community in January 1844, it seems never to have occurred to Ripley or Dana or any of the other Brook Farmers that the Association might have fared far better standing on its own two legs rather than allowing itself instead to be piggybacked on the narrow shoulders of men like Albert Brisbane, Parke Godwin, Horace Greeley, and the New York Associationists.

There was certainly plenty of interest in Brook Farm among *The Harbinger*'s readers. A letter printed in the number for August 30, 1845, is representative. A correspondent from Newport, Rhode Island, asked: "Could you not give in the Harbinger an account of your mode of living at Brook Farm, your occupations, relations together, results and experiences?"[23] The letter's insertion in the paper, however, was only to provide the opportunity for Ripley to remind readers that "we are more anxious to discuss principles, than to exhibit results." But interest in Brook Farm remained high, and on December 20, 1845, Ripley reassured *The Harbinger*'s readers that life in the West Roxbury Association was about as good as it generally gets. Uncharacteristically, he spoke quite feelingly about the community:

> The life, which we now lead, though, to a hasty and superficial observer, surrounded with so great imperfections and embarrassments, is far superior to what we have ever been able to attain under the most favorable circumstances in Civilization. There is a freedom from the frivolities of fashion, from arbitrary restrictions, and from the frenzy of competition; we meet our fellow men in more sincere, hearty, and genial relations; kindred spirits are not separated by artificial, conventional barriers; there is more personal independence, and a wider sphere for its exercise; the soul is warmed in the sunshine of a true social equality; we are not brought into the rough and disgusting contact with uncongenial persons, which is such a genuine source of misery in the common intercourse of society; there is a greater variety of employment, a more constant demand for the exertion of all the faculties, and a more exquisite pleasure in effort, from the consciousness that we are laboring not for personal ends, but for a holy principle.

Before turning his attention to more general matters having to do with the Associative movement nationally, Ripley summarized his personal observations about Brook Farm life: "We are conscious of happiness which we never knew, until we embarked in this career."[24] These are truly remarkable statements by George Ripley in light of the fact that they were made at the very moment that Brook Farm was being battered by a series of crises, the likes of which had never before been experienced in the community. Mary Ann Dwight's assessment of the situation in the Association was quite a bit different from Ripley's. Less than two weeks before his glowing words appeared in *The Harbinger,* Dwight confided to her friend Anna Parsons that the Brook Farmers had reached their "severest crisis."

10

"Our Severest Crisis"

In a letter to Anna Q. T. Parsons on September 28, 1845, Mary Ann Dwight confided to her good friend that "we have had lately a shaking up, as it were, a little sifting out. Some deep and important questions have been agitated. Some [Brook Farm associates] will leave who ought to leave. The selfish should go—they who are not devoted, who cannot give their all." That the trouble to which Dwight refers was even more serious than her remarks suggest is clear from Parsons' reply. After a page and a half of gossipy chitchat in her response dated October 18, 1845, Parsons abruptly asks: "Has anything occurred with you to give rise to the report 'that B[rook] F[arm] has failed'[?]—Have any of the disaffected left?"[1] Whether Brook Farm's internal problems early that autumn were due to the unwillingness of certain associates to contribute their fair share of work to the Association—as Dwight's statements seem to indicate—there's no question that William Henry Channing's presence at Brook Farm in September and October 1845 only served to further inflame the embers of discontent that had been smouldering for some time in the West Roxbury community.[2]

Channing spent a good deal of time at Brook Farm that autumn because he was substituting for Theodore Parker at the latter's Spring Street Church in West Roxbury. After finishing up there each week, he would walk over to the Farm and encourage the Brook Farmers to establish regular Sunday religious services in the community. He even embellished his appeal to them with a "sketch of a temple of worship to be raised here on Brook Farm, as he saw it in his mind's eye . . . There stands that holy temple . . . of circular form, lighted from above, with its pictures of the infant Jesus, of the crucifixion, and the resurrection—with its white marble altar."[3] His efforts were rewarded on October 12 when twenty or so associates, including John S. Dwight, Sophia Ripley, Nathaniel Munday, Fanny Macdaniel, and Mary Ann Dwight, removed themselves from the regular Sunday meeting and followed the charismatic Channing into a separate parlor of the Eyrie in order to prepare for the "religious movement now taking place here."

Mary Ann Dwight was quite surprised that more Brook Farmers didn't follow (including her future husband, John Orvis), and she protested to Anna Parsons that "we want no other exclusiveness than this—to protect ourselves, if we can, against the presence of those who would come only to scoff and ridicule." Just who those persons were Dwight doesn't indicate. She did recognize, however, that "it seemed many people didn't like the withdrawal from the Eyrie parlor."[4]

Most of the Fourierist Phalanxes, Carl Guarneri has noted in his magisterial study of the Fourierist movement in America, guaranteed religious freedom and promised "perfect religious tolerance" in their constitutions.[5] Brook Farm was no exception, so it's no wonder that some members of the community were upset about Channing's revivalist efforts at the Farm. Long before the conversion to Fourierism, the Association's original "Articles of Agreement" included an Article that stated: "No religious test shall ever be required of any member of the Association; no authority assumed over individual freedom of opinion by the Association, nor by one member over another." This statement was repeated verbatim when the first constitution was drafted in January 1844, although, interestingly enough, it was deleted when the constitution was revised in May 1845 upon the occasion of the Association's formal conversion to a Fourierist Phalanx. No matter what the period of the community's existence, however, Brook Farmers would have identified themselves almost to a person with some form of Protestantism, a good many—including George Ripley, Charles Dana, and John S. Dwight—Unitarian in their basic beliefs. There were exceptions, of course. Jean and Eliza Palisse were Catholic, the Macdaniel women were Swedenborgians, and Alfred Peppercorn, Brook Farm's butcher, was, according to one recent arrival, "more like an infidel than any other man I ever saw."

That religious worship at Brook Farm had always been very informal was particularly noted, for instance, by a visitor to the Association back in July 1842, who told his brother that "[John S.] Dwight hoes corn Sundays. Some sail, some walk, some hear [Theodore] Parker preach." Sophia Eastman, writing to her family one year later in July 1843, made this memorable observation: "I regret to say that many have no [religious] principles at all. But very few attend church on the Sabbath, and it is a fact they do knit and sew." Another member of the community, who spent nearly two years at the Farm in 1843 and 1844, recalled later that "we [the Brook Farmers] paid no special attention to [religion]. Nearly every Sunday we met to listen to the reading of Swedenborg's writings; but many different sects were represented among us. Sunday was in general a day of recreation and enjoyment." And S. Willard Saxton, a young printer who moved to the community in April 1845, remarked afterward that "in religious matters there was the greatest freedom of thought."[6]

Channing's instigation of a religious revival at Brook Farm reached a climax on October 19 when he enlisted the support of George Ripley, John Allen, John Orvis, Peter Kleinstrup, and a few other associates in addition to the twenty or so who responded so quickly to his first appeal the week before. Even neighbors like Frank Shaw and Josiah Wolcott joined a committee to determine what kind of religious services would be most suitable for the community. Some wanted quiet prayer, others preferred only music, and still others readings from the scriptures. Three things, however, were clear: several of Brook Farm's leading members agreed with Channing that "without the religious element no attempt at association could possibly succeed"; a room on the west side of the nearly completed Phalanstery would be devoted to religious worship; and "Mr. C[hanning] will not be considered as a priest—we do not want a priest." Channing himself agreed to provide "such books [of worship] as we would want,—Mr. [James Freeman] Clarke's and the Swedenborgian ritual or book of worship." Mary Ann Dwight told Anna Parsons that "at the first service we desire to have only our group (I don't use the word technically) present,—that is, only the *interested,*—the sincere worshippers." "Most carefully will we guard against sectarianism," Dwight assured Parsons, "against dead forms."[7]

While the Brook Farmers were devoting their attention to the community's spiritual well-being, however, they failed to protect themselves against something even more potentially disruptive to the Association's welfare than weekly religious services. While William Henry Channing was admonishing Brook Farm's faithful, John Allen's son Fred was visiting his aunt in Boston where he came in contact "with Mr. Milton Clark, the fugitive slave—who boarded there" and who passed along an infection to the young boy. Both Allens returned to the community right after the visit, unaware for more than a week that Fred's nagging cough and congestion weren't from a cold at all: he had contracted smallpox. "Every body [at Brook Farm] was exposed before we knew what ailed him," John Allen noted afterward.

"Many had never been vacinated." "Our carelessness," Mary Ann Dwight ruefully acknowledged on November 23, 1845, "has been very blamable."

The height of the contagion occurred between November 9 and 23. At first, the Allens were quarantined alone in the Cottage under the watchful eye of Rebecca Codman (the younger), whom Allen thought was "a heroine—a sister of charity . . . a most sublimely affectionate and devoted spirit." Then new cases started erupting every day. As the smallpox spread, about thirty associates—nearly one-third of the community—had to be confined to the crowded rooms of the Cottage, which was "turned inside out" to isolate those with serious symptoms from the rest of the Association. At the onslaught of the disease, Fred Allen's entire body was "but a complete running sore—there is scarcely a spot of the surface that is not filled with the virus."[8]

As it turned out, he was not the most seriously afflicted. The three most severe cases were contracted by Louis and Jane Ryckman's son, James; a new arrival at Brook Farm named George Lloyd; and Jean Palisse's wife, Eliza. Mrs. Palisse, according to Mary Ann Dwight, was "so changed, people who see her say you would not know her to be a human being."[9] Other residents in the community who had to spend time at the Cottage in November were Nathaniel Munday, a tailor; several of Brook Farm's students, including Kate Sloan, Alfred Perkins, and Henry Atwood; and Ephraim Capen, head of the community's Britannia-ware industry. James Kay's son, Allie, Lucas and Jose Corrales, and Charles King Newcomb all managed to escape the disease. So did all the members of the Ripley, Dana, and Dwight families.

One indication of just how fragile relations between associates had become is Mary Ann Dwight's surprisingly heated and protracted disagreement with George Ripley in November over the outbreak of the disease. At the beginning of its spread, Dwight was quick to charge her fellow associates with hysteria because she thought that they were

The "Cottage." The Cottage provided living quarters, classrooms, and, when smallpox struck the community, a place to quarantine the sick. It survived until 1985, when it was destroyed by fire.

mistakenly attributing every headache and sniffle to smallpox. "It's the greatest absurdity in the world," she wrote to Anna Parsons on Sunday, November 9, 1845, which was the very same day that she first snapped at Ripley because he had urged her sister Fanny to isolate herself in the Cottage. Ripley did so because Fanny Macdaniel "gave it as her opinion that Fanny [Dwight] had the disease." Mary Ann told Ripley that her sister merely had "one of her old colds," and so his appeals for her isolation were "ridiculous, nonsensical, and unreasonable." Besides, Fanny Macdaniel knew nothing about smallpox, and

Dwight would not jeopardize her sister's health by having her moved to the Cottage. Ripley said that if Fanny wouldn't go to the Cottage, then both she and Dwight ought at least to seclude themselves in their room at the Pilgrim House. Dwight thought that "this was equally ridiculous and absurd, [and I] told him that to allay the panic of the people I would stay up for meals and not go among folks." Apparently the disagreement didn't end here, though, because Dwight boasted to Parsons later in the letter: "Oh! I said worse and harder things still to Mr. Ripley."

Dwight refused to stay in her room for meals, as it turned out. Her insubordination carried over to the next day when she appeared at the Hive for dinner. "Mr. and Mrs. Ripley looked in consternation," she informed her brother Frank on Monday, November 10, "but not a word has been said to me." Ripley spoke to Dwight right away the next morning, however. She was waiting table at breakfast when Ripley called her aside and asked her again not to endanger the associates. This prompted more sharp words between the two. Ripley appealed to Dwight not to wait table at all, and not to come to the dining room either. But Dwight was as adamant as before: "I told him it was of no use . . . I told him I'd say no more, I would not waste words with him and walked off."[10] Women at Brook Farm during the earlier days of its existence—Georgiana Bruce, Anna Alvord, Almira Barlow, for instance—would have found such behavior inconceivable.

By the end of November, and with no new cases of smallpox for more than a week, John Allen was able to step back and assess some of the losses caused by the spread of the disease: "It broke up our school, damaged our industry—and frighted away for the time being, the timid members. In a pecuniary point of view it could not be less than two or three thousand dollars, that this sickness has injured us."[11] A discouraged Mary Ann Dwight told Anna Parsons on November 23 that "we have fallen upon the critical time." It was also clear

now that the long-awaited Phalanstery would not be finished that winter. "How we need capital!" she complained to Parsons. What Dwight
didn't tell Parsons is that money was so tight that a yoke of oxen from
among the Farm's few remaining animals had to be sold that month
(for $100), and that there were not even enough funds available for the
Brook Farmers to enjoy a traditional Thanksgiving dinner. Fortunately, Amelia Russell recalled afterward, the situation at the Farm "in
some way came to the ears of two of our neighbors [almost certainly
Frank Shaw and George Russell], who supplied us with the turkeys,
etc., necessary. We had never before, not even in the days when we
gave up coffee, been so low in our exchequer."[12]

As if the community's internal difficulties weren't troubling enough in
late November 1845, there were pressing external developments as
well. George Ripley was notified in late November or early December
1845 that Nathaniel Hawthorne had filed a lawsuit against both him
and Charles Dana seeking to recover the $524.05 on the promissory
note that the two Brook Farmers had co-signed way back on October
7, 1842, which was originally to have been paid in full thirty days later.
Hawthorne wrote to George Hillard, Esq., on September 6, 1845, asking his friend to "proceed with the matter, as promptly and forcibly as
possible." Hawthorne had "dunned" Ripley on several different occasions, but to no avail. "The time is come when the note [Ripley and
Dana's] must positively be held."[13]

Ripley didn't deny Hawthorne's claim. He wrote on December 8,
1845, to his wife Sophia's first cousin Richard Henry Dana, Jr., seeking advice, unaware that Hawthorne's lawsuit was already being heard
in a Cambridge courtroom that very same day. Ripley acknowledged
right away in his letter that "we do not dispute the debt," and he
noted that "there are [other] claims of this kind against us . . . to the
amount of 8 or 900 dollars."[14] Ripley claimed that "we have made ev-

ery exertion in our power to meet [Hawthorne's] demand," but his real concern now was whether he and Charles Dana—who was not related to the Boston lawyer—could legally be held liable for the debt. Since the act of incorporation the previous March 1845, "the Phalanx assumes all the indebtedness which we had incurred on account of the Association. Mr. Hawthorne's claim comes under this class; that is, he claims of us; and we of the Phalanx, to be made good."

Ripley also wanted the Boston lawyer to know that Hawthorne had voluntarily advanced the money in question "towards building one of our houses, which was undertaken and planned with a view to his living in it himself." After Hawthorne withdrew from the community in 1841, he exchanged some of his stock for the promissory note in October 1842, which Ripley and Dana co-signed "in our private capacity." Since neither Ripley nor Dana had any real personal property themselves, Hawthorne would be better advised, Ripley naturally thought, to transfer his claim against him and Dana to the community: "If Mr. Hawthorne would sue the Phalanx, we should prefer it, and in that case he might get hold of some property." Hawthorne, in fact, would "get hold" of nothing, even though the court later awarded him $560.62, plus costs of $25.28, for a total judgment of $585.90.[15]

Confidence in Ripley and Dana's ability to continue to lead Brook Farm was at an all-time low in early December 1845. Several associates even initiated "enquiry meetings" into the administration of the Phalanx, prompting Mary Ann Dwight to note solemnly in a December 7 letter to Anna Parsons that "it must be a sad state of things that calls for such measures." Dwight recognized, however, why associates were "ready to give up if matters cannot be otherwise managed, for they have no hope of success here under the past and present government. All important matters have been done up in council of one or two or three individuals, and everybody else is kept in the dark." One serious problem, Dwight recognized, was that "we have not had business men to conduct our affairs." Another was that the community continued to be "perplexed by debts, by want of capital to carry on any business to advantage." That was why the Phalanstery, the construction of which had begun during the summer of 1844, remained unfinished that winter. No wonder Dwight gloomily told Parsons: "We have reached . . . our severest crisis."

Two days after this grim pronouncement, on December 9, 1845, George Ripley received a letter from Albert Brisbane indicating that the Brook Farmers should not expect any financial assistance from New York Associationists because they were shifting their support to the North American Phalanx in Red Bank, New Jersey. Ripley had written twice to Brisbane just a few days before—on December 3, and again on December 5—appealing for relief in the aftermath of the crisis caused by the outbreak of smallpox. He told the New Yorker that $15,000 would enable the Brook Farmers to pay off some of their more urgent debts (it's not known whether Ripley included Hawthorne in this category), and would relieve some of the severe financial pressure on the community. (Dwight also told Parsons in her December 7 letter that "we must have $10,000 at least, before spring, or we may as well die.")

Brisbane acknowledged Ripley's "views upon the necessity of developing Brook Farm," but he quickly noted that his fellow New Yorkers thought that "you had made up your mind to bring things to a close [at Brook Farm]." Charles Dana, after all, had said as much just a month before when he wrote describing the difficulties brought on by the outbreak of smallpox in the Phalanx. The New Yorkers also "feared that [Ichabod] Morton might be foreclosing his mortgage."[16] Undoubtedly the most discouraging part of Brisbane's letter, however, was his announcement that the "the New Yorkers who have any money, [Horace] G[reeley], [Edmund] T[weedy], [Marcus] S[pring], etc., are all interested in and pledged to raise ten thousand dollars for the North American Phalanx to pay off its mortgage." As for Ripley's appeal for $15,000, "you might as well undertake to raise dead men," Brisbane said, "as to attain any considerable amount of capital from the people here." What a difference just one year had made. On December 14, 1844, it will be recalled, Mary Ann Dwight happily reported to Anna Parsons that New York Associationists were "beginning to see the need of concentrating their efforts on some one undertaking, and it is to Brook Farm that they look."

George Ripley certainly didn't need any more bad news in December 1845, but, like the creditors showing up at the front door of the Hive, it came anyway. After his good friend William Henry Channing's religious exertions had to be postponed when smallpox struck the community, Channing, already exhausted before his arrival at Brook Farm in October from his numerous religious and reformist activities, had something of a mental breakdown in December. "Indeed the anxieties and mental sufferings which I underwent with and for you [the Brook Farmers] was the cause perhaps, as much as all else, of my breaking down," the former Unitarian minister told John Dwight.[17] Channing would not be able to return to Brook Farm until late February 1846. He would confine himself to his home in Brattleboro, Vermont.

The discouraging news from Channing came on the heels of a disappointing letter from another of Ripley's cherished friends, Theodore Parker. Parker wrote that December to say that he was thinking about transferring the responsibility for the education of his ward George Colburn, who had been a student at the Brook Farm school almost from the beginning, from the Association to a nearby district school. He didn't say what prompted the idea, but it was probably suggested by Parker's wife, Lydia, who was Colburn's aunt, understandably reacting to the scare of smallpox in the community. Whatever the reason, Ripley must have felt personally wounded, even betrayed, by his good friend Parker's proposal.[18]

Smallpox, lawsuits, unrelieved financial pressures, dissatisfaction and discontent inside the community, disappointment and disaffection among supporters outside the community—no wonder Mary Ann Dwight characterized the turn of events that autumn and early winter of 1845 as "our severest crisis."[19] She herself managed to recover her spirit and determination, however, just a few days after when all the members of the Association gathered at the Hive on Wednesday evening, December 10. Everyone was "firm" and "*full of confidence* that we *shall* and *will*" eventually succeed at Brook Farm, she wrote to Anna Parsons after the meeting. "We are not dead here, but live—our hearts are firm and true, our courage good, and our hands ready for action." It must have been this December 10 meeting, too, that inspired George Ripley's surprising effusions about Brook Farm in the December 20 number of *The Harbinger* (noted in Chapter 9), which he concluded with this statement: "We are conscious of happiness [at Brook Farm] which we never knew, until we embarked in this career."[20] Mary Ann Dwight, in any case, obviously couldn't know that the full import of her words about the Brook Farmers' resolve and mettle would be tested right away, for what would truly prove to be the community's "severest crisis" was about to take place.

11

Fire

The night of Tuesday, March 3, 1846, was one of those brilliant evenings that often occur during winter months in New England. There was little to no wind, the air was crisp and distinct, and the sky was perfectly clear. Even though the moon would not be full until the 12th of the month, the immense canopy of stars overhead cast the snow-covered meadows and pastures that surrounded Brook Farm in a bright blue light. Earlier in the day a fire had been kindled in a stove in the basement of the Phalanstery to warm the corps of carpenters who were about to resume their labors on the much-anticipated "unitary dwelling" that would soon enable all the members of the community to live together under one roof. The first report of fire came in the evening around 8:45. Less than two hours later, all that was left of the nearly completed Phalanstery were charred bricks and Roxbury pudding stone from the building's foundation, and a smouldering heap of ashes.

Construction of the Phalanstery had been ongoing since the summer of 1844. Its anticipated completion in the summer or autumn of 1846 would have climaxed an ambitious—if not financially prudent—building program that had first begun in 1842 with the Eyrie. The importance ascribed to the Phalanstery in the community's future operations was symbolized by the decision to situate the building in the center of the Phalanx. It was located about one hundred yards just below the Eyrie on a large terrace that provided "a most extensive and picturesque view" of the Farm. The Phalanstery was to have been the hub of a wheel, the top spokes of which—moving from left to right—would be the Pilgrim House, the Cottage, the Eyrie, the Workshop, and the Hive.

The 175′ × 40′ building was three stories high, including a very large basement. The basement, as George Ripley described it in *The Harbinger* right after the fire, "contained a large and commodious kitchen, a dining-hall capable of seating from three to four hundred persons, two public saloons, and a spacious hall or lecture room."[1] The second and third stories were divided into nearly one hundred small rooms, the most attractive of which were fourteen suites of apartments, each suite consisting of three bedrooms that opened onto a common parlor. It was hoped that by the first of October 1846, "the edifice would be prepared for the reception of a hundred and fifty persons, with ample accommodations for families." This would enable the one hundred or so people now in the community to live together in a single building, much like bees in a hive. A portion of the second floor had already been set aside for a chapel, which was to have been finished later by private subscription, and in which William Henry Channing was looking forward to conducting regular religious services. Seven thousand dollars had already been invested in the construction of the building for labor, lumber, horse and steam power, drilling a well, hardware, lathing, shingles, and other materials.

Just an hour or so before the fire started to spread, many associates were gathered at the Hive for a "social dance" to celebrate the renewal of work on the Phalanstery. George Ripley himself had not yet arrived for the festivities because, ironically, he was at a council meeting at the Eyrie helping to appoint a committee to superintend the completion of the new building. Charles Salisbury, a trunkmaker turned farmer after arriving at Brook Farm in early 1844, was the first to discover the fire. The twenty-seven-year-old Salisbury, who was the nightwatch that evening, thought at first that the faint light emanating from the second floor of the Phalanstery was from a lamp, but upon entering the building he immediately smelled smoke and realized at once that it was on fire. "From a defect in the construction of the chimney," Ripley reported in *The Harbinger*, "a spark from the stove pipe had probably communicated with the surrounding wood work." The Brook Farmers themselves, as well as their neighbors both near and far away, were immediately on the scene.

Neighbors in nearby West Roxbury arrived right away with their fire engine, "which together with the Engines from Jamaica Plain, Newton, and Brookline, rendered valuable assistance in subduing the flaming ruins." Engines from nearby Dedham, and even from Boston, also made an effort to reach the Farm, but the Dedham engine had to turn back because the recent heavy snows covering the roads had not yet melted enough for the equipment to get through. The Boston engines turned around when it became obvious that they would be too late to provide any help.

Because the Phalanstery was constructed nearly entirely of wood, "the fire spread with almost incredible rapidity throughout the building; and in about an hour and a half the whole edifice was burned to the ground." The Eyrie was also in immediate danger of catching fire, and it too would likely have been destroyed were it not for the "vigorous exertions" of neighbors Thomas Orange and Thomas and George Palmer, whose farms were adjacent to the community. Because the Phalanstery was not yet in use by the Association, "no insurance had been effected." The only things that could be salvaged were "a couple of tool-chests" and a few dollars worth of unused lumber.

By the time that the fire was completely extinguished, more than two hundred people—including the Brook Farmers themselves—were on the scene. Everyone was invited to the Hive, where Peter Baldwin served freshly baked bread that he had just taken from the ovens, intended for the community the following morning. Marianne Ripley brewed coffee for the fatigued and hungry crowd, and Thomas Orange supplied provisions from his own home and bottles of milk that were contributed by Brook Farm's neighbors. George Ripley, ever poised and courageous, mounted one of the dining-room benches and told those assembled that he was glad to give them whatever poor hospitality the Brook Farmers could provide. "But had we known, or even suspected you were coming," he said, as he struggled to relieve the foreboding sense of gloom, "we would have been better prepared to receive you, and given you a worthier, if not a *warmer* reception." The firemen immediately cried out, "Good enough, good enough."[2]

Ripley had to brave the fire without his most devoted associate, Charles Dana, who was away from the Farm on the evening of the disaster. When Albert Brisbane returned to New York City in mid-January 1846 after a brief stay in the community, Eunice Macdaniel had gone with him. A few weeks later, Dana joined Eunice in New York, where, unbeknownst to any of the Brook Farmers, they were secretly married on March 2, the day before the Phalanstery fire. Dana told John Dwight shortly afterward that the wedding "was entirely unexpected to me."[3] Whether Dana was just being cagey because the wedding had really been planned all along isn't known.

Dana returned to the Farm immediately after the fire, and Eunice followed him a week later. Although the marriage took the Brook Farmers by surprise—including a bemused George Ripley—a party to publically announce the union was scheduled for March 19 at the Hive. That morning Ripley wrote to John Dwight, who was in New York City delivering a series of lectures on music in an effort to drum up support among Associationists there. Brook Farm's leader told his younger friend that the marriage "calls forth some amusement" in the

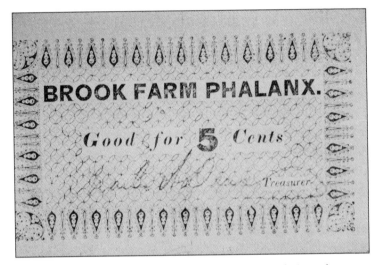

Brook Farm currency. Brook Farm money was printed for internal
community use. Charles Dana's signature appears near the bottom.

community, but that "the people are not altogether well pleased at the
mystery in which it [the marriage] has been kept." Ripley was certain
that "it was an injudicious step, on the part of Charles, I am sure."
Three days later, Mary Ann Dwight notified Anna Parsons that "the
wedding party went off very well," but she also remarked that "about a
dozen of our best people, preferred to stay away." Dwight herself
thought that "the privacy of the wedding, & other circumstances were
unpleasant, or perhaps more than that," but she was glad that Charles
and Eunice had decided to make the marriage public, so she concluded that it "was best to go [to the party], and in kindness and justice make it as agreeable as we could."[4]

By prior arrangement with Albert Brisbane, John Dwight had left
for New York City just a day or two after the fire to deliver his music

lectures. Oddly enough, it turned out to be a rare stroke of good timing (Mary Ann Dwight thought it "one of those providential things"),
for the lecture series gave the Brook Farmer the opportunity to appeal
to prominent New York Associationists for some desperately needed
financial relief following the loss of the Phalanstery. Dwight, however,
was very disappointed by the financial results of the lectures themselves. The problem wasn't lack of public interest. The first of the
four talks attracted about 120 people, and the "audience doubled on
the second night." But owing to the "great expenses of hall and adver-
tising," he told his sister right before returning to the community at
the end of March, "I shall hardly realize over one hundred dollars instead of two."[5]

Dwight was considerably more pleased by the support of the New
York "friends." Horace Greeley, in whose New York *Tribune* Dwight
received enthusiastic notices of his lectures, took a piece of paper and
wrote on it: "I give up all *my* stock *unconditionally,* & will subscribe
besides the first $100 I get which does not belong to some one else."
Several other local friends were also supportive. Marcus Spring gave
up whatever stock he held and promised an additional pledge as soon
as the Brook Farmers determined their future course of action. "Mr
Hicks relinquishes *his* stock—Mr [William?] Manning gives his to
[William Henry] Channing to dispose of as he pleases—Mr Hunt is
willing to do anything—& Mr [George?] Benson of his own accord
said that some effort must be made in New York to help out the subscription in Boston." "You may consider *the whole of the stock held
in New York,*" Dwight happily reported to Ripley, "as cancelled."[6]
Dwight didn't refer to either Albert Brisbane or Parke Godwin among
the forgiving New York subscribers—which is not surprising because
neither man ever supported the community. When it came to providing advice to the Brook Farmers, the two New Yorkers were always ex-

tremely generous. But when it came to putting their money where their proverbial mouths were, neither man could manage to remove his hands from his pockets.[7]

While Dwight was appealing to the "friends" in New York City, the Brook Farmers were preparing to do the same in Boston. "We are pretty much agreed to call together the creditors & holders of loan stock," Dana wrote to Dwight from the Farm on March 15—the day before Dwight sent off the letter to Ripley describing the fruits of his labors. "If they [creditors and stockholders] will do nothing to diminish the weight of interest we now have to pay," Dana said, "we shall have to go through bankruptcy in which case they will get nothing at all, while if they will relax somewhat of their demands their claims will be worth something at least."[8]

Appealing to their numerous creditors for financial relief, however, was one of the few things about which the Brook Farmers could generally agree in the weeks following the Phalanstery fire. March 1846 turned out to be one of the most unsettling months that the community ever experienced. The members of the General Council met privately nearly every evening immediately after the fire to discuss different plans of action. Should the property be given up altogether? Should the mechanical industries be cut back? Which ones, if any, should be retained? Should farming activities be reorganized? What should be the future role of the school in the community? Should associates who weren't earning their keep be asked to leave?

These questions were all related of course to an even more fundamental one having to do with Brook Farm's role in the larger Associative movement, about which there were widely conflicting opinions in the community and elsewhere. If Associationist leaders (not to mention many ordinary adherents as well) in such faraway places as Ohio, New York, and New England had anything in common, it was the generally held conviction that Associationism was a "Providential" movement. It was noted, for example, in *The Harbinger* in the number for August 15, 1846 that "we are convinced, that the Associative movement is a Providential one,—that it fulfills the promises so long unanswered through ages of conflict and suffering; that it opens a new era of justice and peace; that it practically embodies the Christian Law of Love, [and] establishes the liberties and rights of citizens."[9] Some supporters thought that Brook Farm should be the center of that movement. For others, the West Roxbury community was certainly important, but its sacrifice on the Associative altar—if eventually necessary, as it now seemed to many that it would be—would be a regrettable but not an irreplaceable loss.

The majority of the Brook Farmers themselves probably wouldn't have identified with either group. People like William and Mary Ann Cheswell, John Hoxie, Peter and Augustina Kleinstrup, John Cheever, and Jean and Eliza Palisse, for example, were at the community for practical rather than ideological reasons. On the other hand, Mary Ann Dwight, John Orvis, and the members of the Codman family, for instance, would immediately have placed themselves in the first group of those committed to the very end to Brook Farm. To the second group belonged, not surprisingly, New York Associationists such as Albert Brisbane and Parke Godwin but also, more surprisingly, New Englanders William Henry Channing and John Allen. Philadelphian James Kay would have been very sympathetic to the second group, but he still loved the community and its leaders, even though he had just about lost his patience with Ripley and Dana's continual bungling and ineptness in the financial mismanagement of the Association.

Ironically enough, the day before the Phalanstery fire Kay gave vent to his frustration in a no-nonsense letter to John Dwight in which he called a spade a spade instead of an agricultural implement. It was widely known, Kay minced no words, that "you [that is, the Brook

Farmers] have not for a single day paid your way, & have throughout the whole experiment been dependent on . . . the charity of others."[10] Kay had recently been reminded of as much by one of Brook Farm's neighbors (it's hard to imagine that it wouldn't have been either Theodore Parker, Francis G. Shaw, or George Russell) on his most recent visit to the community. Now more than ever it was time to recognize that Brook Farm's chief "business should not primarily be that of realizing Association, so much as that of proving . . . that you are able to pay your own way." Kay urged the following practical measures, which cut directly to the heart of Brook Farm's internal difficulties: the community should be "closed to all [new] applicants"; the administration of the community should be put back into the hands "of the people"; the school should be restored to its original "paramount position"; the "abuses which have made your agriculture an infinite loss" should be reformed; and all associates who could not demonstrate "their ability to support themselves" should be immediately expelled from the community.

Were these steps to be taken, Kay insisted, "then all feuds would cease":

> Then the active supervision of the carpenters over all your interests would commence in a peaceful & productive wielding of the saw, the plane, & the hatchet. *Then* my best friends Mr & Mrs Ripley, Mr Dana & Mr Dwight, forgetting how frequently & strongly they had announced their want of qualification & taste for the arduous & beautiful work of instruction, would discover that it [teaching] was their providential occupation. Then the experienced & the aged would take the place of [the] Jonathan Butterfields & John Orvis' [*sic*] in the management of practical matters. Then, by a divine ne-

> cessity, the indolent would seek other suns in which to
> bask. And then the impure, especially the children, would
> be ejected—no longer defended by the unnatural union of
> Phalansterians and . . . Spiritualists.

This was certainly not the first time, Kay went on, that he had recited his litany of concerns. No doubt aware of Nathaniel Hawthorne's pending lawsuit against Ripley and Dana—and anxious to remind the Brook Farmers that the more than three-year-old debt to Hawthorne was precisely what was wrong with the way the Association was being managed—Kay alluded directly to the title of the former Brook Farmer's popular collection of stories to underscore the extent of his continuing anxiety about the community's future: "This frank & imperfect statement of my views is more than a twice-told tale," the Philadelphia Associationist told Dwight. Kay added that the failure of Brook Farm's leaders to correct the errors of their past ways has "lost you the use & possession of tens of thousands of dollars," as well as a prominence in the larger arena of social reform movements "which would have made you the envy of admiring & opposing multitudes."

In one sense, Kay's letter to Dwight couldn't have been more timely, considering that it arrived just a few days after the fire. For it bluntly addressed the most fundamental and crucial matters that had been squarely facing the Brook Farmers for more than two years—ever since the quiet embrace of Fourierism in January 1844. But what to Kay seemed so perfectly obvious now required extensive and protracted deliberations by the Brook Farmers—notwithstanding Mary Ann Dwight's remark to her brother John in mid-March 1846 that "we incline to his [Kay's] opinions, and find ourselves following his advice." Sophia Ripley, for instance, reported on Saturday, March 14, to the absent John Dwight that the General Council was meeting every night to discuss the viability of the different industries at the Farm and to review their respective accounts. "I think all minds [are] tending towards the decision that it will be best to give up our property," she told Dwight confidentially. One plan was to have the school, *The Harbinger,* and the domestic industry form an "associative center" from which the farm itself would be separated and managed by those who were interested in its operation.

Charles Dana also wrote to Dwight the day after Sophia Ripley did, on Sunday, March 15. Should the Phalanx be forced into bankruptcy, Dana proposed, "we may be able to rent the place at a reasonable rate and continue with a modified organization." Two days after Dana's letter, Mary Ann Dwight followed with one of her own. She told her brother on Tuesday, March 17, that Dana had been arguing in the General Council "that it will be impossible to carry on any mechanical branches or agriculture . . . He would dismiss all but about twenty people, and have only a school and the Harbinger. Miserable!" Dwight herself thought that it was more likely that the sash-and-blind industry would be retained, along with the school, *The Harbinger,* and the farm. She also noted that when Sophia Ripley had written to Dwight just three days before, "the tendency was towards giving up the property. It is now the contrary; we don't mean to give it up if we can avoid it, and the probability is that there will be no difficulty." Poor John Dwight! In a matter of just a few days he received these various and not always consistent reports from Sophia Ripley, Dana, and his sister. As if there weren't confusion enough, a fourth letter arrived for him in New York before the week was over, this one from George Ripley. "We can decide on nothing definite as yet, with regard to our course," Ripley informed his trusted friend on Thursday, March 19. "Every thing, I consider, to be precarious in the highest degree."[11]

The ashes of the Phalanstery finally settled a few weeks later—for the moment, at least. "At last our general plan of operations is fixed," Mary Ann Dwight reported to Anna Parsons on April 24. It was decided that the farm and the school should once again become "the main departments" around which the Association would organize its financial operations. It was also expected that the printing of *The Harbinger* and other Associative pamphlets and tracts would generate additional income. The other "industries" upon which the Brook Farmers had been relying would be abandoned, including shoemaking, tailoring, and the manufacture of sashes, blinds, and windows. The Workshop "we will let if we can." These changes would provide greater independence for the groups remaining in the community: "Each will transact its own business, make its own sales and purchases, etc." To help bring about this greater independence it was agreed as well to "take note of results rather than of hours"—an important modification that signaled a departure from Charles Fourier's system of rewarding individual productivity.[12] For her part, Dwight was excited about her recent election as "chief of the teachers' group which gives me, together with Mrs R[ipley] (chief of the educational service), and indeed more than she, the superintendence of the school. Her health requires that I should give her this relief."

And what of Brook Farm's long-suffering leaders, George Ripley and Charles Dana? Their fidelity to Brook Farm was naturally very strong, but, frankly, both men were feeling the wear of the community's unrelieved financial pressures, not to mention the persistent squabbles and disagreements that had for more than a year too often characterized relations among associates. George Ripley's ambivalent loyalties were already evident in *The Harbinger* right after the fire. One week after reporting the "Fire at Brook Farm" in the number for March 14, he made some telling comments in a March 21 column titled "To Our Friends" by way of introducing a letter sent to the Associationist paper in which the correspondent praised the West Roxbury community: "Upon the firm establishment of the Brook Farm Phalanx," the correspondent proclaimed, "depends in no small degree, the advance of our whole [Associationist] Cause." Ripley acknowledged that through the hard-won efforts of many people in the community, Brook Farm had managed to establish itself as a "centre of influence . . . for the Associative movement." He assured *The Harbinger*'s readers that "we are fully aware of the importance of this," and he exaggerated his own and Dana's commitment to the community when he stated that "nothing but the most inexorable necessity, will withdraw the congenial spirits that are gathered in social union here."

Ripley then added, however, that "we do not altogether agree with the writer, in the importance which he attaches to the special movement at Brook Farm," and he noted that "the discontinuance of our establishment" would not "in the slightest degree" weaken his conviction that the Associative system would eventually be adopted throughout the country. "We have never attempted any thing more than to prepare the way for Association; . . . we have always regarded ourselves only as the humble pioneers in a work, which would be carried on by others to its magnificent consummation." Ripley was even less sanguine about Brook Farm's future prospects just a few weeks after these comments in *The Harbinger* when, on April 16, he remarked privately to Boston Associationist James T. Fisher: "I have never thought that we had here [Brook Farm] the materials to do any thing like justice to the sublime Associative idea; & on that account have often regretted that we have been placed so prominent in the movement."[13] He failed to point out that he himself of course had been singularly instrumental in placing Brook Farm "so prominent in the movement." Evidently Fisher didn't know that less than one year before, Ripley was lobbying vigorously for Brook Farm's recognition as the "model Phalanx" in the United States.

William Henry Channing had privately expressed views similar to Ripley's just a few months earlier, and John Allen did the same right after the Phalanstery fire.[14] The occasion for Channing's remarks on January 18, 1846, was generally to express to John Dwight the extent of his disappointment that his recent "breakdown" had forced him to retreat to his home in Brattleboro, Vermont, rather than standing by the Brook Farmers during their several trials in November and December 1845. He assured Dwight in January that he would return to West Roxbury soon. He had already proposed to Theodore Parker "to take *indefinitely* the supply of Spring-street," Parker's West Roxbury church. Channing then turned to Brook Farm and the Associationist movement. Apparently Dwight had alluded to Brook Farm's importance in the movement by characterizing activities in the West Roxbury community as "living in the centre." "Here," Channing responded, "we either do not understand one another or else we differ in our views." Brook Farm did not have any particularly central importance in the Associative movement. That movement, in fact, was part of an even larger one that—along with all the other reform efforts of the period—Channing regarded as "*Providential.*" "There is no centre[,] no circumference," Channing stated. "*If* Brook Farm can stand it must; *but,*" Channing emphasized, "if it must fall, then by heaven, only a louder, stronger call shall go up for Unity and Brotherhood."

John Allen was ultimately motivated by the same sense of providential purpose as Channing, and right after the destruction of the Phalanstery he urged his fellow communitarians to adopt a similar view. "All that we have and all that we are," he wrote to the Brook Farmers on March 9, 1846, during one of his lecture tours on behalf of Associationism, "belong to the [Associative] cause in which we are engaged." It would be a terrible disappointment, of course, if the members of the Association were forced to leave the place where they had been laboring so assiduously and arduously, but what was of greater importance was not, finally, location, but that together they had "tasted of the fruit from the tree of Unity, [and] of the milk & honey which the spies have brought from the promised land." Allen did not believe that it was "the will of God that the essay of practical Association shall be wrought out on that spot [Brook Farm]," and if the "friends who have aided us" prompted them now to do so, the Brook Farmers should be prepared to move elsewhere and unite with others devoted to the same cause.

It was only a matter of time, of course, before the separate but similar views of people like Ripley, Channing, and Allen would converge with a force that was destined to further weaken Brook Farm's already fatally damaged foundation—and that time arrived at the end of May 1846. The occasion was the quarterly meeting of the New England Fourier Society; the purpose was the organization of a national "American Union of Associationists." At the head of the ranks urging its formation would be George Ripley, William Henry Channing, and John Allen.

12

Beginning of the End

George Ripley made his unofficial break with Brook Farm—in spirit if not in body—at the quarterly meeting of the New England Fourier Society at the end of May 1846. (Charles Dana had symbolically made his break three months earlier when he secretly married Eunice Macdaniel in New York City instead of in the community among his fellow associates.) Ripley's spirit had probably been broken for many months—at least since the previous autumn when the community was racked by internal dissension, smallpox, and a series of legal difficulties, such as Nathaniel Hawthorne's lawsuit in December 1845. It shouldn't be at all surprising—considering Brook Farm's virtually unrelieved history of chronic financial turmoil—that Ripley now turned away from Brook Farm to the national Associative movement for the kind of personal affirmation that had been missing for some time in his capacity as leader of the West Roxbury community.

What made the quiet shift of his priorities easier still was Ripley's heartfelt conviction that Associationism was a providential movement. The former Unitarian minister may have felt called in 1841 to build anew the "city of God" in West Roxbury, but now in 1846, he stated in *The Harbinger* just three weeks after the loss of the Phalanstery, that Brook Farm was merely a practical attempt "to prepare the way for Association . . . We [the Brook Farmers] have always regarded ourselves only as the humble pioneers in a work, which would be carried on by others to its magnificent consummation."[1] That Ripley's personal interests now favored the national Associative movement more than the Brook Farm community was clear at the May 1846 meeting of the New England Fourier Society.

It will be recalled that back in November 1844, Ripley and Dana proposed to the New York Associationists the formation of a "School whose office shall be the propagation and defense of the [Associative] doctrine." Now, more than a year and a half later, there was still no central organization to unify Associationists around the country. Although the future existence of Brook Farm was obviously still uncertain in the spring of 1846, Ripley decided to devote his energies to the national reform movement. If the New Yorkers would not take the lead, then a few of the Brook Farmers would. Ripley put out the call in the May 9, 1846, number of *The Harbinger:* the meeting of the Fourier Society at the end of the month would be devoted to the formation of a "central society" for the purpose of "organizing and directing a system of practical means for the promulgation and realization of the principles of Association."[2] He hoped that plans would also be considered for the formation of affiliated societies, as well as for the "establishment of a permanent fund for the promulgation of the doctrine," for the "organization of an extensive system of Lecturing," and for identifying the "means of increasing and sustaining a system of publications."

The meeting of the New England Fourier Society took place on Wednesday, May 27, at the Marlboro Chapel in Boston. Ripley and his Brook Farm colleagues were so determined to establish a national organization for Associationists that they proceeded to draft a constitution and to elect officers right on the spot, despite the fact that only Albert Brisbane was present among the most prominent leaders of the movement from around the country. But that didn't prevent Ripley,

Dana, and a few others from the West Roxbury community from electing Horace Greeley president of the new organization. Seven other "friends of the cause" (including Philadelphian James Kay, Jr.) were elected vice presidents in absentia.[3] Ripley, Dana, John Dwight, and John Allen had themselves elected to the "Board of Directors" (really, the Executive Committee), along with New York Associationists Brisbane, Osborne Macdaniel, and Edmund Tweedy. Brook Farm supporters Francis G. Shaw, James T. Fisher, and William Henry Channing were elected Treasurer, Recording Secretary, and Domestic Corresponding Secretary, respectively. (Fisher relinquished the position that August or September.) New York Associationist Parke Godwin was elected Foreign Corresponding Secretary.

The name decided on for the new organization was the "American Union of Associationists," which, it turned out, was one of the most ironic titles of any social reform group in antebellum America. Especially in its early stages there was nothing "American" about the organization since it was controlled locally by New Englanders; there was never any "union" in the usual sense of that word among the movement's adherents; and neither were there ever any meaningful cooperative endeavors such as those implied by the term "Associationists." This was immediately apparent even before the ink dried on the newly drafted constitution of the "AUA."

Anticipating the formal announcement of the AUA's formation in *The Harbinger* on June 6, 1846, Parke Godwin forwarded a letter "To the Editors" declining the position of Foreign Corresponding Secretary because of a resolution contained in the new constitution. That resolution—instigated, as Godwin undoubtedly recognized, by William Henry Channing—expressed "horror and detestation of ALL WAR," and called upon Associationists everywhere to pledge themselves "in no way to aid the Government of these United States, or of the several States, in carrying on war against Mexico." In an effort to mollify Godwin, Charles Dana, who reported on the "Convention in Boston—Organization of 'The American Union of Associationists'" in *The Harbinger,* included an editorial disclaimer, noting that "this pledge is to be taken simply as the expression of those persons who favored it at the meeting . . . The Associative School . . . is not united to act against any [particular social evil], however detestable."[4]

The disclaimer, however, didn't satisfy Godwin. He considered the resolution "an expression of the extremest individualism," and, in a postscript to his letter to *The Harbinger*'s editors (sent in care of Dana), he protested to his only real Brook Farm friend that "the time has come . . . when we should take a stand above New England Treason and Fanaticism." Whether Godwin's anger was inspired primarily by his own conviction that the war with Mexico was really a "healthy" aggression to extend "constitutional republican institutions over this whole continent" ("I make no hesitation . . . in avowing that I am an Annexationist," he noted elsewhere in the letter), or his annoyance was prompted by his continuing impatience with William Henry Channing and New Englanders generally isn't clear. Godwin's ire had been roused a few months earlier by a similar but much longer article in *The Harbinger* from Channing's pen.

In a lengthy editorial on "Cassius M. Clay's Appeal" in the October 25, 1845, number of *The Harbinger,* Channing vigorously protested the annexation of Texas, which, he claimed, was the work of the "SLAVE POWER" in the United States, which had "usurped the Legislative, Senatorial, and Executive functions [of the United States government], and which there is every reason to apprehend will command also the Judiciary." Godwin told Dana at that time that he thought Channing's "superficial ravings" were "altogether sectarian and local," and that he had no right to "thrust . . . his own narrow New England notions" into the pages of *The Harbinger,* a journal that supposedly represented the Associative school in America. Godwin was so "pained" by Channing's article that he threatened to withdraw his name as one of *The Harbinger*'s editors. He was particularly disappointed with Ripley. Godwin thought that Brook Farm's leader had "sense enough to see beyond the horizon of the nigger-loving and white-man hating fanatics of the East."[5]

Godwin was even more annoyed, however, by August 1846. His lengthy June letter "To the Editors" had still not appeared in *The Harbinger* (and never would). It had been "cast aside without one word of reference to it in the [*Harbinger*]," Godwin complained to Dana, and this after the New Yorker had asked Ripley personally "to make a brief protest for me." Ripley, in fact, seems to have withheld the letter himself on the grounds that he "did not gather from it that you [Godwin] regarded a statement in your behalf as a thing which *must* be done." Godwin should have recognized that Ripley's allegiance would naturally be with Channing, his longtime New England friend and colleague. (Ripley never had much affection for Godwin anyway.)[6] The point, though, is that Godwin's protest illustrates the divisive regional differences between Associationists in New York and those in New England that ultimately played a significant role in Brook Farm's collapse.[7]

Mary Ann Dwight herself had a distinct sense of shared purposes lost in July 1846, which prompted her, in a letter to her brother Frank, to divide her fellow Brook Farmers into "three classes."[8] Dwight was despondent that summer about the possible collapse of the Association. "I don't mean to be so," she reassured Frank, "even if I see this beloved Brook Farm, this adopted home, draw to an end."[9] The members of the community, however, were now hopelessly divided. One group of associates, Dwight said, consisted of the Ripleys, Danas, and Macdaniels. They were "*promulgators* of the [Associative] doctrine . . . They have taken the doctrine into their heads more than into their hearts." Their real interest was for a "far future"; they were no longer committed to the West Roxbury Association. A second "class" of associates was represented by Dwight's brother, John, and others, like her friend Amelia Russell. These associates agreed that promulgation of Associative doctrine was important, but they were also for preserving Brook Farm "for the *life* we have led together." This class, however, favored individual instead of cooperative enterprise, whereby rewards would be directly commensurate with individual labor. They didn't support a continuation of a system based on associated industries. The third class was the one in which Dwight placed herself, and the one, she thought, that comprised the majority of associates still in the community: those Brook Farmers who were interested in the promulgation of the doctrine, who "love the life here as dearly as any," but who would preserve that life "the only possible way which can produce it, viz., by associative industry." This group thought that the farm—though not primarily farming itself—should be at the center of the community's financial endeavors.

Dwight had good reason in July 1846 to characterize Ripley, Dana, and a few others as "promulgators" of Associative doctrine whose real interests no longer favored Brook Farm. The Farm's two most prominent leaders were fairly often away that summer campaigning for Associationism. It was agreed at the May 1846 meeting of the Fourier Society that one of the best ways to propagandize for Associationism was to send lecturers into the field. At a follow-up meeting of the newly organized American Union of Associationists on June 16 and 17, Dana was formally appointed an agent of the AUA, "to proceed this summer upon a lecturing tour through New York, Western Pennsylvania and Ohio."[10] Dana never got farther west than Massachusetts, but he did speak in Lowell, Massachusetts, on the "New Social Order" at the end of June, and in July he and Brisbane were joined by William Henry Channing, and the three lectured in Worcester and then in Salem, Massachusetts, as well as in Dover and Portsmouth, New Hampshire. Ripley joined Brisbane and Channing in Hingham, Massachusetts, at the end of July for lectures on the "leading doctrines and purposes of the Associative School" in the United States.[11]

Developments closer to home also diverted Ripley and Dana's attention that summer from day-to-day affairs in the community. Along with agents in the field, the campaign to propagandize for Associationism and Fourierism was being waged in the pages of *The Harbinger,* which, through Ripley and Dana's instigation at the AUA meeting in June, had recently been designated "the [official] organ of the American Union of Associationists." Ripley and Dana particularly had high financial expectations for *The Harbinger* after the community's quasi-restructuring in April 1846, but it was clear from receipts in July, August, and September 1846 that the expenses of publishing the weekly paper were regularly exceeding income because its support was limited to subscriptions and the hard work of the Brook Farmers themselves, who had always conducted the paper without any monetary compensation for their editorial labors.

Also demanding more attention were the increasingly hostile attacks in the press on Fourierist and Associative doctrines, particularly those pertaining to Charles Fourier's controversial notions about marriage. Ripley had been willing to continue at Brook Farm after the loss of the Phalanstery mainly so he could urge the Associative movement forward in the pages of *The Harbinger;* instead, he, Dana, and Dwight found themselves responding to accusations such as those in the New York *Observer*—"a religious paper of the Calvinistic school, of large circulation and great influence," Dana characterized it in *The Harbinger* for August 8, 1846. The *Observer*'s charges were annoyingly familiar: "The Associationists, under the pretense of a desire to promote order and morals, design to overthrow the marriage institution, and in the place of the divine law, to substitute the 'passions' as the proper regulator of the intercourse of the sexes." The *Observer* further claimed that Associationists were "secretly and industriously aiming to destroy the foundations of society, and to introduce a system in which the most unrestrained indulgence of the sensual passions is enjoyed and sanctified by the name of virtue."[12]

Charges such as these by the New York *Observer* were hardly new. As recently as this past January 1846, for instance, John O'Sullivan's popular *Democratic Review* printed an article on French Associationist Eugene Sue's novel, *The Wandering Jew,* which was, according to George Ripley, "for barefaced and atrocious misrepresentation of the Associative movement in this country . . . without a parallel among the productions of a partisan and bigoted press." Ripley—who never permitted *The Harbinger* to indulge in mudslinging—was shocked that a journal with so enviable a reputation as that of the *Democratic Review* would publish an article so obviously designed to "appeal to the most shameful prejudices," an article that "would disgrace the most vulgar writer who could be hired to serve the cause of a vindictive, personal controversy." Ripley wasn't the only one upset about the *Democratic Review*'s characterization of Associationism. The Rochester (New York) *Daily Advertiser* agreed with his assessment; it also criticized the *Democratic Review* for publishing "the meanest, most disgraceful, most contemptible [review] that ever appeared in any journal assuming the name of democratic."[13]

Unfortunately, the *Democratic Review* wasn't the only paper making the charges, and Ripley and his colleagues were now responding to them in *The Harbinger* by repeating, "perhaps for the thousandth time," that "Fourier is not our Master, but our Teacher." Associative interest in Fourier was limited to the Frenchman's theories on industrial reform, which were supported for the most part by verifiable evidence and experience. So far as Fourier's speculations on other subjects were concerned, Associationists rejected them.

Such assaults on Associationism led Charles Dana to characterize the New York *Courier and Enquirer,* the New York *Express,* the *Buffalo Advertiser,* and the New York *Observer* as "voracious journals" in his article "Attacks on the Doctrine of Association" in the August 8, 1846, number of *The Harbinger,* and, one week later, Ripley, Dana, and John Dwight were still on the defensive with a "Statement of the 'American Union of Associationists,' with Reference to Recent Attacks." In the very same number of the paper, Ripley responded to the New York *Observer* in a lengthy article in which, again, he tried to explain the Associative position with respect to such widely disparate matters as Fourier's views on the organization of labor and the institution of marriage.

Ripley noted in the "Statement" that "misconceptions, errors, and calumnies are widely circulated in relation to the doctrines of Associationism." Associationists were invariably accused of advocating the abolition of the institutions of marriage, representative government, and the Christian Church. These charges were simply not true. Associationists would not abolish or significantly alter any of these institutions, but they would try to improve them. Marriage in the present state of society, Ripley asserted, was really a form of "legalized prostitution," but it was also "the most sacred and important of existing social ties, and . . . the pivot on which the order of society depends." Associationists considered representative government "the greatest step of modern political improvement." Despite its many imperfections, at least it embodied a part of the idea of human liberty. So far as the Christian Church was concerned, Associationists wanted to see the many hostile and scattered religious sects brought together in one Universal Church, though the reform necessary to effect such a change, they recognized, was not within the province of Associationism.[14]

In other words, far from aiming at the destruction of these institutions, Associationists regarded their preservation "as an indispensable condition of the reform to which we are devoted." The institutions that Associationists condemned as false, corrupting, oppressive, and brutalizing were slavery; the system of labor for wages, which was nothing other than a form of slavery maintained by capitalists; the existing system of commerce, which was wasteful and complicated; prostitution in all its forms; monopoly of the soil; pauperism; war; and competition, which caused hatreds, frauds, jealousies, and lies. Regarding Fourier, Associationists considered him to be the discoverer of the law of universal unity, which would ultimately reconcile these existing evils. No other man ever explained so clearly the great principles of harmony or the formulas for "the organization of all the departments of human activity, according to the divine plan."

These clarifying statements, however, did nothing to lessen the number or intensity of the attacks on Associationism and the Associative reform program. Assaults on Associationist doctrines, in fact, continued right up to the concluding numbers of *The Harbinger* in February 1849. The *American Review, Brownson's Quarterly Review,* and the New York press generally were the most hostile in their denunciations of the Fourierist-inspired social reform program.[15] Ripley invited the New York *Observer* to a formal debate on the merits and aims of the Associative school in America, which debate would consist of six or twelve articles of a stipulated length to be published in full in both papers. The *Observer* never even acknowledged the invitation.

Some papers and magazines, such as the *National Era* (Washington, D.C.), the New Bedford (Massachusetts) *Mercury,* and the *National Anti-Slavery Standard* (New York), were often reasonable in their discussions of Associationism, and Elizur Wright's Boston *Chronotype* and John Allen's *Voice of Industry* (Massachusetts) usually printed articles that supported the utopian socialists and their aims. Even the New York *Herald* and the New York *Mirror* began publishing articles "favorable" to Associationists, though this must have been only a temporary lapse in the usual editorial policy of anti-Associationism in these papers, for Ripley and Dana and their fellow New York editors criticized them more than once in the last three volumes of *The Harbinger.*

The amount of time that Ripley and Dana and even John Dwight spent in the summer of 1846 proselytizing for and defending Associationist doctrines reflects the clear shift in their priorities away from Brook Farm. Their hearts were no longer in the community, especially Charles Dana's, who for some time had been quietly exploring employment possibilities that would enable him to break away from the West Roxbury Association. If there was one "constant" in his life in the five years that he had been at Brook Farm, it was his persistent and embarrassing indebtedness. He had come to the community in the autumn of 1841 without any financial resources and somewhat in debt, and he would leave it in the autumn of 1846 virtually in the same circumstances. He might have managed for a while longer were he still single, but now that he was married he needed income.

There was certainly no financial future at the community. Dana noted this in a letter to Parke Godwin on August 18, 1846, when he acknowledged the importance of getting a "tolerable living" and doing "something towards paying my debts, with me a *desiderium* of the most urgent kind." He had recently contacted Horace Greeley, Dana told his New York friend, but the New York Associationist thought that Dana's "critical talents would do the Tribune no service, and only as a proof reader and translator of foreign journals can he give me a place."[16] Dana hoped for a position in the *Tribune*'s literary department; he certainly wouldn't be able to engage in proofreading because of his poor eyesight.

Dana had also contacted the affable Elizur Wright, owner and editor of the Boston *Daily Chronotype*. The *Chronotype* didn't have the notoriety of Greeley's *Tribune*, wrote Dana, but Albert Brisbane "thinks it is destined to be as influential in its sphere as Greeley's is in his." Brisbane was even thinking about purchasing a one-third interest in Wright's paper, and "wants me [Dana] to go in with Wright as a colleague." Dana, however, was worried that he would be identified with Wright, a man who had "a good deal of general talent and incomparable humour," but who was known for "a variety of crotchets & whimsies; a liberty-party man, a temperance man, a free trade man, & etc." Besides, Dana added, he wanted to be free from "the management and success of the paper . . . having had my fill of responsibility these last three years."[17] But Dana really had no firm prospects in New York City, so he decided to accept the position on the *Chronotype*, where he began work in September or October 1846. Just a few months later, Charles and Eunice Macdaniel Dana severed their ties with Brook Farm for good. Unexpectedly, Greeley had a position for Dana after all as the city editor of the *Tribune*. The newlywed couple moved to New York right after the first of the new year, and Dana assumed his new position in February 1847.[18]

Two of Ripley's other Brook Farm colleagues also abandoned ship in 1846. One of them was Louis Ryckman, the shoemaker from New York who—except for an extended visit to the Sylvania Association in 1844—had been at Brook Farm since early 1843. Ryckman was elected the first president of the newly formed New England Workingmen's Association in May 1845, but his ambitious interests in organizing an Industrial Congress were not really compatible with the more pragmatic concerns of New England's workingmen. Ryckman found greater support for his ideas in New York City in the ranks of the National Reform Association. He left his wife, June, and daughter, Jeanie, temporarily behind at Brook Farm in November 1845, and moved to New York to continue his labors in that city. It was perfectly clear now that any interest at Brook Farm in the activities of New England's workingmen was just one of several different fronts in the comprehensive Associative reform program to which Ripley and Dana were so devoted. When Ryckman set out in February 1846 on a lecture tour throughout New York State on behalf of the National Reform Association, John Allen quickly took over as Ryckman's successor in the New England labor movement.

Allen, another of Ripley's trusted associates, settled for a while at Brook Farm at the beginning of 1845, but, as fond as he became of some of the people there, his heart was never entirely in the West Roxbury Association. Like Ryckman, he was more interested in organizing the burgeoning ranks of New England workingmen. One of the towns in which Allen and his fellow Brook Farmer John Orvis had stopped during their two-man lecture tour in the winter of 1845–1846 was Lowell, Massachusetts. Associationists, Carl Guarneri has noted, were "eager to gain a foothold there . . . because of Lowell's symbolic place as the entering wedge of the factory system."[19] Both Ripley and William Henry Channing had also appeared there in March 1846 as part of a lecture series at the Industrial Reform Lyceum sponsored by the Lowell Female Labor Reform Association, and Channing and Allen returned to the town in May 1846 to help raise funds for the Lowell Women's Association.

Allen decided that this was a good moment to break with Brook Farm. He took editorial control of the struggling *Voice of Industry,* until now the official organ of the New England Workingmen's Association, and almost immediately turned the paper over to the Lowell Associationists.[20] Then in July, he and other local "friends of the cause" reorganized the Lowell Fourier Society and named it the Lowell Union of Associationists, making it in the process an affiliate of the American Union of Associationists. That work accomplished, Allen returned to Brook Farm that autumn for occasional visits, but he didn't have many opportunities to do so because he now was an agent for the AUA.

The once common threads that had held the Brook Farmers together in 1844 and 1845 may have not been the strongest, but nonetheless they had managed to hold. Now in the autumn of 1846, Brook Farm's most conspicuous leaders found themselves marching to the beat of their own different drummers: Louis Ryckman to the National Reform Association; George Ripley and John Allen to the AUA; and Charles Dana to the Boston *Chronotype.* And while William Henry Channing decided that he would renew his interrupted efforts the year before to establish a "Church of Humanity," those efforts would not take place at Brook Farm. The defection of Brook Farm's leaders meant that the community was left without a center of influence and, even more critically, without leadership or direction. John S. Dwight and his sister Mary Ann were willing to try to provide them, but they couldn't agree themselves on the best course of action for the Association.

On September 10, 1846, Bronson Alcott's friend Charles Lane reported that "the industrials [at Brook Farm] are all obliged to leave. They apply to the N[orth] A[merican] Phalanx, but there is no room for them."[21] The exodus from the community had really begun, however, back in May 1846, right after it was decided to cut down the number of people living in the Association. There were about sixty-five associates, boarders, and students at Brook Farm in May—significantly down from the 100 or 110 people who had been there just a few months before. In June 1846 the number dropped from sixty-five to fifty-one, and then to approximately thirty in each of the months of July and August. The numbers increased a bit in September, but, more critically, the number of students returning to the Brook Farm school did not. Only about twelve were there in May; the financial journals indicate that only about this same number returned to the community in September. The school, it had been hoped in the weeks following the fire, would generate a significant part of the income necessary to maintain the Association. It was clear by September 1846 that that was not going to happen. Word of the community's internal problems had obviously spread to Brook Farm's neighbors.

George Ripley was no stranger to disappointment and heartache in the five-plus years of the community's existence, but November 1846 brought one of the most difficult days of his life. On the 5th of that month, the several hundred volumes that comprised his personal library—and whose easy availability in the Hive and later at the Eyrie had provided so much pleasure to his fellow Brook Farmers—were sold at auction in Boston to help pay off some of the community's debts. The founder of the most celebrated utopian community in America reportedly told a friend at the time: "I can now understand how a man would feel if he could attend his own funeral."[22] For Brook Farm itself, the "funeral" would not formally take place, however, until the following October 1847. In the meantime, the few remaining associates who were determined somehow to hang on at the Farm were just as determined to continue their social reform efforts—even if that meant moving the center of their activities from Brook Farm to Boston.

13

Back to Boston

In the months leading up to the final dissolution of
the Brook Farm Phalanx in October 1847, many of
the associates still living at the Farm joined forces with other local
friends of the cause and established two organizations that helped to
ease the impending departure from the community and the return to
conventional society. These were the Boston Union of Associationists
(1846–1851) and the Boston Religious Union of Associationists (1847–
1850).[1] The involvement of the Brook Farmers in these two organizations has always been one of the most-overlooked episodes in the history of the West Roxbury community.

The constitution of the American Union of Associationists, drafted
and adopted at the inaugural meeting of that organization in May
1846, called for the "formation of a series of affiliated societies, which
shall be auxiliary to the parent Society, in holding meetings, collecting
funds, and in every way diffusing the Principles of Associationism." It
was the local affiliated societies in fact that became the backbone of
the American Associative movement after May 1846. Without them,
the Associative movement in this country would have been even
more "desultory, isolated and incoherent" than George Ripley, John
Sullivan Dwight, and William Henry Channing thought that it had already become on the eve of the first anniversary of the formation of
the AUA in 1847.[2] Neither is it an exaggeration to say that of the few

dozen affiliated societies that eventually were formed, none came close to matching the comprehensiveness or the effectiveness with which the Boston Union of Associationists (BUA) conducted its activities. If the affiliated societies became the backbone of the Associative movement in America, then the Boston Union was its lifeblood. The marrow of that lifeblood was made up of the Brook Farmers themselves—both present and past members.

Ninety-six people eventually signed the rolls of the BUA after its formation on November 30, 1846. Of that number, slightly more than one-third were Brook Farmers or others who were closely associated with the community. Among the Brook Farmers were four members of the Dwight family, including John Sullivan and sisters Fanny and Mary Ann, though the latter was now Mary Ann Dwight Orvis, having married Brook Farmer John Orvis in December 1846 (in the only wedding ceremony ever to be performed in the community). Orvis and fellow Brook Farmer John Allen continued in 1847 to travel thousands of miles across New England, through New York, and into the Ohio Valley region propagandizing the Associationist cause. Allen's name shows up in the BUA membership records, but he never signed the constitution, as was customary, nor is there any record of his payment of the weekly rent.[3]

That is not the case with the Codman family. In addition to John and his sister Rebecca and brother Charles, their mother also signed the constitution and attended many of the BUA's meetings. Rebecca Codman eventually married Brook Farm printer Jonathan Butterfield, also a BUA member, whom she met a few years before when each joined the community. Butterfield's participation in the BUA was very active right through 1848. The BUA especially attracted a good variety of Brook Farm's workers. Peter Baldwin, the baker, joined, as did Thomas Blake and Willard Saxton, both of them part of the Brook Farm corp of printers; William Cheswell, a carpenter; and Henry

Trask, a carriagemaker. Among BUA members closely identified or associated with Brook Farm were devoted supporter Francis G. Shaw, Mary Ann Dwight's favorite correspondent Anna Q. T. Parsons and her sister Helen, John S. Dwight's future bride-to-be Mary Bullard (a frequent visitor to the West Roxbury community), Brook Farm stockholder Josiah Wolcott (whose two paintings are among just four surviving contemporary views of the community), and the much-beloved William Henry Channing.[4]

It's fair to say that no individual in either the BUA or the Boston Religious Union of Associationists (BRUA) exerted more influence or authority on the Unions' activities than William Henry Channing, who served simultaneously as president of the BUA from 1847 to 1849, and spiritual leader of the BRUA between 1847 to 1850. The surviving records of the BUA and the BRUA give powerful testimony to Channing's impact on both these organizations, yet his commitment to both Unions was at times disruptive. Channing was one of those interesting individuals whose accomplishments often fell short of his considerable abilities. He combined intelligence and idealism with personal charisma and a passionate devotion to whatever cause he was championing at the moment. However, he seems to have been deficient in practical skill. That was the judgment more than a century ago of Lindsay Swift, who, in his history of Brook Farm, stated that Channing "had an overenthusiasm and lack of definiteness well calculated to wreck any project dependent on him alone to shape its course." More recently, David Robinson observed more sympathetically that "[William Henry] Channing's career leaves us with the sense of enormous talent and energy that never found a satisfactory outlet."[5]

Obviously neither the Boston Union nor the Religious Union was dependent on Channing alone for its success, and it's not the point to attribute the ultimate failure of either organization to Channing. Nev-

ertheless, the records of both Unions show that his prolonged and untimely absences from Boston seriously interrupted their activities
and—so highly was his presence valued by the members—nearly
brought their operations to a halt. Whether that says more or less
about Channing, or about the members of the BUA and the BRUA,
depends on one's point of view.

Between November 1846, when the BUA was organized, and December 1848, when the last affiliated Associative union was formed in
Washington, D.C., between twenty-five and thirty local societies
sprang into existence.[6] At least fourteen of these were located in New
England—eight in Massachusetts, four in Vermont, and one each in
Maine and Rhode Island. Five other unions were established in the
state of New York, including one in New York City and one in Albany.
Two more were formed in Pennsylvania—in Philadelphia and Pittsburgh; and others were organized in Wheeling, Virginia, in Cincinnati, Ohio, and at the Wisconsin Phalanx in Ceresco, Fond du Lac
County, Wisconsin. Many of the more remote local unions in New
England were organized because of the tireless efforts of John Orvis
and John Allen, who spent many months "on the road" preaching the
gospel of Associationism. Even Mary Ann Dwight joined her husband
John Orvis in June 1847 and herself lectured in some of the smaller
towns in Vermont.[7]

Membership in the local societies varied considerably. For example,
Fred Cabot, the recording secretary of the BUA who departed Brook
Farm in December 1845 over a squabble about the community's handling of its financial affairs (Cabot was the bookkeeper), reported at
the first anniversary meeting of the American Union of Associationists
in May 1847 that the BUA numbered forty members.[8] One year later,
Seth P. Chapin stated at the second anniversary meeting that "the
whole number of persons who have been connected with the society
since its organization, is eighty-five; Males fifty-eight, Females twenty-

seven."[9] According to *The Harbinger,* the Philadelphia Union (organized April 7, 1847) had thirty-one men and twelve women members in June 1848, and the Providence (Rhode Island) Union (organized April 16, 1847) reportedly had thirty members in August 1848. Both the New Bedford and Mattapoisett (Massachusetts) Unions (both organized on March 19, 1847) listed twenty members in April 1847, but the Springfield (Massachusetts) Union could manage only four members when it was organized in May 1847. All but two or three of the affiliated societies were organized in a flurry of Associationist fervor within four or five months, between December 1846 and May 1847. Altogether, "perhaps seven hundred persons," according to Carl Guarneri, "enrolled as members of the AUA's affiliated unions during their heyday."[10]

That heyday, in fact, was relatively short, but the Brook Farm-driven BUA was more conspicuous than any other affiliated society in the United States for the impressive range of its activities. It organized and conducted lecture programs featuring the country's leading Associationists, printed Associative tracts and pamphlets for distribution throughout the United States, studied and discussed the principal works of social science at its meetings, planned and presented large-scale celebrations (for the public as well as for Associationists) to commemorate Charles Fourier's birthday, and, in addition to hosting meetings of the Executive Committee of the American Union of Associationists, also sponsored its own conventions for New England Associationists and affiliated societies. Along the way, the BUA was also instrumental in the creation of the "Woman's Associative Union," one of the relatively few organizations in antebellum American society that provided women complete autonomy in the conduct of its affairs.

The Woman's Associative Union (WAU) was established in June 1847.[11] It was the one activity among the many undertaken by the

BUA that most nearly approached the kind of social arrangements that were anticipated by the Associative reform program. John Dwight acknowledged this in his "Letter from Boston to New York" when, in reviewing the BUA's activities since its inception, he corrected himself after dismissing the significance of the activities of the Union's Group of Practical Affairs: "I was wrong . . . in saying that we had *no* practical working of the guaranty principle among us . . . In two ways . . . is this Ladies' movement [the WAU] yielding practical illustrations of the associative principle; in the way of *attractive industrial groups,* and in the way of *combined economy.*"[12]

It's not surprising that the BUA would have the most active women members of all the affiliated societies in the country. For one thing, most of the other unions had great difficulty attracting women members, in part because of conventional domestic expectations and responsibilities, and in part because Associationist doctrines, as was noted earlier, were routinely characterized in the press and in the pulpit as immoral and subversive. It's not surprising that most women chose not to be identified in any way with the movement, despite the important benefits promised them by Associationism. The Philadelphia Union, for example, had only one woman member in the first eight months of its operation. John Allen observed during his lecture tour of New York State in September 1847 that "there are some good women engaged in the cause in Syracuse, [who are] the only *women* we have seen in the State of New York."[13] Even the New York City Union had to struggle to recruit women members. There were none in the first several months of operation, a fact that caused Charles Dana—who was now relocated in New York with his wife Eunice Macdaniel—to confess at the celebration of Fourier's birthday in April 1847 that he could not think of the BUA "without a sense of envy. Their festivities are attended by ladies as all festivities should be, but as ours, by our misfortune, not our fault, are not."[14]

Faithful Brook Farm supporter James Kay was especially envious. It was discouraging, the Philadelphia Associationist told his Boston colleague James T. Fisher in November 1847, that meetings of the Philadelphia Union in the "city of brotherly love" had to be "practically suspended during my absences," but particularly disappointing was the loss of "one of our best members," and "our only lady member." No doubt these circumstances influenced his estimation of the women of the BUA. John Allen told Fisher that "Mr. Kay is constantly talking of the Boston women, regarding them as gifts to our movement but little and less than miraculous and almost giving himself up to tears, that there are no other women in the universe . . . that deserve to be spoken of in the same age with the sisters of charity in New England."[15]

William Henry Channing initially put out the call to women to take an active role in the Associative movement, but it was Mary Ann Dwight, writing from Brook Farm, who provided the first concrete plan of organization that led to the establishment of the Woman's Associative Union. Channing's article on "Woman's Function in the Associative Movement" in July 1846 launched a nearly year-long campaign in *The Harbinger* to enlist women to "set a full example to their sex, by putting forth all their energies in the cause of Unitary Reform." Channing listed specific areas in which women could make contributions to the cause: "We ask them . . . to write tracts on the Rights, Duties and Condition of Women—to form Societies of their own, or to take an active part in our Societies—to circulate our papers—and to obtain contributions for our Funds." Ripley followed Channing's appeal with articles in September 1846 on the "Influence of Association on Woman" and in February 1847 on "Woman's Testimony to Association," in which he explained how Associationism would create an order of society in which "woman will enjoy equal opportunity in all respects, with man, for the highest intellectual cultivation."[16]

These were followed by two letters, each of which was a personal appeal by a woman. The first, printed in February 1847 and signed by an "Angelique Le Petit Martin," briefly discussed the disadvantages of "Woman in the Isolated Household." The second letter, "A Woman's Call to Women," might have been written by Mary Ann Dwight, but more likely it was from Anna Parsons, one of the BUA's most active members. The letter was published in the number for May 8, 1847, on the eve of the first anniversary meeting of the American Union of Associationists in New York City, which was followed a few weeks later by a convention of New England affiliated societies, sponsored by the BUA. In the second letter, "Your Sister" urges women to attend the anniversary meeting, not as "mere passive recipients of the light there to be diffused," but to "unite us firmly . . . into one living body" and to "organize some plan of action."[17]

The plan of action was provided by Mary Ann Dwight, who remained at Brook Farm in the spring of 1847 while her husband John Orvis continued his labors on the lecture circuit on behalf of Associationism. She wrote to Anna Parsons at the end of March and expressed her frustration that, unlike her husband, she herself was not able to promote the Associationist cause more actively. "It is a great trial to me," Dwight said, "to feel so left out as I now do,—and yet I see hardly anything that I can do just now. But I am ready to fall into my place (if there be any for me) wherever I can find it." Dwight had plenty of time in these final days of Brook Farm's existence to ruminate about the matter. She wrote again to Parsons in May 1847, just a week before the BUA's convention, telling her friend that her mind had been "busy with this theme,—*the work of woman in the association cause.*"

Extrapolating from her experience with other Brook Farm women with whom she had formed the "Fancy Group" a few years before to market community-produced goods for Boston and other neighboring areas, Dwight told Parsons that there was "no end to our various useful accomplishments." Some women had skill in cap- or bonnet-making, some in dressmaking, others in plain sewing, and still others were talented vestmakers, or loved to teach music and drawing. Members of the affiliated unions, Dwight thought, should make a pledge not to purchase any item that could be made less expensively among themselves. In return, women would contribute a percentage of their profits to the operating funds of the unions. For her part, Dwight said, she would donate to the BUA "the first *ten dollars* of the profits thus obtained, and fifteen percent of all that shall be thus obtained hereafter."[18]

Thus were seeds planted that quickly grew into the Woman's Associative Union. At the conclusion of the BUA-sponsored convention of New England affiliated societies in May 1847, a committee of ten to twelve women drafted a circular "To the Women Interested in Association." Although it was prefaced with the caution that "we are not yet prepared for any organization," the circular nonetheless called for women to "be up and doing," and it proposed a plan of action directly along the lines suggested by Dwight. It also stressed the importance of communication: "by a friendly interchange of thoughts and feelings, of words and deeds," it was hoped that women would become "a body fitly joined together, and compacted." Anna Parsons, the secretary of the Woman's Union, disseminated the circular to all affiliated Associative unions at the same time that she attempted to establish correspondence with as many women Associationists as she could.[19]

Parsons, whose father always forbade her active participation at Brook Farm, quickly sent out sixty circulars with accompanying letters, which immediately brought back forty-three responses. The most interesting correspondent with whom the BUA women made contact was Elizabeth Blackwell, the sole female member of the Philadelphia Union, who was about to enroll in a program that would have her certified the first woman medical doctor in the United States.

Blackwell first responded to Parsons in October 1847, literally on the eve of her departure from Philadelphia, where she had been denied admission to several medical programs (as well as ones in New York City and Boston). In her letter she noted that she had "endeavored in vain to enlist the assistance of other ladies [in Philadelphia]—they are sadly blind to their true interests."[20]

That was particularly disappointing to Blackwell, who was imbued with deep faith in the promise of Associationism: "Association is to me, the great hope of the world . . .; the strong desire to labor for the cause of Universal Unity is the spring of my action," she told Parsons. Armed with such firm Associationist convictions, she intended someday to open the medical profession to women: "I hope to render our sex a true service. We are more cramped on every side; crowded into a few occupations, with no scope for varied talents, or the acquisition of wealth, and with no chance of escape from the beaten track, hedged in with prejudices and false views of life." Despite the rigors of her medical program (obviously exacerbated by her gender), Blackwell maintained a correspondence with the Woman's Union at least through December 1849.

In the WAU's first annual report dated June 1848, it was noted that a constitution was not formally adopted until December 1, 1847, when "fourteen women gathered to discuss their aims and hopes. Ten women at that time signed the Constitution and during the winter seven others have joined us." It was also noted that a Woman's Union room had been opened in Boston in December 1847, where, with assistance from affiliated societies in Newburyport, New Bedford, Duxbury (all in Massachusetts), New York, Philadelphia, and elsewhere, fancy articles, Associative tracts, and refreshments were offered for sale. The profit after all expenses for these items was $169.78 (receipts of $411.78 less expenses amounting to $242), which was encouraging enough to allow the WAU to ask confidently: "Has it not been truly said, that when woman freed from her own timidity, and the prejudices which her false education, and the atmosphere in which she lives, have bound around her, shall come forth into action, that this movement will receive a new impulse not to be resisted?"[21]

It's interesting to note how the WAU's profits were distributed. Fifty-six dollars was immediately set aside for future operations, $5.75 was spent on gifts, and $25 was deposited in a Mutual Fund. The BUA received $13, the BRUA was given $25, and $15 was donated to *The Harbinger*. The Lecturing Fund of the American Union of Associationists—which, it would have been expected, would directly benefit the efforts of former Brook Farmers John Orvis and John Allen—received a $30 donation. And what of the American Union itself? The Brook Farm and Boston women who comprised the Women's Associative Union didn't set aside even a single cent for the operations of the New York-based AUA.

The success of the Woman's Associative Union is a good illustration of the overall effectiveness of its parent organization, the Boston Union of Associationists. It's not too much to say, in fact, that had the BUA been designated the center of Associative reform operations in the United States, the Associationist movement in America would have been conducted with greater energy and with a greater sense of purpose than it ever managed under the direction of the New York Associationists and the AUA. And interestingly enough, many Associationists around the country recognized that the "friends" in Boston stood a bit taller than those found anywhere else, particularly in New York. When he wrote to John Dwight after his move to that city in October 1847, George Ripley at first referred only to the problems resulting from the transfer of *The Harbinger* ("it seems as if all the petty, unexpected, little imps and demons that could be produced, were hovering over the first steps of the new" paper). Just a month later, however, he was already complaining that "without a stronger infusion of the Boston element [in Associationist activities] we cannot do justice to our ideal." By December 1848 Ripley's litany of woe included the entire Associative movement: "The Affiliated Unions out of the cities," he stated, "are not to be relied on." "The whole movement," he said, "is becoming more and more ambiguous."[22]

The situation among Philadelphia Associationists suggests why Ripley was concerned. When John Allen stopped there at the end of 1847 after a western lecture tour, he was immediately struck by the "bald, naked, abnegating reform spirit of this Quaker city." He stopped in Philadelphia to visit Brook Farm supporter James Kay, the president of the Philadelphia Union. Kay himself had noted back in August 1847 that "the sphere of Philadelphia [was] by no means a congenial one to Association." He made the point again in November 1847 in a letter to Boston Associationist James T. Fisher: there were "zealous" Associationists in Philadelphia, but "this city has no quality which responds to such a movement as ours." Coincidentally, Brook Farmer Fanny Macdaniel—who was now Charles Dana's sister-in-law—made essentially the same point when she wrote complainingly to E. P. Grant, one of the vice presidents of the American Union of Associationists: "were it not that the American Union fails to unite all with whom I have a bond in the Cause, my hopes for the future could know of no check—so earnestly and truly do I find persons alive," she said, now referring to her Brook Farm colleagues in the Boston Union, "to the truths of the doctrine."[23]

As Ripley watched the Associative movement steadily disintegrate under the ineffectual authority of the New York Associationists, he could only appeal to John Dwight that "we must hang together" because "there is little life to grow from except in Boston. Our leading friends here [in New York City] have little courage, little faith, little enterprise, and need perpetual inspirations of life from a higher source."[24] It's too bad that Ripley didn't see the true character of his

New York colleagues much sooner. Had he recognized a few years earlier how unreliable Brook Farm's "friends" there would turn out to be, he might have managed to chart the community's course on a different heading—one that would have enabled it to trim its financial sails on the way to a safer destination than the rocks on which it landed.

The formation of the Boston Religious Union of Associationists on January 3, 1847, just one month after the organization of the Boston Union of Associationists, was the long-delayed expression of the religious impulse that was fired by William Henry Channing at Brook Farm in October 1845.[25] At that time, the religious "revival" he instigated there was interrupted, first, by the outbreak of smallpox in the Association, then by his breakdown from mental exhaustion a month later, and afterward by the destruction of the nearly completed Phalanstery in March 1846, in which was to have been included a chapel for religious worship under Channing's guidance. In the months following the fire, alternative plans to establish a new "Church of Humanity" were considered.

The first detailed public statement announcing the organization of the Religious Union appeared in *The Harbinger* in the number for November 21, 1846. In "Union of Associationists in the Church of Humanity," Marx Edgeworth Lazarus—a Jewish physician turned Associationist whose sister, Ellen, later married Brook Farmer John Allen—stated that it had been proposed to establish a religious union in Boston in order that Associationists might consecrate themselves to the "marriage of science and religion in a true society." To be effectual, Lazarus stated, the Associative movement must "recognize its own religious origin and mission . . . There must be the first germ of the Associative, the Unitary Church; not a church in any narrow, or sectarian sense, but a church in the sense of that profound conviction which we have that all mankind are *one,* and that only in the unity of each with all, can the true God be known."[26] This new church, it was proposed, should be called "The Church of Humanity," a name that was rejected for reasons never indicated.

Lazarus concluded the announcement by stating, "It is moreover the cherished hope of all the friends of the cause . . . that the services of our inspiring and beloved brother, WILLIAM HENRY CHANNING, may be secured, for the initiation and future conduct of this beautiful and solemn worship." Channing agreed right away on December 4, 1846, to serve as spiritual leader of the new organization. Three days earlier, thirty-two individuals pledged various amounts of money "for the purpose of establishing a religious Society" in Boston. These pledges ranged from a high of $100 (from Francis G. Shaw) to a low of $1 (from Brook Farmers Peter Baldwin and Charles Salisbury). The average pledge was between ten and fifteen dollars.

As was the case in the BUA, Brook Farmers were conspicuous among the ranks of the devoted who eventually became affiliated with the BRUA. Eleven of the original twenty-three persons who signed their names to the "Statement of Faith and Purpose" on January 17, 1847, were Brook Farmers—Sophia Ripley, John Dwight, John T. Codman and his sister Rebecca, Jean and Eliza Palisse, Peter Baldwin, Fred Cabot, Lizzie Curson, Hiram Haskell, and Catherine Sloan. (John Cheever also joined just a few weeks later, and so did Mrs. Codman.) Six other members of the BRUA were closely associated with Brook Farm.[27] Thus the Brook Farmers really made up about one-third of the early membership of this organization, just as they did in the BUA. Forty-nine of the seventy-seven persons who eventually pledged themselves to the BRUA were also members of the BUA.

There were, however, some regular Brook Farm names missing on the rolls of the BRUA, among them those of Mary Ann Dwight and John Orvis. At first this seems surprising, considering that Dwight especially was one of Channing's most enthusiastic supporters during the October 1845 revival at the Farm—Dwight and Orvis had in fact just been married by Channing on Christmas Eve 1846 at the Farm. However, Dwight's interest in the religious revival in 1845 was really inspired less by religious fervor than by her hope that it might serve to unify the members of the Association, something that was always of great importance to her while she lived at Brook Farm. Even the arrangements for her wedding were planned with the community in mind. Referring to the ceremony itself, she told Anna Parsons that "I know nothing that could *unite* us so truly [emphasis is Dwight's]."[28]

Even as late as July 1847, with all but a handful of associates having already made their departure from Brook Farm, Dwight still thought that it was important not to let the social fabric of the community unravel completely. She told Anna Parsons that she hoped to attend some of the meetings of the BRUA in Boston, but "you know," she added, "I am for holding on to the *social life* of this dear house [Brook Farm], & I don't like to have our people rush off *en masse,* on Sunday evenings, for any purpose."[29]

Dwight and Orvis, it turned out, were two of a total of twelve Brook Farmers who participated in the BUA but *not* in the BRUA. Of the other ten, nine were men (three printers, three farmers, and three carpenters). The BRUA, for its part, attracted eight Brook Farmers—four men and four women—who never became members of the BUA. In addition to these twenty, ten other members of the West Roxbury community are listed on the rolls of *both* Unions.[30] The point is that the Brook Farmers' presence in these two organizations was obviously conspicuous; it was certainly not limited to the participation of the ten men and women who were enrolled in both organizations.

And what of George Ripley's involvement in the two organizations that fundamentally embodied the very ideals upon which he had established Brook Farm? Ripley is not listed at all on the rolls of the

BUA. He did sign the BRUA's "Statement of Faith and Purpose" on August 23, 1847, but that was just a gesture to demonstrate support for the Religious Union because at this time he was preparing to leave Brook Farm and New England for good. *The Harbinger,* it was decided at the annual meeting of the AUA in May 1847, would be transferred to New York City with the close of the fifth volume on October 30, 1847. Ripley would continue to serve the paper as one of the editorial assistants in New York under the general editorial command of the prickly Parke Godwin.

Ripley himself, in fact, was not at all disheartened on the eve of his departure from the community that he had labored so hard to maintain during the previous six years. He attended the October 17, 1847, meeting of the BRUA (only his third such appearance since the Union's inception) where, it was noted in the minutes, "he spoke very earnestly of the good influences which he thought had gone forth from [Brook Farm] and that although in a pecuniary point of view the experiment had proved a decided failure, he felt that they had all gained immensely in moral strength and certainty of conviction as to the true method of Life by the experiences they had there met with. He said in his experience he never felt as confident of the divinity of the cause of Association and felt a greater determination than ever to live and work for its ultimate triumph."[31]

Brook Farm itself collapsed in October 1847. Both the BUA and the BRUA managed to survive for a few more years, thanks largely to the efforts of the Brook Farmers, who exerted their influence right to the very end—from the formalities for signifying membership in the Unions, to the organization and frequency of meetings, and (especially in the case of the BRUA) to the inclusion of music—in the weekly proceedings. Regarding membership, although there was no probationary period in either the BUA or BRUA such as had been required at Brook Farm, upon admission to either union an individual was expected to sign the constitution or the "Statement of Faith and Purpose," just as Brook Farm probationers had been expected to sign the community's constitution upon their election as associates. During the first two years of its operation, the BRUA, except for the summer months, met twice every Sunday—once in the morning or afternoon for a sermon from Channing on a wide range of topics (typically on subjects having to do with religious humanism), and again in the evening for informal but serious discussion, as well as social conversation and music. (The BUA met weekly its first year, then monthly thereafter.) "Meetings," as anyone living in the community during the "second dispensation" knew very well, were also a regular staple of Brook Farm life, occurring, as they did, every Sunday, and often during the week as well.

As was also the case at the Farm after the conversion to Fourierism, both the BUA and the BRUA relied on "Groups" to focus their activities (for example, a Group of Practical Affairs, a Group of Indoctrination, a Group of Social Culture, a Group of Guarantees, and so on). An even more common feature of Brook Farm life of course was music, which, like the meetings, was never limited to Sundays. On virtually any given evening of the year, sounds of singing and piano-playing might have been heard emanating from the front parlor of the Eyrie. On weekends, when dances and other festivities usually took place, those sounds were heard coming from the Hive. And just as they often did together at the Farm, John Dwight and Mary Bullard (who were wed in 1851) combined their musical talents at meetings of the BRUA. The Religious Union, in fact, had already organized its own choir by the time of its sixth meeting in January 1847. Music was always an important feature of the BRUA's proceedings.

The operations of the Boston Religious Union came to a halt in June 1850; those of the Boston Union ended one year later. To the members of both organizations, one thing by that time had become steadily—even painfully—clear: the Associative movement had been fractured; it was even moribund. The so-called Model Phalanx was never going to be constructed nor, for that matter, was an Associative unitary dwelling—the concept of which so occupied the attention of BUA members throughout 1847 and 1848 (as the Phalanstery had the Brook Farmers for the two years prior to the fatal fire). The American Union of Associationists in 1850 was an organization functioning in name only. Associationism, by then, had lost its urgency and effectiveness so as to no longer be a compelling social force in American society. No doubt it was small consolation, but the members of the BUA and the BRUA—under the determined leadership of the Brook Farmers—were at least able to take satisfaction in the awareness that they had devoted their considerable talents, energy, and zeal to a good cause and an important one, a cause that New Englanders championed with a high-mindedness and sincerity of purpose that regrettably was not to be found among Associationists anywhere else in the United States.

14

"Done with Brook Farm"

In one of those surprising coincidences of timing, the 4th of March 1847 provided a dramatic contrast of fortunes for the two men who had been the mainstays of the Brook Farm community since its earliest organization. On that day in New York City, Charles Dana's wife Eunice Macdaniel gave birth to the couple's only child (a daughter), perhaps even at the exact moment that George Ripley was meeting in West Roxbury to arrange for the disposal of the community that he and Sophia had established nearly six years to the day before. For the normally reserved and intellectually driven Dana, the baby, who remained nameless for more than six months, was "the brightest & sweetest thing that you ever heard of." For the usually determined and always amiable Ripley, his meeting with a handful of Brook Farm's creditors and stockholders was a day that he had certainly never anticipated when he resigned his Unitarian pulpit six years before. That's not to say, however, that he was discouraged or distraught about Brook Farm's impending collapse. He was probably even relieved. On the very same day that he met with Brook Farm's creditors, Ripley was putting the finishing touches to a detailed article on "The Condition and Prospects of the Associative Cause" for the April 3 number of *The Harbinger*. His attention was focused as much on the future of the Associative movement as it was on the community's demise.[1]

Journal *November* 1844

Statement
of the Assets & Liabilities of
Brook Farm Association
November 1. 1844

Assets –

Individual Balances in favor B.F.A.
  in particulars see Journal page: 1803 00
Bills Receivable   284 43
Buildings   6552 67
Cash   14 07
Farm Produce   and Stock p/c Book   949 10
Furniture & Fixtures   "   4413 14
Real Estate   "   22492 60
Sundry Bales on hand   "   955 75   37464 7

Liabilities
Amts due Sundry persons
    and journal page "   13654 77
Bills Payable   for Schedule E on file   1637 66
Joint Stock   5540 .
Sundry Accounts   1596 06 36019 14
    Bal^ce in favor B.F.A. and: H.S. p/c Ledger} Dollars 1445 2
    and Schedule A on file

"Statement of the Assets & Liabilities of Brook Farm Association,
November 1, 1844." From the beginning to the end of its existence,
Brook Farm was plagued with financial difficulties.

Although notice was posted to all of Brook Farm's creditors and stockholders prior to March 4, only Francis G. Shaw and George R. Russell attended the meeting at the Hive, along with a few of the associates still remaining at Brook Farm, among them Jean Palisse, the Association's general mechanic, John Hoxie, who had purchased $60 of stock in October 1845, Jonathan Butterfield, one of the printers with *The Harbinger,* Nathaniel Colson, a shoemaker, and Peter Kleinstrup, the cabinetmaker from Denmark who, until recently, had been in charge of Brook Farm's greenhouse. (Coincidentally enough, all five of these Brook Farmers arrived in 1844 within a few months of each other during the rush to the community after the conversion to Fourierism.) Ripley provided a verbal statement of the Phalanx's financial condition, after which it was "voted unanimously that George Ripley be authorized to let the Farm for one year from March 1 [1847] for $350. and the Keith lot for $100. or more, with such conditions & reservations, as he may deem best for the interest of the Stockholders."[2]

A second important development in 1847 that bore directly on Ripley and Brook Farm's immediate future occurred two months later at the first annual meeting of the American Union of Associationists (AUA) in New York City. The convention, which took place over three days from May 11 to 13, attracted about forty-five delegates from affiliated unions in such places as Philadelphia, Albany, and Pittsford, Vermont. The majority were from the New York Union and the Boston Union, the latter including several Brook Farmers, among them Ripley, John Dwight, John Orvis, and Peter Baldwin. William Henry Channing, John Allen, and Frank Shaw were also present. Among the representatives from the New York Union were former Brook Farmers Charles Dana and Louis Ryckman.

That Brook Farm itself was already considered moribund by Associationists is clear from the report of the Executive Committee of the AUA, which noted that only "*three* of the *Practical Attempts* at Association have survived the immature projects at embodying the true law of society."[3] Those three, the report stated, were the North American, Wisconsin, and Trumbell (Ohio) Phalanxes. (Ripley probably had to bite his tongue hearing Brook Farm implicitly characterized as an "immature project.") Convention delegates recommended, among other things, that a central office be established in New York City to oversee the operations of the AUA, and that the financial responsibility for *The Harbinger* be transferred to the AUA in conjunction with the organization of the central office. *The Harbinger,* it was also agreed, should be formally transferred to the AUA with the close of the fourth volume just a few weeks after the convention.

When the Executive Committee met again in New York just two months later on July 14 and 15 to finalize the arrangements that had been unanimously approved at the May convention, a third development occurred that directly affected Brook Farm's demise. Ripley, Dwight, and Orvis—as well as Allen, Dana, and Channing—all participated in the two-day discussions in New York, in which it was decided that the new central office in New York City would be under the direction of George Ripley, as General Agent of the Union, and that *The Harbinger*—with the close of the fifth and not the fourth volume, it was now decided—would be published simultaneously in New York and Boston, "with Parke Godwin as Editor, assisted by Charles A. Dana and George Ripley in New York, and William H. Channing and John S. Dwight in Boston." Ripley would receive $800 a year for his services as AUA's General Agent and assistant editor of *The Harbinger.* Godwin and Dana would each be paid $150 a year, and Dwight and Channing would receive $500 and $250, respectively, for their editorial labors in Boston.

As if Ripley's commitment to the Associationist cause wasn't already self-sacrificing enough, he also placed himself on three new committees: one to inquire about the practical operations of Associationists in Europe; a second to "inquire and report upon the best mode of applying the Serial Law to the transitional states of Association"; and a third to "classify . . . various attempts at Guarantyism" both in the United States and Europe.[4] Sophia Ripley also intended to devote herself to the cause after the move to New York. She would serve on a committee to consider the best plan for establishing a school based on Associative principles.

When Ripley returned to Brook Farm on July 17, 1847, he must have done so with a sense of some relief, for not only did he have reason to believe that his immediate future, at least, would be secure (something that had always been uncertain at the community), but he also had reason to hope that he would finally be able to put Brook Farm's protracted demise behind him in October. If he was at all sentimental or nostalgic about the community to which he had devoted himself so tirelessly and selflessly for the previous six years, there is no record of it in this period.[5] He had little time, in any case, to indulge such sentiments: there were still nineteen more numbers of *The Harbinger* to get out in order to complete the fifth volume, and the responsibility for doing so rested entirely on the shoulders of those who remained at Brook Farm.

The problem, Ripley well knew, wasn't the paper's production. Even though head-printer Thomas Treadwell had departed the community in early April 1847 with his wife and two sons, the rest of the corps of printers—Jonathan Butterfield, Edgar Palisse, Willard Saxton, and Charles Codman—were still living in the community and had no plans yet to leave. Instead, the difficulty confronting Ripley and the always devoted and reliable John Dwight was soliciting material to fill the triple columns of the sixteen-page weekly paper. John Allen, it turned out, contributed only two items for the fifth volume, which is all that William Henry Channing managed to provide. John Orvis eventually sent along nine items—several of them reports on his and Allen's lecturing activities in New York and Vermont. Charles Dana, however, didn't contribute a single item to the fifth volume, and neither did Parke Godwin or Albert Brisbane, the last of whom would not be seen or heard from at all in the months leading up to Brook Farm's final collapse.[6] That Ripley and Dwight had precious little time between July and October 1847 for anything other than *The Harbinger* is dramatically indicated by the fact that 110 of the 143 original items that appeared in the fifth volume of the Associationist paper (literary and musical reviews, editorials, and reports on Associationism and Associative activities, for instance) were written by these two men. Ripley contributed sixty items, Dwight fifty.

The pressure of *The Harbinger*'s publication notwithstanding, there was one other important "duty" that summer for Ripley in his capacity as leader of the Brook Farm Phalanx, and that was to meet one final time with the community's stockholders and creditors. Brook Farm's "official" demise might be dated from this meeting on August 18, 1847, even though the Ripleys and several other Brook Farmers didn't leave the community until October. As he had done in March, Ripley notified all of Brook Farm's stockholders and creditors prior to the meeting, but surprisingly few showed up. Neither Frank Shaw nor his brother-in-law George Russell attended, although Russell authorized Theodore Parker to represent him. Peter Kleinstrup and Jean Palisse were once again present, and Amelia Russell and Marianne Ripley also attended this meeting, along with James Kay, Jr., and a Samuel P. Teal. The surviving minutes of the brief meeting—recorded by Palisse—note that "it was then voted unanimously, That the President of the Phalanx [Ripley] be and is hereby authorized to transfer to a board of three Trustees, the whole property of the Corporation for the purpose and with power, of disposing of it to the best advantage of all concerned." It was also voted unanimously, the minutes further state, that Theodore Parker, George Russell, and Samuel P. Teal "compose that board of Trustees."[7]

In the weeks following Ripley's final action as president of the Brook Farm Phalanx, quite a few associates lingered on at the community. As late as the end of September and the beginning of October 1847 there were probably more than twenty there and, on any given day, even as many as thirty might be found at the Hive, the Pilgrim House, the Cottage, or the Eyrie, although most of the rooms in these much-used buildings were now eerily empty. Brook Farm's printers— Jonathan Butterfield, Edgar Palisse, Willard Saxton, and Charles Codman—had to stay because of *The Harbinger*. But both of Palisse's parents—Jean and Eliza—also remained at the community, as did Codman's family, including his parents and sister and brother— John, Rebecca, Sarah Rebecca, and John T. Peter Kleinstrup's wife, Augustina, and his daughter, Louisa, also remained with him at the Farm. The Dwight family, too, continued to reside there, including Mary Ann, who was still in her old room in the Pilgrim House, which she now shared with her husband John Orvis when he wasn't on the road on one of his frequent lecture tours. The colorful John Cheever was also one of the last remaining Brook Farmers, as were George and Sophia Ripley themselves.

On the eve of his departure from West Roxbury, Ripley made one final appearance in Boston to attend yet another meeting of the Executive Committee of the AUA beginning on October 10, 1847. It was a memorable occasion, not only because it attracted several leading Associationists from around the country, but also because, uncharacteristically, it featured an evening social gathering that included members of the Executive Committee, "the ladies and gentlemen" of the Boston Union and the Boston Religious Union of Associationists, and the Brook Farmers still remaining at the community. It was as if those who would be staying on in Boston and New England after the meeting was over understood that the participants would never assemble again in quite the same way. They were determined that the four days of activities would leave a lasting impression. And they did. John Dwight characterized them in *The Harbinger* a few weeks later: "Of all the interesting public meetings which have been held by Associationists in Boston in times past, few have been more successful, [or] more happily sustained from beginning to end."[8]

Many of the out-of-town participants arrived early and began the week by attending both the public and private Sunday services of the BRUA, where, in the morning, they enjoyed "the holy and exalting music of Mozart and Haydn" and the "manly eloquence" of William Henry Channing, and then, in the evening, "were welcomed into the circle, and by the mystic symbol of joining hands helped . . . renew the pledge of faithfulness to our life-purpose." The next two days were devoted to reports and discussions about future prospects of the Associationist cause. These were followed on Tuesday evening by a social gathering at the home of Boston Associationist James T. Fisher, which again featured choruses of Mozart and Haydn and songs of Beethoven and Schubert as a prelude to the brief celebratory toasts "to Association," "to the Phalanstery," "to Fourier," "to Woman," "to Beauty in Nature and Art," and "to Universal Unity." The meetings concluded on Wednesday evening, October 13, at a public gathering at Washington Hall on Bromfield Street in Boston. There the many friends of Association listened to remarks "from the impulse of the moment" by Ripley, Dwight, Channing, and John Allen. If Ripley had any reservations about his departure a few days hence from West Roxbury, they weren't evident that evening. According to the account in *The Harbinger,* he referred often in his comments to "the breaking up of the life at Brook Farm." Whatever were his own personal sentiments about the community's collapse, Ripley, "on the eve of entering a new sphere of labor for the same great cause, appeared in all his indomitable strength and cheerfulness, triumphant amid outward failure."

George Ripley left Brook Farm a few days later, on October 19, with his sister Marianne and two or three others from the community. Three days later, on October 22, Sophia Ripley followed her husband to New York, accompanied by John Cheever and several other associates, at least one of whom was on his way to the North American Phalanx to live. D. H. Jacques, a member of both the BUA and the BRUA, stopped at the West Roxbury community around this time and noted that "The 'Eyrie' is nearly deserted. The 'Cottage' and the 'Pilgrim House' will soon be without tenants. The swarm which thronged 'The Hive' is scattered, and yonder stands the blackened walls of what was dignified by the name of 'Phalanstery.'"[9] On October 24, 1847, Willard Saxton wrote to his father and noted that there were not more than "ten or twelve persons at the table" in the Hive at mealtime.[10] The Dwight family had left that very week for nearby Jamaica Plain. John Dwight "has a room in the city, and will stay there most of the time this winter." Only the Codman family would remain at Brook Farm during the winter. As for the young Saxton and the other out-of-work printers, "we shall get through our work here Wednesday or Thursday," he told his father, "and then," he added finally, "we have done with Brook Farm."

Epilogue

There are several postscripts to Brook Farm's troubled history. One has to do with its creditors, another with the physical site of the community in the years following its collapse, and yet another with the later activities of Brook Farm's leaders. A word or two also needs to be included about the various causes of Brook Farm's failure, as well as, even more important, of its success.

Resolution of the community's financial entanglements is somewhat easier to document than the psychic costs of the utopian experiment on Brook Farm's leaders. After the departure of George and Sophia Ripley and others in October 1847, only the members of the Codman family—that is, John and his wife Rebecca and two of their three children, Sarah Rebecca and Charles—and Mary Macdaniel—mother of Fanny and Eunice—stayed on at Brook Farm through the winter of 1847–1848. The Farm was sold at public auction on April 13, 1849, to John L. Plummer for $19,150. Three days later Plummer conveyed the property to the city of Roxbury, which was anxious to relocate the existing almshouse in town to the more secluded surroundings of the Farm.

Plummer was chairman of a Joint Special Committee appointed by the Roxbury City Council to report on Brook Farm's suitability for the almshouse removal. It was noted in the "Report of the Joint Special Committee" in April 1849 that there were still "encumbrances,

consisting of mortgages and an execution, amounting to $17,445.25"
on the property. In fact, there were four mortgages, and they totaled
$14,500. The execution was for $2,096.05, and it was due to Anna
Alvord, who provided nearly all the funds for the construction of the
Cottage in 1842. All of Brook Farm's mortgagees, and the execution to
Alvord, were immediately settled by the city of Roxbury. Among
Brook Farm's thirty-two known creditors, ten made no claim against
the community, and nine claims were not allowed. The other thirteen
claimants were paid varying amounts from the money remaining after
satisfaction of the mortgages and the execution.[1]

The community site underwent immediate changes after Brook
Farm's collapse. After serving as an almshouse for a few years, the
Farm was purchased by Ripley's former Unitarian colleague James
Freeman Clarke, and was then transformed into Camp Andrew at the
beginning of the Civil War. On the eve of assuming command of the
controversial Fifty-fourth Massachusetts (all Negro) Infantry, Colonel
Robert Gould Shaw trained for combat at Camp Andrew, where he
had played so often as a child with his brothers and sisters. Writing to
his mother on May 19, 1861, Shaw noted that it was "very odd to be at
Brook Farm. The cottage is the only one of the old houses that remains. There is a new house on the site of the 'Hive,' and these two
are the only ones now standing."[2] Both these buildings managed to
survive until the second half of the twentieth century because of the
long-term stewardship of the Lutheran Church, which purchased the
property in 1871 and converted it into an orphanage. The building on
the site of the original farmhouse that was known as the Hive was destroyed by fire in 1973. The Cottage stood for twelve more years before it too was consumed by flames in 1985. Both fires appear to have
been acts of vandalism.

Of what might be called the psychic costs to Brook Farm's leaders,
these are obviously difficult to assess. It's true that George Ripley and

Charles Dana went on to have distinguished careers after Brook Farm's demise. However, though no one was so well qualified to provide an internal history of the community, it is a striking fact that neither of these men ever put pen to paper to vindicate their earlier efforts—to celebrate what was, at the very least, a noble and worthwhile experiment on behalf of humanity. They did not do so, almost certainly, because it was simply too painful to revisit the mound of ashes amid which lay the high ideals and faith in man's perfectability that genuinely animated each man during all but the last of the Brook Farm years.[3]

Ripley followed Dana to New York City in October 1847 and joined his colleague on the staff of Horace Greeley's New York *Tribune*, where he remained until his death on July 4, 1880. In the intervening years, Ripley conducted the *Tribune*'s book review column, which he handled with the same high-mindedness and dignity of purpose for which he had been respected during *The Harbinger* years. He and Dana collaborated on the popular and financially successful *New American Cyclopaedia: A Popular Dictionary of General Knowledge* in 1863, which earned both men a nice profit and, according to one commentator, enabled Ripley to pay off the remaining debts still lingering after Brook Farm's collapse. The success of the sixteen-volume *Cyclopaedia* evidently prompted some of Brook Farm's creditors to recall "their twenty-year-old debts and [they] dunned Ripley for free copies to compensate for their losses in his transcendental socialist enterprise [Brook Farm]."[4]

Sophia Ripley, too, found personal satisfaction during her New York years, though this turned out to be tragically brief. Much of her happiness came from the comfort that she found in the hierarchal authority of the Catholic Church, the religion to which she converted almost immediately after she moved to New York. Her conversion is one of the striking ironies of the Brook Farm story. Only a few years before, it will be recalled, Sophia's democratic iconoclasm made her an active participant in Margaret Fuller's "Conversations" for women, an attendee at meetings of the "Transcendental Club," and a supporter of women's rights with essays like the one on "Woman" that appeared in the January 1841 number of the *Dial*. In any case, she developed breast cancer in 1859, apparently from a fall "while stooping to pick up something behind her marble topped bureau." Sophia Ripley died on February 4, 1861. Ripley returned her body to Boston, and the funeral took place at the Purchase Street Church, which would have pleased Sophia because it had been converted to a Catholic Church just a few years before her death.

Immediately after the burial in the Dana family tomb in Cambridge, Ripley shared with her uncle, Richard Henry Dana, Sr., some of his most personal thoughts about the woman to whom he had been married for nearly thirty-four years: "Surely such perfect unworldliness, such wonderful freedom from selfishness, such singular integrity both of mind and heart, such a lofty spirit combined with such sweet womanly grace, was never found in so beautiful a union before." Ripley later married a wealthy German woman some thirty years his junior who, according to Lindsay Swift, "brought him many years of wholesome companionship." The marriage enabled Ripley to enjoy two well-deserved excursions to Europe, the first in 1866 for six months, and the second three years later for a year and a half.[5]

Charles Dana was nearly seventeen years younger than his lifelong friend Ripley, and he died seventeen years after his former Brook Farm associate. In many respects, their careers after the demise of the West Roxbury community followed parallel tracks, for Dana achieved as much if not more notoriety in the New York journalistic world as the owner and editor of the New York *Sun* from 1868 to 1897. Dana, too, spent important time in Europe, though he first journeyed there much earlier than Ripley when Horace Greeley sent him to France,

Germany, and Austria in 1848 to report on the social unrest in those countries, something that he did on a weekly basis for many months, and not just for the *Tribune* but for four other papers as well, including, for a short time, *The Harbinger*. Dana split with Greeley over differences having to do with the Civil War, prompting the influential *Tribune* owner to fire his managing editor in 1863. Dana subsequently was appointed Secretary of War in 1864. When the Civil War ended, Dana purchased the New York *Sun* (after a brief stint in 1865 with the *Chicago Republican*) and turned it into one of the most powerful and respected newspapers in the United States during the last three decades of the nineteenth century.[6]

And what of the lives of the other approximately 200 or so individuals who, at one time or another, made their way to Brook Farm for a day, a week, a month, or even a year or more? For most, their dreams and aspirations were written on the wind; there are no known surviving journals, or letters, or other records to document their later endeavors—or, for that matter, even their brief time at Brook Farm. For a few others, some information is available, especially for those who went on to write their names large in the annals of nineteenth-century American life and letters.

John Sullivan Dwight, for example, remained in Boston after *The Harbinger*'s transfer to New York in 1847 to serve as the New England editor of the Associationist paper. Although he was to have received an annual salary of $500, it's unlikely that he was ever paid anything near that amount. It's a moot point, in any case, because *The Harbinger* collapsed in February 1849, at which time Dwight took over three columns of Elizur Wright's *Boston Chronotype* on behalf of the American Union of Associationists. He had already become very active in both the Boston Union of Associationists (BUA) and the Boston Religious Union of Associationists (BRUA). In 1851 he married Mary

Bullard, whom he had first met at Brook Farm and who, like Dwight, participated actively in the late 1840s in the BUA and the BRUA. Dwight's "Musical Review" column in *The Harbinger* represented the first important music criticism in the history of American journalism, so it's not surprising that the former Brook Farmer established *Dwight's Journal of Music* (1852–1881) after *The Harbinger* folded. *Dwight's Journal of Music* was very highly regarded during the twenty-nine years of its existence, and it continues to be cited today in works dealing with American musical history. Dwight remained in New England for the rest of his life. He died in 1893.[7]

Quite a few other Brook Farmers also remained in the area, several of them settling for a while in the town of Concord. Dwight's good friends George William and James Burrill Curtis moved there soon after their departure from Brook Farm in 1843, where they joined at least two other former members of the community, Nathaniel Hawthorne and Almira Barlow. Hawthorne and Sophia Peabody had moved to the Old Manse in July 1842 on the occasion of their marriage. Barlow went to Concord in 1843 with her three sons, Francis, Edward, and Richard—all of whom had been students in the Brook Farm school. Emerson's good friend George P. Bradford soon followed the Curtis brothers to Concord, as did the young seeker, Isaac Hecker.

Other Brook Farmers who later made their way to the town that was home to Emerson, Henry David Thoreau, and the Bronson Alcott family included Minot and Maria Pratt and their children (son John married Anna Alcott in 1860), Marianne Ripley, who established a school near the Pratt home on Punkatasset Hill, and John Cheever, or "Irish John" as he was known at Brook Farm. Carrie Stodder, one the community's earliest residents, Elmira Daniels, a seamstress, and John and Dolly Hosmer also lived for a time in Concord. The Pratts

remained there for the rest of their lives, for many years gathering together those former Brook Farmers who could still be assembled for
an annual picnic. Emerson, Thoreau, and the Alcotts often participated in the festivities.

After leaving Concord, George William Curtis later achieved considerable celebrity, first as the author of a number of popular and
humorous travel books—*Nile Notes of a Howadji* (1851) and *The
Howadji in Syria* (1852)—then as the progressive editor of *Harper's
Weekly*, in whose columns from the "Editor's Easy Chair" he continued to voice his support of such causes as women's rights and industrial reform. Brother Burrill was ordained an Anglican clergyman in
1851 and spent the rest of his long life in England. Isaac Hecker also
devoted his later years to the religious life. After a brief stay in Concord at the home of his friend Henry Thoreau, Hecker founded the
missionary order that is known today as the Paulist Fathers in 1857.[8]

Several other people directly or indirectly linked to Brook Farm
eventually married one another. According to John Codman, as many
as twenty-eight did so. Charles Dana's marriage to Eunice Macdaniel
and Mary Ann Dwight's to John Orvis stand out perhaps from all the
others—Dana and Macdaniel's for the secrecy of theirs in New York
City on the eve of the destruction of the Phalanstery, and Dwight and
Orvis's for the distinction of theirs being the only wedding ever performed at Brook Farm (in December 1846). Fred Cabot, Brook Farm's
bookkeeper and for a time the object of Mary Ann Dwight's romantic
attention, married Mary Lincoln, a frequent visitor to the community,
in 1845. Just a few weeks before the Dwight-Orvis wedding, Mary
Ann Donelly married Brook Farm cabinetmaker Robert Westacott,
but not at the Farm.

Other marriages that can be traced to Brook Farm include Charles
Dana's sister Maria to his wife Eunice's brother, Osborne Macdaniel;

Lizzie Curson, who lived at Brook Farm during its final days, to John Hoxie, one of the printers of *The Harbinger,* who were married shortly after the community's demise; Rebecca Codman to Jonathan Butterfield, another of the community's printers; and John Allen to Ellen Lazarus, the latter a member of both the BUA and the BRUA, whose brother, Marx Edgeworth, was a contributor to the later volumes of *The Harbinger.* Among the earliest residents of Brook Farm, Abby Morton—who later achieved some celebrity as the author of the popular juvenile books that comprised the "William Henry" series—wed Manuel Diaz, another early resident and one of four Spanish-speaking students who were brought to the community in 1841.[9] George William Curtis eventually married Anna Shaw, Robert Gould Shaw's sister and the daughter of Brook Farm friend, neighbor, and financial supporter Francis G. Shaw. John S. Dwight's marriage to Mary Bullard in 1851 has already been noted.

William Henry Channing performed the marriage of Mary Ann Dwight and John Orvis at Brook Farm on December 24, 1846. Channing was beloved by many of the Brook Farmers, and several of them followed the charismatic minister when the Boston Union of Associationists and the Boston Religious Union of Associationists were being organized even as Brook Farm was breaking apart. After *The Harbinger* folded in February 1849, Channing established a weekly paper called the *Spirit of the Age* (1849–1850), but it lasted only eleven months. Not long after the Boston Union and the Religious Union also collapsed, Channing left for England in 1854, where he served a number of radical Unitarian societies during the remaining thirty years of his life. Channing's influence on the Brook Farmers is often cited as one of the major reasons for the community's ultimate failure. That influence, however, clearly has been exaggerated. William Henry Channing had virtually nothing to do with Brook Farm's demise. Channing aside, there is no shortage of reasons to account for the community's collapse—though not all of them were equally consequential.

The two most immediate causes for Brook Farm's failure were the outbreak of smallpox in November 1845, followed just a few months later by the destruction of the Phalanstery. These two events were like the decisive one-two combination of blows that brings a wearied fighter crashing to the ground. And by 1847, George and Sophia Ripley, Charles Dana, Marianne Ripley, and John Dwight—the only ones left at the Farm who had been there during the early days of promise—were quite weary from unrelieved years of struggle having to do, mostly, with the persistent financial pressures that plagued Brook Farm right from the very beginning of its existence. Obviously the financial impact of the smallpox episode on the Brook Farm school wasn't as immediately devastating as the reported $7,000 loss of the Phalanstery, but it proved to be more insidious because enrollment in the school in the months following the outbreak steadily dwindled to just a handful of students. Parents who were hesitant about returning their children to Brook Farm because of the epidemic were understandably even more reluctant to do so after the extensive fire in early March 1846. The financial impact of these two events cannot be overstated.

Brook Farm's demise, however, was the result of more pervasive forces than smallpox and the fire. As difficult as it is—even painful—to point the finger at a man of such fine and rare spirit as George Ripley, it has to be said finally that upon his shoulders must rest the burden of responsibility for Brook Farm's chronic internal difficulties, and thus its ultimate collapse. Ripley always had the very best intentions, and he was the most unselfish of men, but he was nearly as ill prepared for the Brook Farm venture as Amos Bronson Alcott had been for his disastrous and short-lived "Fruitlands" experiment in 1843.

Margaret Fuller was right when she remarked to William Henry Channing in 1840, just a few months before Ripley undertook the experiment, that she wished he might have "a faithful friend in the beginning, the rather that his own mind, though that of a captain is not that of a conqueror."

Ripley arrived in West Roxbury without any farming or business experience whatsoever. It is ironic that the former Unitarian minister who so patiently and deliberately went head to head with Andrews Norton in a protracted pamphlet war over the religious authority of the biblical miracles was guided by impetuous enthusiasm when it came to selecting a dairy farm as the site of his agrarian utopian experiment. Ripley should certainly have recognized that the reason Charles and Maria Ellis's West Roxbury property was, and had been, a dairy farm was because the relative sterility of the soil made it unsuitable for any other kind of farming. The site of the experiment is definitely an important reason why the community failed to prosper.

John Codman and Lindsay Swift claim in their standard treatments of the community that Brook Farm's distance from Boston markets should be counted among the leading causes of the community's failure. However, they overstate the importance of this factor. No doubt the Farm's location did make the transport of goods to and from Boston inconvenient, but, if anything, being just eight miles from Boston should have been an advantage to the Brook Farmers. None of the more than dozen Shaker communities then in existence were so favorably situated near a major city, and neither was the Separatist community in Zoar, Ohio, that the Ripleys had visited in 1838. Ripley's good friend Adin Ballou's Hopedale Community was situated a lot farther from Boston than Brook Farm was, but it survived twenty years longer than the West Roxbury community. Brook Farm's distance from the Boston markets had very little to do with its collapse. Poor judgment did, and that began with the selection of the Ellis Farm as the scene of the experiment.

It is also ironic that a man who had such breadth of understanding in religious, literary, and social matters consistently failed to exercise good practical judgment, patience, and foresight when it came to the community's internal operations and development.[10] The selection of Charles Dana to be second in command and the hasty and financially irresponsible expansion of Brook Farm are just two obvious examples. The situation with Dana was particularly egregious. He was young and inexperienced, and when he came to Brook Farm in September 1841 he didn't have so much as a proverbial penny in his pocket. Although he spent five years in the community, Dana never managed to purchase even one of the three shares of Brook Farm stock that he originally pledged to purchase in 1841. The physical expansion of the community was simply a case of too much too soon. Ripley's "open door" admission policy to the community necessitated the construction of additional space to accommodate the new arrivals. The ambitious and premature building program immediately ran the community into substantial debt, which in turn provided a constant source of pressure throughout Brook Farm's existence.[11]

Some of the debt might have been offset by the school, but, despite early claims that Brook Farm was first and foremost a community of teachers, Ripley never wholeheartedly supported or promoted its educational programs after the first year or so. (The "Brook Farm Labor Record, May 1844–April 1845," shows, for instance, that Ripley devoted 78 percent of his total worktime that year to activities unrelated to the school.)[12] Neither Ripley nor Dana nor anyone else in the inner circle seems to have ever fully appreciated what exceptional educational opportunities and advantages were available at Brook Farm, or, ironically, what a potentially steady and important source of income the school represented. For Ripley especially these were particularly ironic failures of recognition given his original motivation for organizing the community.

Perhaps the greatest irony of all, however, is the most poignant. It has nothing directly to do with Brook Farm's failure, but it should be noted here among the ironies of the Brook Farm story. This one also has to do with George Ripley, who, by the time of the community's collapse in 1847, had been forced pretty much entirely to abandon the original Christian egalitarian principles that had led him to West Roxbury in the first place. It was those very principles that had inspired him during the religious wars that he fought so determinedly with conservative (and often wealthy) Unitarians like Andrews Norton in the 1830s, for whom there was no place in the Church for Transcendentalists of Ripley's stripe who could not accept the central authority of ministers and miracles. By 1845 financial necessity—the relief from which was of course one of the original impulses behind Brook Farm's organization—had forced Ripley to adopt the same stance that had earlier been taken by conservative Unitarians like Norton. In article after article in *The Harbinger* Ripley echoes his support of "a central [Associative] school speaking authoritatively upon doctrinal questions." This from the minister who just a few years before had repudiated doctrines and creeds!

A significant portion of the blame for Brook Farm's failure, however, extends beyond George Ripley, the stony soil of the West Roxbury farm, the smallpox epidemic, and the Phalanstery fire—all the way down to New York City, in fact. Associationists like Albert Brisbane, Parke Godwin, and Horace Greeley deserve a hefty share of it too. Greeley especially exerted early influence. It was Greeley who first urged the Brook Farmers in 1842 to be more egalitarian by recruiting tradesmen and semiskilled workers, and it was also Greeley, just a few months afterward, who recommended that they devote less time to the school: "Your *dependence* on your pupils is a fetter which you ought not to wear another season," he exhorted. "You *must* not." Horace Greeley was already a powerful man in 1842; the Brook Farmers understandably paid attention to what he had to say. And what he said at the end of the year was that they should admit Louis Ryckman to the community, a shoemaker who was the second vice president of the New York Fourier Society.[13]

New York Associationists, including Ryckman, were instrumental in Brook Farm's conversion to Fourierism in 1844, although their interest in the West Roxbury Association never had very much to do with the community's own welfare. Their commitment was to Associationism and Fourierism. Brook Farm's importance to the New York Associationists lay in the fact that it was the only Fourierist community east of the Hudson River and thus it was a valuable inroad into New England in the effort to propagandize the cause. It might be too much to say that men like Brisbane, Godwin, and Greeley purposely teased the Brook Farmers with the prospect of the community's designation—and the implicit financial support that came with it—as the "Model Phalanx" in the United States, but they certainly did nothing to discourage hope in such an eventuality either.

The effect of the conversion to Fourierism in January 1844 was immediate and domino-like, and it contributed to the community's collapse, but Fourierism itself was not one of the major causes of Brook Farm's eventual failure. To be sure, it prompted the departure of educated and engaging Brook Farmers like George Bradford, Georgiana Bruce, Hannah Ripley, Ora Gannett, Anna Alvord, Burrill and George William Curtis, Almira Barlow, Isaac Hecker, and others, and their replacement with dozens of carpenters, shoemakers, and other skilled and semiskilled workers who permanently altered the character of the community. The spontaneous sense of *joie de vivre* that characterized Brook Farm life in the early days was quickly stifled by the weight of the new labor log that was required by the Fourierist regime to record the number of hours and minutes that associates worked each day. The time and energy, moreover, that had to be devoted to efforts to proselytize the Associationist cause compromised and eventually splintered the commitment of Brook Farm's leaders to the goals upon which the community had originally been established. Despite all their determined efforts on behalf of Associationism and Fourierism during the second half of the community's existence, Brook Farm's leaders were notified by Albert Brisbane three months before the fire that destroyed the Phalanstery that the New York Associationists had collectively decided to withhold any further financial support from Brook Farm because they had agreed to devote it instead to the North American Phalanx in Red Bank, New Jersey.

When all is said and done, however, the last word about Brook Farm shouldn't have to do with failure. The Brook Farmers themselves would certainly be the first to say that the community should be remembered for its many important successes. And they do, in fact, in the dozens of reminiscences, recollections, and retrospectives that they have passed along, in not a single one of which, remarkably, is there to be found a really bad word about the West Roxbury community to which so many people devoted a season, or two, or more, of their lives. On the contrary. Women especially found opportunities there for personal growth and development—for what Emily Dickinson referred to in one of her poems as "Amplitude" and "Awe"—that were rarely available to them anywhere else in antebellum American society. Charles Dana may have been exaggerating a bit when he claimed in 1844 that the Brook Farmers had abolished "domestic servitude," but the fact is, even more remarkably, that no accounts by women have survived in which domestic responsibilities in the community are spoken of disparagingly, which is not something that can be said about any of the other antebellum New England communities.

Work may have been undertaken at Brook Farm along fairly traditional gender lines, but it was invariably performed without complaint and even cheerfully because every Brook Farmer knew that work wasn't circumscribed by gender, and that it would be equitably rewarded. A woman might as easily have spent her day ploughing furrows in the fields as she could in the sewing room. A man might spend his pounding sheets and then washing dishes after supper. (Emerson's poke at Brook Farm men is memorable: "it was ordained that the gentlemen-shepherds should wring and hang out clothes; which they punctually did. And it would sometimes occur that when they danced in the evening, clothespins dropped plentifully from their pockets.") All labor at Brook Farm was thought to be dignified, which is why it was always compensated equally between men and women, regardless whether the labor performed was domestic or mechanical, educational or agricultural.[14]

And this same egalitarian principle was at the heart of Brook Farm's progressive educational program too, although at least one of the community's supporters was never very happy about it. When James Kay, whose son Allie spent several years in the Brook Farm school, wrote in March 1846 with a list of reforms that he thought the Brook Farmers needed to adopt for their continued survival, he urged them to eject "the impure—especially the children," from the school.[15] That was a matter, however, about which Ripley was never willing to compromise. Education at Brook Farm was available to any student, without regard to family circumstances, and not because it was an act of charity but because one of Ripley's original ideals was that every person—male or female, young or old—was entitled to the most complete education possible. For children and adults alike, the educational opportunities available at Brook Farm were not to be found anywhere else in the United States.

And did such unusual advantages as these make Brook Farm a heaven on earth? Obviously not. But it needs to be remembered that important things were accomplished at Brook Farm for which George

Ripley had every reason to be justly proud. It really is unfortunate, as Hawthorne was already regretting in 1852, that Brook Farm's leader was never willing to provide a full history of the community. But it was never George Ripley's style to boast about his achievements. He had gone to Brook Farm to do God's work because that's where he thought that it might best be accomplished. It couldn't be done, he was certain, at the Purchase Street Church in Boston over which he had presided for fourteen years. Like Jesus Christ, about whom prior to Brook Farm Ripley had spoken and written on so many occasions, he would labor quietly in West Roxbury to build the new Jerusalem. And like Jesus, he would himself leave no written record of his work.

Remarkably, 150 years after the experiment failed, the Metropolitan District Commission (MDC) of Massachusetts managed to purchase 148 of the original acres that comprised the community and immediately dedicated them to open-space use. Additional land that formed part of Brook Farm's western side, along the Charles River, also remains open and protected today because much of it is still owned by nearby communities. The MDC eventually hopes to restore the historic landscape. There are also plans to develop interpretive trails, but, as of this writing, these have not yet been realized.

In the meantime, walking the actual ground that was Brook Farm, it is easy to recall the drama that played itself out there for more than six years in the reform-minded 1840s. America's most celebrated utopian community may long ago have ceased to exist, but the land continues to be an evocative and enduring reminder today of the faith and spirit that animated what was arguably the most unique decade in American history because it was a decade in which faith in the potential and perfectability of the human condition was conspicuously on display. That faith, of course, was forever shattered just a few years later by the clangor of a "firebell in the night" that forced the nation to turn its attention away from noble schemes for the melioration of humankind to the bloodiest and most divisive conflict that would ever stain American soil. Today, more than a century and a half after the organization of the "Brook Farm Institute of Agriculture and Education," the land still serves as an important reminder of George and Sophia Ripley's dream to build anew the "city of God" on a small farm in West Roxbury, Massachusetts.

Abbreviations

BFB   *The Brook Farm Book: A Collection of First-Hand Accounts of the Community,* ed. Joel Myerson (New York: Garland, 1987).

BFM   John T. Codman, *Brook Farm: Historic and Personal Memoirs* (Boston: Arena Publishing, 1894).

CAD   James Harrison Wilson, *The Life of Charles A. Dana* (New York: Harper and Bros., 1907).

DL   Marianne (Mary Ann) Dwight, *Letters from Brook Farm, 1844–1847,* ed. Amy L. Reed (Poughkeepsie, N.Y.: Vassar College, 1928).

IU-HS   Arthur E. Bestor, Jr., Papers, Illinois Historical Survey, University of Illinois, Urbana.

JMN   *The Journals and Miscellaneous Notebooks of Ralph Waldo Emerson,* 16 vols., ed. William H. Gilman, Ralph H. Orth et al. (Cambridge: Harvard University Press, 1960–1982).

JSD/MB   John Sullivan Dwight Brook Farm Papers, Boston Public Library, Boston, Mass.

KHi   John Stillman Brown Papers, Kansas State Historical Society, Topeka.

LEPP   *The Letters of Elizabeth Palmer Peabody, An American Renaissance Woman,* ed. Bruce A. Ronda. (Middletown, Conn.: Wesleyan University Press, 1984).

LMF   *The Letters of Margaret Fuller,* 6 vols., ed. Robert N. Hudspeth (Ithaca: Cornell University Press, 1983–1994).

LNH   Nathaniel Hawthorne, *The Letters, 1813–1843,* ed. Thomas Woodson, L. Neal Smith, and Norman Holmes Pearson (1984), vol. 15 of *The Centenary Edition of the Writings of Nathaniel Hawthorne,* ed. William Charvat et al. (Columbus: Ohio State University Press, 1963–1997).

LRWE   *The Letters of Ralph Waldo Emerson,* 10 vols., ed. Ralph L. Rusk and Eleanor M. Tilton (New York: Columbia University Press, 1939–1995).

MH   Houghton Library, Harvard University, Cambridge, Mass.

MHi   Brook Farm Papers, Massachusetts Historical Society, Boston, Mass.

NYPL   Bryant-Godwin Papers, New York Public Library, New York.

RWEMA/MH   Ralph Waldo Emerson Memorial Association, Houghton Library, Harvard University, Cambridge, Mass.

SAR   *Studies in the American Renaissance,* ed. Joel Myerson (Charlottesville: University Press of Virginia, 1977–1996).

SPNEA   Society for the Preservation of New England Antiquities, Boston, Mass.

Notes

Prologue

1. *A Farewell Discourse, Delivered to the Congregational Church in Purchase Street* (Printed by Request, for the Use of the Church, 1841), 18–19. Ripley returned one last time to the Purchase Street Church on February 9, 1842 to deliver the "Address to the People" on the occasion of the ordination of his successor, James Ives Tresothick Coolidge. The Purchase Street Society dissolved in May 1847 when the congregation moved to a new location on Harrison Avenue and Beach Street, and the name of the society was changed to the "Thirteenth Congregational Church of the City of Boston." See Octavius Brooks Frothingham, *George Ripley* (Boston: Houghton, Mifflin, 1883), 92–93.

2. Sophia Ripley to John Sullivan Dwight, May 6, [1841], "John Sullivan Dwight Papers," JSD/MB.

3. Ripley to Dwight, July 7, 1840, "John Sullivan Dwight Papers," JSD/MB.

4. Elizabeth Palmer Peabody made the point succinctly when she took it upon herself in 1842 to defend Brook Farm against the charge that the community was made up of Transcendentalists: "But to mass a few protestants together and call them transcendentalists, is a popular cant. Transcendentalism belongs to no sect of religion, and no social party. It is the common ground to which all sects may rise, and be purified of their narrowness; for it consists in seeking the spiritual ground of all manifestations." See "Plan of the West Roxbury Community," *Dial* 2

(January 1842): 371. Clarke's remark is quoted in James Elliot Cabot, *A Memoir of Ralph Waldo Emerson,* 2 vols. (Boston: Houghton, Mifflin, 1887), 1: 249; for Brownson, see "Two Articles in the Princeton Review," *Boston Quarterly Review* 3 (July 1840): 265–323; Ripley's statement is in his *Letter to the Congregational Church in Purchase Street,* which is reprinted in Frothingham, *George Ripley,* 61–91; for the Transcendental Club, see Joel Myerson, "A Calendar of Transcendental Club Meetings," *American Literature* 44 (May 1972): 197–207.

5. Perry Miller, *The American Transcendentalists* (Garden City, N.Y.: Doubleday and Co., 1957), ix. For a detailed review of "The Transcendentalist Controversy, 1836–1840," see Anne C. Rose, *Transcendentalism as a Social Movement, 1830–1850* (New Haven: Yale University Press, 1981), 70–108, and William R. Hutchinson, *The Transcendentalist Ministers* (New Haven: Yale University Press, 1959), espec. 52–97.

6. *Boston Daily Advertiser* 42 (November 5, 1836): 2, col. 5.

7. For Ripley's response, see the *Boston Daily Advertiser* 42 (November 9, 1836): 2, cols. 3–5. For Ripley's review of Martineau, see the *Christian Examiner* (November 1836): 225–254. Elsewhere in the review Ripley also claimed that individual conscience is a more reliable test of the truths of Christianity than the so-called historical evidence of the miracles: "Let the study of theology commence with the study of human consciousness. Let us ascertain what is meant by the expression . . . the Image of God in the Soul of Man. Let us determine whether our nature has any revelation of the Deity within itself." Ripley and the Transcendentalists did not question the authenticity of the miracles attributed to Jesus in the New Testament. Their argument was that Jesus did not perform the miracles for the purpose of confirming the truth of his teachings.

8. After Norton complained that Ripley's review should not have been permitted in the pages of the *Christian Examiner,* the ministers responsible for the Unitarian organ met and reaffirmed the journal's commitment to free speech. Elizabeth Palmer Peabody reported to her sister Mary that "all the Ministers, (Mr. [Alexander] Young & Mr. [John G.] Palfrey excepted) entirely approve of the course Ripley has taken—altho' they do

not generally *believe* with him in regard to the question of *Inspiration*."
See *LEPP,* 183–184.

9. Long before his cranky review in January 1839 of Norton's masterwork, *Evidences of the Genuineness of the Four Gospels* (1838), Brownson had been chipping away at the brand of Unitarianism that was represented by Brahmins like Norton, Frothingham, Bowen, and Palfrey. In September 1834, for instance, he had published a review in *The Christian Examiner* on Benjamin Constant's *De la Religion, Considérée dans sa Source, ses Formes et ses Développements* in which Brownson vigorously criticized religious institutionalism, which no one mistook as anything but a blast against traditional Unitarianism. In 1836 Brownson published his *New Views of Christianity, Society, and the Church,* a carefully wrought historical analysis in which he identified Protestantism, and thus Unitarianism, with Materialism, and Transcendentalism with Spiritualism. After the severe Financial Panic in 1837, Brownson kept hammering away—especially in the pages of the *Boston Quarterly Review,* a journal that he established in 1838—at the privileged and propertied class represented by wealthy Unitarians who were the followers of Norton and his colleagues.

10. For Emerson, see *An Address Delivered before the Senior Class in Divinity College, Cambridge, Sunday Evening, 15 July, 1838* (Boston: James Munroe, 1838), 26–27. For Norton, see "The New School in Literature and Religion," *Boston Daily Advertiser* 43 (August 27, 1838): 2; *Discourse on the Latest Form of Infidelity* (Cambridge, Mass.: John Owen, 1839). For Ripley, see *"The Latest Form of Infidelity" Examined: A Letter to Mr. Andrews Norton* (Boston: James Munroe, 1839); *Defense of "The Latest Form of Infidelity" Examined: A Second Letter to Mr. Andrews Norton* (Boston: James Munroe, 1840); and *Defense of "The Latest Form of Infidelity" Examined: A Third Letter to Mr. Andrews Norton* (Boston: James Munroe, 1840). Norton soon recognized that he did not have the support of many of his Unitarian colleagues and withdrew from the pamphlet war with Ripley in 1840.

11. Perry Miller, *The Transcendentalists: An Anthology* (Cambridge, Mass.: Harvard University Press, 1950), 65.

12. Brownson, "Progress of Society," *Christian Examiner* 18 (July 1835): 352; "Education of the People," *Christian Examiner* 20 (May 1836): 168.

13. Carl J. Guarneri succinctly summarizes economic conditions in the United States in the late 1830s in his magisterial study, *The Utopian Alternative: Fourierism in Nineteenth-Century America* (Ithaca: Cornell University Press, 1992): "In 1837 the commercial and industrial boom of the preceding decades was abruptly terminated by a bank panic whose origins lay in unbridled speculation in cotton, public land, and internal improvements. Within two years credit virtually dried up, banks and state governments defaulted, businesses went bankrupt, farm commodity prices plummeted, and urban unemployment skyrocketed" (66). The subsequent depression following the Panic of 1837 lasted until the end of 1843 ("one of the gloomiest years in our industrial history") and thus served as a powerful force in the rash of community-building that occurred in the United States in the 1840s. The depression also helps to account for the widespread interest throughout the decade in French social scientist Charles Fourier's utopian socialist principles. It should be added, however, that the effects of this depression in the United States seem to have been felt more acutely outside of New England—at least judging from the number of utopian communities that were in existence in the 1840s. If we don't include Shaker communities—most of which were established in the United States in the eighteenth or early nineteenth centuries—there were sixty-six utopian communities in existence at one time or another during that decade. Of these sixty-six, only five were in New England (four in Massachusetts, one in Vermont). The other sixty-one were in Ohio (13), New York (11), Pennsylvania (9), Indiana (6), Wisconsin (6), Illinois (5), Texas (3), Michigan (2), Iowa (2), Missouri (2), New Jersey (1), and Louisiana (1). Moreover, there are very few explicit references to the depression in the correspondence, journals, and diaries of New England writers during this period.

14. *The Temptations of the Times: A Discourse Delivered in the Congregational Church in Purchase Street on Sunday Morning, May 7, 1837*

(Boston: Hilliard, Gray, 1837), 12–13. As early as 1833 Ripley began to make it clear that fundamental to Transcendentalism was a social critique of existing institutions. This conviction is implicit, for example, in his review of James Mackintosh in the *Christian Examiner* for January 1833 (pp. 311–322) when he says that individual "intuitive perceptions are the foundation of moral science, and the ultimate standard by which we settle all questions of practical duty."

15. See David M. Robinson, "William Ellery Channing," *Biographical Dictionary of Transcendentalism,* ed. Wesley T. Mott (Westport, Conn.: Greenwood Press, 1996), 36. The titles alone of some of Channing's works during the period indicate the extent to which he committed his ministry to social reform: *The Ministry for the Poor* (Boston: Russell, Odiorne, and Metcalf, 1835), *Slavery* (Boston: James Munroe, 1835), *An Address on Temperance* (Boston: Weeks, Jordan, 1837), and *Remarks on the Slavery Question* (Boston: James Munroe, 1839) were all published during the second half of the 1830s.

16. William Henry Channing, William Ellery's nephew, provided a neat statement, for example, of the social principle that Transcendentalists were patiently working out in the 1830s, but it did not appear in the pages of the Cincinnati-based periodical known as the *Western Messenger* until April 1, 1841, the very date, ironically, that is usually thought to mark the beginning of the Brook Farm experiment: "In all denominations of Christians," Channing stated, "are many who can no longer resist the conviction, that property should not be the basis of society, that wealth should not be the test of worth, that commerce should not, and need not be a preying of the able upon the weak, of the well informed upon the ignorant, of the cunning upon the simple" (569).

17. Ripley to Brownson, December 18, 1842, in Henry F. Brownson, *Orestes A. Brownson's Early Life: From 1803 to 1844* (Detroit: H. F. Brownson, 1898), 311–315; Ripley to W. H. Channing, April 7, 1882, in Frothingham, *George Ripley,* 302–303.

18. The reason that the Proprietors thought that Ripley's continuing service was essential to the Purchase Street Society was, ironically enough, financial in nature. His departure, it was feared, would likely prompt

other congregants to leave, which would result in an even smaller base of parishioners from whom to solicit operating funds. The Proprietors' response to Ripley was included with his *Farewell Discourse,* which was privately printed by the Society.

19. *LRWE,* 2:297–299.

20. A significant increase in the Boston population between 1830 and 1840 from 61,400 to 84,400 inhabitants (a 38 percent increase) helped to create a cheap labor market, and stimulated increased costs for housing and other essentials. The widespread unemployment that followed the Financial Panic of 1837 also aggravated social conditions. See, e.g., Peter R. Knights, *The Plain People of Boston* (New York: Oxford University Press, 1971), 19–32, espec. tab. II-1.

21. *A Letter Addressed to the Congregational Church in Purchase Street* (Boston, 1840). In October 1847, as Ripley prepared to depart West Roxbury for good—the ashes of Brook Farm at his feet—it's clear that whatever regrets he may have had as he looked back over the previous six-and-a-half years, they had nothing to do with his original decision to leave the Unitarian ministry in 1840. Upon learning that some of the "young [Unitarian] preachers and theological students are deeply interested" in the social reform program known as Associationism and Fourierism, which Ripley adopted at Brook Farm in 1844, the former Unitarian minister said that he "would not attach a greater importance to it than it deserves" because "the Unitarian denomination, as a body, is altogether too fashionable, too aristocratic, too well to do in the world, too fond of the splendors of 'gigmanity,' to authorize the hope, that it will ever go much ahead of the prevailing, canonical opinion in favor of any radical, social changes." See "Unitarianism and Association," *The Harbinger,* October 2, 1847, p. 271.

1. *"Fermenting and Effervescing"*

1. *Claims of the Age on the Work of the Evangelist* (Boston: Weeks, Jordan, 1840), 8. Subsequent quotations are from this work.

2. It's worth noting that William Ellery Channing delivered the "Charge" at Dwight's ordination. Ripley obviously would have informed Chan-

ning of his intention to deliver his letter of resignation the very next day. It seems safe to say that he did so with Channing's blessing.

3. William C. Gannett, *Ezra Stiles Gannett, Unitarian Minister in Boston, 1824–1871: A Memoir* (1875; Boston: American Unitarian Association, 3rd ed., 1893), 219–220. It's significant that Ripley didn't mention Emerson's name, who, it might be expected, would also have served as a model. Ripley's intention, however, evidently wasn't to exchange his pulpit for a lecture platform, as Emerson had done after resigning from the Second Congregational Church in Boston in 1832. He probably had in mind something like the "Church of the Disciples," which would be formed the following year under the leadership of his friend, James Freeman Clarke, or the "Twenty-Eighth Congregational Society," organized in 1845 for Theodore Parker. Both of these became models of liberal Christianity in Boston. Ripley's thinking in 1840 anticipated the organization of these new religious societies.

4. See Emerson to Fuller, May 28, 1840, and Fuller to Emerson, May 31, 1840, *LRWE,* 2:297–299. Ripley was sensitive enough about his own preaching that he devoted several remarks to it in his comprehensive letter to the Proprietors in October 1840. See Octavius Brooks Frothingham, *George Ripley* (Boston: Houghton, Mifflin, 1883), 72–73.

5. Brownson's statements are from the first installment of "The Laboring Classes" in the July 1840 number of *The Boston Quarterly Review,* 358–395.

6. Sophia Ripley to Dwight, August 1, 1840, JSD/MB. Brisbane's book was noticed in the July number of the *Dial.* Emerson told his brother that Ripley had written the brief notice of Brisbane, but it's unlikely that he would have been responsible for all the items in the lengthy "Record of the Months." It's interesting that Parker made no reference in his journal to Brisbane's or Fourier's religious views. In her prefatory article to "Plan of the West Roxbury Community" in the January 1842 number of the *Dial,* Elizabeth Palmer Peabody agreed in "Christ's Idea of Society" that "as a criticism on our society [*Social Destiny*] is unanswerable," but she complained that Brisbane "does not go down into a sufficient spiritual depth, to lay foundations which may support his superstructure,"

and she recoiled at his attempt to "circumvent moral Freedom, and imprison it in his Phalanx" (225). For Parker, see Carol Johnston, "The Journals of Theodore Parker: July–December 1840," (Ph.D. diss., University of South Carolina, 1980), 52. The entry follows one for "Monday 24 August [1840]" and immediately precedes one dated "Sept. 1–2 [1840]."

7. Frothingham, *Theodore Parker: A Biography* (Boston: James R. Osgood, 1874), 56–57. Parker once described himself as "a raw boy with clothes made by country tailors, coarse shoes, great hands, red lips and blue eyes." Quoted in Mary Caroline Crawford, *Famous Families of Massachusetts* (Boston: Little, Brown, 1930), 1:190.

8. I have not included Shaker communities because they were exclusively religious societies rather than "utopian" communities. (Adin Ballou's Hopedale Community was religiously inspired but just as central to its mission was a broad agenda of reform interests.) Besides, the nine Shaker societies located in New England were all established in the eighteenth century. I therefore do not include them whenever I refer to the five antebellum New England communities. In addition to the four communities cited, only one other ever existed in New England during the antebellum period, and that was John Humphrey Noyes's Putney Society, or Putney Community (1843–1848), in Putney, Vermont, which was reincarnated as the Oneida Community in 1848 after its transfer to the state of New York. The Groton Convention lasted for four days, August 12–15. Garrison himself was not at the meeting because he was abroad and didn't return to the United States until August 17. See Otohiko Okugawa, "Annotated List of Communal and Utopian Societies, 1787–1919," in Robert Fogarty, *Dictionary of American Communal and Utopian History* (Westport, Conn.: Greenwood Press, 1980), 173–200.

9. E. P. Clarke may have been the husband of Ann Wilby Clarke, who was one of the participants in a series of ten "Conversations" conducted by Margaret Fuller at George and Sophia Ripley's Bedford Place home in Boston from March 1, 1841 to May 6, 1841. See Caroline W. Healey, *Mar-*

garet and Her Friends (Boston: Roberts Brothers, 1897), who lists Ann Wilby Clarke as the "wife of a Boston bank officer" (19).

10. Parker devoted several remarks to Brownson's essay in his journal, noting, among other things, that "this question, first of inherited property, & next of all private property is to be hand[l]ed in the 19th century." The subject of property, which was one of the most controversial features of Brownson's essay, was also discussed at least at one meeting of the Transcendental Club. See Johnston, "The Journals of Theodore Parker," 18; Joel Myerson, "A Calendar of Transcendental Club Meetings," *American Literature* 44 (May 1972): 204.

11. Johnston, "The Journals of Theodore Parker," 34–47, espec. 47.

12. *Autobiography of Adin Ballou* (Lowell, Mass.: The Vox Populi Press, 1896), 322–323. Ripley and Ballou had been friends for several years. They participated together, for instance, in Orestes Brownson's ordination in Canton, Massachusetts, in 1834.

13. On August 16, Emerson wrote to Margaret Fuller: "I did not tell you of our University which Mr. A[lcott] & I built out of straw the other day . . . We two are quite ready & perhaps Parker[,] Ripley[,] Hedge[,] [George] Bradford & others may be soon . . . to give lectures or conversations to classes of young persons . . . What society shall we not have! . . . We shall sleep no more & we shall concert better houses, economies, & social modes than any we have seen." See *LRWE*, 2:323–324; 7:398–400.

14. Myerson, "A Calendar," p. 206, lists the date of the final meeting of the Club as "*Circa* September 20," but Theodore Parker notes in his journal that it was September 9. I cite Parker's date in the text. Hedge's letter is quoted in Joel Myerson, "The Transcendental Club," *Encyclopedia of Transcendentalism*, ed. Wesley T. Mott (Westport, Conn.: Greenwood Press, 1996), 223.

15. Peabody to Dwight, September 20, 1840, *LEPP*, 245–247. Ripley was present at both meetings, as were Peabody, William Henry Channing, Margaret Fuller, Hedge, and Theodore Parker. Emerson attended only the meeting on September 2. A few others attended one or the other

meeting. See Myerson, "A Calendar," 206. Peabody, whose sister Sophia married Nathaniel Hawthorne in 1842, was involved in many activities associated with New England Transcendentalism, including Bronson Alcott's Temple School and the publication of the *Dial*. She was at the forefront of the women's education movement, conducting seminars for adult women in the early 1830s. In 1840 she opened a bookshop and lending library on West Street in Boston, which quickly became a popular gathering place for the Transcendentalists whenever they were in town. It was here that several of Margaret Fuller's celebrated "Conversations" for women took place, and it was here that George and Sophia Ripley spent more than one afternoon discussing plans to organize their experimental community.

16. Johnston, "The Journals of Theodore Parker," 53.

17. For Emerson's remarks, see *LRWE,* 2:329–330. If Ripley's "purposes" were simply to resign from the Purchase Street Church, Emerson, who was obviously aware of his colleague's resignation letter in May, would never have characterized his reaction to that decision now by saying that he looked at Ripley "with great curiosity."

18. Clarke, *Autobiography, Diary and Correspondence,* ed. Edward Everett Hale (Boston: Houghton, Mifflin, 1891), 133.

19. William H. Fish, *Memoir of Butler Wilmarth, M.D.* (Boston: Crosby, Nichols, 1854), 88–89. Ripley's "associates" would have been the fourteen people whose names are listed on the "Articles of Agreement," the earliest document in which the Ripleys and their followers attempted to define their aims and purposes (see Chapter 3). It's clear from the list of names that George and Sophia's priorities for the new community were religious and educational in nature: eight of the fourteen individuals who pledged their early support were Unitarian ministers (Ripley himself, of course, and Samuel D. Robbins, Lemuel Capen, and Warren Burton) and teachers (Sophia Ripley, Marianne Ripley, and David and Maria Mack).

20. The nature of the disagreement between Ripley and Ballou was fairly common knowledge around Boston. Local abolitionist Edmund Quincy wrote to Maria Weston Chapman on February 25, 1841, for example,

noting that Ballou "required assent to the doctrines of his Standard [of Practical Christianity] for admission, which prevented Ripley from joining him, as he would not sign a creed, though he said he assented to all it contained." Ripley's ever-faithful supporter Elizabeth Palmer Peabody praised Ballou and his followers in her article on "Christ's Idea of Society" in the *Dial* (October 1841), but she added that the "objection" to their plan "is, that admittance as a member is made dependent on the taking of the temperance, abolition, nonresistance pledges, the pledge not to vote, &c. . . . After all is said for it that can be, they must admit that this test makes their community a church only, and not *the* church of Christ's Idea, world-embracing" (226). Even Lydia Maria Child noted in the *National Anti-Slavery Standard* in January 1842 that "the Roxbury Community would probably have united with him [Adin Ballou], had he not deemed it necessary to make non-resistance a test of membership." For Quincy's letter, see the Weston Sisters Papers, Boston Public Library. The year is incorrectly dated. The correct year is 1841, which is when Chapman was in Haiti, which is where Quincy sent his letter. For Child, see "Social Communities," 2 (January 6, 1842): 123.

21. The spirit of the community that the Ripleys envisioned is reflected in the words of encouragement that William Ellery Channing reportedly conveyed to Adin Ballou in February 1841: "I have for a very long time dreamed of an association to which the members, instead of preying on one another, and seeking to put each other down, after the fashion of this world, should live together as brothers, seeking one another's elevation and spiritual growth." Given Ripley's relationship to his mentor Channing, it's hard to imagine that the Unitarian divine didn't communicate a very similar sentiment to his devoted protégé. Channing's remark is quoted in Annie M. Salisbury, "Brook Farm," *BFB*, 241.

22. *LMF*, 2:174. At the very same moment that Fuller was expressing her reservation about Ripley, Sophia was reaffirming her complete dedication to their future plans: "No regret at leaving our pleasant house here [in Boston]," Sophia told Anna Alvord, "can blunt my keen sense of pleasure at being placed in true relations to society[,] at righting myself as I may say." Ripley to Alvord, October 30, [1840], SPNEA.

23. *Emerson: The Mind on Fire* (Berkeley: University of California Press, 1995), 339. In a letter to her friend Caroline Sturgis on October 18, 1840, Margaret Fuller notes that "it seemed that he [Emerson] would be very slow in solving all these problems that are before him now" (*LMF*, 2:163).

24. *JMN*, 7:401–404.

25. Not long after this sincere and frank expression of his own aspirations, Ripley would "recollect" on November 9, 1840, that "you [Emerson] said that if you were sure of compeers of the right stamp you might embark yourself in the adventure [organizing a community]." Ripley must still have been confident about Emerson's support a week after his November 9, 1840, letter because a mutual friend reported to John Dwight that a "New Harmony . . . is probably about to be established by him [Ripley], Emerson, etc." See Ripley to Emerson, RWEMA/MH, ca. 1840; Ripley to Emerson, November 9, 1840, in Frothingham, *George Ripley,* 312; and Samuel Osgood to John S. Dwight, November 21, 1840, in JSD/MB.

26. Sophia Ripley to Anna Alvord, October 30, [1840], SPNEA.

27. For Ripley, see Joel Myerson, "Bronson Alcott's 'Scripture for 1840,'" *ESQ* 20 (4th Quarter 1974): 27. For Emerson, see *JMN*, 7:407–408.

28. Myerson, "Alcott's 'Scripture,'" 251. Emerson made a similar point to Caroline Sturgis just a few days after the meeting at his home; see *LRWE*, 2:350. Fuller's vision of a model community is described in a letter to William Henry Channing; see *LMF*, 2:179–180.

29. Ripley's "charges" at the Boston Athenaeum included the following titles: for October 1840, *Lowe's Elements of Agriculture;* for November 1840, *Forogoths Agriculture,* the *New England Farmer Annals of Education,* and *United States and British Husbandry;* for December 1840, *Gardners Magazine, Massachusetts Agricultural Society, Laudon's Encyclopedia of Gardening, Farmer's Magazine,* and the *Journal of Education.* In 1841 Ripley charged the following: in February, *Journal of Agriculture* (three times), and the *New England Farmer* (five times); in March, the *New England Farmer* (three times). In March he also charged a work on British husbandry and another on horses.

30. For Fuller, see *LMF*, 2:174; for Sophia Ripley, see Ripley to Anna Alvord, October 30, [1840], SPNEA.

31. This is the earliest reference to a set of "articles of association," a working copy of which, judging from his remark that they needed to be approved, Ripley and his supporters had already drafted. For Ripley, see RWEMA/MH.

32. Emerson makes reference in several letters to the pressure that he was feeling about his participation. See, e.g., *LRWE*, 2:364–365, and 7:429–430.

33. See *LRWE*, 2:360; 7:428–430; 2:361, 364–365; and *LMF*, 2:194.

34. Richardson, *Emerson: The Mind on Fire,* 343. Emerson's anxiety about his decision is attested to by his good friend George Partridge Bradford, who wrote in January 1841: "How long it is since I have heard from you [Emerson]; in the meantime you have decided against the Community and are relieved from the perplexity in which you were when I saw you last." For Bradford's letter, see RWEMA/MH.

35. *LMF*, 2:194.

2. Beginnings

1. Sophia Ripley to John S. Dwight, August 1, 1840, JSD/MB. The description from the Brook Farm circular is quoted in Edwin Bacon, *Walks and Rides About Boston* (Boston: Houghton, Mifflin, 1898), 308.

2. The Ripleys did visit the "Society of Separatists of Zoar" (1817–1898) in Zoar, Ohio, for a few days in 1838 and were generally impressed by its operations. They would likely also have quizzed their good friend Orestes Brownson, who had stayed for a while in Frances Wright's "Nashoba Community" (1826–1829) in Tennessee, which was devoted to helping slaves earn money to purchase their freedom. For Sophia Ripley's report on the visit to Zoar, see the *Dial* (July 1841): 122–129.

3. The two communities organized in New England between 1800–1840 were the Shaker Community (1817–1825) in Berkshire County, Massachusetts, and the Pilgrims (1817–1818) in Windsor County, Vermont. Both these communities were religiously inspired. Of the four communities established in New England between 1840–1860, all were organized

around a central unifying principle. Both Adin Ballou's Hopedale Community (1842–1867) in Milford, Massachusetts, and John Humphrey Noyes's Putney Society (1843–1848) in Putney, Vermont, were avowedly religious communities, although Ballou and his followers also embraced a broad social reform agenda. The Northampton Association (1842–1846) in Northampton, Massachusetts, was organized by Garrisonian abolitionists who were committed to antislavery and the establishment of a "nondenominational Christian society." Bronson Alcott and Charles Lane's Fruitlands Community (1843) in Harvard, Massachusetts, was, like Brook Farm and Northampton, a secular community, but the ascetic lifestyle adopted by the handful of its members was imposed with nearly religious intensity. Frederick Douglass's remark about Hopedale and Northampton applies with equal force to Brook Farm: "For harmony, Hopedale had a decided advantage over [Northampton], in that its leaders were of one religious faith, while [Northampton] was composed both of men and women of different denominations, and of those of no religious bias or profession." Quoted in Christopher Clark, *The Communitarian Moment* (Ithaca: Cornell University Press, 1995), 129. The letter in which Ripley's remark about Shakerism appears is printed in *CAD*, 40. For a list of antebellum American communities, see Otohiko Okugaway, "Annotated List of Communal and Utopian Societies, 1787–1919" (Appendix A), in Robert Fogarty, *Dictionary of American Communal and Utopian History* (Westport, Conn.: Greenwood Press, 1980), 173–183.

4. *New England Farmer, and Horticultural Register* 19 (January 27, 1841): 238–239; *Christian Register* 20 (February 13, 1841): 27.

5. Quincy to John A. Collins, January 30, 1841, and Quincy to Chapman, February 25, 1841, William Lloyd Garrison Papers, Boston Public Library (however, I have used the copies transcribed by Arthur E. Bestor, Jr., IU-HS).

6. Whether "Pulpit Rock," which still sits at the northernmost end of the Brook Farm site, is the actual place where John Eliot delivered his sermons, isn't really known. Nathaniel Hawthorne memorialized the rock

in *The Blithedale Romance,* in which protagonist Miles Coverdale imagines, in the chapter titled "Eliot's Pulpit," that he "used to see the holy Apostle of the Indians [John Eliot]." For a brief summary of the history of Pulpit Rock, see Brian Fitzgerald, "Pulpit Rock: a Local Historical and Literary Puzzle," *B[oston] U[niversity] Bridge,* November 10, 2000, p. 3.

7. The designation "Brook Farm" probably grew out of conversation between the early members of the community, but Nathaniel Hawthorne, an original shareholder, is possibly the first to refer to the Ellis property as Brook Farm. His letter to Sophia Peabody on April 28, 1841 is headed "Brook Farm" and precedes by two weeks a similar heading on a letter by Sophia Ripley on May 11. Hawthorne may also have provided the inspiration for the blue "tunic" that became so popular among the men in the community (see illustration in Chapter 3). He told his sister Louisa on May 3, 1841 that "the thin frock, which you made for me, is considered a most splendid article; and I should not wonder if it were to become the summer uniform of the community." See *LNH,* 534, 540.

8. Ripley's journal is among the holdings of the Houghton Library of Harvard University.

9. Margaret Fuller put the date of George Ripley's arrival as March 28; Elizabeth Palmer Peabody, however, told John Dwight that Ripley did not arrive until April 4. Whether Ripley went directly from Purchase Street to West Roxbury on March 28 (the day of his "farewell discourse") is not certain, but he was definitely at the farm a day or two later. Sophia, however, alternated between the farm and the Ripleys' Bedford Street home in Boston until mid-May when she "closed the door of No. 2 [Bedford Street] & cross[ed] the beloved threshold for the last time." See *LMF,* 2:205; *LEPP,* 249; and JSD/MB.

10. Peabody to Dwight, April 26, [1841], *LEPP,* 249; Sophia Ripley to Dwight, May 6, 1841, JSD/MB; Sophia Ripley to Alvord, May 11, 1841, SPNEA. See also Peabody to Dwight, June 24, 1841, *LEPP.*

11. Sophia Ripley to Dwight, May 6, 1841, JSD/MB.

12. For Sophia Ripley, see Ripley to Anna Alvord, May 11, [1841], SPNEA;

see also Ann Weston to Henry and Maria [Chapman], May 18, 1841, Weston Sisters Papers, Boston Public Library; James W. Mathews, "An Early Brook Farm Letter," *New England Quarterly* 53 (1980): 230.

13. For Allen, see Edith Roelker Curtis, *A Season in Utopia* (New York: Thomas Nelson and Sons, 1961), 58; for Sophia Ripley, see Ripley to Anna Alvord, May 11, [1841], SPNEA.

14. For Salisbury, see "Brook Farm," *BFB,* 241; for Doucet, see "Reminiscences of the Brook Farm Association," *BFB,* 235.

15. For Ripley's essay, see the *Dial* (January 1841): 362–366. For the period May 1844–April 1845, the only one for which community labor records have survived, Sophia Ripley devoted 677 work hours to the community's school, 468 hours to what the Brook Farmers later called the "Second Mechanical Series" (see Chapters 6 and 7), 430 hours of labor to the "Domestic Series," 110 hours to the "Mechanical Series," 70 hours to the "Functional Series," and 556 hours to the "Miscellaneous Series." Of the sixty women listed on the labor record for the one-year period, Sophia's 2,311 total work hours made her the thirteenth hardest working woman in the community. For the same period, George Ripley was credited with 2,532 hours of work, making him the second hardest working man at Brook Farm for the year. He devoted 578 hours to the school, 572 to the "Functional Series," 308 hours to the "Agricultural Series," just 34 hours to the "Domestic Series," and 15 hours to the "Mechanical Series." That Ripley had to devote the bulk of his time to the administration of the community is clear from the 1,026 hours that he accumulated in the "Miscellaneous Series." See the "Brook Farm Labor Record, May 1844–April 1845," Brook Farm Papers, MHi.

16. For Bradford, see Mathews, "An Early Brook Farm Letter," 227–229; for Gannett, see "A Girl of Sixteen at Brook Farm," *BFB,* 269–271.

17. *LNH,* April 13, 1841, p. 527, and April 28, 1841, p. 535.

18. "A Girl of Sixteen at Brook Farm," *BFB,* 273. Hawthorne told Sophia Peabody in his May 4 letter that he had placed a flower vase of hers on Ripley's desk rather than in his room because "I never sit there" [i.e., in his room]. *LNH,* 543.

19. Fuller wrote to her brother Richard on April 6, 1841: "You know you are to settle with Mr. Ripley about the cow." *LMF,* 2:207.

20. See *LNH,* 528 and 530–531; see also Nathaniel Hawthorne, *The American Notebooks,* ed. Claude M. Simpson (1972), in *The Centenary Edition of the Works of Nathaniel Hawthorne,* ed. William Charvat et al. (Columbus: Ohio Sate University Press, 1963–1997), 8:203–205.

21. Sophia Peabody to Nathaniel Hawthorne, May 30, 1841, in James Mellow, *Nathaniel Hawthorne in His Times* (Boston: Houghton, Mifflin, 1980), 184; and Rose Hawthorne Lathrop, *Memories of Hawthorne* (Boston: Houghton, Mifflin, 1897), 46.

22. Since the Codman family did not arrive at Brook Farm until April 13, 1844, his claim of 4,000 visitors probably refers to 1844, 1845, or 1846. Most likely it was 1845. For Codman, see *BFM,* 79–81. For meal and lodging charges, see the "Brook Farm Minutes," March 24, 1844, and April 11, 1844, MHi.

23. *LMF,* 2:209.

24. John Codman, *BFM,* 79–81. At a directors' meeting on April 22, 1843, it was "Voted: that Saturday afternoon be set apart for the reception of visiters [*sic*] at the Farm, and that this arrangement be made public." MHi.

25. William Allen, May 3, 1841, quoted in Curtis, *A Season in Utopia,* 58; Sophia Ripley to Dwight, May 6, 1841, JSD/MB; *LNH,* 562. Farley moved in and out of the community during the early years according to the severity of his bouts with depression.

26. *LNH,* 554. Hawthorne's swipe at Burton noted earlier may indicate that the serious and studious Burton—he was the author of three books on religion and a fairly well-received study of *The District School as It Was*—was not widely liked by the other members of the community. Sophia Ripley told John Dwight in early May, for instance, that "if he [Burton] does not add to the charms of our social circle, he does not interfere with them." Ripley to Dwight, May 6, 1841, JSD/MB. Burton returned several months later for another brief stay at the community.

27. Parker came the closest of this group of Transcendentalists to settling at

Brook Farm. (William Henry Channing would eventually spend considerable time at Brook Farm, but not until 1845, and even then not on a regular basis.) Parker had just invoked the wrath of his Unitarian brethren in May 1841 with his controversial ordination sermon on "The Transient and Permanent in Christianity," a sermon that rejected the miraculous authority of the Bible and of Jesus Christ. Unitarians considered themselves the most liberal wing of the Christian Church in America, but very few would ever have agreed that the supernatural authority of the Bible and of Jesus were not essential elements of Christianity. One outraged correspondent to the Boston *Courier* declared that after "The Transient and Permanent," he would rather see all the Unitarian churches in the land brought to the ground than have a man like Parker appear again in the pulpit. It was the hostile reaction of the Unitarian clergy, though, that prompted George Ripley's closest friend to erupt in his journal: "I find that no body of men was ever more completely sold to the sense of expediency."

Parker was persuaded in October 1841 to deliver a series of five lectures in Boston to amplify his views in "The Transient and Permanent." In spring 1842 he collected and published these lectures as his first book, *A Discourse of Matters Pertaining to Religion,* which was, "if anything, even more controversial than *The Transient and Permanent* had been, because in it Parker made his anti-supernatural assumption even more explicit, directly criticized his Unitarian opponents, and commented on Jesus and the Lord's Supper in ways that some found highly offensive." Dean Grodzins, "Theodore Parker's 'Conference with the Boston Association,' January 23, 1843," *Proceedings of the Unitarian Universalist Historical Society* 23 (1995): 68. Most of Parker's Unitarian colleagues treated him like a pariah, and they refused to exchange pulpits with him, an action that deeply wounded the West Roxbury minister. "I have no fellowship from the other clergy," he told one of them. "No one that helped in my ordination will now exchange ministerial courtesies with me; only one or two of the Boston Association, and perhaps one or two out of it, will have any ministerial intercourse with me." (John Sullivan Dwight's courageous willingness to fill in for Parker in February 1842 should be noted here.) By June 1842 Parker was seriously considering leaving his Spring Street congregation and moving to Brook Farm. Maybe, Parker remarked in a letter to a colleague, he would stay in the community and study seven or eight months a year, and then, the other four or five months, "I will go about, and preach and lecture in city and glen, by the roadside and field-side, and wherever men and women can be found." He had been "put down" by his brethren, but his Unitarian colleagues should be certain about one thing: "I will go eastward and westward, and southward and northward, and make the land *ring.*" For the Parker quotations, see John Weiss, *Life and Correspondence of Theodore Parker* (London: Longman, Green, 1865), 1:184.

28. *LNH*, 545–546.

29. The Northampton Association was organized in late 1841 and 1842. Northampton biographer Christopher Clark lists the Macks among the "founders" of that community. See Clark, *The Communitarian Moment*, 24–25.

30. *LNH*, 552–554. The following quotations are from this letter.

31. This wasn't the first time that Dana had to withdraw from Harvard. He was forced to do so at the end of his first year to earn tuition money. He had already shown such academic promise, however, that Cornelius C. Felton, professor of Greek, wrote to the young student urging him to return right away, and promising him financial support from the college: "I advise you by all means to return to college, for with your abilities and honorable purposes it is impossible you should fail of success." Felton then noted that "there is a [financial] fund which is loaned on easy terms." Quoted in *CAD*, 14.

32. For Hawthorne, see *LNH*, 555; for Ripley's letter, see *CAD*, 31. The overcrowded conditions in the community prompted a frank letter from Sophia Ripley to Margaret Fuller in September. The members of the community had just voted whether Fuller's brother Lloyd should be allowed to remain at Brook Farm during the winter. Sophia thought that Margaret would have been very gratified "if you could have heard the expressions of kindness with which almost all spoke" about Lloyd. It was unanimously agreed that he should remain in the community,

though some associates, Sophia added, reached their decision "very *slowly*." Everyone, Sophia said, considered Lloyd's continuing presence at Brook Farm "as a sacrifice of personal comfort" because he occupied one of the largest rooms at the farm by himself. Sophia reminded her friend that Lloyd had originally been accepted in the community in consideration of his labor to be performed, which, in fact, "he has never accomplished . . . Everyone on the place would tell you that it [Lloyd's work] is of no value to us." Neither could Sophia remember that her husband had ever "engaged to furnish L[loyd] permanently with a separate & very large room." This was a "luxury" that could not continue: "we have [already] put ourselves to inconvenience that he might retain through the summer his airy chamber."

Sophia was also sorry that she had "wounded" her friend previously by telling her that she doubted whether Lloyd would ever do anything worthwhile with his life. But since their relationship had always been characterized by frankness, Sophia had to say that Lloyd was hopelessly lazy, a trait of his that she euphemistically described as "a physical incapacity which unfits him for the performance of work of all kinds." Furthermore, his remarks to and actions towards others in the community "indicate deficiency of intellect," evidenced by the "plan & force" with which he delivered them. It was true that he always treated herself and George "with uniform respect," but, Sophia also added, "I suppose I value this less because his insolence is often so great when he is sure there will be no resistance." Sophia Ripley's letter, which runs to nearly five full pages, reflects the candor and frankness that characterized the relationships of many of the women in Sophia and Fuller's social circle—a frankness, it should be said, rarely, if ever, found in the friendships of men like Ripley and Parker, Emerson and Thoreau, or Emerson and Alcott. Sophia Ripley's letter, dated September 23, 1841, is in the Margaret Fuller Papers, MH.

33. "A Member of the Community" [George P. Bradford], "Reminiscences of Brook Farm," *Century Magazine* 45 (November 1892): 142; Hawthorne, *American Notebooks,* 8:203.

34. Georgiana Bruce, *Years of Experience* (New York: G. P. Putnam's Sons, 1887), 89–90. Bruce described the quality of life at Brook Farm during

her two-year residence this way: "Sincerity and devotion were the warp, and cultivation the woof, of the fabric of our lives" (91).

35. *LNH*, 553.

3. Organization

1. *Dial* 2 (July 1841): 125. Sophia's brief essay on "Painting and Sculpture" was also published in the July 1841 number.

2. *LEPP,* April 26, 1841; June 24, 1841.

3. Ripley to Emerson, November 9, 1840, RWEMA/MH.

4. *Lectures on the Elevation of the Labouring Portion of the Community* (Boston: William D. Ticknor, 1840), [82].

5. Brook Farm commentators invariably overlook the "Articles of Agreement" and focus on the "Articles of Association" as the earliest community documents. They were not. The "Articles of Agreement" predate by several months the "Articles of Association," which were not approved until September 29, 1841. Georgiana Bruce, for example, notes in *Years of Experience* (New York: G. P. Putnam's Sons, 1887) that "one day in the spring [of 1841] . . . Mr. G[annett, who employed Bruce] came home with a written copy of the constitution [i.e., the "Articles of Agreement"] of the Brook Farm Association in his hand" (89). John T. Codman also notes that "before the Association started from Boston a constitution was drawn." Codman then provides a full copy of the "Articles of Agreement and Association between the members of the Institute for Agriculture and Education" (*BFM*, 11–15), although he omits the names of Francis Farley and Maria Mack. He also does not include the names of Charles A. Dana and Sylvia Allen, but that's because they were not among the original subscribers. William Allen, too, refers to a "constitution which prescribes the duty of the members" in a May 3, 1841, letter to his fiancee, Sylvia Farrar. And George Willis Cooke, in *John Sullivan Dwight: Brook-Farmer, Editor, and Critic of Music* (Boston: Small, Maynard, 1898), 51, states that the "Articles of Agreement" were "drawn up in Boston during the winter of 1840–41." Internal evidence supports Cooke's statement.

6. However impatient Peabody was with Ripley's unwillingness to bring

Brook Farm to the attention of the public, she would never have been so bold as to publish her letter without first securing his blessing. There's no way either that Ezra Stiles Gannett, the *Monthly Miscellany*'s editor, would have failed to notify his good friend about the letter. Ripley was evidently happy about the way Peabody described the community in her letter because she followed it with "A Glimpse of Christ's Idea of Society" in the *Dial* (October 1841), in which journal her essay on the "Plan of the West Roxbury Community" appeared the following January 1842.

7. "The Community at West Roxbury, Mass.," *The Monthly Miscellany of Religion and Letters* 5 (August 1841): 113–118.

8. "Articles of Agreement and Association between the Members of the Institute for Agriculture and Education." These Articles, which are located at the MHi, provided the basis for Brook Farm's first constitution in January 1844.

9. Peabody's article in the *Dial* (October 1841) was also intended to prepare the way for her January 1842 essay, "Plan of the West Roxbury Community." In "A Glimpse of Christ's Idea of Society" she doesn't mention Brook Farm by name. Peabody argues that the "ground Idea of the little communities"—so far there were only two of non-Shaker origin in Massachusetts, and readers of the *Dial* obviously knew that she was referring to Brook Farm because Peabody had just dismissed the Hopedale Community for being too secular—"must be Education," by which she meant, good Transcendentalist that she was, nothing less than the "unfolding of the individual man into every form of perfection, without let or hindrance, according to the inward nature of each." Or, as she put it more memorably in January, "LEISURE TO LIVE IN ALL THE FACULTIES OF THE SOUL." The only way to achieve this ideal was to make certain that moral and religious education were the "indispensable condition and foundation" of community life, which was indeed the case at Brook Farm, the very point of her later essay in January 1842.

10. The preamble is taken from the text of the "Articles" at the MHi.

11. "Plan of the West Roxbury Community," *Dial* 2 (January 1842): 361–365. There were three "categories" of residency at Brook Farm: member/associate, boarder, and student. Boarders and students were not

entitled to any profits or guarantees provided to the members of the Association. To become an associate, a resident first had to serve a probationary period, which was usually two months. Once a probationer was formally approved by a majority vote of the members, he or she was vested in the community. A much faster way to become a member of the Association was simply to purchase one or more shares of stock.

12. See the "Articles of Agreement," especially Article VI, and the Brook Farm "Minutes," October 30, 1841, MHi, in which the information immediately following may be found.

13. The "Articles of Association," like the "Articles of Agreements," are in the MHi.

14. Immediately after the meeting to adopt the twelve "Articles of Association," officers were elected to the four "Directions." There is no mention at all, however, of "Directions" in the "Articles of Association"—as the Association members knew, the "Directions" had already been discussed in the earlier "Articles of Agreement." Article II of the "Articles of Association" refers to "the main purpose of the Association," but no "purpose" is referred to anywhere in the document. There was no need; everyone in the community also knew that the "preamble" to the earlier "Articles of Agreement" provided a statement of purpose.

15. Although both their names are also listed after the initial fourteen names, neither Charles Anderson Dana nor Sylvia Allen was involved in any way in the early organization of Brook Farm, which is indicated by the fact that next to their names is only the date, "1842 Feb[ruar]y 17." Of the original fourteen names listed on the "Articles of Agreement," three were Unitarian clergymen, and two were teachers. The Rev. Lemuel Capen, who had married a Roxbury woman named Mary Ann Hunting in 1815, spent the years 1827 to 1839 in charge of the Hawes Place Society in South Boston; Samuel D. Robbins, an 1833 Harvard Divinity School graduate (along with William Henry Channing and James Freeman Clarke), was serving as minister of the Unitarian Church in Chelsea in 1840; and Warren Burton, an 1826 graduate of the Harvard Divinity School (with Ripley), is referred to in Chapter 2. See *Heralds of a Liberal Faith,* ed. Samuel A. Eliot (Boston: American Unitarian

Association, 1910), 2:66-67, for Lemuel Capen; 2:106 for Warren
Burton; and 3:336 for Samuel D. Robbins. Mary E. Robbins was the latter's wife.

The two teachers were David and Maria (Brastow) Mack. The Macks—
perhaps discouraged by Hawthorne's reservations about Brook Farm—continued to conduct a private school in Cambridge between July 1841 and January 1842, at which time they gave their support to the "Northampton Association of Education and Industry" near Amherst, Massachusetts, which was
just then being organized. See Christopher Clark, *The Communitarian Moment* (Ithaca: Cornell University Press, 1995), 24-25. Perhaps Marianne
Ripley should also be listed as a teacher. George Ripley's sister was in
charge of Brook Farm's primary education program for children six to ten
years of age. (For more about the Brook Farm school, see Chapter 4; see also
note 22 below.)

George C. Leach was a West Roxbury neighbor who, like Francis Shaw
and George Russell, never formally committed himself to Brook Farm, although he was involved in its affairs off and on until its collapse in 1847. Sylvia Allen married William, the community's head farmer during the early
months of its existence.

16. It was subsequently decided to reduce the cost of an individual share of
Brook Farm stock from $500 to $100.

17. Dana wrote to his sister on September 17, 1841, explaining that "I pay
for board by labor upon the farm and by giving instruction in whatever
lies within my capacity." One year later, on September 22, 1842, he wrote
to Hannah Ripley and stated that he was depressed about his debts, "my
perpetual torment," which, he complained, "stand before me as ugly &
burdensome as the nightmare." See *CAD,* 31, 33; and KHi.

18. In addition to George and Sophia Ripley's personal savings, the couple
arrived in West Roxbury with a generous gift of $500 donated by
Ripley's Purchase Street congregants. Sophia wrote to John Dwight on
May 6, 1841, and informed him that "many substantial proofs of kindness, & farewell letters were delicately offered in the most affecting
way—a few gentlemen presented us with nearly $500—& the most beau-
tiful garden tools to a large amount." See Ripley to Dwight, May 6, 1841,

JSD/MB. For Charles O. Whitmore, see the "Statement of Assets and Liabilities of [the] Brook Farm Association" for April 1845, MHi, which lists the community's indebtedness to him as $569.43 (principal plus accrued interest).

19. In addition to the "Direction of Finance," three other committees were established immediately after the "Articles of Association" were approved on September 29, 1841: the "General Direction," consisting of Ripley (head), Pratt, and Allen; the "Direction of Agriculture," comprised of Allen (head), Pratt, and Ripley; and the "Direction of Education," consisting of Sophia Ripley, Dana (head), and Marianne Ripley. The four committee heads also served as trustees.

20. *LNH,* 578, 582.

21. The deed is listed in the Norfolk County Registry of Deeds office, Dedham, Mass., in book 133, folio 57.

22. When Marianne Ripley moved to West Roxbury at the beginning of the summer, she brought along most of the students from her school in Boston, including Massachusetts statesman and scholar George Bancroft's two sons, and Orestes Brownson's son, Orestes, Jr. See Chapter 4 for more about the school.

23. Francis Shaw (or Frank, as he was known to his friends) provided $2,000 toward the second mortgage, Sturgis put up $1,500, and George Russell invested $1,000. On March 14, 1842, Sturgis transferred his $1,500 interest in the mortgage to Russell (Norfolk County Registry of Deeds, book 135, folio 58). On February 15, 1843, Russell transferred $500 of his share to Shaw (book 139, folio 198).

24. Apart from the mortgage that they held on Brook Farm, Shaw and Russell's names appear more often in the surviving financial records—which begin on November 1, 1844—than those of anyone else. Not only did both men make frequent short-term loans to the community, but they also regularly employed the Brook Farmers for a wide variety of services, such as carpentry, shoemaking, and tailoring. George Russell also provided financial support for Jose and Lucas Corrales, two of the Spanish-speaking students in the Brook Farm school. What made Shaw and Russell's support so important is that they paid their bills promptly and

in cash, unlike the Brook Farmers, who, throughout, relied heavily on a system of credits and barters.

25. *American Notebooks,* ed. Claude M. Simpson (1972), in *The Centenary Edition of the Works of Nathaniel Hawthorne,* ed. William Charvat et al. (Columbus: Ohio State University Press, 1963–1997), 8:222.

26. Sophia Ripley to Fuller, September 23, 1841, Margaret Fuller Papers, MH.

27. Minutes, October 30, 1841, MHi.

28. George Ripley to Emerson, December 17, 1841, RWEMA/MH.

29. Robert D. Richardson, Jr., *Emerson: The Mind on Fire* (Berkeley: University of California Press, 1995), 343.

30. Ripley to Emerson, December 17, 1841, RWEMA/MH.

4. The Seeds of Fourierism

1. Ripley himself noted in early August 1842 that "we number now about seventy souls, of whom some fifteen are associates, the remainder pupils, boarders, and persons whose labor we are obliged to hire." Many boarders and students, however, did not pay the full rate of $4 per week to live in the Association. Several of them, in fact, paid nothing at all, contributing their labor instead in return for lodging and meals. From the beginning Ripley's practice was to set individual charges on an ad hoc basis. The brothers George William and James Burrill Curtis, for example, who arrived at Brook Farm in the spring of 1842, arranged to pay only $3 per week each in return for three to four hours of daily work. Moreover, not all boarders were financially dependable. When Almira Barlow and her three sons were quietly forced out of the community in November 1843, for instance, Barlow left the Brook Farmers with an unpaid bill for $141.18, which she never later paid. See the "Statement of Assets and Liabilities, November 1844," MHi.

2. Ripley to Dana, April 10, 1842, in *CAD,* 50.

3. For "Pulpit Rock," see Chapter 2, note 6.

4. It was not possible to accommodate all the students at the Eyrie. Several remained at the Nest. It may be that the Eyrie was reserved for the more unruly ones because minutes of the directors' meeting for January 28,

1843, state: "It is ordered, that no entertainments be held by pupils in their rooms."

5. Ripley is quoted in Orestes Brownson, "Brook Farm," *United States Magazine and Democratic Review* 11 (November 1842): 481–482. Burrill Curtis, who had arrived with his brother at Brook Farm two months earlier, told his father on July 9, 1842, that the school was "the principal source of revenue at present." See Joel Myerson, "James Burrill Curtis and Brook Farm," *New England Quarterly* 51 (1978): 405.

6. To appreciate just how exceptional it was to have three college-educated teachers in the school, it might be noted that none of the other antebellum New England communities had more than one college-educated person involved in their educational program. At Hopedale, for example, only Adin Ballou's daughter Abbie had any formal educational training, but she didn't graduate from the state normal school in West Newton until 1848. And in the Northampton Association, the only two people with any teaching experience were David and Maria Mack. Mack did graduate from Yale in 1823, but he seems to have been the only college-educated member of the Northampton Association who was involved in the community's educational program. At Fruitlands, neither Bronson Alcott nor Charles Lane, its leaders, were college graduates. There was no educational program at John Humphrey Noyes's Putney Community in Vermont. See Edward K. Spann, *Hopedale: From Commune to Company Town* (Columbus: Ohio State University Press, 1992), 85–95, and Christopher Clark, *The Communitarian Moment: The Radical Challenge of the Northampton Association* (Ithaca: Cornell University Press, 1995), 114–116.

7. One visitor to the community in the summer of 1842 remarked that she "never saw children at once so happy and so little in the way of other people." Quoted in Brownson, "Brook Farm," 481–496. It's not clear whether Margaret Fuller's youngest brother Lloyd was one of those happy children, but his note to his brother Richard on June 22, 1843— "I belong to history [*sic*], elocution, composition, and french conversation classes"—indicates the kind of program available to students enrolled in the school. Margaret Fuller Papers, MH.

8. *BFB*, 332.

9. If we can believe a young student-boarder named Sophia Eastman, who arrived at Brook Farm in July 1843, three married women were in the community at that time who were not living with their husbands: "It is nothing uncommon for people to get married and then part from there [*sic*] husbands," Eastman wrote to her parents on July 25, 1843. "There are three who board here and there [*sic*] husbands have left them." Since Barlow didn't leave Brook Farm until November 1843, presumably she is one of the three women that Eastman has in mind. A transcribed copy of Eastman's letter is in IU-HS.

10. Ripley is quoted in Cleveland Amory, *The Proper Bostonians* (New York: E. P. Dutton, 1947), 104; for Spring, see Lillie Buffum Chace Wyman and Arthur Crawford Wyman, *Elizabeth Buffum Chace, 1806–1899: Her Life and Its Environment* (Boston: W. B. Clarke Co., 1914), 1:92–93.

11. Gannett, "A Girl of Sixteen at Brook Farm," *BFB*, 278. Ripley's remark about the Curtis brothers is quoted by Gannett.

12. Burrill Curtis attended but never graduated from Brown. See the *Historical Catalogue of Brown University, 1764–1904* (Providence, 1905), 612. See also Edward Cary, *George William Curtis* (Boston: Houghton, Mifflin, 1900), espec. pp. 15–38, which is the source of the biographical information included here; and William Charvat, *Emerson's American Lecture Engagements* (New York: New York Public Library, 1961), 18–19. George William Curtis was also the celebrated author of several travel books, including *Nile Notes of a Howadji* (1851) and *The Howadji in Syria* (1852).

13. *JMN*, 8:217. Emerson may have been miffed because Caroline Sturgis, for whom he felt more than ordinary affection, was living in the community that spring of 1842. See Burrill Curtis's remark below. For Emerson's relationship with Sturgis, see Robert D. Richardson, Jr., *Emerson: The Mind on Fire* (Berkeley: University of California Press, 1995), 327–329.

14. Although she probably didn't intend to criticize them when she said of the Brook Farm women that they "wrote of their happy life [there] as a

college-like experience, replete with a popular vegetarian diet, clubs, weekend trips to nearby Boston, and regular lectures by such people as Margaret Fuller and Ralph Waldo Emerson" (172), Carol A. Kolmerten's remark in *Women in Utopia: The Ideology of Gender in the American Owenite Communities* (Bloomington: Indiana University Press, 1990) effectively demeans them by suggesting that it was primarily social rather than intellectual interests that drew them to the West Roxbury community. For Dickinson, see "She rose to His Requirement—dropt" (#732), *The Complete Poems of Emily Dickinson,* ed. Thomas H. Johnson (Boston: Little, Brown, 1960), 359.

15. For Curtis, see Myerson, "James Burrill Curtis and Brook Farm," 408; for Bruce, see Georgiana Bruce Kirby, *Years of Experience* (New York: G. P. Putnam's Sons, 1887), 97; for Dana, see ibid., 98; and for Gannett, see "A Girl of Sixteen at Brook Farm," 275.

16. Swift, *Brook Farm: Its Members, Scholars, and Visitors* (New York: Macmillan, 1900), 53.

17. Redelia Brisbane, *Albert Brisbane: A Mental Biography* (Boston: Arena Publishing Company, 1893), 171. Fourier expounded his views on love in Part 2 of the *Traité,* which constitutes the fourth volume of *Oeuvres complétes de Charles Fourier* (Paris, 1841–1843; retitled *Theorie de l'unité universelle,* vol. 3, particularly pp. 363–579). Hawthorne read this work as part of his preparation for writing *The Blithedale Romance.* See Julian Hawthorne, *Nathaniel Hawthorne and His Wife* (Boston: Houghton, Mifflin, 1884), 1:268–269. Caroline Sturgis (Tappan) also had a copy. See *The American Notebooks,* ed. Claude M. Simpson (1972), in *The Centenary Edition of the Works of Nathaniel Hawthorne,* ed. William Charvat et al. (Columbus: Ohio State University Press, 1963–1997), 8:446. Biographical information about Brisbane is from Redelia Brisbane and from Arthur Eugene Bestor, Jr., "Albert Brisbane—Propagandist for Socialism in the 1840's," *New York History* 28 (April 1947): 128–158.

18. Ripley to Charles Dana, April 10, 1842, *CAD,* 50.

19. Emerson told his brother that Ripley wrote the "Record of the Months," a lengthy column of reviews that included a brief 209-word notice of

Brisbane's book. It's unlikely, though, that Ripley would have provided all the material for the column. Emerson's name, in fact, is written on the annotated copy of the *Dial* used to microfilm the periodical for the "American Periodical Series, 1791–1900." The review in the *Dial,* by the way, is positive, but in her article, "A Glimpse of Christ's Idea," for the October 1841 number of the *Dial,* Elizabeth Palmer Peabody charged that Brisbane "does not go down into a sufficient spiritual depth, to lay foundations which may support his superstructure . . . Our imagination . . . rebels against this attempt to circumvent moral Freedom, and imprison it in his Phalanx." George Ripley would certainly also have been aware of Peabody's reservation. For the "Record of the Months," see the *Dial* 1 (October 1840): 264–272; for Peabody, see the *Dial* 2 (October 1841): 214–228.

20. *United States Magazine and Democratic Review* (June 1842): 566.

21. Dana's poem is a variation of a Petrarchan sonnet, and though it is infused with transcendent urgings to the reader to recognize "the great waves of God that through us swell," and "yield to the Only Fair," these admonishments are rigidly bound in very non-Transcendental iambic pentameter and the fixed rhyme scheme of the sonnet form. Newcomb's tale, on the other hand, is so abstract and ethereal that even the most devoted Transcendentalist might have been confused about its meaning. "The First Dolon" concerns a wispy and unsubstantial young boy who encounters a "crazy man" in the woods. Though Dolon and this mysterious man never exchange so much as a single word, the latter, "on the evening of the third day," plunges a knife into the youth's breast, and then throws "himself prostrate before the rock as before an altar." End of "tale." Presumably only Newcomb understood the meaning of this little allegory, although Emerson evidently found it interesting enough since he published it in the *Dial.*

22. Brisbane's note is written on the third page of Horace Greeley's letter to Emerson, May 26, 1842, RWEMA/MH.

23. See *JMN,* 8:208–210.

24. "Fourierism and the Socialists," *Dial* 3 (July 1842): 88. The following quotations from Emerson and Brisbane are from this article.

25. This is the earliest reference to what would later be known at Brook Farm as the Phalanstery—Charles Fourier's word for the large central unitary dwelling in the Phalanx.

26. Ripley might have "justified" the loans in his own mind because neither Alvord, who was elected a member of the Association on June 13, 1842, nor Morton, who became an associate on December 31, 1842, required the placement of an additional mortgage on the property, and neither expected immediate repayment of the money that they put forward. Besides, Brook Farm's financial obligation to investors like Alvord and Morton was very ambiguous—as Nathaniel Hawthorne would himself soon discover. Charles Dana's statement to prospective Brook Farmer John Brown in January 1842 suggests the nature of the ambiguity: "Any family that wishes to join us, must bring a sufficient sum of money to build a house for itself and enlarge the operations of the farm and school sufficiently to give it employment." For their part (and for Hawthorne, too), Alvord and Morton did indeed expect eventually to be repaid. Both individuals are listed on the earliest surviving "Statement of the Assets and Liabilities of Brook Farm Association, November 1, 1844," MHi. According to that "Statement," the amount owed by the community to Alvord, at that time, was $1,628.75; indebtedness to Morton was $4,654.84. After Brook Farm collapsed and the site of the community was sold, Anna Alvord received an execution for $2,096.05, which must have included some interest, as well as, it would appear, additional money that she subsequently must have loaned to Ripley. Morton wasn't as fortunate. He received a mere $641.81 from the settlement. See Dana to Brown, January 12, 1841[2], KHi.

27. Hawthorne originally invested $1,000 for two shares of Brook Farm stock in April 1841. Evidently, $500 was refunded to Hawthorne after he withdraw from the community at the end of 1841, but apparently he agreed to wait a while for the balance of his investment in order not to force the Brook Farmers into a difficult financial situation. Thus the promissory note for $524.05, which represents the original $500 plus some interest. Hawthorne's letter of resignation to Dana is quoted in *CAD*, 45–46.

28. Greeley's letter to Dana is quoted in *CAD,* 40–42. Dana wasn't the only visionary to whom Greeley expressed his cynicism about human nature. He told Elijah P. Grant that the latter's difficulties organizing the Ohio Phalanx in Bellaire, Ohio, were due to the "faithlessness, selfishness, and baseness of Man as we find them." A transcribed copy of Grant's June 24, 1844, letter to Greeley—in which Grant quotes Greeley—is in IU-HS.

29. Greeley's letter to Charles Dana is dated October 10, 1842. See the Horace Greeley Papers, Library of Congress.

30. Dana probably never recognized or appreciated the irony of his involvement with Hawthorne. In January 1842 he responded to an inquiry about residence at Brook Farm from his friend John Stillman Brown in Buffalo. The impoverished Dana told Brown that should he decide to move to West Roxbury, "the amount of money that will be necessary we cannot say exactly.—it cannot however be less than three thousand dollars." Considering Dana's own financial circumstances at Brook Farm, he was hardly in a position to dictate such extravagant financial terms to prospective associates. Brown's wife Mary was a bit miffed at this. She told her husband that "Dana knew very well . . . that we had not 3000 dollars to invest" in the community, adding that the Brook Farmer must have written his letter to Brown "under the influence of a bright sun." See Dana to Brown, January 12, 1841[2], and Mary Brown to John Brown, July 5, 1842, KHi.

31. Dana to Hannah Ripley, September 22, 1842; see also John Brown to Mary Brown, September 12, 1842. Both letters are in KHi.

32. For Ballou's letter, see *BFM,* 143. See also the *Autobiography of Adin Ballou* (Lowell: Vox Populi Press, 1896), 323, 326–327, 342–343.

33. Frederick C. Dahlstrand, *Amos Bronson Alcott: An Intellectual Biography* (Rutherford, N.J.: Fairleigh Dickinson University Press, 1982), 190; David P. Edgell, "Bronson Alcott's 'Autobiographical Index,'" *New England Quarterly* 14 (1941): 710–711; *LRWE,* 3:96.

34. *LRWE,* 3:98. David Mack, who with his wife Maria first pledged themselves to Brook Farm, asked Hawthorne to join the Northampton Community, which the Macks and a few other antislavery proponents had

just organized in April 1842 on 500 acres of land about two-and-a-half miles from Northampton, Massachusetts. Hawthorne declined Mack's invitation, saying in a letter on May 25, 1842 that "circumstances of various kinds have induced me to give up the design of offering myself as a member [of the Northampton Association] . . . I am troubled with many doubts (after my experience of last year [at Brook Farm]) whether I, as an individual, am a proper subject for those beneficial influences [of community life]." *LNH*, 552–554.

35. For Curtis, see November 4 and 5, 1842, and November 9, 1842, in Myerson, "James Burrill Curtis and Brook Farm," 412–413. Ripley knew that Burrill had ready cash because he had just made a loan to the Brook Farmers in September.

36. Hawthorne's impressions in this and the next paragraph are from his journal. See *American Notebooks*, 8:201–202.

37. Kirby, *Years of Experience*, 151. When Georgiana Bruce asked Charles Newcomb whether he had ever seen Fanny Elssler dance, he was quite shocked. "Georgie," he replied, "how *can* you, how *dare* you venture to put such a question to me . . . Don't you know that she is—a vile creature?" One week later Newcomb snuck off quietly to Boston to see Elssler dance. He was so captivated by her performance that he purchased a lithograph of the dancer, which he promptly placed between the engravings of Jesus Christ and Ignatius Loyola that were hanging on the wall of his room in the Eyrie. See Kirby, 106.

38. Fuller's comments are quoted in *Memoirs of Margaret Fuller Ossoli*, ed. William Henry Channing, James Freeman Clarke, and Ralph Waldo Emerson (Boston: Phillips, Sampson, 1852), 2:73–78. For "There is no end to her talk," see the letter of October 27, 1842, in *BFM*, 260.

39. Burrill Curtis recounts the details of the incident for his father. See Myerson, "James Burrill Curtis and Brook Farm," 414–415. The very next morning Brook Farm's teamster and his wife both passed out from fumes caused, again, by improperly disposed-of wood cinders.

40. Details of Christmas and New Year festivities are in Myerson, 414–416; Kirby, 151–152; and Amelia Russell, *Home Life of the Brook Farm Association* (Boston: Little, Brown, 1900), 15–17. Among the Brook Farmers at

the end of 1842 there must have been a few temperance advocates because at a community meeting on October 20, 1842, it was decided that
"the association will not hereafter furnish wine or ardent spirits to any
associate on any occasion."

41. Ripley to Dana, March 18, 1842, *CAD*, 39–40.

42. Greeley to Dana, December 13, 1842, Horace Greeley Papers, Library of
    Congress.

43. "Association," New York *Tribune*, December 30, 1842, p. 1.

5. The Winds of Change

1. See the minutes of the directors' meetings, January 7, 1843–November
   12, 1843, and those of the community meetings, September 29, 1841–
   April 23, 1845, both at MHi. When not indicated in these notes, subsequent references to the minutes are indicated in the text by dates of community meetings.

2. In addition to early retrenchment efforts and the weekly financial report
   listing receipts and expenditures, on March 25 the directors "Ordered:
   that at the end of the first week of each month a statement of debts of the
   Association not secured be laid before this board." For Curtis, see Joel
   Myerson, "James Burrill Curtis and Brook Farm," *New England Quarterly* 51 (1978): 417.

3. The three other "industries" upon which the Brook Farmers relied until
   the community's collapse were tailoring (which included "fancy work"),
   the manufacturing of pewter whale-oil lamps and teapots, known as Britannia ware, and the construction of sashes, doors, and blinds. See
   Chapter 7 for more on Brook Farm's industries.

4. In addition to the $12,000 in mortgages and the nearly $5,000 owed to
   Morton, the Brook Farmers were also indebted to Anna Alvord, who
   herself provided a good faith loan of approximately $1,600 to construct
   the Cottage. See also Chapter 4, note 26.

5. For Emerson, see *LRWE*, 3:112–113, and *JMN*, 8:375 n.95. For Bradford,
   see Sterling F. Delano, "George P. Bradford's Letters to Emerson from
   Brook Farm," *Resources for American Literary Study* 25 (1999): 26–45.
   Williams didn't come to Brook Farm until early June 1843, and she even-

tually became a member of the Association in February 1844. She died in December 1844, the only death to occur in the community during its history. According to Minot Pratt's son Frederick, she was buried "on a lovely knoll" at the Farm (probably behind the Pilgrim House and the Cottage). See *BFB, 332.*

6. In his April 11, 1843, letter to Emerson, Bradford briefly refers to Fourierism and even uses the Frenchman's specialized vocabulary when he refers to "Integral" communities. Interestingly enough, an anonymous correspondent from nearby Watertown wrote on February 4, 1843, that he was "induced to address" the Brook Farmers "at the request of several gentlemen . . . for the purpose of inquiring into the principles of *Fourier's plan* for meliorating the condition of the human race." For Bradford, see Delano, "Letters to Emerson," 31; for the correpondent, see Octavius Brooks Frothingham, *George Ripley* (Boston: Houghton, Mifflin, 1883), 133.

   Retrenchment efforts continued throughout 1843. At the August 5 directors' meeting, for example, it was "Voted, that the General Direction be authorized to take measures to raise funds for the Association; That Minot Pratt be a Committee to make an examination of the income derived from and the expenses incurred by the Cows; That Bryant Hill be a Committee to ascertain whether the number of individuals, who work for their board and tuition cannot be reduced." Then on September 24 it was decided at a community meeting that "the use of coffee be discontinued after the expiration of a few days."

7. Morton and Diaz were eventually married, Morton achieving celebrity in later years as the author of the "William Henry" series of books for children.

8. Zoltan Haraszti provides a full account of the Barlow-Dwight relationship in *The Idyll of Brook Farm* (Boston: Trustees of the Public Library, 1937), 19–22.

9. For Hecker's diary, see *Issac T. Hecker: The Diary,* ed. John Farina (New York: Paulist Press, 1988).

10. Hecker to "Brothers," January 26, 1843, Isaac Hecker Papers, Paulist Fathers Archives, Washington, D.C.

11. For a list of the seventeen communities, see Robert F. Fogarty, *Dictio-*

nary of American Communal and Utopian History (Westport, Conn.: Greenwood Press, 1973), 183–186. For Emerson, see *The Correspondence of Emerson and Carlyle,* ed. Joseph Slater (New York: Columbia University Press, 1964), 283.

12. See the New York *Daily Tribune* for October 28, 1842, p. 1, and January 27, 1843, p. 1. See also John Humphrey Noyes, *History of American Socialisms* (1870; reprint, New York: Hillary House, 1961), 451.

13. Henry Wright, who had also returned to America with Alcott and Lane the previous October, soon became disenchanted with his companions' extreme ascetic views, and was now in New York City helping Brisbane proselytize for Fourierism. See, e.g., *The Pathfinder,* May 27, 1843, p. 212.

14. David M. Robinson, "The Political Odyssey of William Henry Channing," *American Quarterly* (Summer 1982): 166.

15. O. B. Frothingham, *George Ripley* (Boston: Houghton, Mifflin, 1883), 84.

16. Frederick C. Dahlstrand, *Amos Bronson Alcott: An Intellectual Biography* (Rutherford, N.J.: Fairleigh Dickinson University Press, 1982), 197; *Louisa May Alcott: Her Life, Letters, and Journals,* ed. Ednah D. Cheney (Boston: Roberts Brothers, 1891), 35.

17. Brook Farm Minutes, October 29, 1842, MHi. For Lane, see "American Correspondences," *New Age, Concordian Gazette, and Temperance Advocate* 1 (September 1, 1843): 90.

18. Hecker to "Mother and Father," February 22, 1843, Hecker Papers, Paulist Fathers Archives. On the eve of his final departure from Brook Farm in August, Hecker recorded in his diary his joy in being at Brook Farm for six months, noting that the skull cap he was wearing was "made with the hands of one [i.e., Almira Barlow] who has come nearer to my heart than any other human being than I have ever become acquainted with." "Hecker Papers, August 13, 1843.

19. Hecker to George Hecker, May 12, 1843, Hecker Papers. For diary entries, see *Isaac T. Hecker: The Diary,* 110 and 113.

20. Sophia Ripley to Emerson, July 5, [1843], RWEMA/MH. Emerson had just assumed editorship of the *Dial* from Margaret Fuller. Sophia's remark about the current number being "really the first Dial we have had"

was probably not intended as a swipe at Fuller, who was the first editor of the quarterly.

21. Sophia probably had in mind the Alcotts, the Hawthornes, Ellery Channing, and perhaps Henry Thoreau, all of whom were living in Concord, but she may also have been thinking of the gifted women who were living nearby, such as Margaret Fuller, George Bradford's sister Sarah Alden Bradford Ripley, Elizabeth Hoar, to whom Emerson's brother Charles had been engaged when he died unexpectedly in 1836, and Caroline Sturgis—not to mention Emerson's wife Lidian, and her sister, Mary Brown. Sophia Ripley to Emerson, July 5 and July 29, 1843, RWEMA/MH.

22. Ripley to Pratt, July 22, 1843, Fruitlands Museums, Harvard, Mass. Pratt's letter to Ripley has not survived, but the substance of it is perfectly clear from Ripley's response.

23. A transcribed copy of Eastman's letter, dated July 25, 1843, is in IU-HS. Eastman did take a poke at Marianne Ripley, describing her as an "old maid and . . . one of the most precise beings I ever saw." She was much more impressed by George Ripley. She thought he was "one of the most beautiful men I ever saw . . . I think I never saw a man who would gain the love of another as soon as he will."

24. Ripley notified Phineas Eastman on November 24, 1843, that "for a long time" the Brook Farmers had thought that his daughter "was not adequate to the work of this place." Neither was his daughter, Ripley added, "sufficiently advanced in the common branches of education, to enable her to pursue our course, to advantage." See Henry W. Sams, *Autobiography of Brook Farm* (Englewood, N.J.: Prentice Hall, 1958), 85–86.

25. Ripley and his associates had no misgivings, however, about the departures of other residents of the community. At the August 13, 1843, directors' meeting, for instance, it was "Voted that Elizabeth Stevens and Charlotte Wood be informed that their longer residence here is thought inexpedient."

26. In the early 1840s "Association" simply referred to a community of persons living together under one cooperative arrangement or another, such as the members were doing, for example, at the Marlborough Associa-

tion (1841–1845) in Marlborough Township, Ohio, the Northampton Association (1842–1846) in Northampton, Massachusetts, the Teutonia, or McKean County Association (1842–1844) in Ginalsburg, Pennsylvania, and, of course, at Brook Farm itself. As Albert Brisbane's continuing propaganda campaign on behalf of Charles Fourier and his system of "social science" steadily attracted more and more adherents, however, Associationism and Fourierism (and thus the designations "Associationist" and "Fourierist") became increasingly more synonymous. This may be the reason why the Skaneateles Community, founded in 1843 in Mottville, New York, the Bethel Community, established in 1844 in Bethel, Missouri, and, a few years later, John Humphrey Noyes's Oneida Community, organized in 1848 in Kenwood, New York, avoided the word "Association" in their names in order to distinguish themselves from Charles Fourier and his utopian social theories (see note 28 below). At the "General Convention of the Friends of Association in the United States" in New York City in April 1844, even the participants, who accepted Fourier's industrial views, approved a resolution that stated in part: "We do not call ourselves *Fourierists* . . . We do not receive all the parts of [Fourier's] theories," especially those that Fourierists themselves considered "conjectural," such as the Frenchman's controversial notions about sexual relations between men and women. While they were advocates of Fourier's plan for industrial reform, the participants wanted it to be known "That the NAME . . . by which we desire to be always publicly designated, is 'The Associationists of the United States of America.'"

27. Brook Farm was the only Fourierist community ever established in New England. As noted in the previous chapter, the respective religious or ideological commitments of the other four New England communities— Ballou's Hopedale Community, the Northampton Association organized by Garrisonian abolitionists, Alcott and Lane's Fruitlands, and John Humphrey Noyes' Putney Society—made them inhospitable to Fourierism. Beyond New England, twenty-five Fourierist communities would be organized by 1846—seven of them in the state of New York, four in Ohio, three each in Pennsylvania, Illinois, and Wisconsin, two in Indiana, and one each in New Jersey, Michigan, and Iowa. Noyes and his fol-

lowers, it might be noted, were forced to move their base of operations from Vermont to Kenwood, New York, in 1847 ("Putney conservatism expelled it") where the Oneida Community was born in 1848, and where it survived until 1881. Noyes later remarked that he and his followers "steadfastly criticised Fourierism," though they "have always acknowledged that they received a great impulse from Brook Farm." See Brownson to Isaac Hecker, September 2, 1843, Hecker Papers, and Noyes, *History of American Socialism,* 614–616.

28. "Social Science," New York *Daily Tribune,* August 30, 1843, p. 1. Technically, this marks the beginning of the "New England Fourier Society," though it would not be formally organized until January 15, 1844. See Charles Dana to Isaac Hecker, [August 27, 1843], Hecker Papers.

29. It was almost certainly this new emphasis on "industrial" operations— and not any fear of scandal—that prompted the Brook Farmers to decline well-known sex and health advocate Mary Gove's proposal in September 1843 to deliver a series of eighteen lectures at the community in return for her daughter Elma's tuition at the Brook Farm school. If anything, the Brook Farmers would have been receptive to Gove's offer, if only because she was associated with Albert Brisbane, who listed her in the first number of his new paper, *The Phalanx,* in October 1843 as one of its future contributors. Gove had recently tried her own hand in the journalistic world, but she and Henry G. Wright and Almira Barlow's estranged husband David Hatch Barlow managed to publish just two numbers of a periodical called the *Health Journal and Independent Magazine* before it collapsed in April 1843. Its subscription list was turned over to Brisbane for *The Phalanx,* which also listed Barlow in the first number as a future contributor. The decision to decline Gove's proposal on behalf of her daughter, in any case, was economically and not socially motivated. The last thing that the Brook Farmers needed was a lecture series. What they needed was a series of industries that could immediately generate some much-needed income. For Gove, see the Brook Farm Minutes, September 1843, MHi.

30. Ripley to Hecker, September 18, 1843, Hecker Papers.

31. Potential financial supporters would hardly have been inspired to invest

in the community if they had heard that the chimney of the Cottage collapsed in November because Charles Dana forgot to underpin it when he dug the cellar for the dwelling. His carelessness, George Ripley's cousin Mary Brown reported on November 20, 1843, to her husband, John, "will cost us as much to rebuild it as it did to alter the dining room [in the Hive]." KHi.

32. *The Present* 1 (September 1843): 1. Channing announced at the end of the first number that subscribers to Parke Godwin's *The Pathfinder,* another journal sympathetic to the doctrines of Charles Fourier, were being transferred to *The Present.* Godwin, the son-in-law of William Cullen Bryant, launched his weekly paper on February 25, 1843, but it died right away with the June 3, 1843, number because "the circulation is too limited to warrant the great expense of a weekly edition" (227).

33. Mary R. Brown to John Stillman Brown, November 20, 1843, KHi; Sophia Ripley to Margaret Fuller, n.d., Margaret Fuller Papers, MH. Internal evidence indicates that Sophia Ripley's letter had to have been written in late October or November 1843.

34. See Kenneth Walter Cameron, ed., *The Massachusetts Lyceum during the American Renaissance* (Hartford, Conn.: Transcendental Books, 1969), 158; Henry David Thoreau, *Journal,* vol. 1, *1837–1844,* ed. John C. Broderick et al. (Princeton: Princeton University Press, 1981), 277–278; and Walter Harding, *The Days of Henry Thoreau* (New York: Dover Publications, 1982), 156.

35. Delano, "Letters to Emerson," 39–40. The real reason for Bradford's letter was to apologize for allowing Thoreau to depart the community "in the midst of a snowstorm; and [we] have had fears that he may have suffered in his throat in consequence . . . We [the Brook Farmers] accused ourselves of great thoughtlessness or want of hospitality."

6. Reorganization

1. The account in the New York *Tribune* was reprinted in Albert Brisbane's *The Phalanx,* January 5, 1844, pp. 46–47. See also William Lloyd Garrison's *The Liberator,* January 5, 1844, p. 3.

2. C. C. Burleigh to J. M. McKim, December 29, 1843, "Anti-Slavery Let-

ters Written to W. L. Garrison and Others," Boston Public Library
(MS.A.1.2., vol. 13, p. 68). Burleigh was the corresponding secretary
and traveling agent for the Eastern Pennsylvania Anti-Slavery Society;
McKim was the publishing agent for the Society.

3. *The Phalanx,* January 5, 1844, pp. 46–47.

4. *Boston Daily Evening Transcript,* December 26, 1843, p. 2; *Boston Courier,* January 3, 1844, p. 2.

5. For the full text of Fuller's poem, and for the quotations from Fuller, see
Zoltan Haraszti, *The Idyll of Brook Farm* (Boston: Trustees of the Public
Library, 1937), 26–27. For Ellery Channing's poem, see *The Transcendentalists: An Anthology,* ed. Perry Miller (Cambridge: Harvard University Press, 1950), 381–382.

6. Brook Farm Minutes, January 2, 1844, MHi.

7. [Marianne Ripley] to John Brown, January 28, 1844, KHi.

8. Sophia's letter to Margaret Fuller is undated, but internal evidence indicates that it was written sometime in the first two weeks of January 1844.
My account of the incident is mainly derived from this letter, located
in the Margaret Fuller Papers, MH. It is also printed in Henrietta
Dana Raymond, *Sophia Willard Dana Ripley* (Portsmouth, N.H.: Peter
E. Randall, 1994), 52–54, though without any contextual framework.
Sophia knew that she didn't have to provide a detailed account to Fuller
because her friend had just spent a few days at the community and was
probably already familiar with the particulars of the incident. When
George Bradford departed the community for good in mid-February
1844, he remarked that "this crisis seems the good time for me to leave."
See Sterling F. Delano, "George Bradford's Letters to Emerson from
Brook Farm," *Resources for American Literary Study* 25 (1999): 41.

9. On September 3, 1843, Ripley's most cherished friend Theodore Parker
delivered "a sermon on the joys of Jesus," followed in the afternoon by
"a sermon of my own stewardship." Together these constituted the
weary Parker's farewell to his West Roxbury congregation. Six days later,
the controversial author of "The Transient and Permanent in Christianity" and *A Discourse of Matters Pertaining to Religion* (1842) set sail
aboard the "Ashburton" for a year-long trip to Europe, thereby leaving

Ripley without the benefit of an objective "witness" at one of the most crucial times in Brook Farm's history.

10. See Dana to Isaac Hecker, January 2, 1844, Hecker Papers, Paulist Fathers Archives, Washington, D.C. Just a few weeks later, on March 7, Dana addressed the members of the New England Fourier Society in Boston and described the goal at Brook Farm this way: "Our ulterior aim is nothing less than Heaven on Earth—the conversion of this globe, now exhaling pestilential vapors and possessed by unnatural climates, into the abode of beauty and health, and the restitution to Humanity of the Divine Image, now so long lost and forgotten." See *A Lecture on Association, in Its Connection with Religion* (Boston: Benjamin H. Greene, 1844), 26.

The Brook Farmers had only the highest regard for Emanuel Swedenborg (1688–1772), the eighteenth-century Swedish theologian, philosopher, and scientist. Ripley and the Transcendentalists had first been introduced to him by Sampson Reed, an 1818 graduate of Harvard. Swedenborg exerted a pervasive influence on the New England Transcendentalists, and Emerson included him in his series of essays on heroic individuals later published as *Representative Men* (1850). Charles Dana and John Dwight indicate what Swedenborg meant to the Brook Farmers. Dana stated in November 1845 that while Swedenborg was "inferior perhaps to Fourier in grandeur and comprehensive sweep of mind, [and was] less mathematical and exact in his forms of expression, he [Swedenborg] carries into his studies a deep Scandinavian reverence, a poetic and religious sentiment with which Fourier was not endowed." Dana had occasion to remark in April 1846 that "no man of sincere and unsophisticated mind can read Swedenborg without feeling his life elevated into a higher plane, and his intellect excited into new and more reverent action on some of the sublimest questions which the human mind can approach." John Dwight also spoke of Fourier and Swedenborg together in June 1847: "Taken together they are the highest expression of the tendency of human thought to universal unity; of the demand for unitary science, in which the soul of man shall feel all sciences co-ordinated to its own living springs of action." See *The Harbinger* 1 (November 22, 1845): 377–378; 2 (April 25, 1846): 315; and 5 (June 12, 1847): 6, respectively. See also

Sterling F. Delano, The Harbinger *and New England Transcendentalism* (Rutherford, N.J.: Fairleigh Dickinson University Press, 1983), 91–96.

11. A copy of the constitution was also printed in *The Phalanx* for March 1, 1844 (pp. 80–82).

12. Among the other matters covered by the By-Laws are the "Admission and Dismissal of Applicants, Candidates, Boarders, and Pupils"; "Personal Property"; "Distribution of Apartments"; "Labor"; "Financial Concerns"; "Education"; "Meetings of the Association"; and "Amendment of By-Laws." For more on Brook Farm's industrial reorganization, see also Chapter 7.

13. *Association; or, A Concise Exposition of the Practical Part of Fourier's Social Science* (New York: Greeley and McElrath, 1843), 44.

14. The surviving Brook Farm financial journals (November 1844–September 1847), it might be noted, are a monument to scrupulous detail. Virtually nothing went unrecorded in the community, whether that be someone being debited thirteen cents for a broken pane of glass, or fifteen cents for a toothbrush from the store, or whether that be someone being credited sixty-six dollars of interest on the stock that he or she owned.

15. Norman Ware, The *Industrial Worker 1840–1860* (Gloucester, Mass.: Peter Smith, 1959), 172.

16. William Ellery Channing, "Likeness to God," in *Transcendentalism: A Reader,* ed. Joel Myerson (New York: Oxford University Press, 2000), 4, 13; David M. Robinson, "William Ellery Channing," *Biographical Dictionary of Transcendentalism,* ed. Wesley T. Mott (Westport, Conn.: Greenwood Press, 1996), 37; Ripley to Ralph Waldo Emerson, November 9, 1840, RWEMA/MH.

17. Amelia E. Russell, *Home Life of the Brook Farm Association* (Boston: Little, Brown, 1900), 55.

18. The six Fourierist communities already in existence in 1843 were the Sylvania Association and the Social Reform Unity in Pennsylvania; the Jefferson County Industrial Association and the Morehouse Union in New York; the Bureau County Phalanx in Illinois; and the North American Phalanx in New Jersey. Thirteen new Fourierist communities were organized in the United States in 1844, the year that represented the

high-water mark of enthusiasm for Fourierism in the United States. (Only four new communities were established in 1845, just two were organized in 1846, and no others were undertaken for the remainder of the decade.) See Robert Fogarty, *Dictionary of American Communal and Utopian History* (Westport, Conn.: Greenwood Press, 1980), 183–195.

19. Ripley cited this same amount when he wrote to Isaac Hecker in September 1843, but it's not clear how he came up with it. When the Farm was sold at public auction in 1849 after the community's collapse in 1847, the selling price was $19,150, and that included a workshop and a greenhouse that were not yet constructed in January 1844. In addition to the land and existing dwellings at Brook Farm, Ripley evidently included in his estimate such things as financial pledges—like the one still owed by Charles Dana—furniture, fixtures, and other improvements, and outstanding balances in favor of the community, such as the $141 still owed by Almira Barlow. Ripley to Hecker, September 18, 1843, Hecker Papers, Paulist Fathers Archives. Many years after Brook Farm's collapse, Frederick Cabot—who was the community's bookkeeper and thus was in a position to know—stated emphatically that the Brook Farmers "never had a 'capital of about thirty thousand dollars.'" Cabot's letter, dated May 1877, is quoted in John Humphrey Noyes, "What Killed Brook Farm? And Who?" *The American Socialist* (May 31, 1877), p. 1.

20. "Phalanx" is Charles Fourier's term for the ideal community that he envisioned.

21. Dana to Hecker, "Thursday afternoon" [March 1844], Hecker Papers.

22. Emerson to John Sterling, January 31, 1844, *LRWE*, 7:585; Sophia Ripley to Emerson, January 17, 1844, RWEMA/MH.

23. Linck Johnson, "Reforming the Reformers: Emerson, Thoreau, and the Sunday Lectures at Amory Hall, Boston," *ESQ* 37 (4th Quarter 1991): 235–289, provides an excellent discussion of the lecture series.

24. See William Charvat, *Emerson's American Lecture Engagements* (New York: New York Public Library, 1961), 20; *LRWE*, 7:585; Marianne Ripley to John S. Brown, January 28, 1844, KHi; and *JMN*, 6:491–492.

25. Lane's January 16, 1844, letter to Hecker is in the Hecker Papers. For

Abba Alcott, see *The Journals of Bronson Alcott*, ed. Odell Shepard (Boston: Little, Brown, 1938), 157. Since her husband was, at this time, arguably the most progressive educator in the United States, it's not surprising that Abba wasn't unduly impressed with educational practices at Brook Farm.

26. For Bradford, see Delano, "Letters to Emerson," 41; for Bruce, see her memoir, *Years of Experience* (New York: G. P. Putnam's Sons, 1887), 179; for Russell, *Home Life*, 80–81. The word "dispensation" is not coincidentally used by both Bradford and Bruce. It is a Fourierist term, explained by Madame Gatti de Gamond, a French Fourierist, in an essay titled "The Third Dispensation" that Channing printed in *The Present*, (November 15, 1843), pp. 110–121. Early Brook Farm residents like Bradford and Bruce employed the phrase "first dispensation" to distinguish between the periods before and after the influx of mechanics and tradesmen and the adoption of Fourierist ideology at the Farm.

27. *Early Letters of George Wm. Curtis to John S. Dwight*, ed. George Willis Cooke (New York: Harper and Brothers, 1898), 154.

28. Brook Farm Minutes, November 18, 1843, MHi. At a community meeting on February 18, 1844, it was voted "that no person shall be considered a member of the Association until he has offered his name[,] place and date of birth[,] and previous occupation to the Constitution." The following were the first to affix their names to the new constitution in February 1844: George and Sophia Ripley; Marianne Ripley; Minot and Maria Pratt; Charles Dana; Louis and Jane Ryckman; Amelia Russell; John S. Dwight; Christopher List, an attorney; William Jackson Davis, a carpenter; Anne M. Dana (Charles's sister); Charles Salisbury, who listed himself as an "Agriculturalist"; and John Mitchell, a shoemaker. Five more people signed the constitution in April, seven in May, nine in June, six in July, fourteen in August, three in September, one in October, two in November, and five in December 1844. MHi.

29. Ripley to Brown, November 6, 1843, KHi.

30. It was only Thoreau and Emerson whose talks were hostile to the communitarians. Charles Dana, in fact, also participated in the program. He delivered a lecture on "Association" on March 17. Thoreau pre-

sented his talk a week earlier on March 10, and Emerson had spoken two weeks before, on March 3. For the full list of speakers and talks, see Johnson, "Reforming the Reformers," 239–241.

7. The Second Dispensation

1. Dana did acknowledge that "the magnitude of [the reorganization] is now first dawning upon me; it calls for such a sound and panoplied wisdom that I should despair if I had any time to do so." Dana to Isaac Hecker, [March 7?], 1844, the Hecker Papers, Paulist Fathers Archives, Washington, D.C. Dana's letter is dated March 1, 1844, but that date fell on a Friday in 1844, not a Thursday, as the letter is headed. March 7, 1844 was a Thursday. For Brook Farm, see the "Brook Farm Minutes," February 29, 1844, March 23, 1844, March 24, 1844, and March 25, 1844, MHi.

2. For example, the names of six men who were elected associates in 1844 appear on the "Petition to the Senate and House of Representatives of the Commonwealth of Massachusetts" to abolish capital punishment: John Sawyer, a broker; Jonathan Butterfield, a printer; Castalio Hosmer, a shoemaker; Frederick Cabot, a bookkeeper; Thomas Treadwell, a printer; and George Pierce, a mechanic. George Leach, who also signed the petition, was one of George Ripley's earliest supporters. His is one of the fourteen names listed on the original "Articles of Agreement."

3. There are at least two fairly obvious reasons why Brook Farm attracted so many single women. One is simply that it was very conveniently situated just eight miles from central Boston, which made going to and leaving Brook Farm a lot easier than at the other four New England communities, namely Hopedale, Northampton, Fruitlands, and the Putney Society, all of which were located in rural areas. A second reason, as was noted in Chapter 4, is that there were opportunities for personal growth and educational enrichment at Brook Farm that were simply not available to women at the other antebellum New England communities. As Carol A. Kolmerten points out in her study, *Women in Utopia: The Ideology of Gender in the American Owenite Communities* (Bloomington: Indiana University Press, 1990), "the women at Brook Farm enjoyed

the best advantages that American culture had to offer its single women" (175).

In his study, *Hopedale: From Commune to Company Town, 1840–1920* (Columbus: Ohio State University Press, 1992), Edward K. Spann states that "although a few [Hopedale women] were single, most were wives and mothers" (68). The situation at the Northampton Association was very similar. According to Christopher Clark in *The Communitarian Moment: The Radical Challenge of the Northampton Association* (Ithaca: Cornell University Press, 1995), only eight single women resided in the community, and four of them eventually married while they were at Northampton (126). Apart from Bronson and Abba Alcott's four young daughters, there was only one single woman at the short-lived Fruitlands, and she was summarily dismissed from the ascetic association when it was discovered that she had secretly eaten some fish. Very little information has survived regarding women at John Humphrey Noyes's Putney Society in Vermont, but Noyes himself notes in his *History of American Socialisms* (1870; reprint, New York: Hillary House Publishers, 1961) that his earliest supporters were his own and his brother's wife and his married sisters and their husbands (615). In 1848 Noyes and his followers left New England and moved to New York where he launched the Oneida Community. For Fruitlands, see Frederick C. Dahlstrand, *Amos Bronson Alcott: An Intellectual Biography* (Rutherford, N.J.: Fairleigh Dickinson University Press, 1982).

4. "Brook Farm Labor Record, May 1844–April 1845," MHi. This is the most comprehensive surviving Brook Farm labor record. It is a monthly account for all 127 persons—sixty-eight men and fifty-nine women—who performed at least one hour of work at Brook Farm during the period indicated. Two other surviving labor records are the "Group of Dinner Waiters" for May 3, 1845–April 4, 1846, and the "Printing Group" for the period April 18, 1846–October 3, 1846.

5. Upon admission to the community, the first month was spent as an "Applicant," the second as a "Candidate," at the completion of which Candidates "may be admitted as Associates on the nomination of any Associate" (By-Laws, Article 1). Exceptions to the two-month probationary period were occasionally made. As was noted in the previous chapter, it

was agreed at a community meeting on February 18, 1844 that "no person shall be considered a member of the Association until he has offered his name[,] place and date of birth[,] and previous occupation to the Constitution."

6. The "parts which individually we reject" certainly would have included Fourier's notions about love and sex in the Phalanx. Jonathan Beecher neatly characterizes the "new amorous world" in his comprehensive biography of Fourier: "the ultimate goal of the Phalanx was not merely to satisfy man's physical needs; it was to liberate man's instincts, to ensure all men and women an emotional and erotic life immeasurably freer and richer than a repressive civilization could ever provide . . . To realize this vision, Fourier argued, what was necessary was a new set of laws and institutions that would promote the most diverse kinds of erotic gratification while at the same time integrating the sexual drives into the whole fabric of man's collective life." See Beecher, *Charles Fourier: The Visionary and His World* (Berkeley: University of California Press, 1985), espec. 297–317. See also *Oeuvres complètes de Charles Fourier*, 12 vols. (Paris: Editions Anthropos, 1966–1968), espec. vol. 7: *Le Nouveau monde amoureux,* ed. Simone Debout-Oleskiewicz (Paris: Editions Anthropos, 1967).

Brook Farm itself, in fact, was immediately identified locally as a Fourierist community. A correspondent for the *Boston Investigator,* for instance, noted in the paper for May 1, 1844, that Brook Farm "has since become a Fourierist Association in every sense, and is now radically organizing for an extensive and useful sphere" (1). The Brook Farmers themselves always resisted the identification. Fifty years after the community's collapse, bookkeeper Frederick Cabot was still protesting that "although the Brook-Farmers have been popularly called 'Fourierists' they never called themselves so, and they never blindly accepted Fourier as a Master." Quoted in "What Killed Brook Farm? And Who?," *The American Socialist,* May 31, 1877, p. 169. The proceedings of the New York Convention are reported in *The Phalanx,* April 20, 1844, pp. 103–116.

7. See *The Phalanx* March 1, 1844, p. 84, and April 1, 1844, pp. 98–100.

8. Dana's remarks were reported in *The Phalanx,* April 20, 1844, pp. 113–115.

9. Dana was not exaggerating either. One of the distinguishing features of Brook Farm life is that women, whether single or married, neither complained nor were critical of the community's domestic expectations or requirements, which was not the case at least at two of the other four antebellum New England communities. The *Journal of Commerce,* for example, would never have said about Brook Farm, as it did about the Northampton Association, that "almost all the ladies" in the community were "unhappy and dissatisfied with their situation"—sentiments certainly also shared by Abba Alcott at Fruitlands, since virtually all of that community's domestic responsibilities rested on her shoulders. For the *Journal of Commerce,* see Clark, *The Communitarian Moment,* 124.

10. Fourier's notions about the "passions" first appeared in America in Brisbane's *Social Destiny of Man: or, Association and Reorganization of Industry* (Philadelphia: C. F. Stollmeyer, 1840), Chapter 12, "The Passions," 157–180. See also Brisbane's comments in his 1843 pamphlet, *Association; or, A Concise Exposition of the Practical Part of Fourier's Social Science* (New York: Greeley and McElrath, 1843), especially "Adaptation of the Groups and Series to Human Nature," 53–55.

11. In *Social Destiny of Man* (1840), Albert Brisbane defines a Group as a "squad, company or a little corporation; it is an assemblage of persons, three, seven, twelve or more, freely and spontaneously united for any purpose, either of business or pleasure. *But in strict theory, we understand by Group a mass leagued together from identity of taste for the exercise of some branch of Industry, Science or Art* . . . The Series are distributed in the same manner as the Groups; the former operate on Groups, as Groups operate on individuals. A Serie should contain at least five Groups" (115, 118). Brisbane modified the number of Groups required for a Series in his 1843 pamphlet on *Association,* where he notes that "a Series must contain at least three Groups" (44).

12. Unfortunately, the labor records do not indicate the "Groups" in which individuals accumulated their hours. I gratefully acknowledge the work of Carol Felton Capitani, whose master's thesis at Villanova based on the "Brook Farm Labor Records, May 1844–April 1845" was completed under my direction in 1999. Capitani carefully sorted through and provided preliminary tabulations of men's and women's work patterns at

Brook Farm, which considerably eased my own subsequent examination of this material.

13. Unless otherwise indicated, all quotations from Mary Ann Dwight refer to *Letters from Brook Farm, 1844–1847*, ed. Amy L. Reed (Poughkeepsie, N.Y.: Vassar College, 1928). Rather than continually intrude upon the narrative, I have tried to provide dates in the text of each chapter should the reader wish to consult a specific Dwight letter. In this instance the "pretty severe cases" letter is dated April 14, 1844, and the "came near dying" letter, May 11, 1844

14. Gannett's letter, ca. May or June 1844, and Curtis's letter, dated June 27, 1844, are among the Hecker Papers, Paulist Fathers Archive, in the collection designated "Letters Received by Father Hecker." Gannett's letter is #28, Curtis's #32. Gannett's letter has no dateline and no postmark, but since Hecker visited Brook Farm at the end of May 1844—see "Letters to Father Hecker's Family," #37—Gannett's letter must have been written in late May or in June.

15. Sumner was the youngest brother of Charles Sumner, the Boston lawyer who became widely celebrated throughout New England for his spirited opposition to the South generally, and for his vehement opposition particularly to the Fugitive Slave Law and the Nebraska-Kansas bill. Horace Sumner was aboard the ill-fated *Elizabeth* when it sank off Fire Island in 1850, killing Sumner, Margaret Fuller, and her husband and child.

16. Joel Myerson, ed., "Rebecca Codman Butterfield's Reminiscences of Brook Farm," *New England Quarterly* 65 (December 1992): 622; Amelia Russell, *Home Life of the Brook Farm Association* (Boston: Little, Brown, 1900), 118; Frederick Pratt, "Accounts of Brook Farm," *BFB*, 331.

17. For the children, however, daily life at Brook Farm was mostly just plain fun—when, that is, they weren't working or devoting their time to school lessons. Frederick Pratt, for instance, fondly recalled years later "the coming of Annie, Louisa, and Elisabeth Alcott one day and the jolly time we children had together, and the use made of our boys' wheelbarrows or wagons in carrying the girls about." See *BFB*, 332.

18. *DL*, 19; Fanny Dwight to brother Frank, June 2, 1844, MHi.

19. The "Brook Farm Minutes" indicate that eleven committees were appointed between March 23, 1844–December 22, 1844. Women were in-

cluded on seven of them, though on only two committees did women outnumber men: the committee to consider improvements in the washing and ironing departments (July 7) consisted of three women and two men, as did the Retrenchment Committee (November 10). No women were appointed to the Building Committee (July 26) or to the committee charged (December 22) to examine the financial report for the previous fiscal year. Mrs. Rebecca Codman, however, joined four men on the committee that investigated allegations against a cabinetmaker, Robert Westacott (November 24), and Fanny Macdaniel sat on the committee that was charged (December 22) to revise the constitution. Not surprisingly, Sophia Ripley sat on four different committees during this period, and Marianne Ripley served on three. Brook Farm Minutes, March 23, 1844, June 2, 1844, July 7, 1844, July 25, 1844, July 26, 1844, November 10, 1844, November 24, 1844, and December 22, 1844, MHi. When Brook Farm was incorporated as a Fourierist Phalanx in May 1845, the new constitution called for a "Council of Arbiters" that would consist "of seven persons, the majority of whom shall be women." See Chapter 8.

20. The "Brook Farm Labor Record, May 1844–April 1845," MHi, lists the names of 127 adults—no children were included—who were at the community for all or for a part of that twelve-month period. Not all of them were there, however, at the same time. The population fluctuated from month to month. The largest number of people at Brook Farm was ninety-two in November 1844. The smallest number was sixty-six in August 1844. The monthly average for the year was seventy-nine. There are no surviving records to provide an exact comparison of populations with either the Hopedale Community or the Northampton Association, but Spann's study, *Hopedale*, notes that the Census of 1850 listed 163 people in the Milford community, seventy of whom were younger than eighteen years of age (89), and Clark observes in *The Communitarian Moment* that the population at Northampton in the summer of 1843 was "just over one hundred," of whom thirty to forty were children (115). The population at all three Massachusetts communities, in other words, was roughly about the same.

21. *DL*, 40–42; Ripley's letter, dated September 11, 1844, is in JSD/MB.

22. See *The Phalanx*, August 10, 1844, p. 244, and July 13, 1844, p. 205. Brisbane's letter from Paris is dated June 13, 1844, but it was not published until July 13, 1844.

23. Brownson to Hecker, September 24, 1844, Hecker Papers.

24. For Brownson, see the following in *Brownson's Quarterly Review:* "No Church, No Reform. *Addressed Especially to the Fourierists*" (April 1844): 175–194; "Church Unity and Social Amelioration" (July 1844): 310–327; and "Fourierism Repugnant to Christianity" (October 1844): 450–487. Parke Godwin, who was assisting with the editorial chores of *The Phalanx* in Brisbane's absence, wrote to Charles Dana on July 12, 1844, to apologize for not responding sooner to a letter from the Brook Farmer: "I have had my hands so full of Brownson and other business that I have not found time or strength to reply to your interesting letter." For Godwin's response to Brownson, see *The Phalanx*, June 29, 1844, p. 195; July 13, 1844, pp. 197–204; and July 27, 1844, pp. 213–220. For Godwin to Dana, see NYPL.

The campaign against Charles Fourier especially targeted the Frenchman's views on marriage. The Boston *Daily Evening Transcript,* for example, copied an item titled "A Fourierite Marriage" on March 13, 1846 (p. 2, col. 4), reporting that a couple living in John Collins's Skaneateles Community in New York supposedly made a pledge "to pass their lives together, without the ordinance which is usually thought to constitute legal matrimony." Four days later, on March 17, the Boston *Post* (p. 1, col. 5) ran the very same item for its readers. Then on March 23, 1846, the *Daily Evening Transcript* copied another item on "Brisbane on Marriage" (p. 2, col. 2) from the *Vermont Chronicle,* in which that paper claimed that the New York Associationist's refutation of a charge in the *Democratic Review* that Fourierism would undermine the institution of marriage actually supported the belief that Fourierism was "anti-Christian and of licentious tendency."

25. See Dana to Godwin, October 30, 1844, NYPL.

8. From Association to Phalanx

1. Brook Farm's financial records do not indicate the source of the $10,000 subscription. It may have been a combination of pledges by several New

York Associationists, such as Horace Greeley, Marcus Spring, Edmund Tweedy, and others. In December 1845 Albert Brisbane reported to George Ripley that the New Yorkers were withdrawing financial support from Brook Farm in order to pay off a $10,000 mortgage on the North American Phalanx in Red Bank, New Jersey. Whether this $10,000 is the same as that referred to in the "Notice to the Second Edition" of the constitution isn't known. Nor is the reason why the reported pledge was subsequently withdrawn. As early as his October 30, 1844, letter, Dana confides in Parke Godwin that "we are[,] too[,] disappointed of a considerable sum, which puts us in a 'fix.'" See the *Constitution of the Brook Farm Association for Industry and Education, West Roxbury, Mass. with an Introductory Statement. Second Edition, with the By-Laws of the Association* (Boston: I. R. Butts, 1844); and Dana to Godwin, October 30, 1844, NYPL. Dana-Godwin correspondence that is dated in the text without further citation can be understood to refer to the Bryant-Godwin Papers, New York Public Library.

2. "Address," *The Phalanx* 1 (December 9, 1844): 294.

3. Godwin was also preoccupied at this time with the forthcoming congressional election because he had been nominated by the National Reform Party to represent the 5th Congressional District.

   Among the resolutions presented to the Rochester convention delegates by Godwin was one—"for the purpose of securing a more uniform system of internal organization"—calling for an active correspondence between existing Associations and the Central Executive Committee in New York City, the approval of which served further to affirm the importance of operations there. For Godwin and Fourier, see especially his letters to Dana dated May 18, 1844, and July 12, 1844, NYPL. Dana had already shared his concern with Godwin back in May 1844 about the proliferation of new Associations and their potential to draw attention away from Brook Farm. Godwin agreed with Dana when he sent the Brook Farmer a letter on May 17, 1844, saying, by way of closing, that "I am clearly of your opinion that no more associations should be attempted."

4. Dana to Godwin, October 30, 1844, NYPL.

5. Brook Farm Minutes, September 22, 1844, MHi. All subsequent quota-

tions from the community's meetings that are dated in the text without
further citation refer to this source.

6. Only a limited number of delegates from each local association were permitted to vote. As Norman Ware points out in *The Industrial Worker
1840–1860* (Gloucester, Mass.: Peter Smith, 1959), despite agitation in
Massachusetts in the early 1840s regarding child labor laws, "no legisla-
tion was obtained to shorten the hours of labor of adults in Massachusetts until 1874, although some reductions were made by the corpora-
tions as a result of the ten-hour agitation" (127).

7. The remark about Ripley in the Boston *Investigator* was quoted in the
Workingman's Advocate for October 26, 1844, p. 3. The remarks from
the *New England Operative* were quoted in the *Workingman's Advocate*
for November 2, 1844, p. 3. Mike Walsh may have been beloved by his
fellow workingmen, but Parke Godwin thought that he was "*a great
brute!*" He also told Charles Dana, in a letter dated November 8, 1844,
that Walsh was "a perfect incarnation of destructivism and diabolical de-
mocracy," and that the Irishman was "th[or]oughly *unprincipled,*—mor-
ally and intellectually." NYPL.

8. Dana to Godwin, October 30, 1844, and Godwin to Dana, November 8,
1844, NYPL.

9. The situation at the Ohio Phalanx is a case in point. Elijah P. Grant, the
head of the Ohio Phalanx in Bellaire, Ohio, complained to Charles Dana
in January 1845 that the "most serious evils" that he had to deal with in
his efforts to organize the community were insufficient capital, "a want
of refinement and kindness of feeling among the Associates," and the absence of "sufficiently exalted conceptions of the object to be attained."
Grant then continued: "The most serious evil of all perhaps is, the want
of a sufficient number of intelligent managers, possessing practical skill
and expansive views . . . I feel the want of energetic and intelligent co-
operators, and unless I can enlist in our movement some of the higher
class of minds at the East, I know not but I shall be constrained to abandon [the community]." Grant to Dana, January 6, 1845, transcribed copy
in IU-HS.

10. *The Social Reformer and Herald of Universal Health,* to cite its full title,
had just been launched by John Allen and Joseph A. Whitmarsh on Sep-

tember 1, 1844, as a bimonthly, but the paper was obviously already encountering difficulties, given Dana's comment to Godwin. Dana to Godwin, November 20, 1844, NYPL. Allen's offer to transfer *The Social Reformer* wasn't entirely altruistic, however; he wanted a stake in the West Roxbury community. He seems to have bartered his printing press for five shares of Brook Farm stock. See the Brook Farm financial journals, April 1845, MHi.

11. *DL,* 52.

12. *DL,* October [10], 1844, p. 44; Brownson to Isaac Hecker, September 24, 1844, the Hecker Papers, Paulist Fathers Archives, Washington, D.C.; and Fuller to Bruce, October 20, 1844, *LMF,* 3:236–237. It didn't help either that the Pilgrim House was nearly brought to the ground on October 10, 1844. This was the second fire there (the first was in December 1842); it was caused by a new "air-tight stove" that John Codman had installed in Mary Ann Dwight's room just the day before the incident. Rebecca Codman immediately alerted several of her associates and the fire was quickly extinguished, but not before a section of plaster had to be knocked out in the ironing room below her bedroom, which revealed "a flame 10 inches broad which must (had there been a short delay) have fired the house, but water was thrown on and it was stopped." *DL,* 44; Brownson to Hecker, September 24, 1844.

13. This "solution" to the problem of extras at table is typical of the short-sightedness with which the community's financial affairs were managed. Apart from the important fact that the Brook Farmers needed whatever cash they could get their hands on, deferring charges for extras meant that no payment might be made at all because members often departed the Association before the annual dividend was actually settled. Departures were so common in fact that it was voted on March 20, 1845, that "those persons who have withdrawn from the Domain without the consent of the several Directions have virtually ceased to be members of the Association."

Mary Hosmer was the wife of Castalio Hosmer, who came from New Bedford, Massachusetts, with his brothers Charles and Granville (and his wife Anna), and his sister Laura. (They were probably not related to Dolly or John Hosmer, who came from Concord.) Cynthia Hastings was the wife of Buckley, Brook Farm's grocer and purveyor. William Cheswell was a carpenter (Mary Ann was his wife), as were Job Tirrell and Jeremiah Reynolds. Peter Kleinstrup was a cabinetmaker and talented botanist (Augustina was his wife) who took over the newly constructed greenhouse in the autumn of 1844. James Clapp was a bricklayer. All of these people arrived at Brook Farm during the busy six months following publication of the new constitution in January 1844.

14. *DL*, 51.

15. Brook Farm Minutes, December 22, 1844, MHi.

16. Pratt returned to West Roxbury and worked a full month in March 1845 along with his wife Maria (their children did no work after February 1845), at which time the popular and hardworking family departed Brook Farm for good. Their departure is discussed later in this chapter.

17. "Convention of the New England Fourier Society," *The Phalanx*, February 8, [1845], pp. 309–317.

18. Parsons to Mary Ann Dwight, January 18, 1845, MHi.

19. *DL*, December 22, 1844, p. 55; *The Phalanx*, February 8, [1845], p. 320; Russell, *Home Life of the Brook Farm Association* (Boston: Little, Brown, 1900), 94; *BFM*, 90–91. The anonymous "obituary"—"Reflections on Returning from a Funeral in Association"—in *The Phalanx*, designated simply 'S.,' was written by Catharine M. Sloan, who first came to Brook Farm in May 1844 and was, like Williams, a seamstress. See *DL*, February [27?], [1845].

20. *DL*, January 15, 1845, p. 64; January 19, 1845, p. 67.

21. This report, according to Philadelphia Associationist James Kay, was evidently an extended version of a defense of "Association" that Dana had originally written to a woman named Mary from Buffalo, New York, to whom he hoped to become engaged, until, that is, she decided that she was no Associationist, and that Brook Farm was no place to begin a marriage. See Kay to Isaac Hecker, March 24, 1845, Hecker Papers. Dana wrote to Hannah Ripley, George's cousin, a few weeks before the Fourier Society meeting in January and reported that he had received a letter from Mary in which "she bids me a last farewell, & does not ask me to write to her again, or even speak of it." Dana recognized, he also told Hannah, that Mary "must be unhappy in such a mode of life as my wife

must move in,—not with repining & longing looks back to the poor comforts that she has left behind, but with joy & strength & indomitable zeal." See Dana to Hannah Ripley, [December 21, 1845], KHi.

22. See *The Phalanx*, February 8, [1845], pp. 309–317, for a full report of the convention proceedings.

23. *DL*, January 26, 1845, p. 70.

24. Mary Ann Dwight provides a full account of this evening. See *DL*, January 27, 1845, pp. 72–76.

25. Parke Godwin would hardly have agreed with Cabot's sentiment. In his letters to Charles Dana in the months immediately following Brisbane's return to America, Godwin took one swipe after another at his New York colleague. By contrast, Brisbane seems to have been fairly well liked by Brook Farm's leaders. After a subsequent departure from the community on April 10, 1845, for example, Mary Ann Dwight told Anna Parsons that "Mr. Brisbane . . . leaves a void here that must be felt until his return" (*DL*, 90). In the same letter, Dwight notes that Brisbane "has won our [Brook Farmers'] hearts" through his entire devotion to the cause of Association (91). Godwin's animosity towards Brisbane not only reflects the nature of his own acidulous personality; it also indicates the problem with the New York Associationists generally: they were never a unified group.

26. The group included Nathaniel Hawthorne, George P. Bradford, Almira Barlow and her three sons, and Burrill and George William Curtis. Isaac Hecker had also been there in 1844, living as a boarder in Henry Thoreau's house.

27. Pratt's letter to Ripley is in *BFM*, 150. Despite their increasing unhappiness at Brook Farm, Maria and Minot Pratt were among the community's hardest-working members for the period between May 1844 and April 1845—the only year for which a detailed labor record has survived. For the twelve-month period, Maria was the tenth-hardest-working associate at Brook Farm, and Minot was the eighteenth among 127 associates and probationers whose names appear in the labor record.

28. For Ripley's remarks, see *BFM*, 157.

29. Brook Farm Minutes, April 8, 1845, and May 3, 1845, MHi. From the point of view of George Ripley and the other trustees of Brook Farm, the

primary advantage of incorporating the community was that it reduced the potential conflict over the property rights of individuals who might choose to leave the Association because incorporation meant that the land now belonged to the corporation and not to the individuals who comprised the community.

30. The Ripleys certainly weren't the only associates invested in the community. Many other associates owned Brook Farm stock, although most could only afford to purchase it incrementally. The financial journal for April 1845 shows, for example, that Mary Dwight had thus far invested $52 toward the purchase of a single share; daughters Mary Ann and Fanny had managed $20 apiece; and son John, just $12. Charles Dana's sister Maria owned 32/100s of a share by virtue of the $32 that she had accumulated since becoming a member of the Association in February 1844. Cabinetmaker Peter Kleinstrop, however, owned six shares of stock worth $600. Dry-goods purveyor George W. Houghton and mechanic George Pierce each held two shares, and Jonathan Butterfield, a printer, and Henry P. Trask, a carriagemaker, had one apiece. Right after the conversion, two new applicants, Samuel Alfred Adams and Charles D. Fitch, invested $250 and $500, respectively. George W. Hatch, who was in charge of the sash-and-blind manufacturing industry, is on the books holding $500 worth of stock, although, as John Allen did with his printing press, Hatch may have bartered for all or part of his five shares. See the Brook Farm financial journals for April 1845 (the end of the second quarter), July 1845, and October 1845 (the end of Brook Farm's fiscal year). MHi.

31. *Constitution of the Brook Farm Association for Industry and Education, Second Edition*, 4.

32. The Brook Farmers were always eager to pursue any activity that might be a potential source of income. The "fancy work" of Mary Ann Dwight, Amelia Russell, and other Brook Farm women has already been noted (see Chapter 7). There was also a modest demand for tailoring, plain sewing, and dressmaking in 1845, though none of these provided the kind of substantial and regular income that could meet the community's considerable needs and expenses. Neither did the occasional translations of notable foreign works, nor did the mustard-seed venture in-

spired by fellow Associationists at the North American Phalanx in Red Bank, New Jersey. The new greenhouse constructed behind the Cottage in 1844 in the hope that the floral business might be profitable never generated any significant income either.

33. Today, ironically enough, a pair of Brook Farm whale-oil lamps in good condition might cost as much as $1,500—not because of their intrinsic worth but simply because they were manufactured at the community in relatively limited numbers.

34. J. B. Kerfoot, *American Pewter* (New York: Bonanza Books, 1924), 156. For Codman, see *BFM*, 208.

35. The attractive and engaging Almira Barlow is a good example. She departed the community with her three sons in 1843 leaving behind unpaid charges for board and instruction in the amount of $141.18, which, it appears, Barlow never did settle with the community.

36. The carpenters and cabinetmakers did generate income, however, when they were employed by their West Roxbury neighbors, which they occasionally were, especially by George Russell and Francis Shaw, who relied on the Brook Farmers for repairs and renovations around their homes. Russell, for example, paid $42.23 in the spring of 1845 to have the carpenters build trellises and fences on his property, and Shaw paid $500 in February 1845 for an addition on his property, and another $38 the following month for the construction of a library table and a cornice for a bookcase.

37. Codman, *BFM*, 208; Lindsay Swift, *Brook Farm: Its Members, Scholars, and Visitors* (New York: Macmillan, 1900), 43–44. Swift also remarks that "lumber could not be bought in large quantities; furthermore, it could not be kept on hand long enough to become properly dried, and the vexation of customers whose doors shrank was great and justifiable."

38. Doucet, "Reminiscences of the Brook Farm Association," *BFB*, 233–234; Swift, *Brook Farm*, 43–44; Codman, *BFM*, 208.

9. The Harbinger

1. It turned out, in fact, to be nearly a year and a half before the "American Union of Associationists" was organized in Boston in May 1846, but the

record should show that the earliest overture for a new "school" was first proposed by the Brook Farmers in November 1844. Despite the fact that internal conditions at the West Roxbury community were already critical in May 1846, Ripley and a few other Brook Farmers converted a quarterly gathering of the "New England Fourier Society" in Boston into an organizational meeting and established the American Union of Associationists—even electing several prominent New York Associationists officers in absentia. See Dana to Godwin, November 20, 1844, NYPL. All subsequent quotations in this chapter from the Dana-Godwin correspondence are from the NYPL. See especially Dana to Godwin, February 20, 1845, and [March 1845]; and Godwin to Dana, February 14, [1845]; [March 21, 1845]; April 26, 1845; April 28, 1845; May 12, 1845; June 14, 1845; and June 18, 1845.

2. The letter, in the NYPL, has no address, no place, and no date—other than "Monday 17th." Internal evidence indicates that it was written in March 1845. In fact, March 17, 1845, was a Monday.

3. *The Pathfinder* survived from February 25, 1843, to June 3, 1843.

4. Ripley himself was so anxious to undertake the new venture that he told Jonathan Saxton, who contributed one item to the first volume of *The Harbinger,* that although it might still be a few weeks before publication of the new paper commenced, "I think . . . that we shall make a beginning next week." Ripley to Saxton, March 31, 1845, IU-HS.

5. Dana specifically mentions Emerson and Parker as possible contributors in a letter to Godwin on February 20, 1845, NYPL. *The Harbinger* was published weekly. Every six months it was bound into a volume of twenty-six numbers. Volume 1 covers the period June 14, 1845–December 6, 1845; Volume 2: December 13, 1845–June 6, 1846; Volume 3: June 13, 1846–December 5, 1846; Volume 4: December 12, 1846–June 5, 1847; and Volume 5: June 12, 1847–October 30, 1847. (Volumes 6 through 8 were published after the paper was transferred to New York.) All but the incompleted eighth volume include the names of the contributors to the volume as well as a full index. For an index to Volume 8, see Sterling F. Delano and Rita Colanzi, "An Index to Volume VIII of *The Harbinger,*" *Resources for American Literary Study* 10 (Autumn 1980): 173–186.

6. Additionally, Ripley and Dwight co-authored, with William Henry Channing, five articles on the "Anniversary Meeting of the American Union [of Associationists]" for Volume 4.

7. Godwin complained to Dana on August 1, 1845, that "you must not yet insist upon my writing for you much. I should be glad to do so, were it within the possible of possibilities. From 6 in the morning till late at night I work." NYPL.

8. Emerson's letter to Dwight has not survived, but it is quoted at length by George Willis Cooke in his biography, *John Sullivan Dwight: Brook-Farmer, Editor, and Critic of Music* (Boston: Small, Maynard, 1898), 103–105. Several years before, Emerson had grown just as impatient with Victor Cousin, the French eclectic philosopher who became the rage in the mid-1830s for Transcendentalists like Orestes Brownson and Ripley himself. Emerson found Cousin's eclecticism to be merely "pompous." Emerson is quoted in *The Transcendentalists: An Anthology,* ed. Perry Miller (Cambridge: Harvard University Press, 1950), 107.

9. In Chapter 1, I mark the demise of the Transcendental "movement" with the final meeting of the "Transcendental Club" in September 1840. Technically, the "newness"—as Transcendentalism was known around Boston in the 1830s—was never formally a "movement" at all. But to the extent that men like Ripley, Emerson, Hedge, and Brownson stood on recognizably common religious and philosophical ground, the collapse of the Transcendental Club marks the point at which they were no longer able to occupy that ground together. For a discussion of the *Dial,* see Joel Myerson, *The New England Transcendentalists and the* Dial (Rutherford, N.J.: Fairleigh Dickinson University Press, 1980); for *The Harbinger,* see Sterling F. Delano, The Harbinger *and New England Transcendentalism* (Rutherford, N.J.: Fairleigh Dickinson University Press, 1983).

10. Gohdes, *The Periodicals of Transcendentalism* (Durham, N.C.: Duke University Press, 1931), 111.

11. George Joyaux, "George Sand, Eugene Sue and *The Harbinger,*" *The French Review* 27 (December 1953): 124.

12. For a discussion of the "ten-hour movement" in Massachusetts and New

England during the 1840s, see Norman Ware, *The Industrial Worker 1840–1860* (Gloucester, Mass.: Peter Smith, 1959), 125–148. For specific reports in *The Harbinger* having to do with the activities of the New England workingmen, see the following: "Address to the Workingmen of New England, by L. W. Ryckman," 1 (June 21, 1845): 21–22; "Working Men of New England," 1 (July 19, 1845): 112; "New England Working-men's Convention," 1 (September 27, 1845): 255–256; "The Working-men's Protective Union," 2 (December 13, 1845): 15; "The Working-men's Movement," 3 (June 20, 1846): 30–31; "Workingmen's Protective Union," 3 (October 31, 1846): 336; "The Workingmen's Protective Union" (reprint from the *Voice of Industry*), 4 (May 1, 1847): 326; and "Protective Unions," 5 (October 16, 1847): 304.

13. All citations are to *The Harbinger:* Ripley, "Brook Farm Lecturers," 2 (February 21, 1846): 175; Dana, "The Campaign Begins," 3 (July 11, 1846): 80; Dana, "Industrial Feudalism," 3 (July 25, 1846): 112; Ripley, "American Labor," 3 (September 12, 1846): 223; and Brisbane, "Industrial Reform," 3 (October 10, 1846): 287. Occasionally, poems having to do with labor were included in *The Harbinger,* although most of them were reprinted from other sources because the poetry column was the most difficult to provide for. See, for instance, "The Laborer," 1 (July 26, 1845): 103; "The Mechanic," 1 (October 25, 1845): 313; "The Sentimental Manufacturer to the Factory Girl," 3 (October 24, 1846): 306; "The Laboring Man," 5 (August 7, 1847): 131.

14. Margaret Fuller's *Papers on Literature and Art* (1846) was the only one of her works to be reviewed in *The Harbinger*. She sailed for Europe that year as foreign correspondent for Horace Greeley's New York *Tribune*. John Dwight praised *Papers*—which combined some of Fuller's earlier contributions to the *Dial* with a number of critical notices that she had written for the *Tribune*—but he criticized her style, noting that it was marked by the same hurriedness that characterized her conversations. See *The Harbinger,* September 26, 1846, pp. 249–252.

Brook Farm friend and neighbor Theodore Parker received a lot more attention than Fuller in *The Harbinger*. Five of his works were reviewed. Charles Dana used the occasion of his review of *The Idea of a Christian*

Church—Parker's ordination sermon upon his installation as minister of the Twenty-Eighth Congregational Church in Boston in January 1846—to criticize the Christian Church for its failure to take a more active role in social reform activities (1846; 2:157–158), a criticism that he leveled more broadly against the American government when he reviewed Parker's *A Sermon of War* (1846; 3:75–76). Ripley reviewed three of Parker's sermons for *The Harbinger: A Sermon of the Perishing Classes in Boston* (1846; 3:361–363), *A Sermon on Merchants* (1847; 4:137–138), and *A Sermon of the Dangerous Classes in Society* (1847; 4:377–379). His reviews of the first two of these gave Ripley the opportunity to lash out himself at the Christian Church, specifically at the "snow-white Pharisees," the "Ponderous doctors of divinity," and the "sleak and studious Scribes" who remained silent in the midst of widespread oppression and evil in contemporary society.

15. For Channing's complete review, see *The Harbinger* 3 (June 27, 1846): 43–44.

16. For Story, see *The Harbinger* for February 7, 1846, pp. 142–144; for Dana, see ibid., April 4, 1846, pp. 268–269; and for Dwight, see ibid., January 16, 1847, pp. 91–94.

17. See Sidney P. Moss, *Poe's Literary Battles* (Durham, N.C.: Duke University Press, 1963). For Dana's review, see *The Harbinger,* 1:73; for Dwight, see ibid., 1:410.

18. Poe, "Brook Farm," *Broadway Journal,* December 13, 1845, pp. 27 and 32.

19. The following quotations about *The Harbinger* refer to the five volumes published at Brook Farm. See *The Harbinger,* 6:104.

20. Ripley characterized the Brook Farmers as "the humblest of pioneers" on different occasions; see, e.g., *The Harbinger* for August 30, 1845 (1:192) and for March 21, 1846 (2:237). For "centre of influence" references, see, e.g., Charles Dana to Parke Godwin, November 20, 1844, NYPL; and George Ripley, "To Our Friends," *The Harbinger,* March 21, 1846, p. 237.

21. "The Fountain in the Palace: A Story Told to the Brook Farm Children" (1:24–25) has nothing at all to do with the community; two other references are in letters of inquiry about Brook Farm (1:192 and 2:237–238);

one reference is an announcement about "Brook Farm Lecturers" (2:175); and another is George Ripley's report of the fire that destroyed the Phalanstery (2:220–222). The most extended personal remarks in *The Harbinger* about Brook Farm appeared on December 20, 1845 (2:29–30), but these have nothing to do with the community's internal operations.

Ripley and his colleagues would have been understandably encouraged by the paper's early financial returns, which might have reinforced their conviction that the thing to be emphasized was Fourierism and not the Farm. Expenses for the first volume of *The Harbinger* (June–December 1845) were approximately $255, which included such items as labor, paper, postage, and mailing labels. Income for the same period, however, amounted to slightly more than $1,000. Practically every associate in the community, by the way, took a subscription to the paper.

22. Even members of other Fourierist communities around the country looked to Brook Farm for leadership. The head of the Wisconsin Phalanx spoke for many Associationists nationwide when he noted in a report that "we had hoped to see something in the Harbinger, which would be a guide to us in this branch of our [educational] organization. We look to the Brook Farm Phalanx for instruction in this branch, and hope to see it in the Harbinger for the benefit of ourselves and other Associations." See *The Harbinger* 1 (September 6, 1845): 208.

23. *The Harbinger,* 1:192.

24. Ibid., 2:29.

10. "Our Severest Crisis"

1. For Dwight, see *DL,* September 28, [1845]; for Parsons, see October 18, 1845, MHi. Unless otherwise indicated, *DL* is the source for all Mary Ann Dwight quotations dated in the text.

2. An insidious sort of "elitism" seems to have been present in the community throughout much of its existence. Georgiana Bruce and George P. Bradford's supposedly playful references to a "first dispensation" to distinguish those early Brook Farmers who came to the community in the pre-Fourierist days before the arrival of the mechanics and tradesmen is

one example. Another is the remark of Sophia Eastman, an unsophisticated young woman who came to Brook Farm in July 1843 and immediately noted "that there is an aristocracy prevailing here . . . many complain of being neglected. I think there should be a distinction made, but
you know it is against their principles." It should also be noted here that
Mary Ann Dwight was persuaded to attend a party at the Hive in March
1846 to celebrate the anniversary of the arrival of William Cheswell because she didn't want to offend the Brook Farm carpenter, who "has always looked with a jealous eye upon the aristocratic element." (In May
1845, Mary Ann Dwight changed the spelling of her name to Marianne,
but I have retained the original spelling throughout.) While Dwight was
condescending to Cheswell, Philadelphia supporter James Kay was admonishing Brook Farm's leaders to recognize that "the introduction of
the *people* into the practical administration of [Brook Farm's] government" was one of the essential "measures" that needed to be taken if the
community hoped to survive much longer. George Ripley, in fact, had
been steadily circling the wagons, so to speak, around the administration
of Brook Farm. See Eastman to "My dear Parents and Sisters," July 25,
1843, IU-HS; *DL,* 161, espec. 164-165; and Kay to John S. Dwight,
March 2, 1846, JSD/MB.

3. Channing substituted for Parker on October 5, 12, and 19, and again on
November 2 and 9, 1845. See Dean Grodzins and Joel Myerson, "The
Preaching Record of Theodore Parker," *SAR* 1994: 93. For Channing's
sketch, see *DL,* "The last day of summer" [1845], p. 116.

4. *DL,* October 19, 1845.

5. Guarneri, *The Utopian Alternative: Fourierism in Nineteenth-Century
America* (Ithaca: Cornell University Press, 1991), 168.

6. *BFM,* 269; Aria S. Huntington, *Memoir and Letters of Frederic Dan
Huntington* (Boston: Houghton, Mifflin, 1906): 69. A transcribed copy
of Eastman's letter is in the Arthur E. Bestor, Jr., Papers, IU-HS. For the
unidentified Brook Farmer, see "The Hopedale and Brook Farm Communities," *The American Socialist,* June 22, 1876, pp. 101–102; for Saxton, see *BFB,* 323.

7. Dwight, *DL,* October 19, 1845, pp. 123–124.

8. For John Allen, see his letter to Mehitable Eastman, dated November 2 and [3] and December 1, 1845, a transcribed copy of which is in IU-HS. The Brook Farmers always prided themselves on their ability to turn a clever pun, but John Allen's on his son's smallpox is certainly among the most memorable. He reported to Eastman that his son Fred was "horribly pitted" from the disease, and that he "will probably always be sadly *defaced.* (I cannot resist the pun)," he acknowledged.

9. See *DL,* November 23, 1845, p. 133.

10. Amy L. Reed, the editor of *Letters from Brook Farm, 1844–1847,* states that Mary Ann Dwight" was correct in her assumption that none of her own family had or would have the disease." *DL,* 132.

11. The decision to convert the Cottage into a temporary hospital did have an effect on the Brook Farm school because students usually met there for instruction. Allen's remark that the smallpox "broke up our school" is somewhat misleading, however. The disease did require Brook Farm's teachers to find other locations to meet with their "scholars," but it didn't force the school to discontinue operations. That said, parents must have been understandably nervous about their children's continued presence at the Farm. Allen to Mehitable Eastman, November 2 and [3] and December 1, 1845, IU-HS.

12. See *DL,* 133; Brook Farm financial journal for November 1845, MHi; and Russell, *Home Life of the Brook Farm Association* (Boston: Little, Brown, 1900), 120–121. On September 24, 1843, it had been "voted that . . . the use of coffee on the breakfast table be discontinued." MHi.

13. See Robert F. Metzdorf, "Hawthorne's Suit against Ripley and Dana," *American Literature* 12 (May 1940): 235–241.

14. Ripley's letter to Dana is in the Dana Family Papers, MHi.

15. *The Blithedale Romance,* his satiric romance of utopian ventures notwithstanding, Hawthorne still recalled his earlier days at Brook Farm with affection. He remarked in a letter on January 23, 1847, to Henry Wadsworth Longfellow, his classmate at Bowdoin College, that he would happily sit for a proposed portrait dressed in the blue tunic that was such a popular piece of clothing among the Brook Farm men. "Gladly would I appear before men and angels in that garment; but on leaving

the Manse, I bequeathed it to Ellery Channng." Hawthorne, *The Letters,
1843–1853,* ed. Thomas Woodson, L. Neal Smith, and Norman Holmes
Pearson (1985), in *The Centenary Edition of the Works of Nathaniel
Hawthorne,* ed. William Charvat et al. (Columbus: Ohio State University Press, 1963–1997), 16:197.

16. Ichabod Morton did not hold a mortgage on Brook Farm, but the community owed him nearly $5,000, which is the amount that he put up in 1842 to construct the Pilgrim House. For Brisbane's letter, see *BFM,* 144–146.

17. Channing's letter to Dwight is in JSD/MB.

18. Ripley responded to Parker on January 2, 1846. The language of his brief reply—alternately incredulous and melodramatic—makes clear the extent of his personal disappointment. "We [the Brook Farmers] were all very much astonished at your proposal, & can scarce believe that it was prompted by your better judgment. To say nothing of the exposure of sending a lad like him [George Colburn] four miles on foot over a bleak road through storm & cold at this inclement time of the year, we could never consent to take the physical charge of a pupil in our family [the Parkers evidently wanted Colburn to continue to board at Brook Farm], while his moral & intellectual culture was entrusted to other influences." This and Ripley's other terse remarks had their intended effect: Colburn was not withdrawn from the Brook Farm school. See the George Ripley Papers, MHi.

19. Ripley would also have been very discouraged had he known about E. P. Grant's assessment of Brook Farm. Grant, the president of the recently collapsed Ohio Phalanx in Belmont County, Ohio, spent several weeks at the community in September and October 1845. He left on October 18, 1845, entirely disheartened. "Brook Farm can scarcely succeed," he told a friend on December 12. To another friend he was more specific in a January 1846 letter. He had gone to Brook Farm with realistic expectations: "I did not expect to find perfection there—on the contrary I looked for much imperfection, accompanied with scanty means—but the appearance of things was so much more unsatisfactory than I expected that I was completely discouraged." Grant's disappointment had much

to do with the state of Brook Farm's several industrial enterprises, all of which the former New Englander found to be "miserably unproductive and unprofitable." Grant politely understated what all along had been among the most serious problems at Brook Farm: "I think that . . . Mr. Ripley and Mr. Dana misapprehend some points of great practical importance" in the operation of the community's industrial enterprises. Grant was also quite dismayed by "the consideration that so many interesting and devoted people were laboring and sacrificing themselves to so little purpose." See Grant to Jerrey Doty, December 12, 1845, and Grant to James D. Thornburg, January 28, 1846, Elijah P. Grant Papers, University of Chicago.

20. For Dwight, see *DL*, December 12, 1845, pp. 139–142; for Ripley, see *The Harbinger* 2 (December 20, 1845): 29.

11. Fire

1. "Fire at Brook Farm," March 14, 1846, pp. 220–222. Unless otherwise noted, quotations are from this account by Ripley in *The Harbinger*. Boston newspapers reported the fire long before Ripley did in *The Harbinger*. *The Chronotype* (p. 2, col. 4) and the *Boston Daily Evening Transcript* (p. 2, col. 3), for example, noticed it in their columns the very next day on March 4, 1846, but that's all they did—provide a brief notice. The *Boston Daily Advertiser* (p. 2, col. 4), the *Boston Courier* (p. 2, col. 1), and the *Boston Atlas* (p. 2, col. 1) included short notices of the loss on March 5, 1846. The only major Boston paper not to report the fire was the *Boston Post*.

2. S. Willard Saxton, "A Few Reminiscences of Brook Farm," *BFB*, 325.

3. Dana to Dwight, [March 15, 1846], JSD/MB.

4. Ripley to John S. Dwight, March 19, 1846, JSD/MB; Mary Ann Dwight to Anna Parsons, *DL*, March 22, 1846.

5. Dwight's letter to Mary Ann, [March 25, 1846], is in JSD/MB. From Dwight's proceeds would have to be deducted his expenses to New York—$10—and the cost of outfitting the Brook Farmer for the four lectures—$5.81 for a belt, suspenders, a coat, and other clothing. See the Brook Farm financial journal, March 1846, MHi. See also Mary Ann Dwight to Anna Parsons, *DL*, March 22, 1846.

6. John S. Dwight to Mary Ann Dwight, [March 25, 1846], JSD/MB. The letter is partially quoted in George Willis Cooke, *John Sullivan Dwight: Brook-Farmer, Editor, and Critic of Music* (Boston: Small, Maynard, 1898), 112–114.

7. The Brook Farm financial journals are surprisingly silent about the stock holdings of New York Associationists—surprising because the journals provide scrupulous detail (thanks to the meticulous bookkeeping of Fred Cabot) about every conceivable aspect of the community's operations, including the names of stockholders. The ease with which the New York Associationists relinquished their stock in Brook Farm suggests, in any case, that their holdings in the community were not very extensive. Brisbane's lack of financial support of Brook Farm is particularly egregious, considering that he owed the West Roxbury community more than seventy-five dollars in room and board charges for his periodic visits to Brook Farm in the spring of 1845, a debt that he still hadn't paid the following October. Luckily for Brisbane, John T. Codman didn't know about the indebtedness. He was never one of Brisbane's champions. He recalled that Brisbane "labored hard with the [Brook Farm] Society" in the early months of 1845 "to change its name to Phalanx, and to push the movement as far as possible into the formulas and organization described by Fourier," which, Codman was quick to add, "did not advance it [Brook Farm] a single step in material or spiritual progress, and acted, as in the case of the constitution, as a dead weight, owing to the burdensomeness of its details, which called for too much labor to keep the accounts of so complex an organization." *BFM,* 74.

8. See Dana to John S. Dwight, March 15, 1846, JSD/MB. Extraordinary as it sounds, Brook Farm's creditors may have forgiven the entire $7,000 of Association indebtedness incurred by the construction of the Phalanstery—according, that is, to Mary Ann Dwight. Ripley, Dana, and a few other Brook Farmers met with local creditors in Boston on April 7. Dwight notes that the intention was to "make this proposition to the creditors, viz. [namely] that they would convert $7,000 of debts into partnership stock." The creditors instead, she says, relinquished "entirely $7,000 of debts," and they also promised not to impose any additional financial pressures on the Brook Farmers until the community

managed to recover from its devastating losses from the destruction of the Phalanstery. One of the creditors with whom the Brook Farmers met that evening was Ichabod Morton, a former trustee of the Association, to whom the community still owed nearly $5,000, the amount that Morton had provided in 1842 to construct the Pilgrim House. Morton didn't dismiss any of that debt on this occasion, but he was "perfectly ready to assent to anything that we [the Brook Farmers] asked."

It seems very odd, however, that no other corroborating accounts of such remarkable generosity have survived. The most obvious explanation is that Dwight was simply confused or unclear about the actual financial arrangements. A more likely scenario is that creditors like Morton agreed to postpone future credit payments and dismiss additional interest charges. The reason, by the way, why the Brook Farmers would have offered partnership stock rather than loan stock is because the former did not provide a fixed interest annually, which the latter did. Moreover, any interest accruing to partnership stock was not credited until all the Association's expenses had been met.

The Brook Farmers were no strangers to legal actions against them. George Ripley, it should be remembered, remarked just a few months before the fire, in his December 15, 1845, letter to Richard Henry Dana, Jr., concerning Nathaniel Hawthorne's lawsuit, that "there are claims of this kind against us, exclusive of Mr H[awthorne]'s, to the amount of 8 or 900 dollars." For Dwight, see Dwight to her brother Frank, April 7, [1846], *DL*: 162–163; Dwight to Anna Parsons, April 19, 1846, *DL*: 163–166; and Dwight to Anna Parsons, April 24, 1846, *DL*: 166–169, from which the quotations above have been taken.

9. "Statement of the 'American Union of Associationists' with Reference to Recent Attacks," *The Harbinger*, 3:152. The characterization of the Associative movement as "providential" shows up frequently in the correspondence of the Brook Farmers right after the fire. See, e.g., Sophia Ripley to John S. Dwight, March 14, 1846, JSD/MB, and William Henry Channing to Edward Phillips, June 24, 1846, transcribed copy in IU-HS. Even the very first resolution of the newly organized American Union of Associationists would state that Associationism was a "Providential movement."

10. Kay to Dwight, March 2, 1846, JSD/MB. Unless otherwise noted, quotations are from this letter.

11. See Mary Ann Dwight to John S. Dwight, *DL,* March 17, 1846, p. 154; Sophia Ripley to John S. Dwight, March 14, 1846, JSD/MB; Dana to John S. Dwight, March 15, 1846, JSD/MB; and George Ripley to John S. Dwight, March 19, 1846, JSD/MB.

12. That is, an individual's contribution to the community would no longer be measured—or rewarded—by the number of hours and days he or she worked, but by the actual profits accruing to the community from the individual's labors. All, in short, were now expected to "justify their existence" in the Association in financial terms. See Dwight to Anna Parsons, *DL,* April 24, 1846, pp. 166–169.

13. James T. Fisher Papers, MHi. Interestingly enough, just two days before Ripley's remarks in *The Harbinger,* Charles Dana—at a wedding party in the Hive on Thursday, March 19, to celebrate his and Eunice Macdaniel's secret marriage a few weeks earlier in New York City—"expressed his deep faith that the cause of Association and the work of Association must and would to some extent be carried on here at Brook Farm." Mary Ann Dwight regarded Dana's expression of "deep faith" in "Association" as a sign of his continuing commitment to Brook Farm, but Dana himself certainly would have enlarged upon the qualifying phrase, "to some extent," had he known that Dwight thought that he intended to remain at the West Roxbury community. See *DL,* 162.

14. Channing to Dwight, January 18, 1846, JSD/MB; Allen to "My very dear, dear friends," March 9, 1846, Abernethy Library, Middlebury College, Vt. (however, I have consulted the transcribed copy in IU-HS).

12. Beginning of the End

1. "To Our Friends," *The Harbinger,* 2:237.

2. "The Associative Movement—Its Present Condition—Practical Measures—Meeting in May," *The Harbinger,* 2:346–337.

3. In addition to James Kay, Jr., the other six vice presidents were Peleg Clarke, Coventry, Rhode Island; Frederic Grain, New York; E. P. Grant, Canton, Ohio; Charles Sears, North American Phalanx; Benjamin Urner, Cincinnati, OH; and H. H. Van Amringe, Pittsburgh, PA.

4. Godwin, "To the Editors of The Harbinger," June 5, 1846, NYPL; Dana, "Convention in Boston," *The Harbinger,* June 6, 1846, p. 411. Godwin's letter, in fact, was never published in the paper.

5. See Godwin to Dana, October 24, 1845, and November 4, 1845, NYPL. For Channing's editorial, see *The Harbinger,* 1: 317–319.

6. Godwin to Dana, August 12, 1846, NYPL; Dana to Godwin, August 18, 1846, NYPL. It's not difficult to imagine what Godwin's reaction must have been when, just a few weeks after his June 5, 1846, "Letter to the Editors," Ripley published the Brook Farmers' friend Christopher Pearse Cranch's antiwar and antislavery "Sonnet—On the Mexican War" in the July 18 number of *The Harbinger.* Shortly after *The Harbinger*'s transfer to New York, Ripley, who also went to New York, complained to Dwight in a letter dated December 7 and 8, 1847, about certain difficulties in that city: no material had been received from W. H. Channing; Dana (now a correspondent for *The Harbinger;* see note 18 below) felt confined by the secular department of the paper; and Ripley himself was bogged down with various details. Godwin, Ripley remarked, was "fruitful, genial, and altogether in earnest, but is not altogether inexhaustible; and without a stronger infusion of the Boston element, we cannot do justice to our ideal." Seven months later, on July 14, 1848, Ripley informed Dwight that Godwin had just had a son, who, Ripley said, "I hope will not turn out . . . like its father." On October 18, 1848, with *The Harbinger* on the verge of collapse, Ripley would tell Dwight that Godwin "has never shown any vital paramount interest in it [*The Harbinger*] and does not love it well enough to write for it without a consideration."

After the paper's demise in February 1849, New York Associationists considered the possibility of publishing a new journal. Apparently they asked Ripley for his support, for he informed Dwight on March 26, 1849, that he could not work on any publication with Godwin, a man who was "too much of a Caliban or Cannibal, to make cooperation with him pleasant. Indeed, I don't see . . . how anyone can work under him, or over him, or with him, without extreme annoyance; and for himself he decidedly prefers to write or fight (which with him is pretty much the same thing) on his own." For Ripley's letters to Dwight, see JSD/MB.

7. Dana would say to Godwin that "it seems an unfortunate thing to open the [Associative] movement thus just commenced with a public evidence of [internal] dissension in our body." Dana to Godwin, August 18, 1846, NYPL.

8. Dwight seems to have written only two letters from Brook Farm in July 1846. See *DL,* July 28, 1846, and July 1846 (dates estimates), from which the following quotations have been taken.

9. Apparently there was a formal breakup of the community of some sort at the end of July because Lizzie Curson also noted in a letter to her sister on August 4, 1846, that "they had held a meeting a few days before and dissolved the Association." See Stephen Garrison and Joel Myerson, "Elizabeth Curson's Letters from Brook Farm," *Resources for American Literary Study* 12 (Spring 1982): 20.

10. "Meeting of the 'American Union of Associationists' in Boston," *The Harbinger,* June 27, 1846, p. 47. That the AUA was, at this point, nothing other than Ripley, Dana, and a few others speaking with a different voice is indicated once again by the absence at this meeting of any Associationists outside of New England. Likewise, when Ripley, Dana, and Dwight published a "Statement of the 'American Union of Associationists,' with Reference to Recent Attacks" in *The Harbinger* on August 15, the statement was signed by all the officers of the Union except those not consulted, which happens to have been all the New York Associationists and a few others from elsewhere around the country. In other words, the only people actually consulted in drafting the statement were the Brook Farmers and their local supporters.

11. "Association Meeting at Hingham, Mass.," *The Harbinger,* August 1, 1846, p. 127.

12. See "Attacks on the Doctrine of Association," *The Harbinger,* August 8, 1846, p. 143.

13. See *The Harbinger,* 2 (January 3, 1846): 60, and 2 (January 10, 1846): 79.

14. It's a good thing that they did recognize it, too. According to *The American Almanac and Repository of Useful Knowledge for the Year 1846,* there were more than twenty-five Christian denominations in the United States in 1845. The list of denominations—along with number of churches (28,074), ministers (32,563), and communicants (4,458,554)—

is cited in the *Communitist* 2 (January 22, 1846): 92. For more on Fourier and marriage, see Chapter 7, note 24.

15. For the *American Review*, see *The Harbinger*, 5:28, 43, 58, and 73; for *Brownson's Quarterly Review*, see 6:84 and 8:92; for the New York press, see 1:189, 2:44, 3:143, 4:14, 5:31, 161, and 287.

16. Dana to Godwin, August 18, 1846, NYPL.

17. For Dana, see letter dated August 18, 1846, NYPL. Dana is either confused about the amount of time that he'd spent helping to produce *The Harbinger* (a little more than a year), or he is including time spent earlier helping with Albert Brisbane's *The Phalanx.*

18. *CAD,* 58–61. Neither Charles nor Eunice Dana's names appear in the Brook Farm financial journals after August 1846. Dana did double-duty while he worked for Greeley on the New York *Tribune.* He became the "foreign correspondent" for *The Harbinger* after its transfer to New York in November 1847 with the close of the fifth volume. For Volume 6, for instance, he contributed forty-one items, and for Volume 7 he provided fifteen articles—many of them under the heading "European Affairs."

19. Guarneri, *The Utopian Alternative: Fourierism in Nineteenth-Century America* (Ithaca, N.Y.: Cornell University Press, 1991), 303.

20. One of the advocates for labor reform in Lowell was Mehitable Eastman, whose daughter Sophia spent several months at Brook Farm in 1843. See *The Harbinger,* 4:208, and Sophia Eastman to Mehitable Eastman, July 25, 1843, IU-HS. For Sophia Eastman at Brook Farm, see Chapter 5.

21. Clara Endicott Sears, *Bronson Alcott's Fruitlands* (Boston: Houghton, Mifflin, 1915), 140-141.

22. Quoted in *BFM,* 235. The title of the auction catalogue is "Catalogue of a Select Private Library, Containing About 1,000 Volumes, of Very Valuable Theological, Philosophical, and Miscellaneous Books: In the English, French, and German Languages." The catalogue, however, only lists about 536 titles.

13. Back to Boston

1. The records of the Boston Union are in the MH; the records of the Boston Religious Union are in the MHi. A more detailed discussion of

the activities of the two Unions is Sterling F. Delano, "The Boston Union of Associationists (1846–1851): 'Association Is to Me the Great Hope of the World,'" *SAR* (1996): 5–40; and Sterling F. Delano, "A Calendar of Meetings of the 'Boston Religious Union of Associationists,' 1847–50," *SAR* (1985): 187–267.

2. Ripley, Dwight, and Channing co-authored three articles for *The Harbinger* ("American Union—Anniversary Meeting—Affiliated Societies") in an effort to inspire greater interest before the first anniversary meeting of the American Union in May 1847: see 4:287, 318, and 384. For the American Union of Associationists, see also "Convention in Boston—Organization of the American Union of Associationists," *The Harbinger* 2 (June 6, 1846): 410–411.

3. To become a member of the BUA a person was expected to sign the constitution and to pledge a weekly amount to the Union's general fund. These pledges ranged from a low of two cents to a high of fifty cents per week (the latter amount pledged by James T. Fisher and Josiah Wolcott). The average weekly pledge was about ten cents. William Henry Channing and John Dwight each pledged twelve-and-a-half cents.

4. Both of Wolcott's paintings are currently at the MHi, though one of them continues to be privately owned. The other two contemporary views of Brook Farm appear as part of the cover design of this book. The originals of these latter views are miniature watercolors by Mary Ann Dwight, dated November 1845, and owned by Dr. Ivan Gilbert.

5. Swift, *Brook Farm: Its Members, Scholars, and Visitors* (New York: Macmillan, 1900), 217; Robinson, "The Political Odyssey of William Henry Channing," *American Quarterly* 34 (Summer 1982): 165–184, espec. 183. See also Delano, "The Boston Union," espec. 14–16 and 26–27.

6. In *The Harbinger* for December 16, 1848 (7:54) it was noted that the "friends" in Washington, D.C., had formed an affiliated union there, which, "we trust will not be the last if it is the first, south of Mason and Dixon's line." The exact number of affiliated societies is difficult to pinpoint. Charles Crowe, in his biography of Ripley, claims that there were thirty-three. Carl Guarneri, in his detailed study of Fourierism in nineteenth-century America, is more cautious in his estimate and says that

there were "at least twenty-eight." Both Crowe and Guarneri cite unions for which there seems to be only a single vague reference in *The Harbinger*, suggesting—to me, at least—that if any one of such unions was in fact established, its existence was so temporary as not to deserve being counted. See Crowe, *George Ripley: Transcendentalist and Utopian Socialist* (Athens, Ga.: University Press of Georgia, 1967), and Guarneri, *The Utopian Alternative: Fourierism in Nineteenth-Century America* (Ithaca: Cornell University Press, 1991), 410.

7. See Dwight to Anna Q. T. Parsons, July 4, 1847, MHi.

8. *The Harbinger*, May 29, 1847, p. 389.

9. The actual number of signatures on the membership rolls, however, was ninety-six: sixty-one men and thirty-five women. See *The Harbinger*, May 13, 1848, p. 13.

10. Guarneri, *The Utopian Alternative*, 242. See also *The Harbinger*, May 13, 1848, pp. 64 and 128; *The Harbinger*, May 29, 1847, pp. 385 and 472.

11. Although the Woman's Associative Union was organized and began to function in June 1847, it did not formally adopt a constitution until the following December 1847 (see *The Harbinger*, 5:14–16, 7:61).

12. For John Dwight, see *The Harbinger*, December 25, 1847, p. 61.

13. Social pressure, of course, was not limited to women. John Allen, in writing to Anna Parsons about his lecture tour in Rochester, New York, noted that "the few friends [in that area] have been . . . ridiculed as insane Fourierists, and persecuted for being so till they are . . . absolutely afraid to do anything openly for the cause lest they should be hissed or scoffed at or thrown out of employment." Allen to Parsons, September 17, 1847, Abernethy Library, Middlebury College, Vt. And James Kay, president of the Philadelphia Union, complained a month earlier to the members of the Boston Union that he "feared that the charges so freely made in some of the papers of the immorality of our doctrines had prevented and would tend to prevent ladies from joining" the local Associative unions. Minutes, BUA, August 18, 1847, MH. See also letters from Allen to Parsons in the records of the Philadelphia Union of Associationists, Harriet P. Sartain Papers, Historical Society of Pennsylvania, Philadelphia.

14. For Charles Dana, see *The Harbinger,* April 24, 1847, p. 316.

15. Kay to Fisher, November 26, 1847, James T. Fisher Papers, MHi; Allen to Fisher, [no date], Fisher Papers, MHi.

16. See *The Harbinger,* July 18, 1846, p. 95; September 26, 1846, pp. 252–253; and February 13, 1847, p. 158.

17. See *The Harbinger,* February 27, 1847, p. 191; May 8, 1847, p. 351.

18. Dwight to Anna Parsons, March 29, [1847], *DL,* p. 177, and Dwight to Parsons, May 17, 1847, MHi.

19. See "The First Annual Report of the 'Woman's Associative Union,'" *The Harbinger,* June 24, 1848, p. 61.

20. Blackwell to Parsons, October 29, 1847. The original of this and two other Blackwell letters to Parsons are in the Abernethy Library, Middlebury College. I have relied, however, on transcribed copies of the letters, which are in IU-HS. I am grateful to John Hoffman, curator, for bringing the latter to my attention. See also *The Harbinger,* June 24, 1848, p. 61.

21. See *The Harbinger,* June 24, 1848, p. 61.

22. See Joel Myerson, "New Light on George Ripley and the *Harbinger*'s New York Years," *Harvard Library Bulletin* 32 (Summer 1985): 323, 328.

23. [Allen to Fisher, no date], Fisher Papers, MHi; Minutes of the Boston Union of Associationists, August 18, 1847, MH; Kay to Fisher, November 26, 1847, Fisher Papers, MHi; Macdaniel to Grant, December 12, 1847, Elijah P. Grant Papers, University of Chicago Library.

24. Myerson, "New Light," 334.

25. Plans were already in motion for the Religious Union, in fact, in very early December 1846. Thus the BUA and the BRUA were organized virtually at the exact same time.

26. That the BRUA managed to be true to its mission of religious pluralism is suggested by this entry in the records for December 5, 1847: "It was suggested . . . that it would be interesting to know the names of the various denominations of religious belief the members either now or formerly belonged to . . . It was found that the following were represented [at that evening's meeting]: 1 Presbyterian, 3 Orthodox Congregationalist, 1 Baptist, 1 Methodist, 11 Unitarian, 3 Universalist, 1 Catholic, 2 Ra-

tionalists, 1 [undeciphered], 1 Transcendentalist, 1 Swedenborgian, 1 Jewish and two Sceptics." MHi.

27. The six were Channing himself, of course, Anna Q. T. Parsons and her sister Helen, Josiah Wolcott, Mary Bullard, and James Kay, Jr. I am not including Elizabeth Palmer Peabody because she didn't formally join the BRUA until some time after its inception, even though she attended and participated in many of the meetings in 1847 and 1848.

28. Dwight to Parsons, *DL,* December 15, 1846, p. 176.

29. Dwight to Parsons, [July 1847], MHi.

30. The ten Brook Farmers who were members of the BUA but *not* the BRUA were Jonathan Butterfield, William Cheswell, Charles Codman, John Drew, Fanny Dwight, James Bryant Hill, Minot Pratt, S. Willard Saxton, Henry Trask, and Robert Westacott.

    The eight Brook Farmers who were members of the BRUA but *not* the BUA were John Allen, John Cheever, Lizzie Curson, Peter Kleinstrup, Eliza and Jean Palisse, Sophia Ripley, and Catherine Sloan.

31. Delano, "A Calendar of Meetings," 215–216.

14. "Done with Brook Farm"

1. Dana to Hannah Ripley, September 5, 1847, KHi; *The Harbinger,* 4:267–269.

2. Minutes, March 4, 1847, MHi.

3. For a full report of the proceedings, see "Annual Meeting of the American Union of Associationists," *The Harbinger,* May 29, 1847, pp. 385–392.

4. See *The Harbinger,* July 24, 1847, p. 111, and Mary Ann Dwight to Anna Q. T. Parsons, July 18, 1847, MHi.

5. It was noted in the previous chapter that Ripley spoke about Brook Farm without regret at the October 17, 1847, meeting of the Boston Religious Union of Associationists.

6. Brisbane was not present at any of the important Associative meetings in 1847, including the May 1847 meeting in New York City, the meeting in July 1847, also in New York, and the meeting in Boston in October 1847. See *The Harbinger,* May 29, 1847, pp. 385–392; July 24, 1847, p. 111; and October 23, 1847, pp. 316–317.

7. Minutes, August 18, 1847, MHi. An indenture was formally drafted on September 6, 1847, between the Brook Farm Phalanx and Theodore Parker, George R. Russell, and Samuel P. Teal whereby the Phalanx did "hereby give grant bargain sell convey transfer assign and set over unto the said Parker Russell and Teal the Trustees . . . of said Corporation" in order to dispose of the property and settle Brook Farm's debts. The indenture was legally filed on October 2, 1847. See the Records in the Norfolk County Registry of Deeds, Dedham, Mass., book 8178, folios 268b and 269a. Samuel P. Teal was a Brook Farm stockholder. He owned $400 worth of shares, plus interest that was owed him. See the Brook Farm financial journal, April 1845, MHi.

8. "The Meetings in Boston," *The Harbinger,* October 23, 1847, pp. 316–318. The information about the meetings is from this article, and from the minutes of the BUA (MH) and the BRUA (MHi).

9. *The Voice of Industry,* October 22, 1847, p. 2. The Brook Farmers who were on their way to the North American Phalanx might have been John Glover Drew, a farmer from Plymouth, Massachusetts, or Nathaniel Colson, one of the community's several shoemakers. Both of these men's names show up on the list that concludes *A History of the First Nine Years of the North American Phalanx . . .,* written by Charles Sears in 1852, which is reprinted in John Humphrey Noyes, *History of American Socialisms* (1870; reprint, New York: Hillary House, 1961), 467.

10. Saxton, October 24, 1847, IU-HS.

Epilogue

1. "Report of the Joint Special Committee on the Removal of the Alms House and the Purchase of 'Brook Farm'" (City Document No. 3; Roxbury: Joseph G. Torrey, 1849); "Report of the Joint Special Committee on the Buildings at Brook Farm, and a New Almshouse" (City Document No. 6; Roxbury: Joseph G. Torrey, 1849). Charles M. Ellis, of West Roxbury, wrote to George Ripley on August 15, 1849, to report on the "mode in which the several claims have been disposed of" of the thirty-two creditors whose names Ripley himself had earlier supplied. Of the thirteen creditors to whom some settlement was provided, nine were paid a total of $1,031.11, including Nathaniel Hawthorne, who re-

ceived a "dividend" of $70.80, Philadelphia Associationist James Kay, who was given $132.13, and Ichabod Morton, who received $641.81, which was obviously only a small portion of the $4,654.84 that he had loaned the Brook Farmers seven years earlier for the construction of the Pilgrim House. Hawthorne, it will be recalled, was awarded a judgment against Brook Farm in March 1846 for $585.90, but it seems that he never received more than the $70.80 dividend cited in Ellis's letter. It is possible, of course, that Ripley further compensated Hawthorne at a later time. Evidently he did later compensate the other four remaining creditors cited in the letter, the amount of the settlement to whom, according to the letter, was to have been $352.94. For Ellis's letter, see MHi.

2. *Blue-Eyed Child of Fortune: The Civil War Letters of Colonel Robert Gould Shaw,* ed. Russell Duncan (Athens: University of Georgia Press, 1992), 101. It's not known what brought down the Pilgrim House, the Eyrie, the Workshop, and the Hive.

3. Former Brook Farmer Nathaniel Hawthorne was one of the very earliest to urge Brook Farm's leaders to write the community's history. In the Preface to *The Blithedale Romance* (1852), Hawthorne said that it was his "most earnest wish that some one of the many cultivated and philosophic minds, which took an interest" in Brook Farm, "might now give the world its history." Brook Farm's leaders, he noted, were the best qualified to "convey both the outward narrative and the inner truth and spirit of the whole affair." Ripley himself remained silent about Brook Farm throughout his life, except for the following poem, which is often attributed to him, and which appeared in the *Christian Examiner* (42 [May 1847]: 343–344) a few months before the community's ultimate collapse:

"The Angels of the Past"

My buried days!—in bitter tears
    I sit beside your tomb,
And ghostly forms of vanished years
    Flit through my spirit's gloom.

In throngs around my soul they press,
    They fill my dreamy sight
With visions of past loveliness
    And shapes of lost delight.

Like angels of the Lord they move,
    Each on his mystic way,—
These blessed messengers of love,
    These heralds of the day.

And as they pass, the conscious air
    Is stirred to music round,
And a murmur of harmonious prayer
    Is breathed along the ground.

And sorrow dies from out my heart
    In exaltation sweet,
And the bands of life, which she did part,
    In blessed union meet.

The past and future o'er my head
    Their sacred grasp entwine
And the eyes of all the holy dead
    Around, before me, shine.

And I rise to life and duty;
    From nights of fear and death,
With a deeper sense of beauty
    And fuller strength of faith.

In 1895 Charles Dana gave an address at the University of Michigan on the social reform fervor that swept through the United States in the 1840s, in the course of which remarks he referred briefly to Brook Farm. See James Harrison Wilson, *The Life of Charles A. Dana* (New York: Harper and Brothers, 1907), 525–534. Nothing more than these brief references to Brook Farm was ever said by either man about the West Roxbury community.

4. Henry Golemba, "George Ripley," *Dictionary of Literary Biography:*

American Literary Critics and Scholars, 1850–1880, ed. John W. Rathbun and Monica M. Grecu (Detroit: Gale Research, 1988), vol. 64: 200–206. For Ripley, see Octavius Brooks Frothingham, *George Ripley* (Boston: Houghton, Mifflin, 1882); Charles Crowe, *George Ripley: Transcendentalist and Utopian Socialist* (Athens, Ga.: University of Georgia Press, 1867); and Henry Golemba, *George Ripley* (Boston: Twayne, 1977).

5. See Henrietta Dana Raymond, *Sophia Willard Dana Ripley* (Portsmouth, N.H.: Peter E. Randall, 1994), 87–89, and Swift, *Brook Farm: Its Members, Scholars, and Visitors* (New York: Macmillan, 1900), 142–145.

6. The standard biography of Dana is James Harrison Wilson, *The Life of Charles A. Dana,* cited above.

7. The standard biography of John Sullivan Dwight is George Willis Cooke, *John Sullivan Dwight: Brook Farmer, Editor, and Critic of Music* (Boston: Small, Maynard, 1898). Like Charles Dana, Dwight provided some brief remarks about Brook Farm many years after its demise. See the *Christian Register,* March 9, 1882, pp. 5–7.

8. See Joel Myerson, "James Burrill Curtis and Brook Farm," *New England Quarterly* 51 (1978): 396–423; Gordon Milne, *George William Curtis and the Genteel Tradition* (Bloomington: Indiana University Press, 1956); Josephine Latham Swayne, *The Story of Concord* (Boston: Meador Publishing Co., 1939); and Joel Myerson, ed., *The Brook Farm Book: A Collection of First-Hand Accounts of the Community* (New York: Garland, 1987) (cited elsewhere in these notes as BFB).

9. James Sturgis, the brother-in-law of Brook Farm supporter Francis G. Shaw, recalled many years after the West Roxbury community's demise that he went to the West Indies in 1841 on business, and "in the spring [of 1842] I came home from Puerto Rico bringing four Spanish boys, none of whom could speak English." Shaw recommended that Sturgis take the four boys to Brook Farm, which he proceeded to do, living himself in the community for eight months. In addition to Manuel Diaz there were two brothers named Jose and Lucas Corrales (who were sponsored by George R. Russell, another West Roxbury neighbor and Brook Farm supporter). I have not been able to identify the fourth boy.

A Jose Lopez is listed as a student-boarder at the school in 1846, but this is probably not the fourth boy because the date of his association with the community is so much later than that of Diaz and the Corrales brothers. For Sturgis's recollection, see the *Christian Register,* March 9, 1882, p. 7.

10. Ripley was always fearful about sharing administrative authority in the community, something that James Kay admonished the Brook Farmers about in March 1846, the day before the Phalanstery fire: "The introduction of the *people* into the practical administration of the government," Kay said, was one of the "measures which are primary, & preliminary" to Brook Farm's continued survival. A few months before Mary Ann Dwight expressed the same concern. Many of the associates were "ready to give up if matters cannot be otherwise managed, for they have no hope of success here under the past and present government. All important matters have been done up in council of one or two or three individuals, and everybody else kept in the dark (perhaps I exaggerate somewhat) . . .—our young men have started 'enquiry meetings,' and it must be a sad state of things that calls for such measures." From the very beginning, those who wielded administrative authority in the community were only Ripley's most trusted supporters, such as his wife Sophia, his sister Marianne, Charles Dana, Minot Pratt, and one or two others, who were reelected year after year to the General Direction, the Direction of Finance, and the Direction of Education.

    For Kay, see his letter dated March 2, 1846, JSD/MB; for Dwight, see *DL,* December 7, 1845, p. 137.

11. For example, Fred Cabot, who as Brook Farm's bookkeeper was in a position to know, afterward stated that by the time the community converted to Fourierism in January 1844, it had already "proved a pecuniary failure," and that, Ripley's statement to the contrary at that time notwithstanding, "They [the Brook Farmers] never had a 'capital of about thirty thousand dollars.'" See Cabot's letter dated "May, 1877" in the *American Socialist,* May 31, 1877, p. 1.

12. The labor records for May 1844–April 1845 are among the Brook Farm Papers, MHi.

13. In an article entitled "What Killed Brook Farm? And Who?" in the *American Socialist* for May 31, 1877, editor John Humphrey Noyes devotes two full columns to supporting the view "that Horace Greeley was the man who killed Brook Farm" (169–170), although the reasons he cites have nothing to do with the matters just noted. See also Greeley to Charles Dana, August 29, 1842, quoted in Wilson, *Dana,* 40–42; and Greeley to Dana, December 13, 1842, Horace Greeley Papers, Library of Congress, Washington, D.C.

14. Although it has been pointed out in more than a few studies of Brook Farm (by way of criticism) that women chose their work along traditional gender lines, the real point to make isn't about choice; it's about opportunity. It's not about whether women devoted a significant portion of their worktime to, say, mechanical enterprises or to agricultural pursuits. The important point to make is that Brook Farm provided opportunities to and never discouraged women from participating in any work activity that might promote formation and growth of their individual character—what Transcendentalists like Dr. Channing, Elizabeth Palmer Peabody, Bronson Alcott, and Margaret Fuller routinely referred to as the unfolding of character and "self-culture." For Emerson, see "Historic Notes of Life and Letters in New England," *Complete Works of Ralph Waldo Emerson,* ed. E. W. Emerson (Boston: Houghton, Mifflin, 1904), 10:366–367.

15. Kay to John Dwight, March 2, 1846, JSD/MB.

Acknowledgments

The generous support of both the National Endowment for the Humanities and Villanova University enabled me to undertake this project in earnest. Support from the NEH was in the form of two Travel to Collections Grants, as well as a Fellowship for College Teachers and Independent Scholars. Thanks to Rev. Kail Ellis, OSA, Dean of Liberal Arts and Sciences, and Dr. John Johannes, Vice President of Academic Affairs, Villanova more than matched the NEH Fellowship, and that enabled me to devote an entire year to Brook Farm free from the responsibilities of teaching, student advisement, and committee work. I am very grateful to both the Endowment and Villanova University.

Research is invariably a collaborative process, and I have benefited beyond measure from the cooperation and knowledge of the staffs at numerous libraries and repositories, especially the Houghton Library of Harvard University; the Massachusetts Historical Society; the Rare Books and Manuscripts Division of the Boston Public Library; the West Roxbury Historical Society; the Fruitlands Museums; and the Library Company of Philadelphia. I owe special thanks to John Hoffman, Leslie Perrin Wilson, the late Marcia Moss, Philip J. Lampi, and Dennis Laurie, who on more than one occasion helped me discover various Brook Farm–related treasures at, respectively, the Illinois Historical Survey, the Concord Free Public Library, and the American Antiquarian Society. It's also a pleasure to thank Don Fennimore and the Winterthur Museum and Amanda Lange and Historic Deerfield, Inc., for their assistance and cooperation. I long ago lost count of the number of requests cheerfully and doggedly fielded by Phylis Wright and Anne Ford in Villanova's Inter-Library Loan department. Bernadette Dierkes and Donna Blaszkowski in Instructional Media Services deserve acknowledgment too for their careful preparation of several of the plates for this book. It is a pleasure to extend my thanks as well to the reference staff of Falvey Memorial Library for their unfailing support and assistance.

I am also greatly indebted to several colleagues for their thoughtful reading of different portions of the manuscript. Robert D. Richardson, Jr., was enthusiastic about the project from the beginning, and he later provided a humbling red-pencil edit of one of the opening chapters, raising important questions along the way that helped to shape later chapters. Wesley T. Mott brought his own sharp critical eye to some of those chapters. Gary Collison's patient reading of and his detailed and insightful comments about several middle chapters were enormously helpful to me. Joel Myerson also commented on a section of the manuscript, but my debt to him extends well beyond his reading. For many years now I have benefited from his unfailing generosity and support, and it is a pleasure to acknowledge it here. For the Brook Farm project, Professor Myerson shared his transcribed copies of Mary Ann Dwight and Isaac Hecker's extensive correspondence, and he also provided Boston city directories that enabled me to identify some of the more elusive Brook Farmers as well as a few of the local merchants with whom the community had dealings.

I am also very grateful to the two anonymous readers at Harvard University Press whose detailed criticism of the entire manuscript prompted important contextual revisions that have helped to make the Brook Farm story more complete. That gratitude extends as well to Kathleen McDermott, Kathi Drummy, Richard Audet, and the editorial staff at Harvard University Press. Kathleen McDermott was immediately interested when I first contacted her about Brook Farm, and her continued enthusiasm for the project was a source of inspiration throughout the editorial process. Kathi Drummy patiently fielded questions and coordinated the organization of the illustrations in the book, and Richard Audet did a meticulous job of copyediting.

I had long felt the spirits of the Brook Farmers hovering about this project, but when a complete stranger named Ivan Gilbert unexpectedly called one day to say that he had found heretofore undiscovered watercolor images of the community that he wanted to share with me, I knew right away that the book was destined to be written. The two images of Brook Farm buildings that appear on the dust jacket of this book were painted by a member of the community in 1844. Dr.

Gilbert's pleasure sharing them is a reflection of his generous nature, and also a fitting tribute to the spirit of unselfishness that animated the Brook Farmers themselves, particularly the founders, George and Sophia Ripley.

A few other individuals deserve recognition too for their role in helping to shape this book. Robert Murphy was a matchless source of interesting and important information about antebellum life in West Roxbury, much of which he shared on our ramblings together at the Brook Farm site. Over the years Nancy Osgood's interest in Brook Farm has led her into the nooks and crannies of many New England archives both on and off the researcher's beaten path, and she has always happily shared the fruits of all her careful labors. I have also benefited from numerous conversations with Patricia Cohen and Dean Grodzins, whose work, respectively, on antebellum American reformers Mary Grove and Theodore Parker has intersected in surprising and interesting ways with my own on Brook Farm. Sol Kleinman, Wayne Bremser, Jim Milano, Ed Mathias, and Tom Massey displayed remarkable patience as they helped me work through the Brook Farm financial records. I wish that I could name all the graduate research assistants with whom I've worked over the years, but Carol Felton Capitani, Larissa Dudash Lee, Tom Jackson, Susan Johnson, Christopher Smith, and Michelle Wetzell deserve special mention because of their valuable assistance with the Brook Farm project. Conversations with many other colleagues and friends—particularly Philip Kubzansky, Charlie Cherry, and Paul Abbate—have helped me more than they will ever know because their thoughtful interest in my work so often clarified important matters related to Brook Farm. Charlie Cherry also provided much appreciated additional support and assistance in his capacity as Chair of Villanova's English department, as did the department's splendid support staff, Susan Burns, Cindy Farrell, and Madeline DiPietro. To Sidney P. Moss and Robert E. Wilkinson I am indebted, as always, in more ways than I can say.

When all is said and done, this book would certainly never have been written without the unwavering support and encouragement of my wife, Maris. She lived with the Brook Farmers more years than the community itself existed, and her lively interest in every stage of the project was a source of continual inspiration. My other cheerleaders have been the beloved members of my family—Rachel, Debra, Randy, Adam Judd, and Stacie—who were eager to hear the story of Brook Farm, and never doubted that I could tell it.

Index